COMMUNISM, DEMOCRACY,
AND CATHOLIC POWER

BEACON STUDIES IN FREEDOM AND POWER

1947

THOMAS JEFFERSON: *Champion of Religious Freedom; Advocate of Christian Morals*
By HENRY WILDER FOOTE

1948

ESSAYS ON FREEDOM AND POWER
By LORD ACTON
Selected and with an introduction by Gertrude Himmelfarb; preface by Herman Finer

1949

AMERICAN FREEDOM AND CATHOLIC POWER
By PAUL BLANSHARD

CORNERSTONES OF RELIGIOUS FREEDOM IN AMERICA
Edited, with an introduction and interpretations, by JOSEPH L. BLAU

1950

THE AMERICAN TRADITION IN RELIGION AND EDUCATION
By R. FREEMAN BUTTS

1951

THE WALL OF SEPARATION BETWEEN CHURCH AND STATE
By CONRAD HENRY MOEHLMAN

THE ATTACK UPON THE AMERICAN SECULAR SCHOOL
By V. T. THAYER

COMMUNISM, DEMOCRACY, AND CATHOLIC POWER
By PAUL BLANSHARD

COMMUNISM, DEMOCRACY,
and
CATHOLIC POWER

Paul Blanshard

Boston · THE BEACON PRESS · 1951

Copyright 1951
By PAUL BLANSHARD

First Printing, April 1951
Second Printing, May 1951

BOOKS BY PAUL BLANSHARD

AN OUTLINE OF THE BRITISH LABOR MOVEMENT

WHAT'S THE MATTER WITH NEW YORK
with Norman Thomas

DEMOCRACY AND EMPIRE IN THE CARIBBEAN

AMERICAN FREEDOM AND CATHOLIC POWER

COMMUNISM, DEMOCRACY, AND CATHOLIC POWER

Printed in U.S.A.

I have sworn upon the altar of God eternal hostility against every form of tyranny over the mind of man.

THOMAS JEFFERSON

Contents

Preface ix

1. PATTERN AND PANORAMA 1
2. THE KREMLIN STRUCTURE OF POWER . . . 23
3. THE VATICAN STRUCTURE OF POWER . . . 43
4. THE DEVICES OF DEIFICATION 65
5. THE KREMLIN AND THOUGHT CONTROL . . 84
6. THE VATICAN AND THOUGHT CONTROL . . . 105
7. THE KREMLIN AND THE VATICAN VERSUS THE PUBLIC SCHOOL 131
8. DISCIPLINE AND DEVOTION 159
9. THE MANAGEMENT OF TRUTH: THE KREMLIN . 183
10. THE MANAGEMENT OF TRUTH: THE VATICAN . 212
11. THE STRATEGY OF PENETRATION: THE KREMLIN . 243
12. THE STRATEGY OF PENETRATION: THE VATICAN . 263
13. THE AMERICAN ANSWER 287

Appendix 302
    I. The Mussolini-Vatican Agreements of 1929 (*Excerpts*)
    II. The Roosevelt-Spellman Correspondence

Bibliography 313
Notes 316
Index 333

Preface

MY ORIGINAL INSPIRATION for this book came from reading the lectures delivered at Butler University by the well-known scholar, Professor George La Piana of Harvard, and published in the *Shane Quarterly* (1949) under the title, "A Totalitarian Church in a Democratic State: the American Experiment." Professor La Piana spoke in those lectures of the "impressive parallelism of theoretical principles and of institutional features in a totalitarian church and in a totalitarian state." He pointed out that "the totalitarianism of the Catholic Church differs from that of the state, because it has a spiritual content and a spiritual purpose which are completely lacking in the latter," but that nevertheless there is a real structural parallel between this Church as an organized system of power and the totalitarian states bent on expansion and domination.

I have applied that suggestive remark of Professor La Piana to one segment of the problem, the three-way struggle between the Vatican, the Kremlin, and democracy; but its elaboration and interpretation are wholly my own.

Two noted experts on Russian affairs have reviewed the portions of this book which deal with Communism — Warren B. Walsh, Chairman of the Board of Russian Studies at Syracuse University, and Frederick C. Barghoorn, Associate Professor of Political Science at Yale University. I am grateful for their constructive suggestions, but I am entirely responsible for any opinions expressed or for any errors in the text. Kenneth Dailey, of Syracuse University, has also helped me materially with research among Russian documents.

Over a period of several years, the editor of the Beacon Press has contributed to my files a mass of revealing material from Communist and Catholic periodicals published in this country and abroad, together with many helpful quotations from democratic periodicals. Edward Darling of the Beacon Press has been immensely helpful to me in many ways, especially in the period when I was overseas. The officials of the Baker Library at Dartmouth have been unfailingly generous with their literary treasures.

Although I have relied heavily on documentary material in this study, no survey of such a subject would be complete without on-the-spot observation. My previous studies had included five periods of observation in Europe and two in the Orient, with a short period of residence in Moscow;

but it was the weekly magazine *The Nation* which made it possible to gather together all these past threads of observation and experience into a book, by sending me to Europe in 1950 as its special correspondent in Rome for the Holy Year. Some of the incidental facts in this book appeared in *The Nation* late in 1950 and early in 1951, but very few paragraphs have been used bodily. I am grateful to *The Nation* for the opportunity of renewing and strengthening my knowledge of the operations of both the Kremlin and the Vatican in Europe.

Not the least of my acknowledgments should go to my wife, Mary Hillyer Blanshard, for constant assistance and encouragement.

In the appropriate places in the Notes I have expressed appreciation to the publishers who have granted permission to quote briefly from their works. All students working in the field of Soviet policy owe a special debt to the Joint Committee on Slavic Studies for the translations from the Russian press contained in the *Current Digest of the Soviet Press*. Most quotations from the Russian press used in this volume have been taken from these translations, and I wish to express my thanks for permission to use them.

Unfortunately it would not be wise to mention all of my friends in Italy who have helped to gather facts pertinent to this study, but I can mention Professor Giovanni Pioli, of Milan, formerly an official in the Roman Curia, and now a tireless advocate of human freedom; and Ernestine and Anthony Caliandro, of Naples, who helped to show me the seamier side of Vatican policy among the people of southern Italy.

PAUL BLANSHARD

COMMUNISM, DEMOCRACY,
AND CATHOLIC POWER

1
Pattern and Panorama

PROBABLY NO ASPECT OF WORLD AFFAIRS is more carefully avoided by American writers today than the fundamental resemblance between the Vatican and the Kremlin. The meaning of that resemblance has never, so far as I know, been systematically examined or interpreted. Those writers who have approached the subject in passing have skirted its edges warily and avoided the disturbing central facts.

This book, I hope, will serve as an introduction to a neglected theme, an exploration into undiscovered country. Its aim is ambitious, but its pattern is very simple. I undertake to examine in detail two powerful institutions of our time, the Vatican and the Kremlin, selecting for comparison and contrast those features which seem to have significance for democracy. Then I ask: Given these facts of resemblance and disparity, what should be the policy of western democracy in dealing with such institutions? My purpose is to bring the present three-way struggle of Communism, political Catholicism, and democracy into clearer focus in the hope that the analysis will contribute to a consistent American policy for dealing with both the Vatican and the Kremlin.

The importance of the subject scarcely needs emphasis. Our whole western civilization is being threatened by Kremlin power, and we are already marshaling all our forces against the day of catastrophe. At this critical moment an alleged ally, the Vatican, has come forward offering substantial assistance in the war against Communist aggression. The Vatican is certainly one of the most important organizations of our time, and its opposition to Kremlin aggression is undoubtedly sincere. Are we justified in accepting its proffer of partnership? Should we welcome Catholic moral leadership in the desperate fight against Communist advance?

In a sense this whole book is an attempt to marshal the facts necessary for an answer to those questions. I believe that a knowledge of the comparative backgrounds and continuing tactics of both the Kremlin and the Vatican is essential to any sound judgment concerning our role in the three-way struggle. Certainly we cannot prudently make an alliance with the Vatican or with any other world power unless we know where our prospective ally stands on the fundamental issues of democracy. Otherwise we may find that our alleged ally is really an enemy.

In the past we Americans have been rather careless and sentimental in making our international alliances. We have tended to accept as a friend anybody who happened to be at the moment an enemy of our enemies. When the United States Senate voted a loan to Franco's Spain in 1950 over the opposition of President Truman, the Washington *Post* described the theory that "the enemy of your enemy is your friend" as a "theory entertained only by primitive minds . . . utterly at variance with logic or common sense." Our experience in recent wars gives point to that judgment.

In the First World War, we plunged in with solemn pledges against annexations and punitive indemnities without ever stopping to examine the annexationist treaties which had been written by our allies before we entered the conflict. In the Second World War, we accepted Joseph Stalin as an ally in good faith partly because he had been welcomed by other allies before we entered the war, and then we proceeded to co-operate with him without requiring reciprocal co-operation from him and without providing proper safeguards against his anti-democratic post-war designs.

Will we make the same kind of undiscriminating commitments in the next stage of the war against Communism? There are signs that we are in danger of doing precisely that. We seem to have forgotten the possibility that a victory even for the right principles may be transformed into a defeat if the triumph is scored in co-operation with anti-democratic forces. We have already encouraged the formation in Europe of a political bloc which includes many reactionary elements ranging from the fascist regime of Franco to the rightist parties of Italy. At the heart of that rightist political bloc stands a complex organization, the Roman Catholic church-state, a unique blend of personal faith, human compassion, clerical exploitation, and submissive ignorance. It is a vast empire of churches, schools, hospitals, orphanages, monasteries, political parties, clerical-dominated governments, labor unions, embassies, newspapers — a world system of culture, discipline, and loyalty which in many respects outweighs in influence any single nation in the world. Its dual relation to Communism on the one hand and to western democracy on the other is worthy of much more scrutiny than it has yet received.

How far should we go in making concessions to such a church-state in order to hold its allegiance to an anti-Communist front? If we defeat Communism in alliance with such a power, what kind of world will our victory secure? Will it be a world capable of continued resistance to totalitarian power? Will the Vatican gain increased prestige from co-operation with us in the emergency, and then use that prestige to weaken our democratic culture?

It is because I accept the most pessimistic answers to these four questions that I have written this book even during a war period. In fact, I believe that wartime, when men tend to become too sentimental about the qualities of their allies, is precisely the time when a book like this should be written. It should help to serve as an antidote to the traditional wartime illusion that men who hate our enemies are *ipso facto* friends of democracy — and simultaneously it should help to reveal the moral peril behind the military might of our enemy.

A Total War of Ideas

Our primary shortcoming, it seems to me, is that we tend to oversimplify the complex war of ideas which is now shaking the world and try to reduce it to a single conflict, the black-and-white struggle between Communist villainy and American democracy. Such an oversimplification makes us blind to the fact that there are other facets of the struggle and that democracy is faced with other enemies besides Communism. It makes us blind also to the fact that millions of little Communists think they are fighting for democracy when they are fighting for the Kremlin, and that some of our own allies have little respect for democracy. If we cannot disentangle these facts from the present confused situation, and interpret them accurately, we may find ourselves losing a war because we have won it without having a proper understanding of all the forces in the struggle. What shall it profit a nation to win a war for democracy when its sacrifices are turned into a victory for reaction?

I am concerned in this book with disentangling only one feature of this complex situation, the inter-relationships between Communism, democracy, and Catholic power. In the process of the analysis, I use American democracy as a yardstick for measuring the merits and defects of both Communism and political Catholicism; but this does not mean that I assume perfection in our democracy, or pre-eminence in our economic system, or superiority in our predominantly non-Catholic way of life. Good Americans and good democrats may believe in collective enterprise or in the Catholic way of life or in any other pattern of economic or moral behavior and still be good Americans and good democrats, so long as they accept the fundamental thesis on which our whole way of life is based — namely, that the majority of the people have the right to determine our future by free choice based on free discussion, with certain inalienable rights guaranteed to minorities. Such freedom of choice based on free discussion is the only sacred thing in the unique mixture of nobility and egotism which we call Americanism, and it is the only thing which we have a right to use as a yardstick in measuring the Vatican and the Kremlin.

Readers of my previous writings will not need to be reminded that when I speak of the Roman Catholic Church and the Vatican, I am not generally speaking of the Catholic people or of the Catholic mystical faith. Catholicism as a theory of the relationship between man and God is beyond the scope of this discussion, and I make no attempt to consider it or to discuss the truth or falsehood of contemporary Christianity as religion. In general, it is political Catholicism as a world power which concerns me in this book. The Catholic people are not responsible for the great structure of political, diplomatic, medical, and cultural authority which has been built upon their sincere personal faith. They do not make its policies or direct its programs. American

Catholics, particularly, know little about its world-wide significance, and it is an accident of history that they have been born into association with it.

If we are fair-minded enough to exempt the Catholic people from blame for the totalitarian policies of the Vatican dictatorship and to respect the Catholic faith as genuine and sincere, we should also be fair-minded enough to acknowledge that there is a distinction between the Communist hierarchy and the Communist masses, and that not all Communists are equally responsible for the aggressive policies of the Kremlin. It is, of course, very difficult to display cool impartiality when we are looking down the muzzle of a gun. The tendency in discussing Communism in the United States today is to see who can shout the loudest in the negative without stopping to acknowledge that Communism, like Catholicism, is also an amalgam of good and evil which has become for millions of men a fanatical religion. History shows that men cannot kill a religion with a sword, and that nothing can destroy a false religion except superior ideas. If, as Arnold Toynbee says, Communism is "a Christian heresy" which rejects western man's code of values and "preaches an alternative way of spiritual life," then nothing will defeat it except a competing philosophy which embraces whatever positive values Communism offers to man, and which offers in addition those values that have been overlooked or denied by Communism.

I happen to believe that democracy as a system of free choices and a gospel of free minds is the only competing philosophy which has any chance of defeating Communism; but I believe that the defeat can be accomplished only if men recognize that they are engaged in a war of ideas which is even more fundamental than the war of bombs, and that the war of ideas embraces the whole field of democratic versus totalitarian thought. The struggle of democracy against the Kremlin is one phase of the war of ideas, and the struggle of democracy against the Vatican is another. The underlying issue in both phases of the struggle is the same — the rule of the world by free minds.

To meet the threat of the right as well as the threat of the left, we apparently need what a number of liberal leaders have called "Operation Mental Hygiene." The phrase was used in a manifesto, "We Put Freedom First," issued by the executive committee of the Congress for Cultural Freedom, which met in Berlin in

June 1950 to draw up a liberal program for the defeat of Communism. The manifesto said:

> Communism in its present form has become a phantom ideology. It has as little to do with Socialism as the Medieval Inquisition and the reign of the Borgias with the teachings of Christ. Our civilization can be saved if only the hypnotic power of this phantom is broken. This is not a task which any political party or group can achieve alone. It is an Operation Mental Hygiene which can be accomplished only by a joint effort of the educated classes — of the men in public life, in the arts and letters, in the universities and elementary schools, in the trade unions and professional organizations — who determine the intellectual climate of the nation.[1]

The great question before western man, it seems to me, is whether Operation Mental Hygiene will go far enough. In fighting the Kremlin, democracy is being tempted to dilute its own gospel of freedom with a Vatican gospel of authoritarian reaction. The Vatican offers ready-made a competing set of loyalties which have been hallowed by twenty centuries of tradition, and a competing reservoir of anti-Communist strength in its 350,000,000 adherents. But an honest analysis of facts indicates that the Vatican is on the democratic side only for the duration of the emergency because the Kremlin is on the other side. Bertrand Russell put the truth with bluntness and candor in a lecture at Columbia University in November 1950, just after he had been awarded the Nobel Prize. He declared that it is a "dangerous error to think that the evils of communism can be combated by Catholicism," and he described the shortcomings of Communism in the terminology of Catholicism as follows:

> Adherence to a rigid and static system of doctrine, of which part is doubtful and part demonstrably false; persecution as a means of enforcing orthodoxy; a belief that salvation is only to be found within the church and that the True Faith must be spread throughout the world, by force, if necessary; that the priesthood, which alone has the right to interpret the Scriptures, has enormous power, physical east of the Iron Curtain and spiritual over the faithful *in partibus;* that this power is used to secure an undue share of wealth for the priesthood at the expense of the rest of the population; and that bigotry, and the hostility that it engenders, is a potent source of war.

"Every one of these evils," said Mr. Russell, "was exhibited by the Catholic Church when it had power, and would probably be exhibited again if it recovered the position it had in the Middle Ages. It is therefore irrational to suppose that much would be gained if, in the defeat of communism, Catholicism were enthroned in its place."[2]

The Struggle of Titans

Having said these introductory words about the purpose and pattern of this book, I am ready to plunge into a discussion of what I have called the three-way struggle. The participants in the struggle are the Vatican, the Kremlin, and western democracy. The struggle is taking place on three fronts, Vatican versus Kremlin, Kremlin versus democracy, and Vatican versus democracy.

I propose to spend few words in describing the direct battle between the Kremlin and American democracy because mountains of books and oceans of ink have been devoted in the last few years to this theme. Virtually every literate person in the United States knows the central facts of America versus the Soviet Union. Accordingly I shall use those facts only as background material for discussing the character of Soviet power and the relationships of the participants in the three-way battle. How did the Kremlin and the Vatican get that way? How did it happen that they became bitter antagonists? To answer these questions, it will be well to take a brief flash-back to the beginnings of Bolshevism.

The Vatican and the Kremlin have been mortal enemies since 1917, when Lenin and Trotsky launched the world's first socialist soviet republic. The new government was always hostile to ecclesiastical power, and the Vatican was only one villain in its religious rogues' gallery. Its policy was flatly and unashamedly anti-religious, and it drew its anti-religious inspiration from Karl Marx himself, who had described religion as an opiate and as a counter-revolutionary force. The Sixth Congress of the Comintern, meeting in Moscow in 1928, expressed the Marxian doctrine quite candidly when it said: "One of the most important tasks of the cultural revolution, affecting the wide masses, is the task of systematically and unswervingly combating religion — the opium of the people. The proletarian government must withdraw all State support from the Church, which is the agency of the former ruling class."[3]

That Marxian phrase, "the opium of the people," occurs over

and over again in the literature of Communism. The Bolsheviks made sure that the people of Moscow would remember it by inscribing it on a brick wall in one of Moscow's chief squares. Lenin never favored the destruction of religion by law — he was too shrewd to make martyrs of the priests — but he called on all his followers to ridicule and denounce it. "We demand," he said, "the complete separation of the church from the state in order to combat religious darkness with a purely ideological, and exclusively ideological, weapon, our printed and oral propaganda." Probably his most striking comment on the subject was one that he made in 1905 when he called religion "a kind of spiritual gin":

Religion is one of the forms of spiritual oppression that everywhere weighs on the masses of the people, who are crushed by perpetual toil. . . . To him who toils and suffers want all his life religion teaches humility and patience on earth, consoling him with the hope of reward in heaven. And to those who live on the labor of others religion teaches charity on earth, offering them a very cheap justification for their whole existence as exploiters and selling them at a suitable price tickets for admission to heavenly bliss. Religion is the opium of the people. Religion is a kind of spiritual gin in which the slaves of capital drown their human shape and their claims to any decent human life.[4]

Stalin has been almost as frank on the subject of religion as Lenin was. In talking to an American trade union delegation in 1927 about his government's attitude toward religion, he said that "all religion is something opposite to science," and that Communist Party members who "hamper the complete development of anti-religious propaganda" ought to be expelled. Then he asked rhetorically: "Have we suppressed the reactionary clergy? Yes, we have. The unfortunate thing is that it has not been completely liquidated."[5]

In a large part of Russia there were no Roman Catholic priests to be liquidated, since the Roman Church was very weak in Russia proper. It had at least 4,000,000 members, aside from its great strength in Russian Poland, and most of the 4,000,000 were concentrated in Lithuania and the Ukraine. Its Ukraine division, a Uniate branch of the Eastern rite, was taken over bodily after World War II "on its own initiative" — so the Kremlin said — into the Communist-controlled Russian Orthodox Church. Today Roman Catholic activity in the Soviet Union has almost disappeared.[5a]

Lenin and Trotsky naturally devoted their first great anticlerical campaign to the church of the Tsars. The Russian Church was disestablished and forbidden to maintain its own schools; priests were denied voting rights as citizens; Communist Party members were directed not to support organized religion; Communists who were caught going to church even for marriages and baptisms were ruthlessly purged. The Union of Militant Godless, with official backing, poured out vitriolic anti-Christian and anti-clerical propaganda, and, on the whole, the propaganda was strikingly effective in turning away the younger generation from the church.[6]

All this anti-religious effort was carried on under a constitution which guaranteed religious freedom. It is true that some Russians were left free under that constitution to practice some features of their religion. Public worship was permitted, and the churches which were allowed to function at all were frequently filled to capacity with worshipers. The first Soviet constitution decreed complete separation of church and state and declared that "freedom of religious and anti-religious propaganda is recognized for all citizens." But in practice there was only as much religious freedom as the Communist leaders permitted. The non-devotional activity of the Church was strictly limited, and even the devotional features were frequently suppressed when a political excuse could be found for the suppression.

Intermittent streams of anti-Church propaganda poured from the Union of Militant Godless in Moscow, and the streams were turned off or on according to the directions of the Politburo. The emphasis and tempo of the anti-religious drive changed from year to year, but throughout the whole span of Russian revolutionary rule, there is no evidence that the fundamental outlook of the Communist leaders has changed. In 1950 the work previously carried on by the Union of Militant Godless was taken over by the Soviet Society for Political and Scientific Research, which launched a campaign against the "medieval Christian outlook." "The struggle against the gospel and Christian legend," said the chairman of the new drive, "must be conducted ruthlessly and with all the means at the disposal of Communists."[7]

The Soviet government has not seen anything inconsistent with its constitutional pledge to separate church and state and its constant intervention into religious affairs to stifle, direct or manipulate church activity. It proclaimed in the "Stalin Constitution" of 1936: "Freedom of practice of religious cults and freedom of anti-religious propaganda is recognized for all citizens." "Freedom of practice" is a very vague phrase, and it has never been interpreted liberally enough to guarantee to Russian churches the commodity which is described as religious freedom in the United States. The government has never pretended to be impartial as between religious sects. In 1923 it promoted a schismatic branch in Russian Orthodoxy called the "Living Church," and in 1943 it rehabilitated the Russian Orthodox Church and made it virtually an arm of the Soviet regime, restoring the synod of the church to some of its former glory. Organized religion, in Communist eyes, is a corrupting social force which should be used or ignored according to the current needs of the Communist movement; and if it cannot be destroyed by a frontal attack, it should be captured by boring from within.

The most devout believer cannot deny that the Russian Orthodox Church contained social evils which have been condemned by many Christian churchmen in the western world. The Russian Church had a long and reactionary record. After the Spiritual Regulation of 1721, when the Russian Orthodox Church had become the official national church, the priests were completely subordinated to a corrupt ruling class. How far they shared the corruption of their masters is a matter of opinion, but there is no doubt that they helped to bolster the old regime. They took active part in reactionary political movements and used personal pressure to keep the peasants from revolt. In their miserable parish schools they fed their pupils a medieval diet of obscurantism and orthodoxy. They brought a similar anti-scientific attitude into the Russian public schools where they were entrusted with the teaching of religion and morals.

Here is a passage on loyalty to the Tsar, taken from a catechism which the Orthodox priests used in Russian public schools in the 1890's. It is interesting to notice that it is an almost exact counterpart of the catechism used later by the Roman Catholic Church in support of Franco in Spain:

Question. How should we show our respect for the Tsar?

Answer. We should feel complete loyalty to the Tsar and be prepared to lay down our lives for him. We should without objection fulfill his commands and be obedient to the authorities appointed by him. We should pray for his health and salvation, and also for that of all the Ruling House.
Question. With what spiritual feelings should we fulfill these commands?
Answer. According to the words of the Apostle Paul, "Not only for wrath, but also for conscience' sake" (Rom. 13:5), with sincere esteem and love toward the father of our land.
Question. What should we think of those who violate their duty toward their Sovereign?
Answer. They are guilty not only before the Sovereign, but also before God.[8]

It is not surprising that Lenin, long before the revolution, called the leaders of the Russian Church "advocates of serfdom in surplices." Professor Michael Florinsky has declared that "a majority of the Russian clergy were obedient tools in the hands of their ecclesiastical superiors, who themselves were tools of the government."[9] The Third Duma had forty-five clergymen, none of whom belonged to the radical or liberal parties, while the Fourth had forty-eight, of whom forty belonged to the most reactionary parties. This conservative alignment was not surprising, because the Orthodox Synod had instructed the clergy to preach sermons supporting the government, and to attend election meetings for a similar purpose.[10]

Professor Pitirim Sorokin — who was a member of the old Russian Orthodox Church and who escaped from the Bolsheviks with a price on his head — has pointed out that the Russian Church before the revolution was "well-nigh completely identified with the Russian nation. In its absence the structure of Russian society and culture would have been as inchoate and incomprehensible as that of medieval Europe without Roman Catholicism."[11] Professor Sorokin's analogy is especially useful in understanding the competitive position of the Roman Catholic and the Greek Orthodox churches in Europe. The two churches were not parallels, but they were natural and historical rivals. They had been identified with competing states and competing civilizations.

The Struggle Between Wars

From the end of World War I to 1937, the Vatican and the Kremlin engaged in a series of tentative maneuvers which never reached a formal decision — partly because the Vatican always hoped for the defeat of the Bolsheviks and the restoration of Russian rule to an upper class with which it might bargain successfully. It was willing to bargain with Bolshevism, but there was no reciprocal desire for bargaining in Moscow. The Bolsheviks appeared to be quite willing to regard Roman Catholicism in their country as a purely historical phenomenon. Since they have never exchanged representatives with the Vatican, they have had few contacts with official Catholicism on the diplomatic level.

During the years immediately following the Russian revolution the Vatican apparently believed that a deal was possible through which the Soviet Union would permit Catholic activity on its soil in return for neutrality in matters of international policy. Both Benedict XV and Pius XI seemed to have some hope that Roman Catholicism might fill the spiritual vacuum created by the widespread destruction of the Russian Orthodox Church. A group of propaganda and missionary bodies was set up, designed to enter Russia and reap the ecclesiastical harvest if and when the Bolsheviks opened their doors — or collapsed from their own incompetence.

At the Genoa Conference in 1922, when the Bolsheviks made their bow to foreign diplomacy, the Vatican, hoping to work out a compromise with Lenin, tried unofficially to persuade European representatives to induce Russia to grant complete freedom for religious propaganda. Louis Fischer, in his work *The Soviets in World Affairs,* tells how Chicherin, Soviet Commissar for Foreign Affairs, met the King of Italy and the Archbishop of Genoa on an Italian cruiser and drank a toast to the co-operation of the Kremlin and the Vatican in Russia under a policy of the separation of church and state.[12] When nothing came of the toast or the Vatican's dreams of compromise, the relations between the two organizations became steadily worse.

By 1937, blunt-spoken Pius XI in his encyclical *Atheistic Communism* penned one of the most bitter denunciations of Communism ever issued, and boasted that the Papacy "has called public attention to the perils of Communism more frequently than any other public authority on earth." Pius XI went on to say that "Communism, moreover, strips man of his liberty, robs human personality of all its dignity, and removes all the moral restraints that check the eruptions of blind impulse. There is no recognition of any right of the individual in his relations to the collectivity; no natural right is accorded to human personality, which is a mere cogwheel in the Communist system."[13]

It is interesting to note that Pius XI considered this subordination of man under Communism to be wrong primarily because it was subordination to the *wrong agency,* an exclusive subordination to the "community." On this point he said: "In man's relations with other individuals, besides, Communists hold the principle of absolute equality, rejecting all hierarchy and divinely constituted authority, including the authority of parents. What men call authority and subordination is derived from the community as its first and only font." Pius XI, who had signed the Vatican Concordat with Mussolini in 1929, and who wrote this attack on Communism shortly after Mussolini's conquest of Ethiopia, revealed no comparable indignation over the subordination of his country to the fascist "community."

If Pius XI had known what World War II was to bring forth, he might have been even more bitter against Communism than he was. World War II, and the realignment of power which came afterwards, gave the Soviet Union its opportunity to strike at Catholic strength in middle and eastern Europe. As the Soviet forces swept westward, Catholic power for the first time confronted a total enemy using all the resources of modern communication to destroy it. The friendly governments in these regions, which had treated the Papacy with some deference, rapidly disappeared. The first casualties were Poland and the Baltic States. Eventually came Rumania, East Germany, Hungary, Czechoslovakia, Yugoslavia, and Bulgaria. In the end the Kremlin came into authority over at least 45,000,000 members of the Roman Catholic Church who had not been subject to its rule before 1939. The Baltic States and parts of Poland succumbed to Russian control before the Soviet Union entered the war, as a result of the Hitler-Stalin deal of 1939. The rest of conquered middle Europe was acquired by the Kremlin at the end of the war, or shortly afterwards, either by force of arms or by Communist political penetration.

The Vatican Meets Defeat

What happened to the Catholic Church in these countries as

the Soviet steam roller lumbered westward? It will be many years before the full story can be told, but its main features are already known to the world.[14] It will be enough here to note that everywhere throughout the conquered sections of middle and eastern Europe the Vatican and the Kremlin joined in mortal combat, and the Vatican in every case met complete or partial defeat. The tactics of battle varied from country to country, but the spirit of the antagonists did not. The struggle was described by the Vatican as a battle of religion against atheism, but it was from the beginning much more than that; it was an all-out struggle for survival between two cultures and two systems of power. The Communists, through controlled regimes that were established by arbitrary and undemocratic methods, legislated against traditional Catholic practices in parochial education and ecclesiastical marriage. The priests struck back with appeals to the wrath of God. The left-wing governments deprived some churches of their property and stripped many leaders of their special privileges. Great landed estates were taken away from religious orders, and many monasteries closed. The Catholic press was curtailed, censored, or suppressed. Catholic Action groups were disbanded as a threat to public order, and many Catholic charitable institutions were confiscated or closed. Thousands of Catholic priests who rebelled were punished for treason or disloyalty. Archbishop Stepinac went to prison in Yugoslavia and Cardinal Mindszenty in Hungary. Many lesser priests suffered a worse fate.

We shall see later that the Communist case against some of these clerics was not wholly lacking in merit, because freedom of education and economic justice were involved in the dispute together with religion; but the Communist *method* of prosecuting its enemies had no merit. It revealed a fundamental contempt for democratic processes. The fact that the Catholic Church in many disputed zones had become an ally of monarchy, feudalism and economic reaction could not excuse the Communists for their denial of due process of law to their priest-victims.

In most cases the Kremlin was clever enough in extending its territory not to make a frontal and official attack on religious liberty as such. It concentrated its attack on the Church as a great landowner or as an enemy of public education or as a promoter of specious "miracles." Actually, most of the churches in conquered eastern Europe were left free to continue their services of worship, and many of the priests collected the same salaries from left-wing governments that they had previously collected from conservative governments. In several countries the strategy of the Soviet attack was so adroitly planned that compromise agreements were reached with Catholic bishops. Poland was the best example of this partial compromise, and the Hungarian hierarchy was also maneuvered into a compromise. The Polish Catholic bishops finally signed an agreement with their left-wing government in April 1950 without the previous approval of the Vatican, and Hungarian bishops followed suit in a similar manner in August 1950.[15] These incipient movements toward national Catholic independence have caused consternation at the Vatican. There is nothing the Pope fears more than a kind of Catholic Titoism that would attempt to preserve the moral and spiritual values of Catholicism while repudiating Roman dictatorship.

In several countries the Communists have already succeeded in splitting the local Catholic hierarchy by organizing a dissident, national Catholic bloc which has defied the Vatican's right to control its policies. In Rumania, which had a 1927 concordat with the Vatican, the left-wing government terminated the concordat and brought an entire section of the Roman Catholic Church into the Rumanian Orthodox Church, controlled primarily by Moscow, taking at least 1,500,000 members away from Rome. A significant break toward a local-controlled Catholic church in Czechoslovakia came in early 1951 when a pro-government bishop began to ordain pro-government Catholic priests without Vatican approval; several other bishops joined with the first dissenter.

Everywhere the spirit of the struggle between the Kremlin and the Vatican has been uncompromising on both sides. Each antagonist in its propaganda campaign has represented the other as the epitome of all evil. Neither antagonist has compromised unless compelled to do so. The Church's submission to left-wing governments in countries like Poland and Hungary has been, in the last analysis, a forced submission, and if the Kremlin has treated the Church respectfully in any country, the treatment has been due not to friendship but to sagacity. The Kremlin has in most cases used the pretext of freeing the people from an external, reactionary power, claiming that its own particular brand of external power is neither reactionary nor dictatorial. Wherever the Kremlin has found it feasible, it has treated Catholic priests as enemies of the people and taken over as many of their social and educational functions as possible. Wherever the Church has dared, its leaders have fought back with the weapons of boycott and mass demonstration. When these weapons have failed, the hierarchy has been forced to rely on moral condemnation only; and when outspoken public moral condemnation has been impossible, it has reluctantly accepted temporary submission.

At this writing, the issue in middle and eastern Europe is still undecided, but the odds are overwhelmingly in favor of the Soviet Union. The Catholic Church has lost ground in every country where the two antagonists have directly clashed, and Soviet power has steadily increased. The Soviet Union, in fact, during the thirty-four years of the Vatican-Kremlin struggle, has developed from a weak and defeated second-rate power into the greatest military regime in Europe and one of the two greatest military powers in the world. If the forces of Communist China can be counted as part of Soviet military might, the Kremlin now represents the greatest aggregation of mass power in all human history.

During this same period the Vatican has steadily lost power in several parts of Europe and America to the rising forces of secularism, fascism, socialism, and modern science. It gambled on fascism as a potential ally in Italy and Spain, and lost prestige with fascism's defeat. It still holds a top-rank position in Italy, Spain, Portugal, Ireland, and Belgium, and substantial participation in power in the Netherlands, West Germany, and France. But as a total force in world affairs it is probably less important today than it was in 1917, and certainly less secure. Its worldwide empire is declining, while that of the Kremlin is expanding. Its total membership, perhaps 350,000,000,[16] is fourteen times that of the Communist parties of the world, which are estimated at only 25,000,000; but membership is not a very trustworthy gauge of power in modern society. Altogether, the Kremlin rules at least twice as many people as are included in the entire membership rolls of world Catholicism, and its effective military power is incomparably greater than that of the predominantly Catholic nations. The Vatican, in order to protect itself in a material world, must rely on its non-Catholic political allies; it no longer has armies and navies of its own; it no longer reigns in a Catholic continent in conjunction with Catholic princes.

The stakes involved in the Vatican-Kremlin battle are very high, especially for the Catholic Church, and its very existence in eastern Europe depends upon the defeat of the Kremlin. Poland was, until its partition under the Hitler-Stalin pact, the third Catholic country in Europe, with more than 20,000,000 Catholics. Hungary and Czechoslovakia had between them 15,000,000 more Catholics. Today nobody knows how many loyal members are left in these countries, but there is not much doubt that the younger generation is being weaned away from the Church. At least one-eighth of the total world strength of Catholicism is directly involved in the fight, and, in a sense, the prestige of the whole Catholic system of power is at stake in the battle.

It is not surprising, therefore, that since the westward advance of the Kremlin began, the Vatican has been an open advocate of a new holy crusade against the Communist menace. The clerical appeals for war against Russia are always dressed in spiritual phrases and embroidered with the clichés of peace and prayer, but the intent is unmistakable. When the Pope issues an appeal to pray for the Russians, and the Catholic press of the world simultaneously features every act of Soviet aggression and every hysterical denunciation of Soviet policy, the meaning of the papal supplication is self-evident.

The Vatican's "Great Purge"

In this whole battle in eastern Europe between Vatican and Kremlin forces, the Vatican has tried to convince the world that the struggle is primarily between atheism and God; and the Kremlin has worked with equal zeal to convince the world that it is a battle between working-class democracy and reaction. Neither has been wholly successful because, in fact, the struggle is often complex and confused. The official issues, as described by both sides, are frequently not the real issues. The elaborate Communist charges of "collaborating with fascist enemies" which were leveled against Catholic leaders in the iron-curtain countries seemed too pat to be true, even when they had "evidence" to support them. The contrary picture presented by Vatican propaganda seemed also a little too simple and pure, especially for those who were familiar with past Vatican strategy in European countries.

The haggard countenance of Cardinal Mindszenty, pictured in a Communist-controlled courtroom in Hungary as he sat between armed guards, touched the hearts of millions of people in the west when it was reproduced in their newspapers, and the Catholic Church in the United States exploited popular sympathy to the limit. But the western world was not quite so sure about the purity of the cardinal's motives when it was disclosed that — as John Gunther has pointed out — the Catholic Church was the nation's largest landowner, that the cardinal was bitterly opposed to the government's land-reform program, and that he had been receiving a salary from the government twice that of the Prime Minister.[17] Further doubts were raised in many minds when his sympathies with the Hapsburg monarchy were revealed, and when he excommunicated every Catholic legislator who voted to make the nation's Catholic schools into public schools. Perhaps this was a religious fight, and then perhaps it was not. To many an outsider it also looked like a fight between two foreign powers, the Kremlin and the Vatican, for a Hungary that belonged by right to neither.

Similar doubts were raised in many minds when the Vatican attempted to picture the persecution of Catholics in Yugoslavia by Tito as purely anti-religious in character. The lean, dark figure of Archbishop Aloysius Stepinac, when he was imprisoned by the Communists for various political crimes, was pictured very effectively in many western newspapers as a martyr for religion pure and simple, a victim of atheist Communism. There is no doubt that he was a victim of Communist power, but it is also true that he had been associated with some of Europe's most reactionary, pro-fascist forces, including Ante Pavelitch of Croatia, whom the Washington *Post* called quite accurately "the Croatian Fuehrer." The Pavelitch regime was bloody and brutal, but it never drew any severe rebukes from the Vatican. In fact, the Pope had telegraphed a cordial greeting of good wishes to Pavelitch in 1943 after he had been in power long enough for the world to appreciate the nature of his regime. That regime had murdered thousands of Orthodox priests and leaders, and even some of Croatia's Roman Catholics thought that their archbishop deserved something worse than imprisonment for condoning the liquidation of the Vatican's chief religious competitor in the region.[18]

Perhaps, also, it was popular doubt about the character of the Vatican's holy war that induced the Pope on July 13, 1949, to issue a Holy Office decree under which every Catholic sympathizer with Communism anywhere in the world might be excommunicated. The decree attempted to narrow the issue between the Kremlin and the Vatican to religion and religious freedom. Written in the form of official answers to official questions addressed to the Holy Office, the decree pronounced an anathema against anyone in the Catholic world who even read the literature of Communism or co-operated with a Communist organization in any way. It said:

This Supreme Sacred Congregation of the Holy Office has been asked:
1. Whether it is lawful to enlist in or show favor to the Communist Party?
No, for Communism is materialistic and anti-Christian. Besides, Communist leaders, although they sometimes verbally assert that they are not opposed to religion, show themselves, nevertheless, both by doctrine and by action, to be in reality enemies of God, of the true religion and the Church of Christ.
2. Whether it is lawful to publish, read or disseminate books, newspapers, periodicals or leaflets in support of Communist doctrine and practice or write in them any articles?
No, inasmuch as this is prohibited by law itself (of Canon 1399, *Corpus Juris Canonici*).
3. Whether Catholics who knowingly and freely place actions as specified in questions Nos. 1 and 2 above may be admitted to the sacraments?
No, in accordance with the common principles governing refusal of the sacraments to those not having proper dispositions.
4. Whether Catholics, who profess and particularly those who defend and spread, the materialistic and anti-Christian doctrine of the Communists, *ipso facto* as apostates from the Catholic faith, incur excommunication reserved especially to the Holy See?
Yes.[19]

When an excommunication of this character is "reserved especially to the Holy See," it does not mean that the punishment waits on the Pope's order; the excommunication is incurred automatically, and the absolution depends on the Pope's mercy. The condemnation was so broad that it condemned and anathematized millions of "Catholic" Communists. In fact, about two weeks after this decree, the Vatican newspaper *Osservatore Romano* pointed out, in effect, that even a sports writer for a Communist newspaper might be denied the sacraments, and that ordinary Catholics could not read Communist newspapers to inform themselves about the Communist side of any argument unless they had serious or professional reasons to expose themselves to such dangerous thoughts.

The reaction to this anti-Communist decree of excommunication was much more violent in Europe than in the United States. Italy had more than 8,000,000 citizens who had defied Vatican pressure in the April 1948 election and cast their votes for the left-wing bloc when that bloc had been defeated by the Christian Democrat (Catholic) Party. Since the Church claims that 99 per cent of the Italian people are Catholics, the effect of the decree meant that, on the basis of the Church's own reckoning, at least 8,000,000 Italian Catholics were, or might be, subject to excommunication under its terms. France also had a few hundred thousand left-wing Catholic trade unionists who were susceptible of classification as victims of this decree because they persisted in co-operating with Communist-controlled unions. Moreover, the iron-curtain countries of eastern Europe still had a few peasants and workers who continued to pray Catholic after voting for Communist Party slates. The Communists were shrewd enough to base their counter-attack on the Vatican's decree on the "victimization" of these poor workers.

Two weeks after the decree, a Communist-controlled government in Poland declared that it could not be put into force in that country. Nine days later the government passed a law penalizing with five years imprisonment any priest refusing sacraments to a person who co-operated with the government.[20] The left-wing Polish regime was clever enough to use the most approved shibboleths of freedom in announcing its "humane" law. The law prescribes a penalty of five years imprisonment for any person "who misuses freedom of creed by refusing to let another person participate in a religious ceremony because of political, social or scientific activities or opinions."

In Czechoslovakia the left-wing government waited only two days after the decree to announce that anyone who attempted to enforce the excommunication feature of the decree would be prosecuted for treason. Three weeks later the government sent a priest to prison for eight years, allegedly for refusing to administer the sacraments to a dying Communist. The reaction of the outside press was not unanimously favorable to the imprisoned priest in this case. Perhaps that was one reason why similar tactics were not resorted to by priests elsewhere, and the Church virtually suspended the application of the rule that Communists should be denied Catholic sacraments. In Czechoslovakia the Catholic bishops failed to implement the decree on the technical ground that they could not call a full official meeting.

The Communists, in their counter-attack on the decree in *Pravda,* declared that "the Holy Fathers have not belched such mass curses at least since the twelfth century," and that even then "the number of heretics to be burned did not reach such astronomical figures."[21] But the astronomical figures existed only in the imagination of the Communists — and in the loosely phrased terms of the decree itself. After the tremendous initial ballyhoo, the actual enforcement of the decree soon petered out. It became almost impossible for any journalist in Europe to discover any specific Catholic who had been penalized under its terms. About one month after its promulgation a new "interpretation" was issued by the Holy Office, in order, as the New York *Times* put it, "to clarify but in no wise to alter the fundamental principles." "The Holy Office," said the *Times,* "was moved principally by the desire not to withhold the benefits of religion from the children of Communist marriages. It was felt that if all marriages of Communists were indiscriminately barred, many potentially religious children would be driven away from the church. It was also felt that any Communist who accepted the conditions laid down by the church was sure to be at most a lukewarm Communist and therefore not incapable of being won over."[22] This was tantamount to an admission that the original decree was unenforceable. The Vatican had attempted a "great purge," but had discovered that ecclesiastical penalties were not very effective weapons for destroying opposition forces in the twentieth century.

The Washington-Rome Axis

During this whole struggle in eastern Europe it had become increasingly evident that the Vatican could not stand alone against such a determined and militarized power as the Kremlin, and that it must rely chiefly on American sympathy for future safety. (Already America supplies most of the Church's contributed funds.) Catholic propaganda in America became increasingly important. Every incident of Kremlin persecution was dramatized and underscored for American consumption in the hope that the United States would use its power on the Vatican side in the conflict. (The Communists by this time had become so completely hostile to the United States that they made almost no attempt to disguise their depredations for American consumption.)

In terms of power politics the Vatican was quite justified in directing its diplomatic energies toward the United States. During the thirty-four years of continuous struggle between the Vatican and the Kremlin the whole balance of power of the modern world had altered. The traditional Catholic states had declined in military rank. The United States had become the most important single power in international democratic affairs, and it was generally admitted that only the power of the Soviet Union might successfully challenge it in war. In these circumstances Rome looked more and more to Washington. If it could not convince Washington of the justice of its cause, its struggle for survival seemed hopeless.

At the beginning of World War I, the power alignment had been very different. Then Great Britain, Germany, the United States, France, Italy, Japan, and Russia were all substantial military powers. Now the fate of the Vatican, surrounded by Communist and Socialist forces, depends largely on the friendship of the United States. The Vatican is aware that it was American money, mostly taxpayers' money, and the threat of American arms, that saved Catholic forces in Italy from inundation in a Communist tide in 1948, and that it is chiefly American Catholic money today which is paying for Vatican expansion. That is one reason why the Vatican is so desperately anxious to maintain American friendship and to demonstrate to the American people that Rome stands for a way of life consistent with the American democratic ideal.

In the chapters that are to follow I propose to examine that claim in some detail, beginning with a comparison between the basic power structures of the Vatican and the Kremlin.

regime would be a government of law and that his agents would be compelled to respect national law, he replied: "Let all know that I intend to defend the principle of autocracy as unswervingly as did my father."

When the March 1917 revolution began, it took just five days to dispose of Nicholas and his oligarchy. His regime collapsed under the dead weight of its own incompetence and crime and the acute tensions of war. Nobody had worked out a careful plan for its destruction. Some of the strikers who participated in the relatively mild first stages of the March revolution were as much surprised as the Tsar himself when their modest efforts produced the greatest social upheaval in the history of man. Lenin also was surprised. The actual revolution did not follow his blueprints, and when he returned from exile in April 1917, after the first shooting was over, having been permitted to cross Germany in a sealed train, it took him several months to turn the preliminary "bourgeois" revolution into the thoroughgoing Marxian affair that he had visualized.

Although Karl Marx was the godfather of this Bolshevik revolution, he did not draft its battle plan, for he had died almost thirty-five years before it began, and bequeathed to his followers a jumbled blend of brilliant analysis and bad prophecy which became the bible of the European revolutionary working class. His bewhiskered image served as a kind of holy cloud that went before the hosts of his followers in their journey toward the promised land — and the actual direction of the revolution fell to Lenin. Perhaps it was just as well for Lenin that Karl Marx had never attempted to describe in detail the social order which he called socialism. No blueprint drawn in advance could possibly have served as an accurate guide in the long struggle that followed 1917. Lenin changed his blueprints day by day. He did not hesitate to remodel and reinterpret the philosophy of the master when there were gaps in the master's system of thought, although he was shrewd enough to profess that he always followed the principles of Marx even when he was marching sturdily in the opposite direction. His followers found comfort and strength in the conviction that they were obeying the traditions of the Marxian scripture.

As the revolution progressed and the new government gained

in power, it became apparent that its policies were pragmatic even when its professed principles were unchangeable. Its actual machinery of power was adapted from day to day to the needs of ruling a backward people schooled in subjection and nurtured on tyranny.

The Kremlin Pyramid

What kind of power structure has come out of this unique social revolution? On the whole it is tyrannical and cruel, but it is also fluid and adaptable. It makes use of dogma and tradition, but it is never limited by dogma and tradition.

In a sense, the Kremlin power structure is a pyramid with Joseph Stalin at the top. Stalin determines what the Communist Party of the Soviet Union will do, and the Communist Party determines what the Soviet government and the Cominform will do. But Stalin's power is not official and self-perpetuating like that of the Papacy, and he has no right under Soviet law to determine the limits of his own jurisdiction, or to rewrite the fundamental law of his country in order to continue in power. Even the rule of his Party must nominally find some sanction in the loyalty of the great masses of workers and peasants.

Actually, Joseph Stalin is the peak of a whole series of power pyramids which overlap each other and which, together, constitute the real government of the entity known as the Soviet Union. The most important pyramid is that of the Communist Party of the USSR, which serves as a kind of super-government for the Soviet Union and for the Communist movement of the world. The next most important pyramid is the official Soviet government itself, which is a federal centralized government ruling over sixteen Soviet Republics. The third pyramid is that of the Communist Information Bureau, or Cominform, which rules the Communist parties throughout the world. The fourth pyramid is the all-pervading secret police, now active in every country under Soviet domination. Alongside of these four primary pyramids is a whole series of lesser pyramids which also shape up to one peak, Joseph Stalin. There is the Soviet Union's labor pyramid, heading up into the World Federation of Trade Unions, and there are similar pyramids for a vast network of collateral organizations, ranging from military-training squads for small boys to national associations of philologists.

Stalin's dictatorship in this whole scheme of power is an *achieved* dictatorship, not an inherited one. No one knows how much of his authority would evaporate if he should die tomorrow. In fact, it is one of the nightmares of all authors who write about Stalin that he might die before their books go to press. Is he not past seventy — and is not even the flesh of dictators mortal? It is anybody's guess what will happen when he dies. A triumvirate may succeed him, or a single dictator, or there may be a revolution from the right, or a revolution from the left, or, most improbable of all, a Russian social-democratic state.

The best guess is that nothing much will happen to Kremlin power when Stalin dies. The men who operate the Kremlin are disciplined and able leaders who have built a well-knit power machine that may last for generations without a personalized Communist deity at its head.

At present Stalin's dictatorship is so unofficial that there is no description of his role in the laws of his country. It is true that he is Generalissimo, Secretary General of the Central Committee of the Communist Party, Chairman of the Council of Ministers, and First Member of the Supreme Soviet. But even this mighty combination of offices and titles would not in itself give him the right to dictate to the Russian people if he had not built up a scheme of auxiliary controls along with the pretentious offices. Officially the Russian people have a constitutional democracy with a class framework. Officially it protects them from some of the worst abuses of dictatorial power. It will be worth while to look at this official setup to see how much of it is a false front and how much of it is reality.

Democracy — on Paper

The Soviet Union has had three written constitutions since the revolution, one in 1918, one in 1924, and one in 1936. The first one applied only to the Russian Soviet Republic. Nominally the 1936 constitution, often called the Stalin Constitution, is in force today. Actually, as we shall see, no written law in the Kremlin's system of power can be taken at face value. Wherever democracy exists in the system, it is nearly always a paper democracy.

All three of the Soviet's constitutions have been based upon the theory that the Soviet Union is a dictatorship by the working class. In the early days of the new state, city workers were the backbone of the revolution. Councils of soldiers and city workers served as strike committees in the great rebellion in 1905. Lenin was shrewd enough to seize upon these Councils as logical instruments of revolution, and the resultant Soviets of Workers and Soldiers Deputies played a vital part in the 1917 Bolshevik revolution.

Even after 1924, the Soviet Constitution discriminated against large non-proletarian sections of the population, including employers of labor, private traders, rich peasants, priests, and former princes. For a time in the elections for the All-Union Soviets, the Bolsheviks actually gave the city proletariat a five-to-one preference in voting rights over the peasants.

As the Communists grew stronger and more confident, they expanded the base of their electoral system, and in the 1939 Congress of the Communist Party they opened the door to the intelligentsia in the same way that they had previously welcomed the workers and peasants.[2] Today almost everybody in Russia is considered sufficiently proletarian to vote — unless he has committed a crime or tried to form an opposition party. In that case he may be given the opportunity of serving the state in a forced-labor camp.

There are today 111,116,000 voters in the Soviet Union, and 99 per cent of them vote at election time. Nominally, they vote on the basis of universal, secret, unweighted suffrage, one vote for every man and woman who has reached the age of eighteen. Nominally, also, the Soviet Union is ruled by a democratic government with three branches, legislative, executive, and judicial, all controlled, as the British system is controlled, by the elected legislative body. (The Communists do not like our doctrine of the separation of powers.) The Supreme Soviet, the highest organ of state power, is the legislative branch; the Council of Ministers, formed by the Supreme Soviet, is the executive branch; the Supreme Court and the Attorney General, also chosen by the Supreme Soviet, make up the judicial branch.[3]

The Supreme Soviet is elected every four years after a great campaign of public "education" and discussion, and it is supposed to meet twice a year in two large houses for very short sessions. The numbers in each house vary slightly from year to year. One house, the Council of the Union, has 682 deputies elected on a geographical basis from districts with a population of 300,000; the other house, the Council of Nationalities, has 657 deputies and is elected by the constituent republics of the Soviet Union. The whole Supreme Soviet in 1946 had a Communist Party proportion of 81 per cent.

Outwardly this Supreme Soviet has many of the features of a western democratic assembly. Its meetings receive much publicity. Its deputies are hard-working and are besieged by complaints from constituents; they make speeches and travel free on the railroads; they elect their own committees and do a large part of the work of legislation in those committees. Nominally they have much more power than American congressmen. On paper, they can amend the Soviet Constitution, elect the Supreme Court, declare war, and determine the policy of the armed forces. Nominally they elect the oversize Council of Ministers which, in 1946, included sixty-four executives. No court can declare the acts of this Supreme Soviet unconstitutional.

In practice the legislators of the Supreme Soviet leave almost all of the most important decisions to an inner group of members. The Supreme Soviet itself sits only about ten days to two weeks each year, and during the rest of the year its powers are exercised by a thirty-three-man Presidium which does everything but draft permanent laws. It is composed entirely of Communists. It not only issues decrees that are just as important as laws, but also puts them into force even before they have been referred to the Supreme Soviet for approval. Also it serves the nation as a kind of collective president in dealing with foreign powers.

I hope that this description has not given any reader the impression that the government of the Soviet Union should be taken at face value. Actually the reality is quite distinct from the appearance. Nevertheless, there is one feature of the scheme which contains some bona fide elements of democracy. All the great Kremlin agencies have excellent pipelines running down into almost every factory, mine, university, village, and farm in Russia. The flow of opinion in these pipelines is not entirely a one-way affair. The government's contacts with the masses have what Professor Julian Towster might call "opinion-tapping and policy-crystallizing" value. The contacts serve as political barometers and "attraction devices."[3]

Of course, the purpose of the opinion-tapping devices is frequently destructive. The Kremlin's aim in maintaining a pipeline to any particular local group may be the prevention and suppression of honest thinking and accurate information in that group. The Kremlin tends to regard its whole intelligence network as a kind of espionage system. "In our Soviet country," Stalin said once, "we must evolve a system of government that will permit us with certainty to anticipate all changes, to perceive everything that is going on among the peasants, the nationals, the non-Russian nations and the Russians; the system of supreme organs must possess a number of barometers which will anticipate every change, register and forestall . . . all possible storms and ill-fortune. That is the Soviet system of government."[4]

Because of this "barometer" policy, there is a great deal of speech by the Russian masses — but it is not, by American standards, free speech; it is controlled speech. It has therapeutic value in eliminating some of the worst abuses of power, but it is never permitted to go beyond certain limits. In fact, the protests of the Soviet masses are not entirely unlike those of the serfs in the days of the Tsar; they can be heeded or not according to the seriousness of the threat involved. "In general," says Barrington Moore, Jr., in his study, *Soviet Politics — the Dilemma of Power,* "the power of the population to influence the policy of the Communist Party leadership is about equal to the power of a balky mule to influence its driver."[5]

The worst defects of the controlled system show up at election time. Then it becomes apparent that the whole system, with its 111,116,000 voters, is manipulated by a small political bloc in such a manner that genuine popular choice is denied. According to the Constitution, candidates for the Supreme Soviet can be nominated by six kinds of groups, including the Communist Party, and these groups are free to campaign openly for their nominees. In practice the course of the campaign for candidates for the Supreme Soviet is always determined in advance. The Communist Party always "participates" with other groups in selecting candidates. This means that a vigorous critic of the Party's policy is always sifted out at the beginning of the elective process. If, by any chance, the name of a real enemy of the Party slips by the first screening, his name can be vetoed at the next administrative level by an area election commission. The area election commissions are always predominantly Communist. The New York *Times* has even recorded an instance in which a candidate's name was replaced by another name *after* being printed on the ballot.

The Communists are quite shameless and unabashed about this kind of manipulation. They do not accept western standards for free elections, and they make no pretense about it. Ordinarily they do not permit more than one candidate for any office on a ballot, and before election day they force an agreement on a single slate of candidates. If they cannot reach an agreement by suasion, they impose the single slate of candidates anyway. In 1946, Stalin commented that "if people here and there do elect hostile persons, it will show that our propaganda work was organized very badly indeed and that we fully deserve such a disgrace."[6] Usually the "disgrace" is avoided by strenuous manipulation and heavy pressure on lower officials long before the name of a critical candidate has reached a ballot.

In the election of 1946 for the Supreme Soviet, the single official slate of candidates received 99.2 per cent of the vote. In 1950 the percentage was 99.98. In 1946 more than 800,000 votes were cast against the government's slate for Council of the Union; in 1950 only about 300,000 voters ventured to challenge the system in any way. That is a negligible number in a voting list of 111,116,000. The 1950 result was hailed by the Communists as a very "satisfactory" outcome in the "most democratic" election in the world.[7]

The Government Above the Government

What power can compel some 200,000,000 people to accept such a travesty of democracy? The answer is: the Communist Party. In the Kremlin's scheme of power the Communist Party is the government within the government and the government above the government. It has the recognized moral right to determine the fundamental policy of every political and economic unit within which it operates. As the *Agitator's Guidebook* said in 1947: "The All-Union Communist Party of Bolsheviks is the organizing and directing force in the Soviet Government, the heart, brain and spirit of the people, the leader and teacher of the workers."[8] The Communist Party is the party of equality as well as power, a party of superior devotees dedicated to the common good. As one writer put it in *Pravda:* "The Party is the advanced, conscious detachment of the working class, containing all the best elements of the proletariat, armed with revolutionary theory."[9]

The Russian people have been conditioned by a generation of intensive propaganda to accept the Communist Party as the rightful director of the whole national machinery, the authorized governing class of the nation. The Party's claim to leadership is not based on force alone. The organization, as we shall see later, includes men of great competence and intense convictions, fired by a deep but perverted religious ardor. Their exercise of dictatorial power is infused with prodigious energy and genuine devotion to their cause.

The Communist Party originally developed its conspiratorial conception of rule under the guidance of Lenin, when all the revolutionary parties of Russia were outlaws fighting against the Tsar. Lenin, as a good Marxist, taught his disciples that an interim period of dictatorship was necessary to effect the transition from capitalism to socialism. He conceived of the Party as a group of the élite, controlling the mass, and operating the revolution and the dictatorship for the purposes which they held to be valid. The members of the élite were to be well disciplined, resolute, and ready to die for the new society. They were to be entrusted with the task of educating and guiding the masses of the people toward a collectivized world. Their function, as both Lenin and Stalin pointed out, was to form through their dictatorship "a higher type of democracy . . . which expresses the interests of the majority (the exploited) as against capitalist democracy which expresses the interests of the minority (the exploiters)."[10]

Lenin had no patience with the claims of any non-Party groups to share in power. He was ruthless and often unprincipled in opposing non-Bolshevik organizations. A few weeks after the Bolshevik revolution, he lost the first free election for a Constituent Assembly to the opposition parties, winning less than one-fourth of the votes for the Bolshevik Party; but he discarded the result, emphasized the Bolshevik victory in the great cities, and denied that the non-Bolshevik parties had received any mandate from the people.[11] His Red soldiers closed the newly elected Constituent Assembly the day after it convened. Lenin, however, was never so abrupt in dealing with his own party, and he never attempted to attain the supreme dictatorial powers later assumed by Stalin. The central committee of the early Bolshevik Party was not a one-man affair; its debates were relatively free and, during that early period, some genuine differences of opinion were permitted in high places. For a few years the opposition was even allowed to publish its criticisms.

In the gradual process of centralizing power into a permanent dictatorship, Lenin and his successors claimed to be carrying out the one true gospel of Karl Marx. They carefully selected those Marxian gospel passages which confirmed their prejudices. They attempted to make every important decision appear to be a logical fulfillment of the principles of their master's materialism. Their citations seem to be very impressive until one begins to read the equally persuasive Marxian citations of their opponents.

Within two years after the revolution the Bolshevik (Communist) Party became the party of the nation, the directing force of all economic and political policy. At first its role was entirely unofficial. Then, when it had become secure in power, it wrote its mandates into the 1936 Constitution and became officially "the directing kernel of all organizations of toilers both public and state." By 1938 the Party was willing to admit in its official history that the great movement for the collectivization of agriculture in the 1930's was a revolution "from above."[12] This change, according to the official history, was supported by "millions of peasants," but there was no pretense that the movement began with the peasants or was directed by them. The support was described as coming "from below." The millions of peasants who died during the process of forced collectivization were just as dead as if they had been exterminated by the forces of the Tsar.

At no time in this process of growth and development has the Communist Party been an open, people's party in the western democratic sense. Membership has always been a privilege, not a right. Except in wartime, adult applicants for membership are carefully screened before admission, and forced to work for a considerable time as probationers. Those who are too independent to serve with blind loyalty are not usually admitted to final membership — this has been the general rule, except during World War II when the bars were let down for a time in order to secure mass support in time of crisis. In 1950, the Party numbered only 7,000,000 members, about 6 per cent of the voting population of the Soviet Union. They were the devotees, the fanatics, and the saints of the inner temple of Communist faith.

The use of the Party organization as a nucleus and a spearhead makes it clear why no ordinary chart of power structure can explain the Kremlin. The Party is inside of every organized unit in Russian life. It is more like a fanatical fraternity than an American political party. It is something like a Jesuit order or an officers' corps in an army. Since its policies are created at the top, the incoming flow of millions of new members at the bottom does not guarantee that the Party will become democratic. Every new member is compelled in advance of admission to submit to the Communist hierarchy's tests of loyalty.

An organization under such dictatorial control could easily become ossified and static if it were not for the great network of pipelines that run out from central headquarters to all parts of the nation. This contact machinery keeps the Party dynamic. The process of renewal through partial freedom has been well described by Warren B. Walsh and Roy A. Price of Syracuse University in their *Russia: A Handbook:*

> In summary the Soviet Union is governed by a dictatorship, but at least two qualifications must be added to this statement. First, the government is not a tyranny which operates without any regard for the will of the people. Popular opinion, although by no means always decisive, is never ignored by the rulers of Russia. The Party apparatus which transmits orders downward also is equally efficient in transmitting reports of the popular will to the top. These reports may sometimes be overruled, but they are always taken into account. Certain things, such as the form of government, may not be questioned, but within rather narrow and understood limits there is much greater freedom of discussion and criticism in the Soviet Union than is generally recognized by people outside the country.[13]

To stimulate the right kind of discussion in the masses, the Party has official agitators, about 2,000,000 of them throughout

Russia, one for every sixty-five persons in the country over fifteen years of age. They serve as the "spiritual" leaders of every type of cultural and propaganda organization which feeds strength into the Party.[14] In function their activity falls about midway between that of a Tammany leader and a parish priest. During the election campaign of 1946, the Party stepped up its propaganda campaign and appointed 3,000,000 agitators instead of 2,000,-000. For the purpose of inspiring and instructing these professional agitators, the Party publishes a semi-monthly magazine called the *Agitator's Guidebook,* which had a circulation in 1939 of 650,000 copies, the top circulation for Russian journals at that time.

The feeder organizations cover the whole nation and reach every age group. The most important is the Young Communists or Komsomols, numbering perhaps 15,000,000 young people ranging in ages from 15 to 26. Its official name is the All-Russian Leninist Communist League of Youth, and its task is two-fold: to feed new human strength into the Party, and to make all of Russia's younger children sympathetic to Communism. All its officers who serve in the higher echelons must be Communist Party members, and even the secretaries of village branches must be approved by district secretaries, who ultimately come under a leader appointed by the Politburo itself.

The Komsomol organization is the chief recruiting agency for the Party, and it serves as a kind of broad testing ground for all new aspirants to Party position. It admits young members rather freely, without much screening, and then the higher officers watch the new recruits carefully to eliminate those who do not fit snugly into the Party system. In general, the Komsomol organization is an immense success. It played an important part in Russian victory in World War II, and in the various elections for the Supreme Soviets after the war it was strikingly successful in getting out the vote. At the present time, one of its most important tasks is to supervise and foster two groups of younger children, the Pioneers (10 to 16), and the little Octobrists (8 to 11), who serve as a kind of Communist Boy Scout movement, developing habits of loyalty and obedience to the Kremlin.

By the use of similar techniques the Russian labor unions have become as completely subservient to the Communist Party as the Komsomols. "Soviet Trade Unions," says a statute of the Congress of Trade Unions of the USSR, adopted in 1949, "carry on their work under the leadership of the Communist Party, the organizing and directing force of Soviet society."[15] Nominally these statutes of the Russian trade unions give the workers the right to strike and to participate in the control of their unions, but all trade unions are officially operated by Communist-controlled agencies on the basis of the principle of "democratic centralism." In practice they are "speed-up" agencies for Soviet production, using the class shibboleths of free labor. The Central Committee of each union is responsible to the Congress of Trade Unions, and the Congress of Trade Unions is responsible to the Politburo. This is the pattern of Russia's "free" labor system.

The Mysterious Politburo

Although the Communist Party begins at the grass roots of Russian life with political cells in schools, factories, mines, farm co-operatives, and the army, it is topped by the most powerful and aloof group of political leaders in the modern world, the mysterious and sacrosanct Politburo. Names of some of the members of this Politburo have become world-famous — Stalin, Molotov, Bulganin, Malenkov, Beria — but the organization itself is shrouded in secrecy. Technically it is a subordinate commission of the seventy-two-man Central Committee of the Communist Party, but actually it is itself the fountain of all Kremlin power. Its ten to fourteen members rule the whole power structure of world Communism with a sway which is absolute and unquestioned. The Politburo's power runs down to 113,000 Party cells, through the All-Union Party Congress, which is officially the supreme authority of the Party, and through the Party's top bureaus and committees. Technically, the whole Party's structure is built upon elective assemblies and committees, but in actual practice the power is completely centralized in the Politburo.

Gradually, in the years since the revolution, this system of power has become more and more top-heavy. At the beginning, the Party held frequent congresses and conferences, and even represented anti-Stalinist points of view. Then, with the rise of Stalin, it met less and less frequently. Although it is required by its laws to meet at least once in three years, there have been only three meetings in the last nineteen years, and during those years Stalin and his associates have gradually tightened their control over every aspect of the great Communist machine. Now the Politburo is supreme — but in practice the Politburo means the son of a Georgian cobbler, the world's most powerful single individual, Josef Djugashvili.

Around him in the Politburo sit the men who rule the Communist system of power. Although their names are known to the public, their published histories have great gaps in the record. Since the Communist Party controls the nation's publicity machine, only those facts which are of service to the Party are made public. The personal lives of the leaders are often shrouded in great mystery. Even the place of Politburo meetings is a carefully guarded secret, and the roster of rank within the organization is revealed only indirectly in official publicity material. Under its rules every decision is announced as unanimous, and the public never knows whose voice was raised in a defeated minority and promptly silenced by Stalin.

Probably it is safe to say that major issues get thorough discussion behind the closed doors of the Politburo. The men who are sifted upward through the great Party network of power until they reach the pinnacle of Politburo heights are often men of great ability and administrative skill. They have been tested by decades of devotion. "These men," said General Walter Bedell Smith in *My Three Years in Moscow,* "are, in every sense of the word, dedicated men. As a group they represent the most effective form of authoritarian dictatorship, that is, dictatorship by committee. They are, without exception, intelligent, able, disciplined, and indefatigable. I doubt that any statesmen in the world work half as hard as those of the Soviet Union. They are Stalin's men, loyal to him and owe their advancement to him and to his appreciation of their merits and abilities."[16]

For our purposes the important thing to note about this top echelon of Communist power is that it governs its world by its own special type of party responsibility. Party responsibility in the Kremlin system is quite different from party responsibility in a democratic society. Parties in a democracy are responsible to the people. They are subject to the laws made by the representatives of the majority. In the Kremlin system of power all members of the Party are responsible not to the people but to the heads of the Party. The internal government is the supreme government; the external government is a showpiece. The internal government must never yield its point of view to any other group no matter how great the majority against it. Its own sovereignty is the only sovereignty that counts: that is what the Party means by the principle of democratic centralism. First things come first, and the Party is first. Any legislator or bureaucrat who questions that dictum is bound to be expelled from his Party and government post. If he persists in defiance, the secret police trail him down, the People's Court sentences him, and the Soviet's railroads (fourth class) carry him off to Siberia. That is what makes the Soviet Union a police state in spite of its professions of lofty idealism. Lenin said in 1901: "We have never rejected terror on principle, nor can we do so."[17] The new nation which he helped to build has followed his dictum literally.

International Headquarters

The Kremlin's control over world Communism through the Cominform is based on the same principle of rule by a government within a government. Nominally the world Communist movement is self-determining. Each constituent nation with a Communist Party of its own sends delegates to central Communist headquarters, and there the wise men of the movement are supposed to draw up plans for continuing world revolution. In practice the overwhelming superiority of the Communist Party of the Soviet Union in money and men makes all other Communist parties subordinate to it. It is the "Mother Church," and it is also the mint and treasury of world Communism. "In our time," said *Pravda* in January 1949, "one can be a genuine revolutionary and internationalist only by unconditionally defending and supporting the Communist Party of the Soviet Union and the Soviet Union itself."[18]

This subordination of world Communism to Russian power has developed gradually over the past twenty-five years. In the beginning the Socialist internationals, from which the Communist movement broke away, were representative organs of the revolutionary working class. Even the first Communist international, organized in 1919, quite fairly represented the leftist factions in some fifty-eight countries, and the first Communist congress contained many world leaders of considerable independence and idealism.

After Lenin's death and the rise of Stalin, the Comintern gradually lost independence. The turning point came when Stalin was chosen Secretary General of the Russian Communist Party in 1922. He immediately began to establish personal boss rule in the various national units outside of Russia, and Communist leaders from the United States and Europe soon discovered that they were completely helpless in the face of his wishes. Representatives of the Comintern in many countries became virtually Stalin's personal agents, not representatives of their revolutionary constituents.

The full extent of the new boss control was revealed at the 1928 Sixth World Congress of the Comintern at Moscow, when all resolutions were passed unanimously. Behind that unanimity lay not agreement but skillfully manipulated coercion. Within a year after that boss-controlled Congress, Stalin had established so complete a dictatorship over the Communist parties of the world that even in far-away America he could bludgeon a nine-to-one majority in the American Communist Party into ousting the Party's top secretary, Jay Lovestone.[19] Thereafter, he calmly substituted as Secretary of the Party William Z. Foster, whose faction had polled only 10 per cent of the vote at the preceding party convention; and presently he substituted Earl Browder for Foster, and then yanked out Browder to reinstate Foster. Ironically enough, Stalin attempted almost the same maneuver against Tito twenty years later in Yugoslavia, and he failed only because, by that time, the Communists of Yugoslavia knew what to expect when they challenged his dictatorship.

During this period the Comintern became more and more arrogant in dealing with labor parties which approached it in the hope of self-respecting co-operation. The small, left-wing Independent Labor Party of Great Britain asked the Comintern in 1934 in "what way it could assist in the work of the Communist International," and received a brusque reply:

> A party cannot be regarded as sympathizing with Communism unless it fights against the treacherous social-democracy, against the Second International and the reformist leaders of the trade unions and comes out

decisively against all attempts to create new internationals. A party cannot be regarded as sympathizing with Communism unless it sympathizes with the slogan of Soviet power and supports the Soviet Union.[20]

During all these years of the building of Stalin's personal system of power, the representatives of the Comintern were acting as secret revolutionary agents within each nation. In time of war they were spies and in time of peace merely agitators; but the distinction was unimportant, because the Kremlin considered itself in a perpetual state of war against non-Russian civilization. And today the same agents and their successors are playing the same role in virtually every nation in the world, obeying the orders of the Kremlin and attempting to destroy the governments of the countries in which they operate. In describing them it is impossible to draw a dividing line between the intellectual adherents and the military agents, because, in a sense, all the ideological agents of the Kremlin are commandeered by central headquarters as military agents also.

It would be a mistake to think of these Kremlin agents merely as criminals or gangsters, even though their tactics are often criminal; for in their own estimation their ideals are noble and exalted. Their ranks include many devoted dreamers and idealists who regard their work as a holy sacrifice for humanity. Unfortunately for the idealism of these comrades, the ruthless boss rule of international Communism has become more and more apparent in recent years. The atmosphere at central headquarters has changed profoundly since 1919 from flaming idealism to calculated scheming, and the most savage reprisals are directed against any comrades who deviate from the bossed Party line.

By the time of the Hitler-Stalin pact in 1939, the representatives of the Comintern were so universally hated and distrusted by most idealists in the west that the sudden switch to Hitler was considered only a final proof of moral degradation. Distinguished independent socialists like Ignazio Silone of Italy had withdrawn from the Executive, and those who remained were rubber stamps for Stalin. The Comintern in the crisis of 1939 and later in its support of Russian aggression revealed that it was just as amoral as fascism.

When the Soviet Union was forced into the war on the Allied side by Hitler's invasion of Russia, Stalin realized that the western fears of the Comintern were a handicap to Russia. He abruptly abolished the international organization in May 1943, the year of the battle of Stalingrad, and announced a policy of co-operation with other nations. This action, said Stalin, "puts an end to the lie" that "Moscow allegedly intends to intervene in the life of other nations to 'Bolshevize' them."[21] Moscow's western allies received the announcement with cheers, but those who were familiar with Communist history did not take Stalin's pronouncement at its face value. They suspected that he would shift with the political winds when some new opportunity for intrigue was offered. In fact, in 1945, as soon as Allied victory seemed certain, the new co-operative attitude of Stalin evaporated. In the 1945 edition of *The History of the USSR* used in Russian schools, the death of the Comintern was recorded briefly; in 1946 the description of the obsequies was entirely omitted.

The world was not surprised when Stalin launched a new world Communist agency under the auspices of the Politburo in October 1947, after a secret meeting in Poland of the representatives of nine European Communist parties. It was dubbed the Communist Information Bureau, and the title was promptly abbreviated to Cominform. The press of the world made earnest attempts to find out the basic facts about the new organization, but discovered very little, and to this day the life of the Cominform is a veiled mystery. The Communists allege that the Cominform is not a successor to the old Comintern, but a new, purely informational Communist co-operative. It publishes a magazine in many languages under the lengthy and non-euphonious title *For a Lasting Peace, For a People's Democracy,* and the master edition is, appropriately enough, printed in Russian. The magazine started to function in Belgrade, but when Tito began to show some signs of independence, the headquarters were promptly moved to Bucharest.

This new Communist international reveals in striking fashion the sorry decline of world Communism as an independent, international movement with pretensions of social idealism. The Cominform is little more than a transmission belt for Politburo propaganda and orders, and if it is accorded any respect in political circles, the respect is due not to its own accomplishments but to the backing of Russia's armed forces. Intellectually it has reached a new low in docility, and its remaining representatives include only those leaders who have surrendered every vestige of intellectual integrity to Moscow. Most of its leaders, in fact, are devotees who have spent years in special training institutions in the Russian capital. The Cominform rarely bothers to meet, and makes no attempt to represent its constituent movements fairly. Although it is officially supposed to be nothing but an editorial board for a Communist magazine, it steps out of that role at will to perform any emergency operation desired by Stalin. In June 1948 it excommunicated Yugoslavia's Tito from the Communist communion because he had dared to defy his political boss. The story of that excommunication is too long to tell here,[23] but it was immensely illuminating in exposing the final degradation of democratic principles in the top levels of world Communism.

3

The Vatican Structure of Power

THE VATICAN AND THE KREMLIN are both dictatorships. That simple and unpleasant fact, which is as obvious as the sunrise, is so consistently avoided by most "responsible" journalists in the west that millions of people have never faced it. The two dictatorships, of course, have many contrasting features. One is very old and the other is very young. One emphasizes the goals of the next world, the other of this. One is soft and the other is hard. But they are both dictatorships, and no cloudy ecclesiastical effusions can quite conceal that basic fact.

The two dictatorships grew up in different environments and in different centuries, and they are the children of contrasting inheritances. One absorbed many of its characteristics from the Roman Empire, the other from Tsarist Russia. Compared to the Kremlin, the Vatican is a mature and almost static institution. Its policies and doctrines were crystallized and congealed long before the Soviet Union was born.

Although the Vatican lacks the vitality and the dynamic energy of the younger organization, it dominates its subordinate parts so completely that it deserves to be called the most unified and stable government in the world. It faces no threat of violent revolution from within, since dissident priests do not carry guns. It is safe from effective internal criticism because it permits no opposition clerical party to challenge its major policies. It is relatively experienced and guileful because it has had several centuries' head start over the Kremlin in learning the arts of dictatorship. It is serenely confident in its own moral supremacy. As Father Aelred Graham has said about the Church in an authoritative recent symposium, *The Teaching of the Catholic*

Church, "She is the one supra-national force able to integrate a civilization fast dissolving in ruins."[1]

Innocent III brought the Papacy to a pinnacle of prestige and power about seven hundred years before Lenin moved into the Kremlin. It was 363 years ago, in 1588, that Pope Sixtus V reorganized the Roman Congregations and built what the *Encyclopedia Britannica* calls "the foundations of that wonderful and silent engine of universal government by which Rome still rules the Catholics of every land."[2]

The earliest Christians knew nothing about popes, bishops, and ecclesiastical dictatorships. Their communities were apparently quite simple and democratic, with an emphasis upon other-worldly values. Since the Founder of Christianity gave no detailed directives to his followers concerning the methods to be used in building an organization, the Christian Church grew up during the first three centuries after his death in a more or less unsystematic manner. St. Paul, the missionary, did much to transform the simple other-worldly religion of the Founder into an effective engine of power for this world. St. Peter was also important, but nobody knows exactly how important. It is certain that he was not universally recognized by the first Christian congregations as the head of the Church.

Roman Catholic theologians claim that Jesus made Peter the first pope, and they claim support for this theory from the famous passage in the sixteenth chapter of Matthew, part of which is carved on the dome of St. Peter's: "And I say unto thee, thou art Peter, and upon this rock I will build my church; and the gates of hell shall not prevail against it. And I will give thee the keys of the kingdom of heaven: and whatsoever thou shalt bind on earth shall be bound in heaven; and whatsoever thou shalt loose on earth shall be loosed in heaven."

What does this famous passage mean? It occurs in only one of the four gospels, and many authorities believe that it is an interpolation.[3] Certainly it is not consistent with the passage which immediately follows it, and there is nothing else in the teachings of Jesus to indicate that he gave Peter any *exclusive* rank among his disciples. Two chapters later in the Gospel of Matthew he makes the same general grant of power to *all* his disciples.

Whatever may be the truth of the conflicting views of theologians about this passage in Matthew, it is clear that the words of Jesus are broadly symbolic and not definite. His statement does not mention Rome or popes or bishops or any ecclesiastical machinery of power. It contains no specific sanction for a centralized dictatorship or papal infallibility or a Vatican diplomatic corps. It has been inflated into a kind of Magna Charta for Vatican dictatorship by reading into it a whole library of meaning which is not there.

The first Christians knew nothing about the alleged primacy of Roman bishops, and some of the first "popes" of the Roman church were buried in the catacombs as simple bishops, without any papal inscriptions on their tombs. The idea that Roman bishops should be made into popes developed slowly and gradually as a result of historical forces and population movements. The early church needed some central authority to rule its quarreling factions and to mobilize the clergy for effective work; and metropolitan Rome seemed the most logical place for the seat of that authority. There is no evidence in the Bible or in other early Christian literature that the structure of power which actually developed in the Roman Catholic Church ever had any necessary connection with Christianity, or that the founders of the first churches contemplated anything like the Papacy.

It has often been said that the real founder of the Roman Catholic Church was the Emperor Constantine, who was baptized on his deathbed in the year 337. Certainly his conversion changed the whole future of the Church. He admitted Christianity to the status of an authorized government religion in 313, and one of his successors of the fourth century, Theodosius the Great, made Christianity the sole official religion of the Empire. Ever since then, the practical union of church and state has been one of the cardinal tenets of Roman Catholic policy. Trading on the advantages of that policy, the Church was gradually transformed from an informal association of believers into a great ecclesiastical empire, patterned in structure after the Roman Empire. Later on it became an important temporal power itself, and acquired armies, navies, diplomats, and considerable stretches of territory. For several centuries it held sway over princes and kings, and for several other centuries it was completely dominated by princes and kings.

Pope Gelasius I laid the basis for the modern Catholic theory of church and state in the fifth century when he evolved the notion that the world is divided into two spheres, one to be controlled by the Church and the other by the civil power. According to his theory, both powers derived their authority from God Himself, the separation was effected by Christ, and human beings must "give to each its due."[4] Gregory VII carried papal claims farther in 1075 by explicitly declaring that popes have the right to depose emperors; and five years later he gave a demonstration by deposing Henry IV and absolving all Henry's followers from their oath of allegiance to him on the ground that if popes could "bind and loose in heavens, so also they could take away and grant kingdoms, principalities, and all other possessions of men, according to men's merits." He claimed that "the Pope stood to the emperor as the sun to the moon."[5]

Boniface VIII issued in 1302 the boldest and most presumptuous statement of papal dominion over the world, his encyclical *Unam Sanctam;* but his reign actually marked the beginning of papal decline. Claiming at the time of his jubilee in 1300 that he was both a pope and an emperor, he had two swords carried in front of himself in his official processions to symbolize this dual majesty, with the official contention that "the temporal is subject to the spiritual."[6] The Papacy has never yet renounced the symbolism of those two swords, since it still claims to be both a church and a state. It did not renounce its status as an important European temporal and military power until it was compelled to do so by force of arms.

From Coronations to Infallibility

At the height of papal power, the popes conferred crowns on the ruling monarchs of Europe and did much to direct the policies of their governments. It was Leo III who crowned Charlemagne Emperor of the West — not Charlemagne Leo III. Other emperors kept coming to Rome for their coronations for about six hundred years. Even Napoleon Bonaparte planned at one time to be crowned in St. Peter's, but changed his mind because of a dispute with Pius VII.

In the slow process of growth and adaptation, it took many centuries for the present elaborate structure of Vatican power to jell. The "engine of universal government" was not at first either silent or wonderful. Papal dictatorship was often faced with bitter opposition, and sometimes very questionable methods were used to sustain it. One of the important factors in establishing the temporal power of the Papacy was the famous "Donation of Constantine," a document which purported to show that Constantine had given to the Pope all the provinces of the Western Roman Empire. It was circulated for centuries before it was finally discovered that somebody had forged it at Rome during Charlemagne's time. Even when the Roman bishops were finally recognized as leaders of the Church, they had at first very little power, and they were not given the undisputed right to choose other bishops until the nineteenth century.

The final totalitarian structure of the Church, the structure which exists today, was not perfected until the corruption of the Middle Ages had produced the Reformation, and that Reformation had in turn produced a counter-reformation within the Church in the direction of more centralized authority. While the rest of the world was busy with the great expansion and development of modern liberalism and science, the Papacy, working under the influence of the Jesuits, tightened its grip on every branch of the Church and stood fast against the tides of modern culture. Seminaries and religious orders directly dependent on the Papacy expanded into a great network of ecclesiastical power. Throughout the world the Jesuits acted as promoters and intelligence agents of papal absolutism, reporting to the Pope on any movement among the clergy that might weaken his authority. Laymen were given no power over the papal machine except on one occasion, the Council of Constance in 1414, and that was because a pope and an anti-pope were quarreling for authority, and each of them needed lay support to win the struggle.

Gradually, authority in the Church became more and more centralized, and local independence disappeared. The climax came in 1870 when Pius IX, "a kindly man of inferior intelligence,"[7] had himself declared infallible. That was only the final theoretical step in a centrifugal process that had been going on for centuries. Strangely enough, the natal year of infallibility, 1870, was the year when Lenin was born.

In this whole process of growth and adjustment, there was

no clear dividing line between the development of the Church as a religious institution and the development of the Papacy as a worldly sovereignty. Church and state overlapped and fought each other and participated in each other's affairs. The frontier between them changed from year to year according to the power of the reigning pope. The popes played politics with princes and traded bishoprics as astutely as a modern baseball magnate trades good pitchers and batters. The princes frequently nominated the popes and directed their policies, and the popes for centuries accepted the right of princes to veto "undesirable" bishops. The Holy Roman Empire of the Middle Ages was exactly what its name implies, a church-state empire in which, for at least three centuries, the relation of the state to the Papacy was the paramount fact of its existence. The hierarchy patterned its machinery of power after that of the Empire, and the divine right of popes went hand in hand with the divine right of the political upper classes. The Church never ceased to claim dominion over as much of the world as it could subdue.

The Church's chief temporal domain, the Papal States of Italy, originated about the eighth century, and ended in 1870 when the forces of the new Kingdom of Italy marched into Rome, and took over three million subjects from a papal regime which, as the *Encyclopedia Britannica* says, had been "an incompetent theocracy with a corrupt administration." The people of Rome in a plebiscite ratified the transfer of their city to the new Italy by a vote of almost 9 to 1. In 1929 the Vatican got back 108 acres of its former power and glory in the form of the new Vatican City State.

I have taken this brief canter through Church history in order to point up one judgment, that the Catholic dictatorship of the twentieth century is only a natural and logical consequence of the Church's growth in a pre-democratic mold. The Papacy rose to its present pinnacle of centralized autocracy from a background of imperialism and serfdom, and it has never completely shaken off its imperial and feudal past. In the very nature of things it could not be expected to shake off its past. Born in an era when the rights of free peoples were almost unknown in the world, it has never talked the modern language of freedom or adjusted its government to the ideals of freedom. Its culture has always been a strictly controlled, anti-democratic, and authoritarian culture. It has accumulated over the centuries a mass of anti-scientific and anti-social traditions which have been perpetuated largely by tradition and inertia. If we are inclined to be harsh in judging the Church for continuing to cherish these traditions, we must remember that it has come to us from an age when democratic values were almost unknown.

The Blueprint of Power

The Vatican structure of power is a pyramid with a very thin peak, where the Pope is perched in a position of such grandeur and isolation that he is qualitatively detached from the rest of the machinery of power. He is so far above his subordinates that he is more like a public image than a human being.

Directly under him are fifty to seventy cardinals of the College of Cardinals — there have been rumors for several years that the quota will be raised to one hundred. The cardinals hail from many different nations, but they do not represent the Catholic people of those nations, since they are chosen entirely from above in accordance with standards of performance determined by the Vatican.

Under them come the twelve Congregations, three Tribunals, and five Offices of the Roman Curia, which are really bureaus, boards, and courts organized to carry out the administrative and judicial program of the Church. They are made up of cardinals and lesser prelates who operate at the central headquarters of the Church in Vatican City, or in separate buildings in Rome that have acquired a kind of extra-territorial status. Their top personnel are appointed and controlled entirely by the Pope, and the public rarely hears of them.

The top Congregation is that of the Holy Office. It determines doctrine, condemns books, punishes heresy, frames marital and medical policy, and grants certain kinds of dispensations. The Congregation of the Consistory creates new dioceses, examines the reports of the bishops throughout the world, and proposes new bishops for appointment by the Pope. The Congregation of the Oriental Church supervises the churches of the Eastern rite. The Congregation of the Sacraments regulates matters of discipline concerning the seven sacraments, and includes in its work such matters as declaring children legitimate or illegitimate.

The Congregation of the Council supervises the discipline of secular priests and laymen. The Congregation of the Religious supervises all the Religious orders of the world; the Congregation of the Propagation of the Faith manages the missions; the Congregation of Sacred Rites supervises rites, canonizations, relics, and liturgy in the Latin church; the Congregation of Ceremonies regulates ceremonies and protocol in the Vatican Court; the Congregation of Extraordinary Ecclesiastical Affairs handles special matters of great diplomatic importance, such as concordats; the Congregation of Seminaries and Universities supervises all Catholic universities and seminaries in the world; the Congregation of the Basilica of St. Peter is not really a Congregation but a local management committee.

All of these Congregations include staff members and associates who are not cardinals, but the policy decisions are made by the cardinals alone. The whole power of the system comes from the top down. Under the cardinals come the bishops and archbishops who rule the dioceses scattered throughout the world. They are appointed directly by the Pope, on recommendation of the Congregation of the Consistory, but the Pope is under no obligation to follow any recommendation if he wishes to make a personal appointment.

Below these high dignitaries are the priests and nuns and brothers who do the basic routine work of the Church throughout the world. They minister to the sick and comfort the dying and preach brotherhood from the jungles of Africa to the wilds of Labrador, but their selfless service does not necessarily make them citizens in their own commonwealth. They are completely disfranchised on all major matters of policy, and must accept the rule of their bishops or the heads of their religious orders.

At the bottom of the pyramid are perhaps 350,000,000 baptized Catholics throughout the world who have professed allegiance to the Holy See at some time in their lives. Even more than the priests, they are utterly subordinate in the Catholic system of power. They have no representatives of their own choosing in the central administrative machine, and no plenary popular assembly. Their organizations for propaganda and social activity have no right to participate in the making of policy, and they do not even own the church buildings which they pay for.

The Pope is the absolute monarch of this whole structure. Elected for life by a committee of princes, the cardinals, he has exclusive power to appoint new princes as vacancies occur, and the princes have no power to discipline him or to remove him after they have once elected him. They can, of course, attempt to correct him or dissuade him from some unwise course of action, but he is never compelled to accept their advice or to submit his policies to any assembly, elected or appointed. His powers are nominally limited by canon law, but if he chooses to be arbitrary he can remake canon law without calling any General Council of the higher clergy. In any case, his will is supreme over all General Councils, and no pope has bothered to call a session of a General Council in more than eighty years.

In a sense the Pope operates a limited monarchy in which he sets the limits of his own power in consultation with his underlings. He makes no claim at the present time to complete authority over all the various aspects of the lives of his subjects, but he could if he wished extend his power almost indefinitely by deciding to define new territory as primarily "moral." His monarchy is not a constitutional monarchy in the strict interpretation of those words because the Catholic people do not have any constitution protecting them from papal power. They do not even have the right to call a meeting to discuss a constitution that might set democratic limits to the Pope's authority. Without consulting them, the Pope can extend his authority at any moment into any new area of medical or political or economic conduct; and he has done precisely that during the last century in a number of important controversies. He may create a new rule against artificial insemination or a new doctrine condemning socialized medicine or a new stricture against the application of the theory of evolution — and the Catholic people have no recourse against his blunders.

The theory of the Pope's power is that God has given him a divine right to rule the Church, and that the right has come down to him from Christ through Peter, as the first bishop of Rome, and thence to all succeeding popes. The Catholic theologians have some difficulty in explaining how this authority has come down unsullied through the ages without being lost in the shuffle. Several popes in the fourteenth century never came near Rome, but set up their luxurious quarters in Avignon, and during the Great Schism (1378-1417), a rump College of Cardinals backed a series of "anti-popes" with the support of a large part of Catholic Europe.

Catholic theologians never admit that any pope has ever made a mistake in declaring the wrong doctrine true, or vice versa. By definition, a pope cannot make a mistake in matters of faith and morals when he speaks on such matters with due solemnity as pastor of the human race. This argument protects the Pope against all criticism. When, for example, Pope Pius IX said in 1870 that all popes are infallible in matters of faith and morals, he was himself infallible in saying this, and his judgment was retroactive. So, it became a dogma of divine truth that all popes in all ages have always been infallible in making solemn declarations on matters of faith and morals.

This circular type of reasoning is remarkably effective in repelling any attack. Unfortunately, it is a little like the Chinese system of ancestor worship. It consecrates not only all the virtues but also all the mistakes of the past.

The fact that some of the popes of the Middle Ages were notorious political spoilsmen and personal sinners, even in the eyes of Catholic historians, does not in any way affect their infallibility. "The Pope," runs the approved doctrine, "is infallible but not impeccable." An impeccable person is one who possesses "the impossibility of offending God."[8] Not many people in history, even popes, have ever attained this condition of absolute moral sublimity. Hence, a pope may offend God by his rascality, but still be incapable of error when he speaks as pastor of the human race.

The Biblical peg on which Catholic scholars hang the whole theory of papal power is the verse in Matthew 16 which I have already quoted: "Thou art Peter . . ." Catholic theologians also use, together with this passage in Matthew, certain statements of early Church fathers such as Clement of Rome, Ignatius of Antioch, Irenaeus, Caius, Tertullian, and Origen, all calculated to strengthen the tradition that Peter preached in Rome and was buried there after being crucified head downward. On the whole, these passages from early Christian writers strengthen the tradition that Peter visited Rome, but they do not prove much, since they do not provide specific information about the claims of the Roman Church to unique authority.[9]

The Role of the Pope

In these days a pope is much more than a doctor of the Church; he is also an ecclesiastical business man, a master of ceremonies, and a diplomat. He need not be a good preacher, but he must be a shrewd tactician and capable manager of men. He must take care of a vast, polyglot army of ambitious cardinals, archbishops, and bishops. He must spend a great deal of each day as a kind of ecclesiastical showpiece, going through repetitive ceremonies for the faithful. He must deal with Catholic and non-Catholic statesmen in advancing the Vatican program in world politics.

In all of these activities the Pope's role as pastor and prophet is quite secondary. His actual output of sermons and doctrinal discussions does not need to be large, and his thought does not need to be original. In fact, since he must conform to the infallible utterances of his infallible predecessors, he must avoid the appearance of originality as a plague. He has a great staff of assistants to do his detailed work for him, and a world-wide intelligence service to keep him informed on matters of political policy. His work load is enormous, but it is the work load of a diplomat and administrator, not of a pastor of souls.

The present Pope, Pius XII, embodies remarkably well the new conception of papal power in the modern world. He possesses, as the *Little Italian Catholic Annual* says, "a powerful harmony and a rare equilibrium." He is a distinguished leader of considerable charm and dignity, an Italian patrician who moves about easily with people of wide culture. But he has never been the full-time pastor of a church, and he has never served as an ordinary parish priest. He is an ecclesiastical diplomat groomed from childhood for success as an ecclesiastical diplomat.[10] He went directly from the closed Catholic educational system into the office of the Vatican's Secretariat of State, and worked his way up as a political negotiator, Nuncio, Secretary of State, and finally Pope. His encyclicals reflect his origin and outlook. They are narrowly denominational and wholly traditional.

The Pope's supervision over his bishops is necessarily superficial. No human being could possibly remember all of these bishops and guide them personally. He must rely for their selection chiefly on the recommendations of the Congregation of the Consistory, and the members of this Congregation must in turn rely chiefly on the recommendations of local bishops. The Pope, of course, can intervene in any diocese in the world when a policy problem arises, and remove or promote any bishop at will. This power affects the whole operation of the church profoundly and makes it impossible for any anti-papal party to arise to challenge any policy.

Once every five years every bishop in the world must make the long trek to Rome to visit the Holy Father personally and offer homage at the tombs of St. Peter and St. Paul. He must submit a detailed report of his affairs in Latin, "neatly written on opaque paper," and somebody in the Vatican must read these reports so that the Pope will appear to be all-wise and sagacious when he interviews each bishop. To save the Pope from a logjam of visits and reports, the *ad limina* visits of the bishops are staggered on a regional calendar — from Italy one year, from the Americas another year, and so on.

The total supervision of the Vatican over its scattered outposts is phenomenally effective, and the bishops feel that they are working under an all-seeing eye. "Even the private life of a bishop is subject to supervision," says Joseph Bernhart in his comprehensive survey *The Vatican as a World Power*. "Even the lower prelates and pastors are subject to the direct scrutiny of Rome."[11]

This great papal power machine is as overwhelmingly Italian as the power machine of the Cominform is Russian. It is true that at this writing the College of Cardinals has a non-Italian majority, but this fact does not mean much because the central organization which operates Vatican machinery day by day is almost wholly Italian. There is only one non-Italian cardinal who is a resident member of the Curia. The foreign cardinals are nominal members of important Congregations, but they appear at central headquarters very infrequently; the day-by-day decisions are made by Italians, and the operating language of the Vatican is Italian. The Vatican has had no non-Italian pope for more than four hundred years.

The Vatican as an Empire

We shall see later that the Pope has become an institutional figure with qualities quite apart from his physical personality. He has become a synthetic god whose semi-mythical qualities resemble the qualities conferred on Stalin by Communist propaganda.

In one respect, however, the Pope's supremacy is quite authentic and unique. His status is written into Catholic law in such a way that no Catholic has the right to question him. Other dictators of the modern world find it necessary to base their power on some kind of popular sanction or democratic choice; the Pope has no need of such fictions. He rules with calm reliance on his divine right, and he makes no attempt to disguise the undemocratic nature of his sovereignty. His cardinals are princes of the monarchy not only in name but also in fact. Under the Italian Law of Papal Guarantees of 1871, and under Article 21 of the 1929 treaty between Mussolini and the Vatican, cardinals have been granted, while in Italy, honors accorded princes of the blood.

On the top level of the Vatican system, the dynamics of power coincide completely with the structure of power. The real ruler is the nominal ruler, and the Catholic handbooks are quite correct in describing Pius XII as "Gloriously Reigning." No one else approaches him in dignity or power, and no one has the right to challenge his authority. The Vatican, on the whole, rules its imperial territory with complete success. Naturally, in the lower reaches of such a vast and complex system a certain amount of dry rot creeps in because of the entirely undemocratic system of appointments. But the clerical abuses of the earlier days have gradually been reduced, and the Vatican machine continues to be a quite remarkable engine of power.

In terms of political theory the Pope's sovereignty is a special limited imperialism, operating within each nation as a government outside the government, differing in several respects from the standard imperialist techniques of such empires as the British,

French, and Dutch. In the operation of European geographical imperialisms, the central imperial government decides for itself how much authority shall be granted to each one of its colonial peoples. Usually it controls all foreign relations, armaments, and tariffs, and leaves such matters as land taxation and traffic regulation to local colonial bodies.

In the papal variety of imperialism, the Vatican likewise determines what areas of life shall be controlled by the Church, and then the leaders of the Church lay down rules for the conduct of all Catholics within all nations in respect to those particular areas of activity. The Catholic colony in each country is not an independent nation but an imperial segment obedient to the Vatican in a strictly limited sphere. The Vatican, in attempting to control this imperial segment, does not challenge the authority of national governments in such matters as war and the preservation of public order — that is why Catholics are good patriots in both fascist and democratic countries in time of war and in time of peace — but it does assert explicit supremacy over all Catholics in all nations in matters of education, marriage, religion, censorship, and general morals.

Although the Vatican does not claim control over military and criminal policies even in Catholic nations, it is very insistent on one point. The Church and the Church alone has the right to determine what areas the Church shall control. Such a decision, the Church maintains, can never be made by a democratic or by any other kind of civil government. As the *Catholic Almanac* puts it, "the State, as a creature of God, cannot determine the extent of its power but must accept the limitations imposed by God."[12] In practice, the "God" in this rule means God's representative on earth, the Pope.

The new revised edition of the Church's Baltimore Catechism, the most authoritative catechism for American Catholics, says that a government may not prohibit the Church from "legislating in all those matters that pertain to the worship of God and the salvation of souls. If a government commands citizens to violate the law of God they must refuse to obey, for, according to Saint Luke, 'We must obey God rather than men' (Acts 5:29)."[13] The *Catholic Encyclopedia* states the theory of Catholic imperialism in another way: "The definition of an unchangeable dogma imposes itself on every Catholic, learned or otherwise, and it necessarily supposes a Church legislating for all the faithful, passing judgment on State action — from its own point of view of course — and that even seeks alliance with the civil power to carry on the work of the Apostolate."[14]

In one other respect papal imperialism differs from standard imperialism in theory. The jurisdiction of the British, French, and Dutch empires can be accurately delimited because power is contained within geographical boundaries. The geographical boundaries of the Vatican's power are never clearly defined because authority moves with the Catholic population inside all geographical units. Catholics do not live in Catholic reservations. Papal power searches them out wherever they live. In this respect, Vatican imperialism resembles Soviet imperialism.

There is no written constitution of Catholic power, or any bill of rights, as there is for the people of the United States, but there are many papal constitutions and there is the general code of canon law. On the whole, constitutions and canon laws are rules for governing and guiding the Catholic people, or explanations of doctrine, not affirmations of rights of the Catholic people. The *Catholic Encyclopedia* defines papal constitutions as "ordinations issued by the Roman Pontiffs and binding those for whom they are issued, whether they be for the faithful or for special classes or individuals. . . . In fact, a papal constitution is a legal enactment of the ruler of the Church, just as a civil law is a decree emanating from a secular prince."[15] And the *Catholic Encyclopedia* goes on to point out that no acceptance by the Church is necessary for a papal constitution. It just *is*.

> The binding force of pontifical constitutions, even without the acceptance of the Church, is beyond question. The primacy of jurisdiction by the successor of Peter comes immediately and directly from Christ. That this includes the power of making obligatory laws is evident. . . . Bishops, therefore, are not at liberty to accept or refuse papal enactments because, in their judgment, they are ill-suited to the times. Still less can the lower clergy or the civil power possess any authority to declare constitutions invalid or prevent their due promulgation.

The Church theoretically has a legislative body, the General Council of the higher clergy, but these General Councils have been practically abandoned, with one exception, for four hundred years. Even in the days when they were held, they were far from being democratic in their composition. With the exception of the Council of Constance, they were composed of the higher clergy without any lay representation. The Vatican Council of 1870, at which the Pope was declared infallible, is still nominally adjourned, living, apparently, in perpetual hibernation.

If the General Councils are ever resurrected in the future to give the Vatican some appearance of democratic procedure, the Catholic bishops will be confronted by a bizarre rule which makes it virtually impossible for them to disagree with the Pope, a rule which was summarized by Father Aelred Graham recently in the standard work, *The Teaching of the Catholic Church*. He said: "In the event of discussion arising, the final judgment lies with that portion of the Council adhering to the Roman Pontiff, since he is the head of the Church and protected from error by the gift of infallibility."[16] This means in practice that one vote cast by the Pope is always a "majority."

When these undemocratic principles are taught in the Catholic schools in the United States, there is no attempt to disguise the fact that the Vatican is a monarchy, but it is emphasized that there is some democracy in the scheme of control because the humblest man may become Pope.

The Exposition of Christian Doctrine of the Brothers of the Christian Schools once tried to explain away the imperialism of the Church in plausible words for American students in an early textbook. It offered the following questions and answers under the heading "Form of Government in the Church":

From what has preceded, what may we infer to be the form of government in the Church?

It is the monarchical form, pure and simple, for the Pope possesses the plenitude of authority; he is the ecclesiastical heart and head of the whole Church.

Why is this monarchy not absolute, in the common meaning of the term?

Because the Pope can make no change in matters of divine right; besides his infallibility preserves him from doing so.

What aristocracy is there in the government of the Church?

The episcopate, which is of divine institution and without which the supreme pastor cannot govern the Church.

In what sense is there democracy in the Church?

In this, that even the man of humblest origin may attain to the highest of dignities in the Church. Among the great popes and bishops are some who were of very lowly birth and condition.[17]

The American Catholic theologians who drew up this catechism for American students knew that absolute monarchies were very unpopular in the United States, so they attempted to work out a formula which would describe the Pope as something less than an absolute monarch. According to their claim, the Pope has no power to change divine laws. Technically that is correct — the institution of divine law is bigger than any man. But who will tell the Pope which laws are divine? Scripture and tradition, of course, but the Pope has power to create a new "tradition," and no one on earth can tell him it is not a tradition. Hence, if the Pope makes a change in the divine law, it may appear to be a change in the divine law, but actually it is not, because, if it were, the Pope would recognize it and refuse to make it. Is this clear? If not, that is the fault of the good priests who were trying to reconcile infallibility with freedom of choice. They were trying to allow for the phenomenon of change in an "unchanging" system of thought.

In actual practice, change is permitted in the Catholic system of thought by calling it something else. A new doctrine is called a "reinterpretation," and it does not offer any great difficulties in the Catholic system of power because the same man makes and judges the new doctrine. There is no tribunal in the Catholic system for appraising the pronouncements of the Pope in the way our Supreme Court interprets our laws.

Law by Fiat

There is also no legislative assembly of the Catholic people, and all ecclesiastical law is, therefore, law by fiat. Some of it is doctrinal and some of it is disciplinary; some of it is given to the world in bulls and encyclicals, and some of it in the more formal provisions of canon law. But it is all papal law, not people's law.

Pius IX announced papal supremacy to his followers and the world in his *Pastor Aeternus* in 1870, and this "constitution" is now considered the charter of modern papal power. It is a declaration rather than a constitution, and it embodies no detailed regulations. It simply announces papal infallibility as an accomplished fact, pronounces anathema upon any person who questions "the plenitude of this supreme power," and says: "We teach and declare that the Roman Church by divine institution has the supremacy of ordinary power over all the other churches and that this power of jurisdiction of the Roman Pontiff, truly episcopal, is immediate; that the pastors and the faithful, as well separately as collectively, whatever their rite and rank, are subjected to him by the duty of hierarchical subordination and true obedience, not only in matters that concern faith and morals, but also in those that pertain to the discipline and government of the Church spread throughout the world."[18]

This infallible utterance of Pius IX has been supplemented by statements of other popes, extending the papal power into many areas of economic and social life, so that today there is almost no segment of the life of the Catholic people which can be safely and surely described as lying outside the domain of the Pope's authority. Pius XI in his 1931 encyclical, *Reconstructing the Social Order,* protested that it would be wrong for the Church to interfere in "earthly concerns"; but he went on to say of the Church that "she can never relinquish her God-given task of interposing her authority, not indeed in technical matters, for which she has neither the equipment nor the mission, but in all those that have a bearing on moral conduct."[19]

And what matters do not have a bearing upon moral conduct? Pius XI specifically indicates that all social and economic problems have such a bearing, and declares that "we lay down the principle . . . that it is Our right and Our duty to deal authoritatively with social and economic problems." In this same encyclical he delivers sweeping judgments for the guidance of the faithful on such diverse matters as socialism, economic competition, fascist labor organizations, and employers' associations.

It is such sweeping judgments as these that have led one authority to declare that "the universal direct jurisdiction claimed by the Church in the realm of morals in which papal decrees are infallible, can be extended to cover all human actions, all institutions, and all aspects of social, economic and political activities of any community."[20]

The full scope of papal authority can best be appreciated by reviewing the Church's 2414 canons which were finally codified into a Codex under Benedict XV in 1917. From the point of view of American democracy, many of the canons are incredibly restrictive upon the liberty of Catholic citizens. I shall discuss some of those restrictions later. The Code claims superiority over American law in many particulars, and in some respects the Vatican is more open and frank in its claims than the Kremlin. The Code, for example, as it is presented and annotated in a standard work like Bouscaren and Ellis' *Canon Law,* directs American Catholic parents to keep their children out of public schools whenever possible (Canon 1374); declares the marriage of Catholics by American officials entirely invalid (Canon 1094); and makes it compulsory for every Catholic legislator in the United States to oppose liberalizing divorce laws (Canon 1118). We shall discuss some of these encroachments on democracy in more detail when we compare the techniques of the Kremlin and the Vatican in penetrating non-Communist and non-Catholic territory.

The Vatican claims that its canons do not interfere with the laws of states because church laws are religious in nature while the laws of civil governments are confined to "the things that are Caesar's." This conclusion is reached by assuming an entirely unreal division between civil and religious authority. The Vatican, according to Catholic theory, has a primary and divine right of control over all matters of religion, morals, censorship, education, and domestic affairs. The rights of democracy over these areas begin where the Vatican authority ends. Hence, there can be no conflict between Vatican and temporal authority.

This ecclesiastical word-juggling, as we shall see, is quite similar to that used by Communist dialecticians when they argue that there is no conflict between Communism and democracy. Of course there can be no conflict if one party to the dispute has the absolute right to determine the frontiers of authority. The Vatican claims such an absolute right. In practice it operates its own establishments on American soil as extra-territorial enterprises, and then declares that they do not encroach on American sovereignty because they exist under an entirely independent religious sovereignty.

Since judicial power is an attribute of sovereignty, the Vatican has its own ecclesiastical courts with appointed judges who are priests. Laymen may act as lawyers in Catholic courts. but the priests make the laws and sit on the bench. These courts are organized not only in Catholic countries but in non-Catholic countries as well, on the theory that Catholics in every nation should obey their rulings. The best-known Catholic ecclesiastical courts are the Roman Rota, which has general jurisdiction; the Sacred Penitentiary, which has only spiritual jurisdiction and which handles questions involving the use and abuse of indulgences; and the Apostolic Signature, which handles certain kinds of appeals.

The Catholic judicial theory is that Catholic Church courts, by divine right, reach down into every nation in the world where there are Catholics and act for them as arbiters in all such matters as separations, annulments, and the crimes of priests. American law, of course, does not recognize the coercive power of the Church and does not enforce its decrees; but the Vatican insists that American Catholics recognize these courts anyway. It is a mortal sin for an American Catholic willfully to defy the ruling of a Catholic court even when he acts in accordance with the dictates of an American court. The best illustration of this principle is the continued clash between Catholic courts and American courts on matters of divorce. No Catholic court is permitted to recognize an American divorce as morally valid for Catholics.

One reason for the continued maintenance of these separate Catholic courts is that in Catholic countries they are recognized as having certain coercive powers, and they are given supreme authority over all Catholics in matters pertaining to domestic relations, marriage, and inheritance. This recognition of the power of Catholic courts is frequently written into the constitutions of Catholic countries, and in some cases, such as Italy and Portugal, the recognition is embodied in formal treaties between the governments and the Vatican. Under such treaties, and under Canons 120 and 2341, priests and nuns are exempt from trial or suit in ordinary democratic courts, and any Catholic who brings them into court is subject to excommunication.

Priests may serve as judges, but in practice they have little more power than laymen unless they conform to the orders of their bishops. Their appointments, their dismissals, and their promotions all come from above. When they sit down together in a diocesan synod or council, they are prohibited by Canon 362 from taking any action contrary to any ruling by their bishop. Church law says that the bishop is "the sole legislator in the synod." Even the bishops themselves are powerless to take any position contrary to that of the Vatican. American bishops, whose potential power has been regarded with great apprehension by Rome for a long time, may not even hold a plenary session of their own. They have not been allowed to hold an American Church Council since 1884 — that was the Third Council of Baltimore — although Italian bishops are permitted to hold a plenary Council every twenty years.

Perhaps the surprising docility of the American bishops is largely explained by their method of appointment. The appointing authority is wholly un-American, and even the recommending authority, the Congregation of the Consistory, has only one American cardinal in seventeen. Before American priests are recommended by the Congregation of the Consistory for appointment as bishops by the Pope, they are carefully tested for conformity to Roman doctrine and obedience to Roman authority. Any tendency to respect American authority in preference to Roman authority is a fatal obstacle to promotion. The Vatican is as much afraid of national churches as the Kremlin is afraid of national Communist movements.

The Roman system of power is essentially a man's world, as well as a priest's world. Catholic Religious women do most of the routine work of teaching, nursing, and social service in the Church, but all the central agencies of power in the Vatican are without exception male. Even when a woman is made into a saint at St. Peter's, the long procession of dignitaries, headed by the Pope on his portable throne, contains not a single representative of the sanctified sex. There was a strange touch of irony in the fact that when the Catholic party of Italy won the 1948 election from a powerful left-wing bloc, the margin of victory was partly supplied by cloistered nuns who were directed by the Vatican to leave their cloisters for the first time to cast their votes against the Kremlin. Communism, by threatening to destroy the Vatican, gave Catholic women a new standing as citizens in the Italian commonwealth which they had never possessed under male domination in their own religious commonwealth.

This failure to grant citizenship rights to the Religious women who do the basic work of the Church is typical of the whole Catholic system of power. In that system the little people have no rights, only privileges, and the hierarchy confers the privileges. Nevertheless, millions of little people continue in devoted loyalty because, for them, subjection is God's will. Peasants, nuns, brothers, slum-dwellers, mystics, monks, illiterates, priests, dreamers find in the Catholic approach to life a comfort and an inspiration. Their faith is the primary source of Vatican strength. They believe in the Church because for them it symbolizes purity, integrity, sacrifice, and, above all, changeless values in a changing world.

4

The Devices of Deification

SINCE THE RISE OF DICTATORS, the manufacture of gods has become a major political industry. Modern totalitarian rulers have learned to exploit man's hunger for objects of veneration as it has never been exploited before. Mussolini in Italy, Hitler in Germany, and Stalin in the Soviet Union have been exalted into minor deities by techniques of pageantry, publicity, and display that are quite unparalleled in history. The dictators have learned to make effective use of all the gadgets of the machine age in deifying themselves. Their egotism has been served effectively by the loudspeaker, the radio, the motion picture, the kleig light, and television. Today the deification of a leader is recognized as part of the necessary machinery of power in a totalitarian society. George Orwell has immortalized the process in his *1984*.

One interesting result of this new exploitation of the devices of deification has been to eliminate the traditional distinction between political and religious glory. In totalitarian societies it is impossible to tell where political hero-worship ends and religious devotion begins. Totalitarian statecraft has gone over into the field of religion and borrowed some of its most exalted images for political propaganda. Nationalism has become a faith competing with orthodoxy. National devotion has developed its own fanatical prophets and scriptures. Fascism and Communism have tried to supplant Christianity not only as systems of truth but also as systems of moral control. Now the devices of religion are used so openly by Communism that the Communist movement is generally recognized as a competing sect, challenging all the old gods and offering its followers alternative objects of devotion.

In the light of these developments, a comparative description of Vatican and Kremlin devices of deification is in order. Both institutions have developed the most elaborate publicity machines for stimulating in their followers extreme admiration for their two chieftains. It is difficult to say which institution is the more expert in this development, but my own feeling is that the Pope is the champion in this field. Certainly the Vatican is more systematic in its program of deification than any other organization in the world, and its devices have acquired the strength and solidity of ancient traditions. They are accepted today as an organic part of the Catholic faith because they have been associated for centuries with the worship of God and because the Pope is God's Vicar on earth.

The years 1949 and 1950 afforded a unique opportunity for contrasting the techniques of adoration developed by the Vatican and by the Kremlin. Stalin's seventieth birthday, on December 21, 1949, almost coincided with the opening of the Holy Year by Pius XII. In a sense the two leaders staged in December 1949 competing festivals of adulation in which they were the competing objects of honor. Both festivals were prodigiously successful for their own people. Perhaps Stalin's celebration was a little more notable than that of the Pope because the Soviet dictator had a completely controlled system of culture and publicity throughout his whole empire. From Prague to Vladivostok no journalist dared to suggest the thought that the Russian dictator might be anything less than a divinely inspired genius. The Vatican promoted a parallel image of the Pope in its own press, but, outside of Spain, it had nothing to match the iron control of the press in the Soviet orbit.

The Kremlin Trinity

In the Holy Trinity of the Kremlin theology, Marx stands for God, Lenin for Christ, and Stalin for the Holy Ghost. Engels is a demi-god, not quite up to these three. The existence of this trinitarian deity is never specifically acknowledged in Soviet literature, but it is a definite and important part of world Communism. Stalin, as the surviving member of the Communist Trinity, is treated as the Living God.

He began his rapid ascent to the rarified heights of deification in 1920, and since 1929 he has been treated as virtually infallible. His ascent has been somewhat surprising, for he lacks the magnetism and color of prophetic leadership; and he did not reveal any sign in his youth that he would someday be the world's most powerful single individual. Ponderous and sober, rather than brilliant, his method of speech and writing is far from inspiring.[1] Throughout his career he has been a hard driver, a skillful manipulator of men, a tireless administrator. No one has questioned his youthful courage; but in his fighting years he never became a military hero, and later, at the height of World War II, when the fate of the nation hung in the balance before Moscow, he never appeared in the front lines to inspire his men.

As a young man he had been trained for a time in the Theological Seminary of Tiflis, but that was because the Seminary was the chief high school in Georgia, not because he had ever had any hankering for the priesthood. His proletarian background — he was the son of a humble shoemaker — his poverty, his rugged physical power, and his courage united to make him a leader of an entirely different sort from the distinguished, middle-class Lenin and the brilliant man of letters, Trotsky. Where they led men by virtue of their sheer mental superiority, Stalin led men by his mastery of the mechanisms of power. Also he had experience, bitter and instructive experience, and it seasoned him well.

While the patrician, Eugenio Pacelli, was mastering diplomacy and canon law in the protected clerical circles of his home city, and moving upward smoothly toward the papal throne, Josef Vissarionovich Djugashvili was daring death and exile in a running battle with the Tsarist police, a battle which lasted throughout his youth and young manhood. During more than ten years he was a hunted animal, changing names and identities, and almost miraculously preserving his life while he alternately served in the revolutionary underground and labored in Tsarist prison camps. For a time he even acted as a kind of master mind for the "fighting squads" of Bolshevik robbers who looted banks to replenish the Party's depleted treasury. From the age of twenty-three to the age of thirty-four he was arrested and imprisoned six times, sent into exile six times, and escaped six times.

In the beginning stages of the revolution, Stalin was a St. Paul to Trotsky's St. Peter, a crude and ruthless St. Paul, who served as missioner and organizer of the outposts of the Faith. Lenin at one time thought he was too rough and tactless to serve as Secretary General of the Party. In fact, Lenin's famous Testament indicated that he held that view at the time of his death, for in the Testament he said: "Stalin is too rude, and this fault, entirely supportable in relations among us Communists, becomes insupportable in the office of General Secretary. Therefore, I propose to the comrades to find a way to remove Stalin from that position and appoint to it another man who in all respects differs from Stalin only in superiority — namely, more patient, more loyal, more polite and more attentive to comrades, less capricious, etc."

But Lenin's Testament was suppressed over the bitter protests of his widow, and Stalin, three years after Lenin's death, was able to turn even this condemnation by the messianic leader into grist for his own mill. "I am rude toward those who traitorously break their word, who split and destroy the Party," he told a Central Committee meeting in 1927. "I have never concealed it and I do not conceal it now."[2] Oddly enough, the two men who did most to save Stalin's skin by suppressing Lenin's condemnation of him, Zinoviev and Kamenev, were shot for treason to Stalin in the great purge of 1936. Stalin, in spite of Lenin's words, managed to convey the impression to the Russian masses that he was the anointed of the "savior."

Gradually he moved upward in the ranks of Soviet power until he equaled Lenin in popular homage and far surpassed him in the extent of his personal authority. With World War II, Stalin became virtually a Kremlin godhead, using the words of Marx and Lenin to sanctify his authority. Since Marx and Lenin were both quite prolific in voicing many opinions on many sides of many subjects, it was not difficult for Stalin to pluck the appropriate quotations from their works and to use them for justifying any policy he wished to advocate.

While the transformation of Stalin was taking place, Trotsky, who had originally shared honors with Lenin, was demoted to the role of Bolshevik Satan, exiled, and finally murdered. Trot-

glory. He is not obliged to make any campaigns for re-election. He is considered too exalted to meet presidents, generals, or prime ministers outside of the Russian orbit. The period between 1920 and 1950 has been dubbed "the Stalin Epoch." The Academy of Medical Science of the USSR addressed Stalin as "great captain of all victories." Gradually Russian history has been largely rewritten to give Stalin a new and glorified position in his country's annals.

When the great French writer, André Gide, visited Russia in 1936, the Stalin cult had already become so entrenched that Gide was the victim of a bizarre ruling by a Stalinist bureaucrat. He was passing through Stalin's birthplace, the little Georgian town of Gori, and tried to send a telegram of greeting to Stalin through the government telegraph. The local officer in charge would not accept the telegram with its original wording because Gide addressed Stalin simply as "you." Gide was forced to address the Leader, even in a personal wire, as "You Leader of the Workers," or "You Lord of the People."[7]

Stalin's fiftieth birthday in 1929 was a national orgy of government-directed adulation. By the time of his seventieth birthday on December 21, 1949, Cyrus Sulzberger of the New York *Times* declared: "Emphasis is no longer upon either Marx or Lenin. It is upon Stalin, and in the name of Stalin the movement assumes the label of infallibility."[8] The Albanian People's Assembly, under Communist control, voted to erect a statue to "the deity, Joseph Vissarionovich Stalin." The American Communist Party gave Stalin chief credit for winning the war against Hitler, sending a special birthday message to its Leader in which he was conspicuously placed ahead of Lenin: "This victory was possible because the multi-national peoples of the USSR are united in the bonds of true brotherhood. Victory was guaranteed because the Soviet people and their state are guided by the Great Bolshevik Party built by you and Comrade Lenin, and since Lenin's death continuing under your leadership. . . ."[9]

In Moscow, Stalin was called "the greatest military leader of all times and nations (stormy and prolonged applause)." The Academy of Sciences of the Moscow-dominated Rumanian People's Republic announced a symposium to celebrate Stalin's seventieth birthday with papers on the following subjects:

Stalin as Deity

After Lenin's death it did not take Stalin long to move upward to a semi-divine status. The Russian people were not told of Lenin's determination to displace Stalin before he died. Pictures began to appear in all parts of the Soviet Union placing Stalin and Lenin side by side. Always they were flattering pictures, and the lithographs of Stalin looked very much like old Orthodox icons. He became a new Russian saint, an Olympian legend. Within ten years virtually every home, school, store, factory, and office in the Soviet Union had blossomed forth with a representation of Stalin as a figure of godlike proportions. Sometimes there was a great white bust, sometimes an equally impressive oil painting, and there were endless photographs.

Cities and districts were named for the Leader. The Stalin cult of adoration became a recognized part of the national culture, and as soon as the Soviet Union expanded its empire eastward and westward after World War II, the cult was developed in other countries. The same heroic pictures of Stalin appeared in Moscow, Prague, and Peiping. Always the image of the Leader was sublimely glorified. Edgar Snow says he counted Stalin's name fifty-seven times in one four-page issue of a Moscow daily even at the height of the paper shortage in World War II.[5] In 1950, with paper more plentiful, one issue of *Pravda* mentioned Stalin 91 times on the front page alone: 35 times as Josef Vissarionovich Stalin; 33 times as Comrade Stalin; 10 times as Great Leader; 7 times as Dear and Beloved Stalin; and 6 times as Great Stalin. The Yugoslav newspaper which did this bit of research into the processes of deification also recorded the fact that Stalin is commonly described elsewhere in the Soviet press as Great Leader of Mankind; Great Chief of All Workers; Protagonist of Our Victories; and Faithful Fighter for the Cause of Peace.[6]

While this process of aggrandizement was going on in the press, Stalin's public appearances were becoming more rare, and more adroitly managed. In recent years he has never appeared before the Russian public except in well-arranged theatrical settings. His entrances into political congresses have taken on the nature of triumphal pageantry. The common people never catch a glimpse of him in anything less than an environment of

pletely contemptuous of pomp and ceremony, and supremely devoted to the moral ideal of Communist revolution. He hated orthodox religion with every atom in his being and described it as "the thousand-year-old enemy of culture and progress," but he occupied a position in the new Russian society that made it almost inevitable for him to be deified. He would have resented this posthumous deification bitterly if he had lived to see it. He wanted to live and die as a realist, scorning all idealizations except the one idealization which was the core of his aspiration, the Communist society. He regarded popular deities as an abomination, and on some occasions he publicly admitted his own mistakes in a burst of frankness and modesty not characteristic of Stalin. In two letters to Maxim Gorky in 1913 he savagely ridiculed the process of "god-building" by pouring into the god-complex "those ideas worked out by tribes, nations, by humanity at large, which arouse and organize social emotions, and which serve to unite the individual with society." For him it was treason to socialism to make the concept of god palatable by associating it with any ideal of social kindness or humanitarian reform. He scorned such maneuvers as "redecorating the idea of god" and scolded Gorky, saying: "What you have actually done has been to embellish and sweeten the idea of the clericals."[3]

It is one of the supreme ironies of history that Lenin's mummified body and Lenin's sacred memory became the containers for the very complex of ideas which Gorky had described as god. Lenin had expressed a total philosophy for the whole of life, and he had embodied that philosophy in a striking and virile personality. He filled a national need for a new deity. A disillusioned nation which had once paid homage to its Little Father, the Tsar, quickly transferred its devotion to "the great father of the Soviet Revolution," and finally made his marble mausoleum in the Red Square of Moscow the holy of holies of Communist faith.

At the next Congress of the Soviets after Lenin's death, Stalin chanted his sacred vow in the name of the revolution: "Departing from us, Comrade Lenin bequeathed to us the duty of preserving and strengthening the dictatorship of the proletariat. We swear to thee, Comrade Lenin, that we will not spare our energies in also fulfilling with honor this thy commandment!"[4]

sky's successor as the favorite devil of Communist propaganda is a composite individual of large paunch and ugly fangs, known roughly as Mr. Wall-Street-Warmonger.

The elevation of Karl Marx to the role of socialist divinity was not surprising. Although his personal characteristics were far from admirable, he created a new system of thought of immense timeliness and importance. Even before he died, he had become an almost legendary figure throughout Europe. His Jove-like head, his fierce solemnity, his profound dissertations on the movements of man and the meaning of history, all united to lift him above the level of the moral leaders of his age. Yet if he had ever led a socialist parliamentary regime and seen it collapse under his arrogant rule, a little of the magic of his name might have been rubbed off. As it was, he was never called upon to fill in completely the details of his own dream. He concentrated on diatribes against the sins of capitalism, and so much of what he said was true that the deficiencies of his analysis were not immediately apparent. Not until the generation after his death did socialist leaders recognize the fact that he was both a brilliant and a jaundiced philosopher who had oversimplified the universe almost as crudely as the religious prophets he despised.

Perhaps Harold Laski overstated the case when he said that "no tool at the command of the social philosopher surpasses Marxism whether in its power to explain the movement of ideas or its authority to predict their practical outcome." But there is no doubt that Marx's thinking shook the world of the social sciences as profoundly as Darwin's *Origin of Species* had shaken the world of the biological sciences. Marx's philosophy was not wholly sound but almost miraculously timely. It gave to the social discontent of the nineteenth century a gospel, and to the submerged working classes a dream. By the time Lenin had made "Marxism" the creed of the October revolution, Marx the atheist had already become established as the deity of a new world religion.

Lenin himself fitted into the new religion naturally as son and savior. He was a great thinker in his own right, and a great strategist. He was utterly simple in his manner of living, com-

J. V. Stalin — Lenin's Perpetuator in Creating the Theory of the Construction of Socialism

J. V. Stalin — The Theoretician and Leader of the Fight for Peace and Brotherhood among the Peoples

J. V. Stalin — The Military Genius of Our Time

J. V. Stalin — As Mirrored in the Literature of the Peoples of the World

J. V. Stalin — The Teacher and Inspired Leader of the World Proletariat

J. V. Stalin — Coryphaeus of World Science

J. V. Stalin — The Theoretician and Initiator of the Transformation of Nature in the USSR [10]

M. Chiaurelli, writing in *Soviet Literature* on "The Efflorescence of Soviet Art," added a new talent to Stalin's genius, the mastery of art. "Luxuriant has been the efflorescence of the art of the Soviet peoples," he said, "an art replete with lofty ideas and embodied in striking artistic forms. The paths of development of Soviet art, its advance to the summits of mastery have been charted for us by the great Stalin." This was only a routine panegyric compared to the general salutation to the Great Leader:

Father! What could be nearer and dearer than that name?

Soviet people one and all, from Young Pioneers to hoary-headed ancients, call Stalin "our Father."

For like a loving, tender father, like a wise mentor and teacher, Stalin brings up the generation of the new people, builders of Communism.

Multiform is the all-compassing power of Stalin's genius. Not a single field of the creative endeavors of the Soviet people but has been illumined by the rays of his intellect which has pointed the way to the new summits of achievement.

The shoots of all that is new, progressive, beautiful and exalted in our life reach out to Stalin as to the sun. Stalin inspires our people and gives them wings. Stalin's words, Stalin's kindness and solicitude are a source of life-giving strength to millions.[11]

The All-Union Soviet Book Chamber reported simultaneously that Stalin had become the world's most widely read author, with 539,000,000 copies of his works in print in 101 languages. The Kremlin proceeded to boom its favorite author by publishing two million additional colored posters of him and one million personal portraits. Some of the posters read: "Stalin is the People's Happiness," "Glory to Dear Stalin." The state publishing house, according to the New York *Times,* issued forty-five songs about Stalin, and announced that it would soon issue a collection of Stalin folk songs.[12]

"Each one of us," exclaimed a writer in *Pravda* on the occasion of Stalin's seventieth birthday, "alone with himself, wants to confide his innermost thoughts to Stalin, to share both sorrow and joys with him, to dream about the future. . . . Stalin gave us peace of mind based on wisdom: he welded our thoughts and aspirations to the thoughts and aspirations of the people. . . . Whenever the great Teacher points out our mistakes and shortcomings . . . we are thankful and grateful for the penetrating and constructive advice of the brilliant thinker and scholar."[13]

Odes to Stalin appeared by the hundreds, frequently comparing the Leader to some object like the sun. Mikhail Isakovsky wrote:

> He has brought us strength and glory
> And youth for ages to come.
> The flush of a beautiful dawning
> Across our heaven is flung.
> So let us lift up our voices
> To him who is most beloved.
> A song to the sun and to justice,
> A song that to Stalin is sung.[14]

Actually, Isakovsky's effort was not quite so laudatory as that of another poet whose work appeared in *Pravda* in 1936:

> O Great Stalin, O leader of the peoples,
> Thou who broughtest man to birth,
> Thou who purifiest the earth,
> Thou who restoreth the centuries,
> Thou who makest bloom the spring,
> Thou who makest vibrate the musical chords,
> Thou splendor of my spring, O Thou
> Sun reflected of millions of hearts.[15]

Apparently no eulogy is too fulsome for Stalin's ears, even when it comes from his close associates and subordinates in the Politburo. According to G. M. Malenkov, in a long Stalin eulogy in *Pravda*, "the peoples of the Soviet Union and the whole of progressive mankind see in the person of Comrade Stalin their recognized leader and teacher." L. P. Beria echoed the eulogy, and added tactfully: "Comrade Stalin's work is so great and so many-sided that many years would be needed to describe it in due measure."[16] But it remained for the Young Communist League to attain the climax when it advocated falling on good Communist knees to kiss Stalin's "holy footprints." Arthur

Schlesinger, Jr., has quoted the following gem from a 1946 book published by the Young Communist League, presumably describing the ecstasies of its young members when visiting the Kremlin: "Stalin! . . . Here in the Kremlin his presence touches us at every step. We walk on stones which he may have trod only quite recently. Let us fall on our knees and kiss those holy footprints!"[17]

The attitude of the American press toward this Stalin cult and the corresponding cult of the Pope is worth recording. In describing the whole ritual of adoration for Stalin on his seventieth birthday, the American newspapers were gleefully sardonic. The New York *Times* scorned such elevation of the Generalissimo to the stature of a "demi-god" in a manner alien to western thought and feeling, and pointed out that such exaltation had nothing to do with Communism. "Any totalitarian system," said Lieutenant General Walter Bedell Smith, "lives to a large degree on the myth that its leaders are infallible." "There is even a neat parallel between the deification of Stalin and the deification of the Roman emperors," said Joseph and Stewart Alsop, liberal columnists. How carefully all the newspaper writers avoided the one most obvious parallel, the parallel between the deified Stalin and the one deified leader in the world who officially claims infallibility!

Christian Simplicity to Papal Grandeur

The devices used by the Vatican to stimulate veneration for popes and saints have developed over a span of sixteen centuries. In the early days of the Church, there was nothing to parallel the present ecclesiastical magnificence of Rome or its centralized power. Jesus and his followers lived a simple and frugal life without pomp or ceremony, and abjured all the outward manifestations of ceremonial splendor. During the first three centuries of the Church's life, the emphasis of the Church was upon simplicity and devotion. In fact, the spirit of the Church during that period was not wholly unlike the spirit of the first Utopian socialists who despised the conventional forms of worldly power and attempted to realize a dream of economic equality.

After the Papacy had become a great power it took on the grandeur of an imperial court, and the whole attitude of the

Church toward the personalities of the bishops of Rome changed. The popes became royal personages instead of merely supervising bishops. They gradually assumed more godlike gestures and habiliments. They learned to use religious devotion to increase their prestige in both temporal and spiritual realms.

In spite of the doctrine of infallibility, the Vatican has tried to impress the fact upon the world that Catholics do not actually worship the Pope. A careful set of theoretical distinctions has been drawn up to separate worship, veneration, and honor. It is permissible to venerate certain objects but not to worship them.[18] It is proper to *honor* a church leader, *venerate* a saint, particularly the Virgin Mary, and *worship* the deity with full adoration. In theory the grades of veneration, honor, and worship are to be carefully distinguished. But in practice the fixations of worship cannot be subdivided according to priestly dictates. Neither an Andalusian peasant nor a Catholic professor of philosophy can make a feasible working distinction between limited veneration and complete adoration. Admiration, if it becomes uncritical enough, grades imperceptibly into worship.

Regardless of its professions, the whole machinery of the Church is geared to exalt the personality of the Pope to the divine level. He is considered superior to all earthly criticism, and virtually no Catholic ever criticizes him directly. He is, in practice, one of the plural gods of the Catholic system of power, and all the gods in the system, saints and popes, are skillfully used to hold the loyalty of the Catholic people to a great ecclesiastical enterprise. The spirit of that enterprise was well expressed by Leo XIII in describing himself in his encyclical letter on *The Reunion of Christendom:* "We who hold upon this earth the place of God Almighty."

Any visitor to St. Peter's is impressed with the unabashed idolatry of its great religious festivals, and the Pope himself is always the central idol of every ecclesiastical display. Ostensibly his every act in public ceremonies is a tribute not to his own divinity but to the divinity of the God he serves. He is careful not to assert his own deity, and he is officially called "slave of the slaves of God." But in practice he is himself the god of all St. Peter's pageantry, and the Catholic people are the slaves who come to worship him as the Church's divine agent on earth.

Every detail in the vast and complicated system of Catholic ceremonials is designed to promote and strengthen this assumption.

The fundamental attitude of the Church toward the Pope was made especially clear during the great festivities of the Holy Year of 1950. During that year every major celebration in St. Peter's — and I attended many of them — was systematically organized to demonstrate the homage of Catholics to Pius XII. His every appearance in a gorgeous processional was the signal for wild cheers of adulation. Thousands of pilgrims knelt in reverence before his bejeweled figure, either on the stone floor of St. Peter's or on the pavement of the square outside. He was borne into the middle of every celebration seated on his portable throne, carried on the strong shoulders of twelve crimson-clad valets. He was, on the whole, an entirely successful idol for the millions of pilgrims who came to see him, magnetic, sensitive-faced, and graceful.

The devices of deification used by the Vatican in such activities are so familiar that they scarcely need detailed description. Catholics are taught to give the Pope far more honor than the average citizen of a monarchy gives to his king. They are taught to kneel before him when he approaches, and in private audiences they are taught to kiss his hand or ring. All the cardinals bask in his reflected glory, as princes of the Church, and they are officially recognized by the Italian government as princes under the Vatican treaty with Italy. When they visit an Italian warship, they are given the full broadside of an artillery salute.[19]

In the great Easter celebration each year at least 25,000 faithful followers kneel before the Pope as he steps out onto the central balcony of St. Peter's in his white silk vestments and stretches out his hands in the apostolic benediction. But for the Pope, Easter day is like many other days. He has lived for more than a decade in an atmosphere of directed adulation, and his whole life is lived in such a way as to produce among his followers the conviction that he is completely unique among all beings on the planet.

It may be worth while to list some of the elementary practices and beliefs that help to create the papal god-image.

He is God's Vicar on earth, and all Catholics owe obedience to him "as to God Himself."

He has power to declare what is right or wrong by divine fiat, and simultaneous power to consign to eternal perdition any human being who defies his judgment.

He may depose emperors and free their subjects from allegiance to wicked rulers.

He may forgive sins and remit the temporal punishment for them.

He may absolve any human being from the obligation to keep any promise.

He is the only personage in the world who is infallible.

He can consign human beings to hell for violation of divine law.

He can make or unmake saints, and every declaration creating a saint is per se infallible.

He can grant dispensations from all impediments of ecclesiastical law and from the conditional provisions of divine law.

He can make decrees which cannot be annulled by any person on earth.

He may resign without requiring the acceptance of his resignation by any human agency.

He is the only person entitled to have his foot kissed.

He must have a nine-day funeral service.

He is the only one who has the right to be buried in an elevated place in a church.[20]

It would be easy to multiply these practices and beliefs by including the conventions and rules which are used to exalt the Pope as a special personage. He is too exalted to eat with any other human being; anyone who wishes to see him must come to the Vatican; he is never compelled to account to any other human being for the money he receives; he is immune from all legal process in any court; he cannot be impeached or removed; he must never be quoted by any journalist after an interview; he has his own great altar in St. Peter's at which no other prelate is allowed to officiate; he can assert ownership rights over all Church property throughout the world.

Rome, during the Holy Year of 1950, was flooded with pictures, statues, postcards, and medallions of the Pope in quantities rivaling the Moscow output of similar material on Stalin. The papal biography, in myriad saccharine versions, was piled high on the counters of every book store. The whole Catholic system of power throughout the world was methodically organized to promote the Pope as a superhuman figure.

Probably the most important device in papal exaltation is not a deliberately contrived device at all, but an indirect result of papal power. I refer to the fact that throughout the press, radio, and motion-picture world, both Catholic and non-Catholic, a steady process of glorification is going on. The Pope is always favorably represented to the public by pictures, laudatory editorials, and respectful references. His encyclicals may be flat, his policies stupid and reactionary, but no one in the western world says so. It was twenty years ago that the New York *Times* dared to criticize an encyclical of a pope editorially because it undermined the American public schools. Since then several popes have issued shockingly reactionary and anti-scientific pronouncements which, coming from any other source, would have been treated in the American press as clear evidence of personal stupidity. But, however much American editors may disagree, they no longer discuss the fundamental shortcomings of the popes and their Papacy as the sturdy individualist editors of the nineteenth century were wont to do. In a sense, the decline in courage and integrity in the American press in this area is a proof of the success of papal deification.

The Catholic press, of course, continues to exalt the Pope in a manner that parallels the exaltation of Stalin in the Communist press. *Osservatore Romano,* the official organ of the Vatican, is essentially a papal puff-sheet. It devotes a large part of the front page of almost every issue to a list of the personages who are permitted to see the Pope in private and semi-private audiences. Nearly all its many pictures are devoted to showing the Pope in multiple favorable poses. In these columns he is called a "sweet-god" and exalted even more systematically than Stalin is exalted by the Moscow newspapers, *Pravda* and *Izvestia.*

The Catholic press throughout the world follows this same adulatory line with monotonous regularity. No word of doubt about a papal attribute or a papal policy must ever appear in a Catholic journal. In celebrating the anniversary of Pius XII's election as Pope, the *American Ecclesiastical Review,* one of the leading priestly magazines of the United States, announced a series of seventeen articles on His Holiness which were strikingly parallel to the articles on Stalin, which I have cited, from the Rumanian Academy of Sciences. Cardinal Spellman led off with an article on the Pope as "Martyr for Peace." Archbishop Cushing of Boston described his "contributions to the cause of sacerdotal perfections." Bishop Michael J. Ready of Columbus described the Holy Father's "special affection" for the United States. Simultaneously, an American publisher brought out a biography of Pius XII called *Angelic Shepherd*. Its title was accurate.

The Ritual of Display

As the Church has grown in age and power, the Pope has become more and more the center of an elaborate and costly ritual of display. Hundreds of laymen and priests are assigned to humble roles as his theatrical supporters in the great ceremonies of exaltation which take up a large part of his life. Some of those ceremonies outdo in grandeur the greatest royal coronations. The Pope's part in the canonization of saints may be taken as an illustration of the current techniques of obeisance and exaltation. Here are extended excerpts from the official ceremonies prescribed for such canonizations, showing how the role of the Pope has been dramatized in Catholic ritual to the point of deification.[21] I have filled in the name of the first saint I saw canonized at St. Peter's by Pius XII in the Holy Year of 1950, together with a few descriptive phrases of my own (in brackets), but otherwise I have let the record speak for itself. It tells an almost incredible story of the ritualism of display, incredible at least in an age of scientific realism.

Canonization is a ceremony of magnificent solemnity. . . . The Basilica of St. Peter's has, for many centuries, been destined for solemn canonizations. . . . It is a very ancient custom to decorate the Basilica with great splendor on such occasions. . . . The funds of the Cause must defray the expense of the decoration, which consists of banners, candelabra, Latin inscriptions, huge paintings hung from the pillars depicting the approved miracles, and finally the picture of the new Saint. At the end of the apse, in front of the altar of the Chair of St. Peter, the Papal Throne is erected on an elevated platform and alongside it are arranged the stalls for Cardinals, Patriarchs, Archbishops, Bishops, Prelates and dignitaries who take part in Papal functions. In the apse also there are erected tribunes for Royal Sovereigns, the Diplomatic Corps, the Order of Malta, the Pope's relatives, the Roman aristocracy, etc. . . .

The funds of the Cause must supply the frontal for the Papal altar, richly embroidered in gold, the missal and the other ornaments used at the mass. On the facade of the Basilica are placed inscriptions and a large canvas representing the new Saint in glory. . . . Those who have to put robes on for the occasion are assisted by their attendants and, when all are ready, they go into the Sistine Chapel. . . . The Cardinals . . . all wear white damask mitres and their train bearers are vested in croccia, cotta and vimpa. . . . The Prince Assistant at the Papal Throne wears his ceremonial costume with ornaments of lace; the Grand Master of the Sacred Hospice, the Privy Chamberlains of the Cape and Sword, and the Chamberlains of Honor wear the picturesque costume of the early Elizabethan period; the Pontifical Jeweller, who has charge of the Pope's tiaras and mitres, wears a silk cloak, and a sword. [Two extra papal tiaras are carried in the procession, in addition to the one on the Pope's head.]

While the procession is forming, the Pope, accompanied by the Privy Chamberlains, comes to the sacristy of the Sistine Chapel wearing a white cassock and sash, rochet, and red mozetta. He takes off the mozetta and vests in the *falda,* amice, alb, girdle, red or white stole, and large red or white cope embroidered with gold, which is fastened by a gold clasp studded with precious stones. The *falda* is a white silk vestment peculiar to the Pope, consisting of a long tunic and train. The vestment falls over the Pope's feet, and is raised by his assistants when he walks.

His Holiness, wearing the tiara, puts incense into the thurible, and enters the Sistine Chapel preceded by the Papal cross, having at his side the Assistant Cardinal-Deacons and the Prince Assistant at the Throne who carries his train. . . . The Pope, wearing the mitre, sits on the *sedia gestatoria* and receives from the Cardinal Procurator of the Canonization two large painted candles and one small one, one of which he gives to the Prince Assistant at the Throne, while the smallest he carries in his left hand wrapped in a silk veil, embroidered with gold. The grooms and chairmen, wearing their costumes of red damask, raise the *sedia* on their shoulders, and the canopy is spread over the Pope's head. Behind the *sedia* the large fans are carried. The Senior Officers of the Noble Guard, the Palatine Guard, and Swiss Guard, the Privy Chamberlains of the Cape and Sword, the Macebearers, and all those known as *de custodia Pontificis* form the Pope's guard of honor. The Noble and Swiss Guards, clad in full ceremonial costume, bring up the rear of the magnificent procession [which takes about thirty minutes to pass].

On arriving at the doors of the Basilica the Pope is received by the Chapter of St. Peter's, while the choir sings the motet *Tu es Petrus.* When the Pope has entered the Basilica, a triumphal march is played on the silver trumpets. [The procession then advances]. . . .

Immediately the ceremony of the "obediences" commences: the Cardinals approach and kiss the Pope's hand; the Patriarchs, Archbishops and Bishops kiss the cross of the stole placed on the knees of His Holiness, while Abbots in their own right, Abbots General, and the Penitentiaries kiss his foot. . . .

When the dignitaries have taken their place . . . the Cardinal Procurator of the Canonization approaches the Throne accompanied by a Master of Ceremonies and Consistorial Advocate. Arrived at the foot of the Throne, the Advocate kneels and addresses the following words to His Holiness:

"Most Holy Father, The Most Reverend Cardinal N.N., here present, earnestly begs your Holiness to inscribe the Blessed Maria Guglielma Emilia De Rodat in the catalogue of the Saints of Our Lord Jesus Christ, and to ordain that she be venerated as a Saint by all the Christian faithful."

The Prelate Secretary of the Briefs, who is standing on the platform of the Throne, replies in Latin that the Holy Father is very much edified by the virtues of the Blessed, and by the miracles with which Our Lord has made their glory resplendent, but before making any decision in a matter of such grave importance, he exhorts the faithful to assist him in imploring the Divine assistance by the intercession of the Blessed Virgin Mary, of the Holy Apostles Peter and Paul and of all the Heavenly Court. . . .

The Prelate Secretary replies that the Holy Father, convinced that the canonization is pleasing to God, is resolved to make the proclamation: . . . . [as follows]

"In honor of the Holy and Indivisible Trinity, for the exaltation of the Catholic Faith and the increase of the Christian Religion, by the authority of Our Lord Jesus Christ, of the Holy Apostles Peter and Paul, and by Our own; after mature deliberation, ever imploring the Divine assistance, by the advice of Our Venerable Brethren the Cardinals of the Holy Roman Church, the Patriarchs, Archbishops and Bishops present in the Eternal City, We decree and define as a Saint, and We inscribe in the catalogue of Saints the Blessed Maria Guglielma Emilia De Rodat, ordaining that her memory be celebrated with devotion every year in the Universal Church."

. . . The Postulants . . . approach the Throne once more and the Consistorial Advocate, kneeling, thanks His Holiness in the name of the Cardinal Procurator. . . . The Cardinal Procurator ascends the steps of the Throne, kisses the hand and the knee of the Pope and returns to his place. . . . The Consistorial Advocate then kisses the foot of the Sovereign Pontiff.

The Pope rises, takes off the mitre and intones the *Te Deum* which is continued by the Papal cantors. At the same time the bells of the Vatican Basilica give the signal and the bells of all the churches in Rome announce the good news of the Canonization.

It is scarcely necessary to point out that this ritual of display has nothing more to do with original Christianity than the worship of Stalin has to do with original socialism. There is not only no support in Christian tradition for such a use of Christianity, but all the weight of original Christian testimony is against such proceedings. In fact, it would be difficult to discover in all history any person whose life-record and personal habits conflicted more openly with ecclesiastical display and exaggerated ceremonialism than Jesus of Nazareth.

5

The Kremlin and Thought Control

MAN-MADE GODS LIKE STALIN AND THE POPE are the *results* of totalitarian power, the final flowering of a process of cultivated adulation. The question which puzzles many students of Kremlin and Vatican policy is: How does a dictatorship go about persuading free men to accept this sort of thing in the first place? How are the minds of men prepared so that they surrender themselves to a deified Leader?

As far as the Kremlin is concerned, the answer lies in the nation-wide network of thought control. Modern psychologists have learned that the human mind can be so conditioned that it will accept almost anything as true if the conditioning is continuous and skillfully administered. The Kremlin has created machinery for controlling the Russian mind that reaches down into every school, newspaper, theater, publishing house, courtroom, and home in the Soviet Union. It penetrates every laboratory, artist's studio, and music room; and dictates the Party line which the scientists, writers, artists, and musicians must follow if they wish to continue to earn a living.

The social democrats and Communists who made the two great Russian revolutions of 1917 were certainly not unanimous in their desire for a nation in which freedom of speech and the press would be permanently destroyed. They had fought for the rights of free speech and a free press under the Tsars, and the general philosophy of many of them was libertarian. Perhaps the Communists visualized a permanent dictatorship, but their social-democratic allies certainly did not. Karl Marx had advocated the dictatorship of the proletariat as a transition measure in attaining a socialist society, and when such an alleged dictatorship finally arrived in Russia it was still regarded by many of his disciples as a brief prelude before the arrival of a democratic society. The Communist Party of the USSR as late as 1919 declared that measures restricting political rights should be regarded as "exclusively temporary measures."[1]

As the years went by and the dictatorship of the Communist Party, disguised as the dictatorship of the proletariat, became more nearly absolute, the concept of a time limit for a temporary dictatorship dropped out of discussion. The measures for suppressing the opposition were first justified by the excuse that Tsarist power must be torn up by the roots and that in the meantime the new nation must be united in order to resist its enemies. When, after several decades, that excuse wore thin, a complete philosophy of repression was developed. It was based on the primary thesis that a socialist state does not need to give freedom to anti-socialism because anti-socialism threatens the life of the whole community. As we shall see later, the theory of the repression of anti-socialist teaching is exactly paralleled in the Catholic system of power by the teaching that "error" has no rights against truth, and that supreme truth is determined and defined by the Church. Stalin's assault on "rotten liberalism" as an illegitimate threat to "the vital interests of Bolshevism" echoed in principle Pius IX's Allocution seventy years earlier when the Pope arrogantly asserted that the Roman Pontiff had no obligation to reconcile himself with "progress, liberalism and civilization as lately introduced."[2]

The self-righteous Communist gospel of repressing all opposition thought flowered fully in the middle thirties, after some of the great revolutionary enemies of Stalin had been purged through execution. On August 6, 1936, *Izvestia* summed up the Stalin position by saying: "Liberty will be accorded to everybody except those whose acts and ideas oppose the interests of the workers, and those whose object is to demolish the Soviet regime. No lunatics will be able to hold meetings; neither will criminals, monarchists, Mensheviks, Socialist Revolutionaries, etc."[3]

If all "those whose acts and ideas oppose the interests of the workers" are to be silenced, how will the condemned categories be defined, and who will do the defining? The Communists did not bother to explain that they considered themselves competent to be the sole judges in the matter, and that the "lunatics" to be suppressed included all social-democratic and liberal forces, as well as Tsarists. Two months before this statement, *Pravda,* the official Communist Party organ in Moscow, had made it clear what techniques of suppression would be used against any critics. Commenting on the 1936 Constitution, which was supposed to bring freedom of the press to the Soviet people, *Pravda* of June 27, 1936, said: "Whoever postulates the overthrow of the Socialist regime is an enemy of the people. He will not obtain a sheet of paper, he will not be able to cross the threshold of a printing office, should he try to fulfill his wretched purpose. He will not find a hall, a room or a mere corner in which to spread his poison by speech."[4]

Andrei Y. Vishinsky, later Russia's chief representative at the United Nations, confirmed this point of view concerning the meaning of Soviet freedom of the press when he said in 1948 in *The Law of the Soviet State:*

> In our state, naturally, there is and can be no place for freedom of speech, press and so on for the foes of Socialism. Every sort of attempt on their part to utilize to the detriment of the State — that is to say, to the detriment of all the toilers — those freedoms granted to the toilers must be classified as a counter-revolutionary crime to which Article 58, Paragraph 10, or one of the corresponding articles of the Criminal Code is applicable.[5]

Vishinsky made it plain that freedom in the Soviet Union is not something granted to all citizens but only to "toilers." This limitation of privileges to persons who are willing to work, to bona fide workers of hand and brain, would not be so serious if the denials applied only to the willful loafer and the unprincipled exploiter. But under the Communist system the Party determines the definition of the word "toiler," and therein lies the tragedy and the denial of freedom for honest criticism. A "non-toiler" may be a man who is eager to work under reasonable conditions but who considers the rules of a Soviet police state intolerable for honest labor.

In spite of Vishinsky's sweeping utterance, it should not be imagined that *all* criticism is stifled in the Soviet Union. There is a great deal of give and take in the Soviet press concerning the *execution* of any particular government policy. The letters from citizens in the letter columns of the Moscow newspapers are often caustic and acute, and Soviet leaders watch them with real attention. Ordinary citizens are actually encouraged to write letters criticizing the minor bureaucracy, so long as they do not attack high officials or the Politburo's major policies and doctrines.[6] The great Communist newspapers have staffs of correspondents who handle these letters with considerable care, but there is always an understood limit to this type of criticism. The very device of the published letter is frequently used by the Communist dictatorship to manufacture "public opinion" in order to support any side of any question. With complete control of the press and the workers' organizations, it is a simple matter for the government to create a "mass movement" of protest or acclaim for or against any particular position or policy.

Journalists in the Soviet Union who are Soviet citizens take orders from the Kremlin concerning their journalistic output, or promptly disappear into forced-labor camps. They must learn to regard impartiality in reporting as bourgeois objectivism, and pro-government propaganda as news. Non-Russian journalists who write frankly about Soviet conditions are asked to leave the country — or never admitted in the first place. The Soviet government can afford to be arrogant in dealing with foreign journalists because it controls the press so completely that no denial of journalistic rights becomes known to the Russian public if the Kremlin does not make the news public. Even the American journalist, Anna Louise Strong, who had been an enthusiastic advocate of Soviet policy for years and who had been cited as worthy of a Pulitzer Prize by the New York *Daily Worker,* was abruptly expelled from the Soviet Union in February 1949 without a hearing or trial. She could not appeal to Soviet "public opinion" over the heads of the Soviet bureaucrats because there was no such thing as independent public opinion. She could not get from the Soviet government any specification of charges made against her except that she was guilty of "espionage and subversive activity." It was suspected that she was sympathetic to the strictly Chinese aspirations of the Chinese Communists, although there was little evidence to prove this. She had been a completely devoted admirer of Stalin, and had meekly submitted to the revision of her latest, pro-Communist book, *Tomorrow's China,* by the Soviet Information Bureau.[7]

One reason why no critic of Stalinist policy has any free speech in the Soviet Union is that the same power which controls the press also controls all the courts and the interpretation of Soviet law. There is no such thing in Soviet law as an independent judicial conscience. The mind of the judge is not a free mind, and the theories of the law which he interprets are subject to political pressure. As one Soviet jurist expressed it, "the independence of judges in examining concrete cases does not at all exclude the duty to follow the general policy of the government. The judiciary is an organ of state power and therefore cannot be outside of politics."[8] Soviet legal literature follows this same line in subordinating the judicial mind to political forces. "Bold and militant Soviet patriotism," said the *Soviet State and Law* in September 1949, "must become the chief criterion for determining the quality of Soviet legal literature and must be its basic motivating force." The Communists, having destroyed the "oppressive bourgeois State machinery," have given the people no substitute to protect themselves against the abuses of Communist power.

The Subjection of Truth

With such a theory and practice of freedom, it was inevitable that Kremlin control should extend into the fields of education, science, art, and music. Education will be considered in a later chapter — its subjection to the Kremlin is basic in the control of all the arts and sciences.

Economics was among the first casualties because it had an intimate connection with the Marxian outlook. No non-socialist economics has been taught in Russian schools since the revolution, and all social science has been compelled to follow "the correct Marxist-Leninist approach" because only such an approach "makes it possible to avoid bourgeois objectivity." The dictum is quoted from a comment on history in Moscow's *Voprosy Filosofii*,[9] but it applies to all sciences as well. A National Council of Science, composed largely of Communist Party officials, was created as early as 1922; it furnished detailed lecture outlines to professors of science in the universities, and then set Communist students to spy on them in their classes to guarantee that the outlines would be used faithfully.[10]

"There is no such thing as non-class art," said Mayakovsky,

head of the Futurists, in revolutionary Petrograd in 1918, and the new Soviet Union has accepted the dictum completely not only for pictorial arts but for all literature and literary criticism as well. The dictum even applies to poets, for, as Mayakovsky put it, "a poet is not he who strolls about like a curly lamb and bleats on lyrical themes, but he who in our bitter class struggle donates his pen to the arsenal of the proletariat's arms."[11] "Literary criticism must become a means of ideological propaganda, a weapon for the spiritual education of the people,"[12] said A. M. Egolin of the Academy of Sciences of the USSR in 1946. And he quoted Lenin to give sanctity to his opinion: "Down with non-party men of letters! Down with supermen of letters! The cause of literature must become part and parcel of the general proletarian cause, a 'cog' in one single, great social-democratic mechanism set in motion by the entire conscious vanguard of the whole working class. The business of literature must become a component part of organized, methodical, unified social-democratic work."

Basic in the whole Communist scheme of thought control is the fact that there are no privately owned newspapers, magazines, and publishing houses in the Soviet Union, and that no political parties which might develop an opposition press are permitted to function. The press is Communist, and there is no other press. The Soviet Union has 7,200 newspapers with a total circulation of more than 31,000,000, but all the editors sing the same tune.[13] Their general outlook is set forth quite accurately in the two great official Moscow dailies, *Pravda* and *Izvestia,* which represent the Kremlin's policy as faithfully as Rome's *Quotidiano* or the Vatican City's *Osservatore Romano* represent the Holy See and Catholic Action.

According to one observer, scarcely anyone bothers to read the first three pages of a Soviet newspaper, "at least not until he has read and reread the foreign news on the last page":

> The first part of the paper is just too boring — the same thing day after day: a long letter in praise of Comrade Stalin, an account of how the Red October Tractor Plant went over the top in production a month ahead of schedule, and a report on the Hammer and Sickle Collective, which produced three hundred more bushels of wheat this year than last.[14]

In volume the Soviet cultural apparatus is exceedingly impressive. Since the revolution, there has been a prodigious increase in the number of schools, theaters, and published books, and the resultant reduction in illiteracy has been quite remarkable. Moscow alone claims seventy-six publishing houses. When the Kremlin approves the publication of a book, its circulation is likely to be much higher than the circulation of a corresponding book in the United States. Editions of several million copies of Russian books are not uncommon, and some English classics in Russian translation are very popular, particularly if their authors are dead or pro-Communist.

The devices for Communist control of the press are quite unexampled. The denial of paper to offending publishers is one insurmountable barrier which any critic of the government faces. Government agencies operate the whole publishing industry, approve the books, choose the titles, censor the text, market the product, and determine when any book should be withdrawn under fire. It is impossible for any writer, editor, or publisher to earn his living and continue to defy the regime. The right to work does not belong to any independent journalist, unless it is interpreted to mean the right to work in a forced-labor camp. All these measures of repression and control are carried out without any vocal opposition. To read the Soviet press one would imagine that no problem of intellectual freedom ever arose. The control of the press by the Party is described with complete self-satisfaction by the press itself as an evidence of high moral achievement and of "true freedom of speech." The phrase was used in a laudatory editorial by L. Ilyichev in *Pravda* on May 5, 1949, on "The Press — a Mighty Instrument of Communist Education." He said:

> The Soviet press is a press of a new type. It is the expression of Socialist Democracy, the expression of true freedom of speech. The noble role of the Soviet press and progressive functions become particularly evident when one turns to look at the venal bourgeois press.
> Poisoning the minds of the people with reactionary ideas, the bourgeois press opposes all that is progressive and wages unrestrained propaganda for war, racial fanaticism and misanthropy. Particularly zealous is the reactionary American press. . . .
> In the stormy sea of press lies, the Communist, genuinely democratic, newspapers rise up like bastions of truth. . . . Propaganda of the ideas of Leninism is a noble duty of the Soviet press.[15]

On the same day *Pravda* said editorially: "The great founders of the Party, Lenin and Stalin, in laying its foundations were concerned to organize a press that would be a collective propagandist, agitator and organizer of the masses and would serve as a sharp and powerful weapon of the Party and a strong means of the ideological education of the people." *Pravda* compared this noble singleness of purpose with the low moral outlook of the bourgeois press, particularly in the United States:

> In the countries of capital, notorious bourgeois freedom of the press is extolled at every turn. But what freedom of the press can there be, shall we say, in the United States, if the press there is maintained by capitalist monopolies and champions their interests? Freedom of press under capitalism is freedom for the financial magnates to bribe newspapers, buy writers, and fabricate "public opinion."[16]

Until the 1930's, the general Communist control over the press seemed enough to satisfy even the Stalinists, but in the late thirties and early forties thought control was extended officially into the fields of science and art. Heavy-handed commissars who scarcely knew a test tube from a cadenza invaded the realms of physics, biology, opera, and fiction with all the delicacy of a bull in a china shop. Leaders of the Kremlin conducted a national pogrom against independent intellectuals, and simultaneously exalted several scientific charlatans to high places in the firmament of Soviet science. In the late 1930's, all literature, all science, and all art in the Soviet Union came under the supervision of three political henchmen who acted as secretaries of three control groups: the Academy of Sciences, the Secretariat of the Writers' Union, and the Committee for the Affairs of the Arts. According to Philip Mosely, writing in 1938, "Each of these secretaries exercises what is in practice a monopoly right of patronage over his respective field."[17] In effect each secretary became a prelate-censor whose Imprimatur was essential for publication or performance. Since private patronage in art and science had disappeared, and private publication had become impossible, Russian intellectual freedom had been completely destroyed even before the war. After the war, Stalin's grip was tighter than ever.

The most famous case of post-war thought control was that of Lysenko. Trofim D. Lysenko is a hard-working and enthusiastic specialist in agriculture who caught the fancy of Joseph Stalin — as his predecessor Michurin had caught the fancy of Lenin —

because he was a vigorous organizer who could simplify difficult facts into a formula that fitted in with Marxism. He has been called a geneticist, but he was never given any substantial recognition as a scientist by scientists until he found favor with the leaders of the Communist Party, and then his triumph was purely political. He won the favor of the Stalin machine by advocating a theory of heredity which happened to conform to Stalin's notion of what evolution *ought* to be.

During Tsarist days a voluble and earnest man named I. V. Michurin gained a considerable fame in Russia by preaching a gospel of plant improvement for Russian horticulture. His nearest American counterpart was Luther Burbank, who gained similar fame in California a generation ago. Russian horticulture needed improvement so badly that even an unscientific enthusiast could accomplish wonders with it, and Michurin did effect improvements and did stand out in pre-revolutionary days as a critic of Tsarist farming methods. That endeared him to Lenin. Then, in Stalin's regime, his theories became the occasion for the famous Michurin-Lysenko conquest of genetics.

The essence of the controversy was this. The world's greatest geneticists have demonstrated by scientific experiments over a period of many generations that human beings and plants do not pass on their acquired characteristics by inheritance in their genes. What appears to be a passing on of acquired characteristics is merely a reshuffling or an elimination by natural selection. A man who becomes a good baseball pitcher by hard training is not any more likely to pass on his aptitudes to his son than a man who has never thrown a spit ball. A plant which has become hardened by cold weather does not spawn hardier plants because of that experience. What may happen in such a case is that the hardier and more adaptable plants may survive more frequently than the weak ones, and thus the weak ones tend to be eliminated. This kind of adaptation is going on all the time in nature, but it is not a speedy process.

The three most famous names associated with these scientific findings have been Morgan, Mendel, and Weismann. Also, the president of the Soviet's All-Union Academy of Agricultural Science, Nicolai Vavilov, was associated with the theory. He had been Russia's outstanding scientist in the field of genetics.

Stalin never knew much about genetics — but he knew what he wanted, and his hunches were more important in Soviet science than any scientific experiments. He decided that the traditional theories were "reactionary"; they seemed to him too pessimistic and flatly contrary to a revolutionist's faith in the possibility of a quick and effective revolution. He wanted environment instead of heredity emphasized because he believed that this emphasis would strengthen the Marxian interpretation of society. The truth was too "static" for him, so he demanded that it be "adjusted." He wanted the peasants to believe that if they improved a calf, a cabbage, or a cauliflower, the improvement could be passed on to their descendants quickly. The fact that the reverse of this theory had been established by the world's leading scientists did not disturb him profoundly. He had never been a scientist, and he knew nothing about laboratory experiments.

The theory that science should be compelled to serve the ends of Communist planning was not an exclusive conviction of Stalin's. It was inherent in the Communist theory that all truth must be adjusted and adapted to serve Communist ends. The British scientist, Professor Eric Ashby, who spent a year in the Soviet Union in 1945 as a representative of the Australian government, has tried to explain this attitude. He has said that although much of the work of Russian scientists is first class, the Soviet government

. . . is afraid of the atmosphere of urbanity, tolerance, and objectiveness in which western science is done. . . . Russia cannot yet afford to release her scholars into the intellectual climate of western Europe, for in the west the state adopts an attitude of non-intervention toward intellectuals. . . . To the Russian Communist an intellectual worker is in the same category as any other worker. The workers in a boot factory produce the boots the public wants, not the boots they would like to make; and for precisely the same reasons a worker in a laboratory does the research the public wants."[18]

This is the most charitable explanation of the Soviet philosophy of culture which became apparent in the Lysenko case. Lysenko, backed by the Communist Party, opened a campaign within the Academy of Agricultural Science against the established theory of inheritance, and, with scarcely any scientific facts to support his wishful thinking, carried the new illusion to almost unanimous triumph over "reactionary idealistic" biology. Vavilov, forced out of his position as president of the Academy, arrested as a British spy, sent to Siberia, was later imprisoned and died in disgrace. George S. Counts and Nucia Lodge have told the story very ably in their *The Country of the Blind,* and so has Professor H. J. Muller of Indiana University, Nobel Prize winner in science and former geneticist in Moscow.[19] The documents in the case have been assembled and edited by an American botanist, Professor Conway Zirkle, in his *Death of a Science in Russia.*

The state of mind of the Russian scientists, their groveling abjectness before Communist political power, can best be appreciated by quoting several paragraphs from Lysenko's triumphant speech — actually a Stalinist stump speech — before the Lenin Academy of Agricultural Science on July 31, 1948, as published in Moscow's *VOKS Bulletin. Pravda* printed Lysenko's remarks under a lead paragraph which set the keynote of the controversy by describing Stalin as "the greatest scholar of our epoch." Here is Lysenko's oratorical climax:

V. I. Lenin and J. V. Stalin discovered I. V. Michurin and made his teaching the possession of the Soviet people. By their great paternal attention to his work, they saved for biology remarkable Michurin's teaching. The Party, the Government, and J. V. Stalin personally have taken an unflagging interest in the further development of Michurin's teaching. There is no more honorable task for us Soviet biologists than to develop creatively Michurin's teaching and to follow in all our activities Michurin's style in the investigation of the nature of evolution of living beings.

The question is asked, what is the attitude of the Central Committee of the Party to my report. I answer: The Central Committee of the Party examined my report and approved it. (*Stormy applause, ovation, all rise*). . . .

Long live the Party of Lenin and Stalin which discovered Michurin for the world (*applause*) and created all the conditions for the progress of advanced materialist biology in our country (*applause*).

Glory to the great friend and champion of science, our Leader and Teacher, Comrade Stalin.

(*All rise, prolonged applause*)[20]

Two days later, one of the leading biologists attacked by Lysenko, Professor Anton Zhebrak, recanted in words that remind one of Galileo's submission to the Holy Office in 1616:

Since it is the sacred duty of the scientists of our country to march in step with the entire people for the purpose of satisfying their needs and vitally essential demands of their state, of struggling with the vestiges of capitalism, of aiding the Communist education of the toilers, and of moving science ahead without interruption, then, as a member of the Party and as a scientist from the ranks of the people, I do not want to be regarded as a renegade, I do not want to be barred from assisting in the achievement of the noble tasks of the scientists of our Motherland. I want to work within the framework of that tendency which is recognized as forward-looking in our country and with the methods which are propounded by Timiriazev and Michurin. Henceforth I shall strive with all my power to make my works of maximum use to my country, to develop creatively the heritage of Timiriazev and Michurin, to assist the building of Communism in our Motherland.[21]

Twelve days later the top-ranking scientific organization of Russia fell in line and discharged two of its notable officials who had revealed some sympathy for the Morgan-Mendel genetic findings. It declared that it would assume a "leading position in the struggle against idealistic-reactionary teachings in science, against servility and slavishness toward foreign pseudo-science." And the members of the Presidium of the Academy announced in a personal letter to Stalin that the Presidium "promises you, dear Josef Vissarionovich, and, in your person, our Party and government to correct resolutely the mistakes permitted by us."[22]

It should be remembered that this sudden reversal of view by distinguished scientists took place not in regard to a narrowly disputed point in modern science but in regard to a point on which the overwhelming majority of world specialists have been in agreement for a long time. Julian Huxley, whose scientific standing is unimpeachable, has declared: "In repudiating Morgano-Mendelism the Michurinites and the Communist Party of the USSR have repudiated not a mere speculative hypothesis nor a theory motivated by other than scientific reasons, but a large body of tested scientific fact, and a number of well-validated scientific laws." As Sir Henry Dale, former president of the British Association for the Advancement of Science, declared in resigning from the Russian Academy in protest against the new Stalinist genetics, Lysenko is "the advocate of a doctrine of evolution which, in effect, denies all the progress made by research in that field since Lamarck's speculations appeared early in the nineteenth century."[23]

The truth is that the Kremlin is unwilling to face facts concerning the nature of man — as unwilling as the Papacy was to face the findings of Galileo in 1600. It insists on its own anthropology because it has a preconceived notion of what man must be, and it insists on twisting the facts of nature to meet its own specifications. The Communist movement, as Professor Muller has pointed out, is dominated by "the type of mind that sees things as only black and white, yes and no, and so cannot admit the importance of *both* heredity and environment. Believing that it has found the complete answer to all the world's ills, through its particular way of manipulating environment, the Communist Party regards as a menace any concept that does not fit patly into its scheme for mankind. The genes do not fit into that concept, in its opinion, hence the existence of the genes must be denied."[24]

"The USSR," says Julian Huxley, "has officially rejected some of the essentials of the scientific method itself, and has split world science into two hostile camps. . . . Soviet genetics has thus really ceased to be science in the sense in which the scientists of the past three centuries have practised it, and has become a branch of dogmatic theology."[25]

Perhaps the most significant fact in the Lysenko controversy was that not a single scientist in Russia was able to stand up and challenge the right of the Communist Party's Central Committee to determine the truth or falsehood of a fact of genetics. The few recorded speeches of protest reported in the Soviet press were confined to apologies and explanations. The dictatorship over the Russian mind had become so complete that the *right,* as compared to the *wisdom,* of its control was never even questioned. In later chapters we shall see how this control of thought destroys freedom in the schools and corrupts the social sciences and history.

Marxian Music

One might imagine that music would be so far removed from political dogma that composers could work in comparative peace even under a Soviet dictatorship; but in 1948 opera and symphonic music, as well as motion pictures and drama, came under the heavy-handed attack of the Communist Party's Central Committee. "A play, a picture, and a song," according to Communist theory as expressed in *Bolshevik,* "are also propaganda and agitation, although expressed in artistic forms."[26]

The attack on music and musicians made use of the traditional Communist clichés concerning "formalism," "bourgeois decadence," obscure melodies, and all the other criticisms which any ignoramus might make concerning any piece of chamber music. The criticisms were not as shocking as the results.

One could expect a ban on such Allied war tunes as *Tipperary* and *K-K-K-Katy,* on the ground that they were "products of the bourgeois music hall"; but the extent to which serious composers took orders from musically illiterate commissars shocked the most cynical observers. In the musical purge following World War II some of the world's greatest composers offered quick capitulation to politicians, using language that indicated complete intellectual degradation.

Two of these great composers, Dimitri Shostakovich and Sergei Prokofiev, were arraigned in February 1948 by the Central Committee of the Communist Party in a sweeping attack on the Union of Soviet Composers, an attack which bristled with the phrases of political denunciation for purely musical deficiencies. Some of the phrases of abuse in that assault reveal the whole spirit of thought control in the Kremlin system — "anti-popular formalist perversions"; "anti-democratic tendencies in music"; "the cult of atonality, the dissonance and discord"; "enthusiasm for confused, neuro-pathological combinations"; "reeks strongly of the bourgeois music of Europe and America"; "a narrow circle of specialists and musical gourmands"; "the partisans of decadence"; "champions of the most backward and mouldy conservatism."[27]

To an outsider this whole stream of invective is meaningless unless it is understood as the product of almost psychopathic meanness and frustration. Trifling deficiencies are magnified into major crimes, and the attack is delivered with sadistic relish and self-righteousness. The suggestions for reform seem childish, and their authors show little comprehension of the difficulties of creative work. If such a vindictive analysis had been submitted to any ordinary western newspaper by a neurotic young aspirant to the role of music critic, it would have been promptly thrown in the wastebasket. Yet a composer like Shostakovich felt obliged to apologize in abject language; he had been under attack intermittently since 1936, and perhaps he realized that it was useless to fight back:

When today the Party and our entire country, in the words of the resolution of the Central Committee, criticize this direction of my work, I know that the Party is right and I know that the Party is showing concern for Soviet art and for me, a Soviet composer. . . .

With complete clarity and precision the Central Committee of the Party has pointed to the absence in my compositions of the transformation of the character of the people, of that great spirit by which our people live.

I am deeply grateful for this and for every criticism contained in the resolution. All of the instructions of the Central Committee and particularly those which touch me personally I accept as evidence of a severe but fatherly concern about us, Soviet artists.[28]

Prokofiev was not quite so abject as Shostakovich, although he freely admitted past sins and hailed "this resolution which creates conditions for the restoration of the health of the entire organism of Soviet music." He tried to redeem himself promptly with a new opera, but it was sternly rejected as a "typical relapse into formalism." Perhaps the explanation of this harsh treatment was that Prokofiev, although he apologized by letter, did not take the floor at the All-Union Congress of Composers to prostrate himself before his political masters in person. Shostakovich performed this act of personal prostration with conspicuous humility, and apparently his retraction and repentance were accepted, and he still has a hypothetical future as a Soviet artist. But Prokofiev's rejected opera never reached the public, and his admirers may never know what the world has lost.

Examples of this kind of repression and distortion of culture in the Soviet Union can be multiplied indefinitely. The controlled press glories in "purposive direction." The assumption universally accepted (by compulsion) in the intellectual world is that the political dictatorship has a moral right to make judgments in all the fields of learning and art, and that it is the duty of men of culture to submit to these judgments. Even encyclopedias are strictly partisan propaganda weapons. *Pravda* announced in March 1949 that the Council of Ministers had ordered a new Soviet encyclopedia which would "reflect the party line — all the facts will be precise and correct."[29] In *Pravda's* opinion, this would be the "best encyclopedia in the world," perhaps because it would "show convincingly the superiority of Socialist culture over the rotting culture of the capitalist world, expose imperialist aggression and present party criticism of modern reactionary bourgeois lines in the fields of science, technology, and culture."

Painting has become so degraded that, as Alexander Werth has put it in *The Nation,* "the two principal criteria of merit in painting are subject matter and photographic likeness — usually of Lenin and Stalin."[30] "The value of a literary work," said one critic frankly, "is determined in the Soviet Society primarily by whether it assists the people to build Communism." The spirit of the new Kremlin literature was well summed up by V. Yermilov in an article on Stalin as "Great Friend of Literature":

> Then came an epoch that told a writer that his work was necessary to the people, the state, the Motherland, as bread and air are to man. This was the epoch of the triumph of the ordinary people, the stern, exacting, and horny-handed craftsman and master-builder for whom labor and culture are sacred, and it told the writers through the lips of the great Stalin: your labor is particularly valuable for you are the *engineers of human souls.* The writer, an engineer of the human souls, is not an observer of reality, but a builder who shapes life, appraising all the phenomena of life he depicts from the viewpoint of the Bolshevik Party. By his work he supports the new and progressive that comes into existence. The writer of the Stalin epoch considers himself a worker on a giant construction project, a Soviet "factory producing happiness."[31]

In the "factory producing happiness" many of the Soviet's most devoted disciples find themselves increasingly uncomfortable. They never know when an accurate but un-Stalinist historical interpretation will result in the suppression of a whole novel or opera. Alexander Fadeyev's war novel about a Komsomol resistance organization won a Stalin prize, but when it was discovered that he did not give the Party enough credit for organizing the Young Guard in overcoming the panic in the army during the German offensive, *Pravda* severely reprimanded him. The well-known novelist, Konstantin Simonov, tried hard in his *Smoke of My Fatherland* to make his Communist hero come alive, but in spite of himself, his villain was more credible than his hero; so he was publicly humiliated and denounced.[32] It is assumed that almost all British and American literature not produced by Communists is decadent, even when the writers are distinctly progressive in their economic thoughts. Eugene O'Neill was condemned for "glorifying prostitutes and tramps"; Steinbeck, Dos Passos, and Erskine Caldwell for writing books "hyenas might have written if they could type"; Graham Greene for writing "mystical rubbish"; Arthur Koestler for "poisonous saliva squirting over all that is progressive and involved with respect for men"; Stephen Spender for "lack of conviction."[33]

The same attitude is imposed upon the Soviet Union's satellite countries. Mao Tse-tung, leader of Communist China, early in 1950 publicly burned a number of books on Chinese history and poetry because they conflicted with the Kremlin's interpretation of Oriental life. A left-wing labor paper in Hungary, according to the New York *Times,* attacked the library of the Shell Oil Company in that country because it contained "mainly fascist, semi-fascist and destructive bourgeois books, such as the works of Louis Bromfield, Upton Sinclair and Lin Yu tang." By 1951 the Communist-dominated Hungarian regime had banned a list of books and authors which was almost as long as the corresponding list of banned books in Catholic Ireland. The Hungarian anathema was placed upon Louisa May Alcott's *Little Women,* Edgar Rice Burroughs' Tarzan stories, and Dale Carnegie's *How to Win Friends and Influence People.*[34]

Naturally, the English language textbooks used in Russian schools to teach English to Soviet children must be purged of all that is tainted. They should, according to one Soviet foreign-language specialist, "expose the racial discrimination in the Anglo-Saxon countries and paint the facts of the club-law and terror of these imperialistic beasts in colonial and small countries." The specialist, in this case a lady, condemned the conventional English-language texts because they were "filled with the considerations of the usefulness of photography, of the generosity of the rich merchants of Britain, of the philanthropic behavior of the small shop keepers of the U.S.A. leaving all their goods to the poor."[35]

This same type of control for textbooks is developed in satellite countries as soon as the Soviet Union "liberates" them. The Vice-Minister of Education of the satellite government of Poland objected in 1949 to a third-grade arithmetic book because it pictured a street of privately owned stores with a shop owned by S. Baranski in the foreground, and asked the child to count the number of stores in the picture. This was immoral because it gave the child an exaggerated sense of the importance of private enterprise. The same Vice-Minister objected to physics textbooks which mentioned Fulton, Wright, and Watt, but omitted Russian and Polish scientists who were, according to the Minister, equally eminent.[36]

Controlled Culture

Such cultural attitudes result in a completely controlled set of radio programs for the whole Soviet Union and a completely controlled film industry. For a time the Soviet Union attempted to operate its own film industry completely, but it has since permitted the development of tightly controlled private companies. No opposition voice can be heard on the air or on a sound track, and foreign radio programs are thoroughly screened.[37] This screening is not too difficult because most Russians do not have radio receiving sets of the American type, and the sets must be registered by the small minority who can afford them. Most listeners get their radio programs through wired speakers, similar to the wired speakers used in some American hotels, and it is a simple matter for the government to control the centralized broadcasting which supplies such diffusion networks. The Ministry of Communications itself controls the installations of diffusion receiving equipment. But it should not be imagined that the Kremlin loads its air waves with mere propaganda or that it is indifferent to the possibility of raising the cultural level of its people by serious artistic broadcasting. Many of its programs are of great artistic merit, and it planned, by 1948, seven million wired speakers to carry these programs to its vast polyglot clientele of 200,000,000 persons speaking eighty major languages.

For the control of films the Kremlin has in Great Russia the Ministry of Cinematography of the USSR, which was organized in 1946. Like almost everything else in the Soviet Union's cultural life, it is directed by the Central Committee of the Communist Party; and the constituent republics of the Union have their little ministries of cinematography. The Communist Central Committee not only controls the production of films but also intervenes to condemn any existing film which does not appeal to its members as conforming to their political outlook. In 1946, it condemned a film on the Don Basin, *Bolshaia Zhizn*, because "the restoration of the Don Basin is presented as if the initiative of the workers not only receives no support, but was even opposed by state organizations," and because "the secretary of the Party organization in the restored mine is shown in a deliberately ridiculous position."[38] The offending film, of course, was never released to the public.

Usually the making of such films is blocked in advance by the preventive censorship of the Ministry. Those foreign films which are admitted to the country give an entirely distorted picture of life in non-Communist civilizations, and these misrepresentations are generally accepted by the Soviet people because very few Russians are permitted to emigrate from their country to look at the outside world for themselves.

Documentary films concerning Soviet life must never cast aspersions on Russian economic techniques; if they do, they are cut down before release. An unfortunate producer, Y. M. Bliokh of the Lower Volga Newsreel Studios, imagined in 1949 that it would be pleasing to city film addicts if he showed a little crude life among the fishermen of the Caspian and told a film story of their hard struggle to survive. To add a little pleasure to the film, he gave his fishermen a big catch, using some sturgeons that had been previously caught. The picture was suppressed and he was banished from the studios for two years for vulgar "fictitious episodes," and for showing old and backward fishing techniques, when everybody knows that the Caspian fishermen have a strong labor organization and "the most modern fishing methods."[39]

Sergei Eisenstein, perhaps the greatest of the Soviet film directors, in his *Ivan the Terrible* happened to arouse the wrath of the Communist Central Committee because his depiction of Ivan's police was a little too realistic and suggestive of the political police in more recent times. According to the Committee's indictment, he made the "progressive" forces of Ivan "a band of degenerates, similar to the American Ku Klux Klan, and Ivan the Terrible, a man of strong will and character, as weak and spineless, something like Hamlet." Eisenstein confessed his sin in public, declaring he and others had "lost sight of the honorable, militant, and educational task which rests upon our art during the years of great labor on the part of all the people to build a Communist society."[40]

It is hardly surprising, after all these incursions into the fields of culture, that Stalin has even entered the field of philology and laid down a Party line for scholars in that territory. In June 1950, he graciously wrote a number of answers in *Pravda* to questions sent in by "a group of youthful comrades." He reached the surprising conclusion that it is necessary to introduce Marxism into philology. His modest effort was not received modestly by his comrades. Next month the Academy of Sciences and the Academy of Medical Sciences of the USSR united in sending a message to Stalin, the "brilliant leader and teacher of the heroic Bolshevik party, the Soviet people and all progressive humanity," saying:

> As the coryphaeus of science, you are creating works the like of which have never been seen in the history of advanced science. Your work, "Concerning Marxism in Linguistics," is a model of genuine creative science, a great example of the way science must be developed and advanced. This work has brought a turning point in linguistics, has opened a new era for all Soviet science.[41]

Stalin revealed the fact that his preference is for the Russian language and that he thought it was a good thing that Soviet writers had exalted Russian as the coming "world language of Socialism." Many Soviet writers have promptly agreed with him. They contend that English does not have a very bright future because it "became the world language of capitalism." David Zaslavsky, one of the Soviet Union's leading journalists, commented in a Russian Communist literary magazine in 1949 that "no one can call himself a scholar in the full and genuine meaning of the word, if he does not know Russian, if he does not read the works of Russian thought in the original. Russians unquestionably occupy first place in the social sciences. All future advances in these sciences have been determined by the works of genius of Lenin and Stalin . . . it is impossible to be a genuinely educated person without Russian."[42]

This bare summary of Kremlin thought control states only the negative side of the Russian picture. In deference to Communist culture it should be pointed out that there is a positive side. The Soviet Union is very active culturally, and the Communist sections of the world are, for the most part, inspired with that special type of intellectual optimism which arises in a relatively new society. Cultural control is exercised whenever the Party wishes to exercise it, but the repression does not mean indifference to the tools of culture. The Communist Party, with all its faults, is tremendously interested in improving the receiving capacity of the Russian mind. The Soviet government is vigorously fighting illiteracy and at the same time attempting to dispel the traditional folk superstitions of the Russian people. Schools, theaters, and publishing houses are flourishing, and the volume of work produced by Soviet writers and artists is impressive.

But who can say whether a large quantity of controlled culture is better than a small quantity of free culture? One appraisal of Kremlin thought control comes with deadly force from some Yugoslavs who have lived under it. In 1949 the Yugoslav Communists who had broken away to serve under the rebellious Tito published a pamphlet called *Some Questions of Criticism and Self-Criticism in the Soviet Union.* "In every phase which we have investigated," said the pamphlet, "in Soviet science, philosophy, art and literature, as well as in party life, criticism and self-criticism almost never occur except when ordered by the Central Committee of the Bolshevik party and by Stalin himself. . . . Instead of protesting, Soviet philosophers — at a time when the international proletariat expects creative activity from them — are falling into scholasticism instead of defending freedom of science. . . . Monopoly is a denial of socialism. . . . Criticism is a struggle. Monopoly is power without struggle."[43]

6

The Vatican and Thought Control

THE VATICAN THOUGHT-CONTROL MACHINE is a pretty feeble instrument compared to that of the Kremlin. It has no secret police of its own, and it can no longer rely on the thumbscrew and the rack as punishments for heresy. Its worst features are incidental, and they spring more from tradition than from any conscious will to destroy personal freedom. In the field of culture the Vatican is still suffering from the fact that it was born and grew to maturity in a world which denied the fundamental human freedoms to great masses of men.

The Vatican exercises control over the minds of millions of people throughout the world by a triple process: it denies them the right to think freely about certain vital moral problems by cutting them off from vital sources of information; it offers them a limited culture; and it promotes tradition and obedience as substitutes for scientific curiosity. Probably the repressive measures used by the Church against critics are not actually so important in the modern world as the continuing corruption of human intelligence by systematically cultivated superstition.

The belief that men have a right to disagree with their priests is relatively new in the world. Only a few centuries ago most people in Europe felt that ordinary men had no right to challenge established beliefs. The orthodox majority hanged and burned men for rejecting orthodox creeds, and religious controversies commonly ended in violence and bloodshed. Governments compelled their subjects to support state churches and punished their citizens for disagreeing with the teachings of those churches.

Contrary to popular belief, coercion in religious affairs was not immediately abandoned by the first colonists who came to

American shores. In many American colonies men were punished for heresy and compelled to support state churches whose tenets they could not accept. Occasionally an almost insane fanaticism affected a whole community of our forefathers. Nineteen residents of Salem Village, Massachusetts, were hanged for witchcraft in 1691. In Switzerland in 1553, at the instance of John Calvin, Michael Servetus was burned alive at the stake for views that later became known as Unitarian. The Roman Catholic Church, it should be remembered, had no monopoly on intolerance at that time, and it has no monopoly today. In the Middle Ages the Church became the chief engine of intolerance and suppression largely because it was the chief cultural body of that time. Any other ruling church might have been equally intolerant. The state also was intolerant, and its own courts were probably as cruel as, and certainly more corrupt than, the ecclesiastical courts of the Inquisition.

The Papacy began to assert the right of external coercion against unbelievers about the fourth century, and its intolerance increased as it became more powerful. Its claim to the right to suppress opposing thought seemed logical to men at that time because they believed that the Church had supreme moral authority over the whole human race. Although St. Augustine opposed the death penalty for heretics and declared that "no man should be compelled to accept our faith by force," he finally came to accept banishment for heretics; and later leaders of the Church disregarded his statement against compulsion. For exhibition purposes the Papacy preserved the rule that "the Church abhors the shedding of blood," but in practice the rule simply exempted priests from duty as executioners; it did not prevent the Church from turning over heretics to the civil arm of the government, which employed non-priests to light the faggots.

The first person to be killed for heresy was the Spaniard, Priscillian, who was executed in 385. St. Ambrose and other churchmen protested, but a precedent had been set. By 1197 Peter of Aragon was ordering the stake for heretics, and a little later Pope Innocent III was proclaiming the bloody crusade against the Albigenses. Soon afterwards the Papacy organized a continent-wide system for suppressing heresy.

Books were some of the first casualties in the campaign against dangerous beliefs; in fact, it was common practice for Catholic authorities to burn books they considered heretical long before the Inquisition. Under Innocent IV in 1248 twenty wagon-loads of the Talmud and other Jewish books were publicly burned in Paris.[1]

The Inquisition flowered in southern Europe, especially in Spain, France, and Bohemia, and spread to countries like the Netherlands, and even Mexico, where priests and conquistadores united in "Christianizing" the Indians with sword and cross.

The assumption behind the Inquisition was that the Pope, as the highest representative of truth on earth, had a special assignment to search out and punish disbelief. The disbelief might be quite trivial; any deviation from orthodoxy which in the eyes of the clerics seemed important was enough for retributive slaughter. The Waldensians were massacred in a body in Piedmont for advocating Christianity in its pristine form and for opposing such purely clerical contrivances as indulgences, purgatory, and prayers for the dead. When Milton heard of the massacre of the Waldensians, he cried:

> Avenge, O Lord, thy slaughtered saints, whose bones
> Lie scattered on the Alpine mountains cold.

But it was a long time before men struck at the roots of such intolerance by adopting a program for freedom of faith and freedom of thought.

The popes, beginning with Gregory IX, went about the process of searching out unbelievers with great zeal, and they seemed to have no doubt that they were authorized by Providence to punish all heresy. They frequently used traveling monks as doctrinal spies. They appointed special and permanent judges to sit in the Inquisition courts, and too often these judges were Dominican friars who lacked every ingredient of the judicial temperament. Frequently the friars kept the money of the heretics they condemned, which made the bishops very angry because *they* were supposed to get *their* share.[2]

The techniques of prosecution were far worse than those of a modern Communist court. Usually an inquisitor chosen by the Pope would go into a medieval town and start an investigation of suspected heresy by asking the local inhabitants to spy on each other. The inquisitor would frequently direct the parish priest to send in the witnesses with their complaints. Naturally, the complaints poured in. They were primitive mixtures of malice, fanaticism, and distorted truth, representing fact, fancy, and hearsay. The prosecutions were entirely secret. The persons complained of never had a chance to confront witnesses, and witnesses for the defense almost never appeared because they were afraid to testify. Every defendant was presumed guilty until he established his innocence. There were no juries and usually no lawyers for the defense. Innocent III forbade lawyers to appear for heretics, and later popes allowed lawyers to appear only if they were of "undoubted loyalty." Nobody was ever acquitted; the most that a victim could hope for was to have his case filed for further inquiry.

To make sure that guilty heretics did not escape, each victim was threatened with the stake if he did not confess. Then, if he still held out, he was imprisoned for a time and half-starved. Then he was visited by a persistent inquisitor who was experienced in worming admissions out of broken men. Finally, if no other method produced a confession, the prisoner was submitted to torture. Torture was officially introduced by Pope Clement IV, and Clement V drew up a whole set of regulations for personal torture.

Theoretically, it was permissible to torture each heretic only once in order to secure a confession, but the rule was easily evaded by describing the second session of torture as a "continuation" of the first session. Soon, witnesses as well as defendants were submitted to preliminary torture to loosen their tongues and to impress upon them the importance of supplying effective evidence against the accused. Savonarola, the stormy evangelist of Florence, underwent a slight variation in treatment. He was subjected to a form of torture known as the strappado for at least three days before he was finally burned. This device, in the words of H. C. Lea in his famous *History of the Inquisition of the Middle Ages,* "consisted in tying the prisoner's hands behind his back, then hoisting him by a rope fastened to his wrists, letting him drop from a height and arresting him with a jerk before his feet reached the floor. Sometimes heavy weights were attached to the feet to render the operation more severe."[3] Some victims actually died from torture before they could be sentenced and killed. Sometimes a fanatical judge would order a whole company of alleged heretics burned alive — one Dominican monk, acting as a judge of the Inquisition in 1239, sent 180 victims to the flames at one time. The Spanish Inquisition capped all the other national varieties for sadism, and nominally it lasted for more than three hundred years, until 1820. To this day, the name of Torquemada, the chief Grand Inquisitor of Spain, is synonymous in history with cruelty.

It is true that some of the excesses of the Inquisition can be charged to civil governments rather than the Church. The Church usually turned over its victims to civil authorities for execution after they had been pronounced guilty. But the moral, and sometimes the official, responsibility for the punishment rested with the Church. The courts that convicted the heretics were entirely ecclesiastical. The *Catholic Encyclopedia* says that "the predominant ecclesiastical nature of the institution [the Spanish Inquisition] can hardly be doubted. The Holy See sustained the institution, accorded to the grand inquisitor canonical installation and therewith judicial authority concerning matters of faith, while from the grand inquisitor jurisdiction passed down to the subsidiary tribunals under his control . . . the Pope always admitted appeals from it to the Holy See . . . intervened in the legislation, deposed grand inquisitors, and so on."[4]

I am not concerned here with the number of men who had their flesh roasted in the Inquisition. The purpose of inserting this bit of gruesome history is to remind the reader that the Vatican has a background as an instrument of thought control. In fact, it has a much longer record than the Kremlin — although it is probable that more millions have suffered from barbarism in the USSR. The Church emphasizes the fact that for centuries it was the world's chief guardian of culture, and too often it is forgotten that the Church was also for centuries the world's chief executioner of human freedom. Macaulay spoke rather bitterly, but with much truth, when he said of the Church in 1848 that, "during the last three centuries, to stunt the growth of the human mind has been her chief object. Throughout Christendom, whatever advance has been made in knowledge, in freedom, in wealth, and in the arts of life, has been made in spite of her, and has everywhere been in inverse proportion to her power."[5]

The Catholic people of the world have completely repudiated the spirit of the Inquisition, but the Vatican is in many ways the same institution as it was years ago when the Inquisition was in full swing. Its practices have become relatively humane, but its structure of power and its claim of authority over men's minds are essentially the same. It has never had a democratic housecleaning or a real change of administration since the days of the Inquisition. Its leading philosopher is still St. Thomas Aquinas, who taught that the Church had the right to kill heretics. It still exalts Cardinal Bellarmine as "the spiritual father of the Declaration of Independence," although he taught that "freedom of belief is pernicious; it is nothing but the freedom to be wrong." The Holy Office, the central organ of the Inquisition, is still the chief engine of power in the Roman system; it still has grand inquisitors on its staff; and they still try in secret any person charged with heresy. It still enforces the principle that an autocratic agency of papal power has the right to examine men's beliefs and punish them without recourse for disagreement with orthodoxy.

Even today the Church frequently publishes apologetic statements about the Inquisition which reveal a rather startling kinship with the attitude of the medieval inquisitor. Father Joseph Blötzen, the German Jesuit priest who wrote the important article on the Inquisition in the *Catholic Encyclopedia,* after pointing out that only five of twenty-four suspected heretics were burned alive in Pamiers from 1318 to 1324, and that only forty-two of 930 were burned alive in Toulouse from 1308 to 1323, says: "These data and others of the same nature bear out the assertion that the Inquisition marks a substantial advance in the contemporary administration of justice, and therefore, in the general civilization of mankind." Elsewhere in that same official article, Father Blötzen says of the inquisitors: "Far from being inhuman, they were, as a rule, men of spotless character and sometimes of truly admirable sanctity, and not a few of them have been canonized by the Church. There is absolutely no reason to look on the medieval ecclesiastical judge as intellectually or morally inferior to the modern judge. . . . Moreover, history does not justify the hypothesis that the medieval heretics were prodigies of virtue, deserving our sympathy in advance."

The Machinery of Coercion

The existing Vatican machinery for thought control consists of a doctrine, a set of legal regulations, and several instruments of censorship and review. The use of the apparatus of control is based upon the assumption that the Holy See has always had the right of coercing the human mind directly or indirectly in order to effect its salvation. From this assumption it follows logically that the Church may take any step necessary to achieve its purpose. It may prevent falsehood from reaching the human mind in the first place, or it may inoculate the mind against critical truth by using any ecclesiastical serum which seems suitable.

Censorship is the first and necessary element in clerical thought control. The Church, naturally, favors its own system of censorship over that of the state, although in Spain it frequently defers to government censors because they enforce clerical standards. In a country like the United States, where Catholics are in a minority, the Church leaders "do not wish the state to have power to suppress expressions of opinion, because we fear it might abuse that power by suppressing the true and the good along with the false and the bad." But the Church does not fear the suppression of the true along with the false in its own system of censorship because "in the government of the Church of Christ there are sufficient safeguards against the abuse of the power."[6]

This theory is in line with the Catholic teaching that both the private conscience and the conscience of the state are morally inferior to the conscience of the Church. The individual, according to this theory, does not have a right of free protest against the decisions of the Church. Pius IX, in his 1864 *Syllabus of Errors,* listed as one of the principal errors of modern times the belief that "every man is free to embrace and to profess that religion which, guided by the light of reason, he judges true."[7]

From this belief it is easy to go a little farther and declare that movements opposed to the Catholic "conscience" are not entitled to full freedom. "The Roman Catholic Church," said *Civiltà Cattolica* of Rome in April 1948, "convinced, through its divine prerogatives, of being the only true church, must demand the right of freedom for herself alone, because such a right can only be possessed by truth, never by error." Since *Civiltà Cattolica* is the highest Jesuit organ in the world, the reaction in the United States to this pronouncement was one of alarm, especially since the Jesuit magazine went on to declare that "in a state where the majority of the people are Catholic, the Church will require that legal existence be denied to error, and that if religious minorities actively exist, they shall have only a *de facto* existence without opportunity to spread their beliefs."

Several American Catholic writers have expressed acute embarrassment because of this famous article in *Civiltà Cattolica,* but the Vatican has never repudiated it. Would the Catholic Church enforce such discrimination against American Protestants if it gained a majority in this country? The presumption is that it would. Father John Courtney Murray, a noted American Jesuit, has said: "It is probable that nothing has been written in decades better calculated to produce in the United States a blind reaction of total hostility to all things Catholic than the author's ruthlessly simplifying paragraphs on the Church's 'unblushing intolerance.' " Father Murray tries valiantly to square the American conception of freedom with that of the Vatican, and declares that "the totalitarian threat has made it clear that the freedom of the Church is ultimately linked to the freedom of the citizen; where one perishes, so does the other." But the official doctrine of the denial of freedom still stands.

Two Spanish Jesuit writers, whose utterances have never been repudiated, have recently made it clear that European Catholicism still stands for the philosophy of coercion — and unfortunately it is European Catholicism which determines the rules for American Catholicism. According to Father Pablo G. Lopez, S.J., in *Razón y Fe,* a Catholic government in a country where Catholicism is the religion of the state is obliged to see to it "that nothing is done in public contrary to the interests of the Church, either in the way of propaganda, manifestations, etc." And Father Lopez adds:

> Moreover, Spaniards discontented for religious reasons have no right to enjoy more ample religious freedom than they do enjoy. For one reason they are non-Catholics, and therefore in error; and error, even when in good faith, has strictly speaking no right to show itself or be professed. For another reason, the religious ideal of a tiny erring minority ought not to be respected in its public manifestations, when these gravely injure the Catholicism of the immense majority of the nation, and can be prevented without danger to peace.

Another noted Spanish Jesuit has charged in the same magazine that freedom of religious propaganda would open the door to "international Jewry and Masonry" and reduce Spain to the cultural level of the "materialist and pagan Anglo-Saxon spirit"; and added, in praise of religious persecution: "Persecution inflicted on heretics preserved the faith in France, when she was in danger from the Albigensians; preserved it too in Spain, when she was attacked by Lutheranism and other heresies." [8] Both of these Spanish Jesuits have been quoted by Father Murray with disapproval, but there is no indication that the Vatican disagrees with them or sides with Father Murray.

In fact, these reactionary statements by European Catholics should not cause any surprise, because similar claims concerning the monopolistic nature of Vatican rights in respect to truth have been appearing in Catholic publications for years, *in the United States*. Father Francis J. Connell, dean of the School of Sacred Theology at the Catholic University of America, advocated the right to suppress non-Catholic activity in a Catholic country in an official Catholic publication in 1944, and praised the "doctrinal intolerance" (his own phrase) of the Church, declaring that Catholic governments "are justified in repressing written or spoken attacks on Catholicism, the use of the press or the mails to weaken the allegiance of Catholics toward their Church, and similar anti-Catholic efforts. For, by such activities, the faith of some of the Catholic citizens — particularly the less educated — might be unsettled and their loyalty to the Church destroyed. A Catholic government naturally looks at these happenings as grave evils of the spiritual order, from which citizens must be protected, if possible." [9] It is interesting to compare Father Connell's statement with that of Andrei Vishinsky, which I have already quoted, to the effect that in the Communist state "there is and can be no place for freedom of speech, press and so on for the foes of Socialism."

Both Father Connell's philosophy and that of Andrei Vishinsky are paralleled by Franco in Spain. The Catholic Spanish dictator expressed his philosophy on this subject to a United Press writer in 1947:

The fact that our press and radio carry out certain patriotic and moral obligations doesn't mean that there is lack of freedom. There is no freedom against the homeland or against morale. There is no freedom to be hostile toward or insult nations or chiefs of state abroad. There is, however, freedom for all legitimate activity.[10]

Franco falls back on national morale as the excuse to suppress freedom. Father Connell and his confreres in the most reactionary wing of the American Catholic Church plead "the spiritual interests of the Catholic citizens" as their justification. When Father Connell was challenged in 1949 by more liberal Catholic leaders, he replied (italics added):

> I do not assert that the State has the right to repress religious error merely *because it is error;* but I believe that the State has the right of repression and limitation (although often it is not expedient to use it) *when error is doing harm to the spiritual interests of the Catholic citizens.*[11]

Naturally the judgment as to whether any particular idea is "doing harm to the spiritual interests of the Catholic citizens" is arrived at exclusively by the Catholic hierarchy.

The Vatican theory of cultural coercion by a church-state is made even clearer by one of Britain's greatest Catholics, Monsignor Ronald A. Knox, in his *The Belief of Catholics,* published with official Imprimatur. Knox suggests that Catholic countries would be justified in using coercive measures in the future as they have in the past, and that Catholics have a right to demand freedom for themselves while denying it to others:

> Is it just, since thought is free, to penalize *in any way* differences of speculative outlook? Ought not every Church, however powerful, to act as a body corporate within the State, exercising no form of coercion except that of exclusion from its own spiritual privileges? It is very plain that this has not been the Catholic theory in times past. There has been, in Catholic nations, a definite alliance between the secular and the spiritual power. So, to be sure, has there been among Protestant nations. But may it be understood that in our enlightened age Catholics would repudiate the notion of any such alliance in future?
>
> It must be freely admitted that this is not so. You cannot bind over the Catholic Church, as the price of your adhesion to her doctrines, to waive all right of invoking the secular arm in defense of her own principles. The circumstances in which such a possibility could be realized are indeed sufficiently remote. You have to assume, for practical purposes, a country with a very strong Catholic majority, the overwhelming body of the nation. Probably (though not certainly) you would have to assume that the non-Catholic minority are innovators, newly in revolt against the Catholic system, with no ancestral traditions, no vested interests to be

respected. Given such circumstances, is it certain that the Catholic Government of the nation would have no right to insist on Catholic education being universal (which is a form of coercion), and even to deport or imprison those who unsettled the minds of its subjects with new doctrines?

It is certain that the Church would claim that right for the Catholic Government, even if considerations of prudence forbade its exercise in fact. The Catholic Church will not be one amongst the philosophies. Her children believe, not that her doctrines may be true, but that they *are* true, and consequently part of the normal make-up of a man's mind; not even a parent can legitimately refuse such education to his child. They recognize, however, that such truths (unlike the mathematical axioms) can be argued against; that simple minds can easily be seduced by the sophistries of plausible error; they recognize, further, that the divorce between speculative belief and practical conduct is a divorce in thought, not in fact; that the unchecked development of false theories results in ethical aberrations — Anabaptism yesterday, Bolshevism today — which are a menace even to the social order. And for those reasons a body of Catholic patriots, entrusted with the Government of a Catholic State, will not shrink even from repressive measures in order to perpetuate the secure domination of Catholic principles among their fellow-countrymen.

It is frequently argued that if Catholics have at the back of their system such notions of "toleration," it is unreasonable in them to complain when a modern State restricts, in its turn, the political or educational liberty which they themselves wish to enjoy. What is sauce for the goose is sauce for the gander. The contention is ill-conceived. For when we demand liberty in the modern State, we are appealing to its own principles, not to ours.[12]

England's reaction to Monsignor Knox's frank speaking was highly critical. The same type of reasoning, it was pointed out, could have justified the Inquisition. Some commentators remembered Isaac Watts's maxim that a Christian can claim nothing which he is not prepared to concede to others. Many years later, when a new attack was made on Knox and his gospel of intolerance, the London *Times* remarked: "There is something intensely repugnant to the liberal mind in a coalition between priests and policemen for the maintenance of religion and virtue."[13]

Internal Censorship

The doctrine that the Church has a right to use coercion to protect Catholics against cultural taint is enforced within the Catholic community by internal censorship. The Vatican's censorship machine begins with books and extends to magazines, newspapers, motion pictures, and the radio. (It includes schools also, but I shall postpone discussion of that subject until the next chapter.)

"Literature," says the standard American book on canon law, "is morally bad if it endangers faith or morals, and no one has a 'right' to publish such literature any more than one has a right to poison wells or sell tainted food."[14] "The Church," says the *Catholic Almanac* proudly, "has always denounced and repressed all literature tainted with moral evil."[15] Since the Catholic hierarchy creates its own definition of moral evil, many ideas and policies are condemned which seem to non-Catholics quite reasonable.

In conformity with this policy, no Catholic is permitted to read any of the following classes of books, if he wishes to remain a good Catholic. (They are all described in the text and comments of Canons 1384 to 1405 of the Church's Code, and I shall list only part of them here.)

1. Books which directly attack any major Catholic dogma.
2. Books which attempt to overthrow Church discipline in any way.
3. Books which oppose good morals, as interpreted by the Church.
4. Bibles other than the Catholic Bible, and even the Catholic Bible when it is published by non-Catholics.
5. Books which defend heresy in any way.
6. Books which declare that divorce is sometimes legitimate.
7. Books which favor contraceptives, but not the rhythm method of birth control.
8. Books which justify the Masonic order as useful.
9. Books describing new apparitions or miracles not yet approved by the Church.

In the early days of the Inquisition, condemned books were burned indiscriminately. Occasionally there was some conflict in opinion about certain books, and a bishop in one diocese might burn a book which had been warmly praised by a bishop in another diocese. To prevent this kind of embarrassing conflict and provide uniform standards for book burning, Pope Paul IV finally authorized the Holy Office to prepare a systematic index of prohibited books. The first official list was published in 1559.

For some time after that, the Catholic Index was fairly important. Booksellers and publishers did not dare to defy its prohibitions. Then, with the spread of enlightenment and the growth of free education, cultured Catholics began to feel a certain sense of shame concerning a black list which attempted to suppress many of the world's greatest works of philosophy, literature, and science. They began to ask certain obvious questions. Would any serious thinker be deterred from reading Kant, Bergson, and Tom Paine because some priests told him that it was a sin? Then why pretend that a medieval system of censorship could be carried over into a more enlightened period?

Although the Vatican still keeps the Index going, few persons pay any attention to it, except Catholic professionals whose livelihood is at stake. Even Catholic governments do not dare to enforce its standards in nations which are solidly Catholic. In Italy, for example, with its Catholic population, the Christian Democrat (Catholic) regime completely ignores the Catholic Index and makes no attempt to suppress books which are listed on that Index. As I write these words in Rome, an amusing press controversy is raging between the Vatican and the Communists over the publication in serial form in a left-wing daily of Zola's famous novel *Rome*. The Vatican is scolding the left-wing press for publishing a book on the Index, and the left-wing press is scolding the Vatican for medieval prudery. Zola, of course, has been on the Index for decades, with all his works. The Italian people, in spite of their alleged 99 per cent Catholicism, would never think of permitting the Vatican to interfere with their desire to read Zola.

A similar story can be told about priestly censorship in many countries. Educated Catholics tend to ignore it. The Holy Office, in many parts of the world, has been defeated by modern science and democracy. This, at least, is the net result of most of the censorship attempts of the Church in recent years. The Catholic Index is conspicuously alive only as a weapon to be used *inside* the Church, against liberal priests and Catholic professors in Italy and France.

In Great Britain and the United States, the Church attempts to conceal its censorial apparatus as much as possible because of the conflict between Catholic censorship and democratic standards of cultural freedom. The Index is practically never mentioned in public in the west, and it is virtually impossible to buy a copy of it in western countries. Almost no books in the English language have been Indexed since 1900.

But, having once created an Index and having published certain dogmatic judgments on many famous books, the Vatican feels obliged to continue the list. The titles now remaining offer a strange picture. Catholics are prohibited from reading a great many ancient and honorable classics which have been put away on the back shelves of libraries for many years. They must not read Hugo's *Les Misérables* or *Notre-Dame de Paris,* and they are also prohibited from scanning John Stuart Mill's *Principles of Political Economy* or John Wilkin's "Discovery of a new world or a discourse tending to prove that 'tis probable there may be another habitable world in the moon, with a discourse concerning the possibility of a passage thither."[16]

There are almost no heretical books written by non-Catholic writers on the Index, because the Vatican has been unable to keep up with the output of works of this type. Freud, Lenin, Stalin, Karl Marx, John Dewey, and Bertrand Russell are not even honored by name. Voltaire has more banned books on the list than any other author — forty. On the whole, a writer's position on the Index seems to have almost no effect on his popularity. Benedetto Croce has been Indexed since 1934, but he continues to be one of the most influential authors in Catholic Italy.

Press and Priests

This type of censorship of reading matter is effective chiefly among priests, nuns, and the very ignorant. It is also effective in the Catholic press, which is as completely subordinate to the Vatican as the Communist press is subordinate to the Kremlin. The devout Catholic writer, Louis F. Budenz, in describing Kremlin thought control in the Communist movement when he was editor of the *Daily Worker,* said: "All the American Communist leaders with whom I became intimately acquainted had one common characteristic — a form of fright."[17] The same generalization can be applied with equal truth to virtually all Catholic editors. In doctrinal matters they are afraid of their shadows, and they are never quite sure what matters of purely civic and political policy will be considered within the scope of papal discipline. They write on all controversial matters of belief as if a Vatican counterpart of Stalin's secret police were peering over their shoulders. And the counterpart *is* peering over their shoulders! He wears a priest's robe and he speaks gently, but his refusal to stamp the censor's Nihil Obstat on the production of any priest or nun means silence or intellectual exile.

All Catholic publications, of course, are edited and written by men who are dependent for their livelihood on the organizations which own the publications. There is virtually no independent Catholic press anywhere in the world; nor are there, by definition, any independent Catholic publishers. Officially a Catholic publisher is a publisher who accepts the requirement of canon law that his publications should be submitted for review to ecclesiastical authorities if they treat of any subject that might be considered doctrinal or moral. Every book, every issue of every official Catholic magazine, and every article produced by a priest or a nun, even for a non-Catholic journal, must have the approval of a bishop or his agent. No Catholic editor or writer is free to disagree with the Catholic hierarchy on any doctrinal essential, whether it is the Assumption of the Virgin Mary bodily into heaven after her death, or the infallibility of the Pope, or the necessity of birth control in Italy.

It is true that the control of thought in the Catholic system of power is supposed to cover only the fields of faith and morals, but around these fields are adjacent territories of sociology, philosophy, history, and medicine where ecclesiastical morals rule over scientific integrity. In practice the same thought control is exerted in some matters of political and scientific theory as in matters of devotional purity. A Catholic editor is no more free to advocate a humane divorce law than to write a defense of atheism. A Catholic scientific writer who suggests planned parenthood as a solution for the problem of overpopulation receives the same treatment accorded Galileo, except that he escapes physical confinement. The control of editorial policy in Catholic newspapers and magazines is so pronounced that Catholic editorial pages are almost as deadly in their uniformity as the editorial pages of Communist journals. Key phrases and slogans are repeated over and over again. Ecclesiastical authorities are cited in almost every editorial. Whenever a positive new idea is suggested by a Catholic editor, he usually feels obliged to ascribe its origin to some Church leader in much the same way that Communist dialecticians ascribe their best thoughts to Lenin and Stalin. Perhaps one reason for this timidity among Catholic editors is that nearly all publications in the Catholic world are written and edited by priests, and frequently these priests are subjected to the double discipline of the Vatican and their own religious orders.

Even the letter pages of American Catholic papers almost never contain a direct challenge to any major Vatican doctrine or policy. In fact, the limit of Catholic independence on letter pages is quite similar to that in the Soviet press. It is never possible, for example, to find even in the Catholic correspondence columns any direct criticism of the Church's doctrine on birth control or the Church's practices in the manufacture of saints, although these doctrines and practices are probably criticized privately by more millions of educated Catholics than any other tenets of the Church.

Probably the most devastating effect of the system of internal censorship is noticeable in the cultural output of priests and nuns. In a sense the censorship system in the United States takes about 40,000 priests out of cultural circulation by putting them in anti-scientific strait jackets. Their intellectual independence is completely destroyed. In fact, the literature produced by the American Catholic priesthood is a dreary wasteland of unimaginative conformity, more dreary even than typical Communist propaganda. Most Communist diatribes, no matter how fanatical and misguided, discuss serious problems with a certain boldness and dash, and demonstrate a deep concern with social injustice — except the injustice of the Russian Communist regime.

Much of the priestly output of the Church in the United States is incredibly immature and unreal. Every priestly sermon, pamphlet, or book must arrive at one terminus, the current position of the Vatican concerning the subject discussed. Variety of opinion is never permitted in respect to the fundamentals of Church policy. The most patent ecclesiastical frauds in the fields of relics and apparitions must be accepted without a murmur. A priest, scientist, or editor who challenged any of the Vatican's devices for exploiting relics would receive essentially the same treatment meted out to the critics of Lysenko. Actually the Vatican's control over its priests is so complete that there has not even been a parallel to the Lysenko incident in Catholic circles for several generations because there is no opportunity for movements of scientific protest within the priesthood. Any suggestions of intellectual rebellion are eliminated by pre-censorship. The Church permits no free and independent associations of Catholic intellectuals where a dissident movement might gain a foothold.

Strangely enough, American priests have been among the most docile in accepting Vatican cultural controls. An American priest, Father T. T. McAvoy, was able to boast in the *Review of Politics* in January 1948 that "there has never been a real heresy during the three centuries and more of Catholic life within the boundaries of the present United States." It is true that some American bishops in 1870 protested privately against the imposition of the doctrine of papal infallibility upon the Church by Pius IX for reasons of expediency, but they did not challenge it openly when the doctrine had finally been promulgated, and there was no movement for secession in the United States. During the years since World War I, when American priests have been continuously asserting their faith in democracy, not one has publicly declared himself in favor of the democratization of the Vatican, or protested against the fact that the American Catholic clergy have for years been refused permission to hold a plenary council. Their professions of belief in democracy are never applied consistently to their own Church.

European priests have been more courageous in resisting the system of thought control — more courageous but not more successful. The European modernist movement, which arose inside the Church about the turn of the century, promptly collapsed when Piux X subjected it to a disciplinary reign of terror. The famous British Jesuit, Father George Tyrrell, was excommunicated in 1907, largely for criticizing a bitterly reactionary encyclical of Pius X in two articles in the London *Times*. The brilliant Italian scholar, Father Ernesto Buonaiuti, professor of the history of Christianity at the University of Rome, was excommunicated without trial in 1923 by decree of the Inquisition for writing an unorthodox article on the Eucharist, although the official Church censor had passed the article. Alfred Loisy, the Church's great modernist French scholar, saw his works condemned by the Index because his biblical exegesis was too advanced, and then he was excommunicated in 1908.[18] The modernist movement within the Church was too weak to protect him, but it had made such great headway among the French people that Loisy scored a national triumph in spite of his excommunication. The French government offered him the chair of Comparative Religion at the University of Paris. Could anyone imagine a similar offer being made to an excommunicated priest by a public university in the United States?

One reason why American priests do not assert their American rights of free discussion within the Catholic system is that they are screened early in their careers by a special intellectual filter designed by Pius X. Pius X not only demanded that all bishops exercise great vigilance in examining books before publication, but he also directed the establishment in each diocese of a council "to watch carefully the teachings of innovators." In order to help this thought-control council, Pius imposed on all the clergy and on Catholic teachers a special anti-modernist oath, and this oath, imposed by edict, is still obligatory for the clergy of the whole world.[19] It is not merely a loyalty oath, it is an opinion-controlling oath. In four hundred words it commits every priest without qualification to the acceptance of two of the most reactionary and anti-scientific pronouncements ever issued by the Church — the *Lamentabili* and the *Pascendi* of Pius X. It outlaws all expressions of skepticism and prevents any theological student or priest who wishes to remain orthodox from harboring any notion that the "spiritual or religious activity of man" can possibly be a substitute for Catholic dogma. It pledges every priest to avoid the use of the principles of evolution in interpreting the Scriptures. It eliminates from Catholic life every priest, student, or professor who might have liberal cultural tendencies, and it is still imposed *annually* on every professor or lecturer in every Catholic seminary throughout the world at the beginning of each year's work. Even veteran parish priests are required to take the oath anew whenever they start work in a new parish.

The Lay Mind

The Vatican's control of the Catholic lay mind is much less successful than its control of priests, and also much less rigorous. In the United States, particularly, the Church has met complete failure in attempting to suppress critical writings among baptized lay Catholics. Some of the most vigorous and independent writers of America are ex-Catholics who have broken away from priestly control. For the literary men who have chosen to stay behind in the confines of the Church, the policy of censorship is stultifying and oppressive. The Catholic novelist, Harry Sylvester, has pointed out in the *Atlantic Monthly* how heavily Church controls weigh upon the sensitive creative mind. "Why," he asked, "have we produced a group of meechers and propagandists, who are Catholics, however nominal, before they are people, and whose principal concern seems to be not to write truly but to win ecclesiastical approbation?" "There is," he said, "no national literary or artistic group whose mediocrity is quite so monolithic as that of the Gallery of Living Catholic Authors."[20]

An almost equally severe judgment was delivered against British Catholic authors, who must work under the Catholic censorship, by Michael de la Bedoyere, editor of the British *Catholic Herald:* "If," he said, "we apply the test of suitable spiritual reading for enclosed Religious women to the novel, we shall of course simply cease to produce novels worth the name. And that, expressed in an exaggerated way, is our tendency when we review such subjects as literature, art, the drama, the cinema and the like. . . . No wonder that there is no Catholic fiction or drama or art worthy of the name it is only too easily accorded!"[21]

In the world of Catholic book publishing, a system of preventive censorship is used which is applied to manuscripts before they go to press. All Catholic publishers are obligated under Canon 1385 to submit manuscripts to ecclesiastical authorities in advance of publication if these manuscripts treat of moral, doctrinal, or devotional matters. This is a very wide area of control, and its limits are distressingly vague. The leaders of the hierarchy are especially insistent upon exercising their authority over any manuscript which questions the Vatican's centralized power or which discusses such controversial subjects as birth control or divorce with any independent candor. The rule of pre-censorship before publication applies even when both the author and the publisher are laymen and when the manuscript seems "to favor piety."[22] If the author is a priest, his manuscript must be submitted for pre-publication censorship even if it treats only of fly-fishing or wind velocity. And even if a Catholic author's articles are perfectly correct on moral and theological grounds, they must not be submitted for publication to any magazine which consistently criticizes Vatican policies. Jacques Maritain, famous French Catholic philosopher, who had written many articles over a period of years for *The Nation,* conspicuously withdrew in 1950 his permission for that magazine to describe him as a contributor, all because it had published (unrepentantly) my articles on Vatican social policy.

The Church's machinery for preventive censorship of the literary output of Catholics is maintained by each bishop in his diocese, and every sanctioned work, upon publication, must bear the bishop's badge of approval in the form of a stamp by the priest-censor (Nihil Obstat), and the final permission to print, the Imprimatur. Since the priest-censor of each diocese is appointed by the bishop, he is held responsible to the bishop for checking carefully the manuscripts of books to be published in the diocese.

Since the republication in recent years of many shockingly reactionary statements of Catholic prelates which have been issued with a bishop's Imprimatur, American Catholic leaders have been much embarrassed and have been attempting to play down the significance of the Nihil Obstat and Imprimatur on the fly leaves of Catholic books. These stamps, they declare, are not proofs of approval of everything contained in the works. That is true; but they *are* proofs that the work so stamped contains no theological error. The bishops themselves may stamp their Imprimaturs upon works with very little scrutiny, but the censors of each diocese are obliged by canon law to read all works carefully and guarantee that they are not heretical or incorrect. Bouscaren and Ellis in their *Canon Law,* page 717, say that the censor in each case must "clearly approve the publication as regards soundness of doctrine."

Even non-Catholic publishers in the United States usually observe the conventions of this pre-censorship system by sending manuscripts in advance of publication to Catholic critics if those manuscripts treat of Vatican doctrine or policy. In countries like Spain this internal system of censorship is strong enough to prevent the publication of *any* book on the Index.[23] In the United

States the system usually eliminates all books directly critical of the Catholic hierarchy from the lists of America's leading publishers. Fortunately for America's self-respect, there are still in the nation a number of courageous publishers who are more interested in freedom of thought than in conformity and success.

The External Censorship

Naturally, the Church cannot exercise strict supervision over the publication of critical material written by non-Catholics and published in predominantly non-Catholic countries. In general, its only effective weapon for suppressing criticism in non-Catholic countries is the boycott or the threat of the boycott. The punitive boycott is usually directed against editors, booksellers, publishers, librarians, and motion-picture producers through the mechanism of group pressure. Sometimes the pressure takes the form of public denunciation from a Catholic pulpit; sometimes, as in Catholic Ireland, it takes the form of legal suppression by the state of books which are displeasing to the hierarchy. Sometimes the Catholic hierarchy has more restrictive power over cultural freedom in a nominally non-Catholic country like the United States than it has in France, which is claimed by the Vatican as Catholic domain. The strength of Catholic thought control in a country does not depend upon the number of Catholics in a nation but on the organization of those Catholics into a militant cultural bloc in the community.

The principle of Catholic censorship is always the same; the tactics vary according to the country and the medium of information used. Censorship of films is conducted throughout the world by official committees of priests, working under slight disguises, such as the Legion of Decency in the United States or the Centro Cattolico Cinematografico in Rome. In completely Catholic countries like Spain, the censorship virtually destroys all public criticism of Vatican policy. In Spain no motion picture may be exhibited in the whole nation which does not have the official approval of the official censor of the Church. The Spanish censorship of drama is almost as severe. Only one performance of an uncensored play is permitted, and that is permitted only in private clubs. The Spanish Church operates five daily newspapers and more than four hundred other periodicals, and a "religious assessor" from the Church is attached to every newspaper in the country.[24]

In Italy, on the other hand, the Church's censorship powers have never recovered from the long period of comparative freedom between 1870, when the Kingdom of Italy conquered the Vatican in battle, and 1922, when Mussolini came into power. In Italy today the intellectuals are openly contemptuous of the Church's literary and artistic standards, and Italian motion-picture theaters are currently showing at least five times as many Catholic-condemned films as American producers are showing in the United States. On September 2, 1950, the Catholic Action daily in Rome, *Quotidiano,* advertised sixteen motion-picture programs appearing in Rome all of which were rated "E" or "excluded" by the Vatican counterpart of the American Legion of Decency.[25]

Of course the principle of the retributive boycott of persons who circulate "anti-Catholic" opinions is a very old principle in the Catholic system of power. Pope Paul IV, about the middle of the sixteenth century, inaugurated the policy that the Vatican should boycott not only bad books but bad printers. He laid down the rule that no printer who had published a banned book should ever again be patronized by Catholic readers. The Inquisition enforced the rule that the burden of proof was upon any person who came into possession of a heretical book, and failed to burn it immediately or surrender it to his bishop within eight days.[26]

Sometimes the censorial policies of the Vatican in respect to news are more stupid than deliberate. In spite of all its successes in the field of pageantry, the Vatican is singularly inept and secretive in its techniques of public relations. It fails to tell the world adequately of its own activities. The publicity material which it gives to the press is almost nonexistent. Able journalists assigned by the world's great newspapers to Rome are almost completely frustrated by the Vatican's policy of withholding all candid comment on controversial matters. The New York *Times,* which has been more successful than any other world newspaper in persuading the Vatican to talk, recently revealed some of its difficulty in a candid paragraph, carried in an advertisement in *Editor & Publisher:*

As for Vatican coverage, suppose you were covering Washington without benefit of press conferences or press releases other than copies of speeches already delivered. Suppose every government official were sworn never to permit any unauthorized person to peep behind the scenes, and that the entire government was a completely disciplined and compact mechanism carrying out with unquestioning obedience the will of the President. Suppose, finally, that these officials, from top to bottom, felt that their mission transcended all earthly considerations, and knew they could always command a world audience without the aid of the press if they desired. That, roughly, is the job of covering the Vatican.[27]

Outside of the Soviet orbit the reaction of most editors to Vatican secrecy and silence is very charitable. Catholic power is sufficiently great throughout the western world to prevent independent editors from hostile comment, and news about Vatican activity is treated with special kindness. The most reactionary papal utterances are either printed without comment by the great standard journals or, if there is any opportunity for encomiums, lauded in the most circumspect and deferential manner. The deference and the absence of criticism may, in effect, be a serious distortion of truth about Catholic policy. Even the newspapers which print the truth and nothing but the truth about the more reactionary phases of Catholic policy rarely speak the whole truth.

Two illustrations of affirmative and negative distortion may be taken from the New York *Times,* one of the world's most accurate and valuable news organs. The *Times* has rendered a great public service in exposing the repressive tactics of the Church in Spain through the dispatches of two of its top correspondents, Cyrus L. Sulzberger and Sam Pope Brewer, but at home its policy is at times inexplicably timid and vacillating. Probably no Catholic cardinal ever directly threatened the editor of the *Times* with reprisals for telling the truth about Catholic policy, but the pressure of Catholic influence upon that august journal in recent years has produced some flagrant shadings of the news, and it has resulted in the suppression of honest expressions of critical thought concerning Catholic policy.

At a time after World War II when the Vatican was attempting to rehabilitate itself in the esteem of democratic nations after a long period of tolerance for fascism, the *Times* published a short speech by Pius XII to an American trade delegation in Rome, and dressed it up as both an endorsement of democracy and a denunciation of dictatorship. The story is relatively unimportant, as the Pope's speech was unimportant, but it would be difficult to find a more eloquent illustration of the way in which a great newspaper may favor the Vatican in its news columns. This is the story, exactly as it was published, heading and all, in the issue of October 2, 1947:

POPE PRAISES DEMOCRACY

Rome, Oct. 1 — Pope Pius today praised democratic government and condemned totalitarianism in a brief address to members of the United States foreign trade parliamentary committee, who were here investigating conditions in Italy.

It was clear to some of those present at the private audience in Castel Gandolfo that the Pontiff was referring to the Government in the United States as contrasted with the Government in Russia.

The Pope's address follows:

"Your presence, honorable members of Congress, naturally suggests to our mind the importance of government and the very grave responsibility resting on those whose duty it is to govern a nation. The art of governing justly has never been easy for human nature to learn.

"To exploit the common people for the benefit of one individual or group is a temptation to ambitious men who have little conscience to check them; but that is not to govern. Nero's despotism was not government but oppression.

"A just government recognizes that its own power is limited by the basic human liberties of those who are governed and it succeeds only when each one is ready for personal sacrifice in the interest of all.

"What is true of a single nation may be applied to the larger family of nations, which today especially cannot escape close proximity and interdependence. A just and equitable exercise of legitimate government holds the key to the peace of the world. To that noble purpose — the world is more and more restless to attain it — we devote all our energies, our prayers, our work."

It should be noted that there is not a line in the Pope's speech specifically praising democracy or condemning totalitarianism. The speech could very well have been made by any benevolent prince or dictator giving lip service to "basic human liberties." In fact, at the moment the Pope made this speech, he was giving strong diplomatic support to at least three basically totalitarian Catholic regimes — in Spain, Portugal, and Argentina.

The second illustration from the New York *Times* appeared in that journal on April 9, 1950. A responsible reviewer, Philip

Toynbee, had reviewed a book by Lionel Trilling called *The Liberal Imagination,* and the review, after being approved by a responsible book-review editor, was published in the Sunday *Times* book section. The book section goes to press several days ahead of the standard Sunday edition, which contains the editorials and current news. Toynbee's review contained one casual sentence about Catholic reactions to liberal culture: "We are all too familiar with the facile and vitriolic attacks on liberal and democratic culture made by Roman Catholics and members of the political right." That was all. No educated person could doubt the truth of the sentence — there *are* plenty of such attacks on liberal culture by Catholic writers. But the mere statement of such an elementary truth, buried unobtrusively in a scholarly review, caused the president and publisher of the *Times* to write and publish in the same issue with the offending sentence an editorial retraction, apologizing for the statement and rebuking the book-section editor for not eliminating it. Here is the editorial in full:

A Correction

In today's issue of the Book Review, in a review by Philip Toynbee of a book by Lionel Trilling, *The Liberal Imagination,* there appears a reference to Roman Catholics that obviously should not have been made. Every reviewer has the right to express his opinion and that opinion is his rather than the opinion of the *Times.* The editor, however, has the responsibility to delete statements that are inaccurate or offensive. That responsibility should have been exercised in this case. Unfortunately, it was not and the offending sentence was not detected until after the press run of the Book Section had been completed.

Naturally, all fundamental hostile criticism of any group in society is "offensive" to that group. If the limits of criticism suggested in this editorial should be imposed upon all discussion of Catholic power in the United States, the American press would be no more able to speak frankly about the Vatican than the Russian press can speak about the Kremlin.

In the United States, Catholic power also controls advertising sufficiently to eliminate from most leading papers, magazines, and radio programs any mention of works critical of Catholic policy. An American publisher cannot even buy space for advertising an "anti-Catholic" book in several of the leading agencies of American information. There is even a taboo against any suggestion in American advertising that might in any way conflict with Catholic theories. On December 24, 1950, the American Textile Company published in the New York *Times Magazine* a small picture of Joan of Arc, looking rather voluptuous and coy in a suit of armor, spurs, and helmet, with an inscription beneath the picture: "Joan of Arc might never have gotten so burned up had she but known The Lure of Laces by Ametex." A week later, on December 31, the company published in the *Times* an abject apology headed "Nostra Maxima Culpa": "We wrote the ad in all innocence and meant no offense, since we were considering her [Joan of Arc] as the great historical figure she was rather than as the great Saint she is. . . . We are sorry, and it won't happen again."

7

The Kremlin and the Vatican versus the Public School

WE HAVE EXAMINED Kremlin and Vatican thought control in the last two chapters as if they existed in separate compartments. In one respect these organizations occupy the same battlefield, the battlefield of education; and on that battlefield democracy, Catholicism, and Communism are all engaged in a deadly struggle for the mind of the coming generations.

The struggle for control of schools is far more important than anything I have described in the last chapter. As the public school goes, so will go the future of democratic society. The Kremlin believes in partisan Communist education, and the Vatican believes in partisan Catholic education, and each is hostile to the non-partisan public school. Only a powerful and informed democracy can preserve the institution from impairment or ruin by these two hostile and competing organizations. These words may seem to be unduly alarmist in their tenor, but I believe that a review of the world-wide school battle will justify an alarmist view. It may be well to transfer our attention from Europe for a moment and look at the stake of American democracy in the school struggle.

The free public school, supported by all the community and open without discrimination to children of all faiths, has now become an established part of the American way of life. Most Americans would regard it as unthinkable that an American public school should be subject to the control of any political party or church. It is true that in some sections of our country, notably in the southern states, public schools are not free from racial discrimination, and the teaching on many subjects is not free from racial bias. This shortcoming, however, is primarily regional rather than national, and it is not the fault of the public school itself.

On the whole, we are proud that our American public school is the most democratic institution in a democratic nation. No political party dictates our textbooks; no church enters the classroom during the regular hours of school to indoctrinate the children with denominational dogma; and very few public-school teachers owe their appointments to partisan favor or religious conformity. Pressure groups, representing vested interests and fanaticism, occasionally impair freedom of teaching in an American community, but such lapses are rare. Most American cities, towns, and villages strenuously resist any policy which seems to destroy the freedom of teaching in an American classroom, and the American people take it for granted that educational self-government is one of the nation's most precious possessions.

Almost all Americans accept two basic traditions concerning the control of education — that the responsibility for control should rest with the local community, and that the schools should be free from sectarian strife. The experience of European countries with church-controlled education impressed our forefathers unfavorably. They decided that they should have a school system which represented all the people, which was paid for by all the people, and which was open to the children of all the people without discrimination. That decision was probably the most important decision ever made by Americans for American culture.

It is true that the public-school system has many defects. It is underequipped in countless ways. It frequently overemphasizes American nationalism and discriminates against new ideas of social reconstruction. But this is a failing common to democratic institutions. National majorities do not like to have the opinions of national minorities propagated through the schools. The very fact that our schools are controlled by a majority of the people tends to make the loyalties and prejudices of the dominant majority the norm of education. And who has a better right to determine the norm of education than the majority?

One unspoken assumption behind this American public-school system is that the human mind should be left free to examine life fearlessly and arrive at honest conclusions. Truth, it is assumed, is something discovered by search. Apparent error must be examined with candor because it might prove, upon examination, to be the truth. No areas of life should be exempt from human curiosity. No outside institution should be permitted to tell the teacher or the student what are the limits of reason and curiosity in physics, politics, or ethics. Above all, no alien hierarchy or foreign power should be permitted to impose its cultural or moral strait jacket on an American public school.

All these fundamental principles are commonplaces in American education, but it is astonishing how few Americans have applied them as tests to both the Catholic and the Communist conceptions of education. It is apparent on the face of the record that both Catholic and Communist theories of education are opposed to the American concept of the public school.

Education à la Kremlin

The present rulers of the Kremlin have always been in favor of "education," and the development of a comprehensive school system has been one of their chief aims. Nominally, the Soviet Constitution of 1936 gives every Soviet citizen "the right of education," primarily at state expense, and this could represent a great forward step from the days of Tsarist control.

Opinions differ as to the extent of illiteracy in Russia in 1917 when the Bolsheviks took power. The Bolsheviks did not inherit an entirely illiterate nation, but the Russian masses were certainly underprivileged in everything that constituted culture. Chamberlin puts the illiteracy rate at 60 per cent in 1917, and declares that even in the late 1920's some 69 per cent of the people between 16 and 34 were illiterate.[1] Before the revolution the government had adopted a program, to be completed in 1922, for compulsory primary education, and when the Bolsheviks came into power, they acquired a school system that had reached about 70 per cent of the children of school age for at least a few years of schooling.[2]

The Communist movement quickly transformed this school system for its own purposes. Bolshevik leaders went outside the regular school system and conducted great campaigns, in the army, in trade unions, and in peasant groups, against illiteracy among both adults and children. They extended elementary education to the masses with such vigor and persistence that they claim today to reach 34,000,000 children and young people in the various branches of their educational system. They have made education free and compulsory up to the seventh grade. From 1936 to 1940 they provided free higher education also, but they have now amended the 1936 Constitution and inaugurated a system of tuition fees for college training and for the last two years of secondary education.[3]

Probably the Russian Communists have done more in a single generation to overcome illiteracy among their 200,000,000 subjects than the Vatican has done for *its* people since the Middle Ages. In the first twenty-two years of that stormy and troubled generation, the Russians reduced illiteracy to less than one-third of its 1917 level — it stood at 19 per cent in the 1939 census, and it is probably much lower today.[4]

The relative illiteracy in Catholic countries with Catholic school systems — Spain and Portugal are illustrations — is a shocking commentary on the cultural zeal of the two organizations. When the Vatican was reaching the end of its reign as a major temporal power in Italy, the statistics of 1866 showed that Italy was still 78 per cent illiterate and that in priest-dominated Naples the illiteracy was 90 per cent. Professor Salo Baron has pointed out that the Catholic Church in Europe did very little to overcome illiteracy except when it was faced with secular competition from public schools, as in France; and that at the turn of the century the two most illiterate nations in Europe were both Catholic — Portugal and Italy.[5] Italy made tremendous strides in education as soon as it was free from papal domination in 1870, but it could not be expected to work a cultural transformation in thirty years.

Victor Hugo, in a remarkable and rather undiscriminating burst of rage against the Church's nineteenth-century indifference to culture for the European masses, declared that the priests "claim the liberty of teaching. . . . It is the liberty of *not* teaching." And he added, addressing the priests directly:

You wish us to give you the people to instruct. Very well. Let us see your pupils. Let us see what you have produced. What have you done for Italy? What have you done for Spain? For centuries you have kept in your hands, at your discretion, at your school, these two great nations, illustrious among the illustrious.

What have you done for them? I shall tell you.

Thanks to you, Italy, whose name no man who thinks can any longer pronounce without inexpressible filial emotions — Italy, mother of genius and of nations, which has spread over all the universe all the most brilliant marvels of poetry and the arts, Italy which has taught mankind to read — now knows not how to read! Yes, Italy is of all the states of Europe that one where the smallest number know how to read.

Spain, magnificently endowed Spain, which received from the Romans her first civilization; from the Arabs her second civilization; from Providence and in spite of you, a world, America — Spain, thanks to you, a yoke of stupor which is a yoke of degradation and decay.[6]

The *relative* position of Catholic countries on the world's literacy chart is still strikingly low, and the most Catholic sections of Europe — Spain, Portugal, southern Italy, and pre-revolutionary Poland — have continued to appear near the bottom.[7] I point out this fact by way of interpolation because too often the Catholic critics of Communism seem to assume that the Vatican stands for learning and the Kremlin for cultural barbarism. Incidentally, the over-all proportion of illiteracy in predominantly Catholic countries today is at least five times the proportion in predominantly Protestant countries.

The Communists have not been as successful in dealing with higher education as with elementary schools. They have provided a complete system of public education from the kindergarten to the university, but their record in the fields of higher learning has been far from creditable. The professors of the old Russian universities under the Tsar had been relatively independent, even though the universities were official state universities. After the revolution, all independence was destroyed and standards fell sharply. Every professor in the universities who wished to continue teaching had to be re-elected to his post by a committee which operated on the principle that no teacher, even a teacher of classics or mathematics, was fit to teach in the new Russia unless he accepted the socialist ideal enthusiastically.[8] Partisan political control did not prove any more rational under Communism than it would have been under Tsarism. Although the universities have recovered some of their earlier standards of discipline in recent years, they are still far below western democratic levels of scientific scholarship.

The tragedy in the Russian educational success story is that while the Soviet Union has been moving forward in the mechanics of education it has moved backward in educational freedom. It has achieved political control of education in the worst meaning of that phrase. The control over schools is exercised by a centralized Communist political machine which is not answerable to the people of any community and which is primarily concerned not with free culture but with the production of little Stalinists.

"To whom do you owe your happy childhood?" ask the Russian kindergarten teachers of their little four-year-olds. "To Comrade Stalin, hurrah!" they shout back. That is what John Fischer of *Harper's* heard when he visited a Russian kindergarten in 1945, and it epitomizes the whole Soviet system of education.[9] H. G. Wells was told by Stalin in 1934: "Education is a weapon whose effect depends on who holds it in his hands and at whom it is aimed. In Russia the Communists hold the educational gun and it is aimed at 'bourgeois culture.' "[10] The word "objectivity" is openly jeered at in educational circles as an outmoded bourgeois concept. From the moment that a child enters kindergarten, he is taught that "Communist" and "good" are equivalent moral terms, and that "capitalist" is synonymous with evil.

Every textbook in every Soviet school must be reviewed and edited by a Communist Party official or committee in order to eliminate any possible suggestion which might be opposed to Stalin or his ideas. Simultaneously, the children must be taught that their school system is the best in the world. "Only in the Soviet Union," said a Soviet minister of education in 1947, "is the school genuinely democratic and humanistic." When the Soviet minister came to discuss American education in this same statement, he said: "Everything is for sale and everything is to be bought. Whatever brings profit is moral. Such is the code of morality cultivated in the American school. Such is the true content of bourgeois education."[11]

Naturally, every teacher in this Soviet school system must conform to Communist policies or lose his position. There is no independent system of schools to which a rebellious teacher can turn if he loses his position in the state schools. There is no forum which can guarantee him a hearing for his grievances, no newspaper which will print an unbiased account of his martyrdom. Teachers' unions in the Soviet system are, like all Russian labor organizations, dominated by the Communist party. Their interest in academic freedom ends where Party discipline begins.

This tight control extends to the universities, especially in those fields of thought in which Communist pundits have promulgated a dogma. Even the highest department heads must accept dictation from a Communist Party agent without a murmur. Marxism-Leninism must be the guiding principle of all university training, just as the philosophy of St. Thomas Aquinas must be the guide of all philosophical culture in the Catholic system. There is no such person in the whole Soviet educational system as a capitalist professor, since, by definition, a capitalist professor would be an enemy of the state. This latter fact is not usually emphasized by Communists in the United States when they demand freedom for anti-capitalist professors in American universities.

The Communists have not been content with standard schools to impress their outlook upon the Russian mind. They have established a whole network of special schools for adults, designed to equip those adults for effective participation in the Soviet system of power. There are propaganda and training schools for youths, designed to turn youthful energy into Communist channels. There are training schools for adult Communist agitators, headed by an Academy of Social Sciences which trains Party workers for central Party institutions. In the far-flung Soviet empire outside of Russia, the Communist parties of various nations establish training institutions in Marxism-Leninism to aid in the revolution. Frequently, as in the United States, these Party training schools assume the names of venerable local patriots in order to camouflage their essential purpose. In New York, for example, the Communist school of propaganda was called the Jefferson School of Social Science; in Boston, it was the Samuel Adams School; in Chicago, the Abraham Lincoln School.

George Counts, noted American educator, and Nucia P. Lodge, in their little book, *I Want to Be Like Stalin,* have translated and edited for American consumption selected parts of a Soviet manual on pedagogy which reveals in startling fashion the methods by which the Kremlin controls the minds of Russian school children. The Communists are quite unabashed in imposing their whole doctrine in every Soviet classroom. They read Marx into mathematics as blithely as they read him into music. Mathematics, according to the manual, "must reflect our socialist reality"; "physical education in our school is most intimately related to the cultivation of communist morality"; "Comrade Stalin and the Soviet Government watch over every Soviet person." Substantial uniformity of textbooks throughout Russia has been imposed by the Party on the schools through a textbook committee headed by Stalin himself. Every textbook must give "full support to the Communist direction."

Behind these techniques of indoctrination, as Professor Counts has pointed out, lies the theory that there is no such thing as neutral or non-partisan education, and that in the past "education has always been the servant of the ruling class." The school which stands outside of politics is "a lie and a hypocrisy." The teacher who challenges the partisan conception of education is considered anti-social and a menace to Soviet culture. If he persists in a rebellious attitude he is branded as a criminal and sent to a forced-labor camp.

It is natural that this type of control in the schools should be accompanied by a new emphasis upon repressive measures for the discipline of students. Communists would claim that the rigid measures are entirely justified. To those who are interested in progressive standards, however, they seem very old-fashioned and even reactionary. Every Soviet child must memorize paragraph by paragraph a set of rules of conduct in much the same manner in which a Catholic child is compelled to memorize his Catechism. He must observe every rule in the Communist rule book. He must "rise as the teacher or the director enters or leaves the classroom." He must remove his hat on the street even to a male teacher. He must begin his military training in the fourth year of the elementary school. Co-education was abolished in the Soviet school system in 1943 as one step in the "new discipline."

As Communist power has moved westward in Europe, the

Soviet conception of Communist-controlled education has been imposed on all the satellite countries. Catholic schools have been closed in many countries and the students transferred, not to a neutral or non-partisan public school, but to the school of another dogmatic religion, that of the Kremlin, masquerading as a public school. The educational pattern in the new Hungary, Poland, Rumania, Czechoslovakia, and East Germany is as near as possible to that of the Soviet Union itself. In these schools Stalin has become as much a symbol of goodness and intelligence as the Pope has been traditionally in the Catholic schools, and the dogmatic compulsions are even more severe than in the Catholic schools.

In non-Communist countries Communist tactics in education are different. Primarily Communist education inside capitalist countries is education for revolution, designed to develop and focus dissatisfaction with capitalist power. In places like the United States, Communists emphasize almost all the Soviet values and slogans in reverse. Instead of teaching youths loyalty to the national culture, they teach opposition and criticism. They emphasize the right of teachers to individual liberty and the right of students to protest and agitate. They dramatize every act of reprisal against Communists, without mentioning the fact that the right of protest against the established regime is completely denied in the country of Communist dreams.

Behind all Communist activity in the field of education is the conviction that Communists are a morally superior group in the population because of their possession of Communist truth, and that by virtue of the possession of this truth they have a superior moral insight, a capacity to reject error and discern reality. In the theory of Communist education the masses of the people have no independent right to set up an educational system of their own which opposes Communist truth, because Marxism-Leninism is the undisputed fountain of all truth. Hence, in Communist theory, the state may control education so long as the state is the instrument of Marxism-Leninism and so long as it does not attempt to challenge the supervising rights of the Communist Party in the educational world. Accordingly, it is quite fair to say that the Kremlin does not stand for education by the democratic state. It disbelieves in the public school and it stands for the Party school. Its schools are called public schools — but they are *not* public schools.

The Church as Educator

Although the *aims* of Communist and Catholic education are at opposite poles of the cultural universe, the Vatican *theory* of education is an almost exact parallel to the Communist theory. In Catholic educational philosophy, God has given the Church superior rights over the schooling of all Catholics, and an auxiliary right to censor certain aspects of non-Catholic education. No government has the moral or legal right to challenge this supremacy because the right of any government to govern comes from the same source from which the Vatican derives its power. God's grant of authority to the Church takes precedence over the divine grant of authority to civil governments.

The Vatican carries out this policy of superior power in education with the utmost consistency. Wherever in non-Catholic countries the Church is unable to control public schools, it attempts to establish a segregated, competing educational system of its own to teach Catholic "truth" and combat "secular error." It never permits the Catholic people of any particular country to alter this general pattern of educational policy on their own initiative. The policy is world-wide, and imposed without exception by the Church's canon law.

The Church's philosophy of education is, of course, partly an accident of history, a survival of a cultural splendor that has since faded away. For centuries the Church had almost a monopoly of education in Europe. Priestly learning was the highest learning, and clerical philosophy dominated the whole academic field. For the most part, these centuries of Church domination were periods of neglect for the masses. Both princes and popes feared the effect of knowledge on the common people. Slowly, a world of democratic culture developed outside of authoritarian control, but at first even the boldest thinkers left the fundamental dogmas of the Church unchallenged. Even after the Reformation, Protestantism still clung to many authoritarian concepts, and the idea that theology should be exempt from criticism by all other branches of learning still prevailed in many quarters. The concept of free public education, independent of ecclesiastical control, did not develop until three centuries after Luther.

When the American Constitution was written, public education was not mentioned, and it was not until forty years after its promulgation that most Americans began to appreciate the public school as a basic institution of modern democracy.

The Vatican has yielded very reluctantly to the modern movements for free public education, and today it is the world's foremost enemy of the independent public school. It has flatly denied the right of the non-Catholic state to direct the education of Catholic children and it has consistently disputed the claim of the state to establish educational policy for the community.

This is strong language, and it requires documentary proof. Fortunately, the Catholic philosophy of education is so open and explicit that any ordinary student can find abundant proof of its character in any good Catholic book shop. The policy of opposition to public schools is written into canon law in the most specific language, and supported by the most specific theological sanctions. A good Catholic has no more moral right to support neutral, public education than a good Communist has to support western "bourgeois culture." Many American Catholics, probably a majority, actually *do* support public education in preference to Catholic education — but this is because they are good Americans rather than good Catholics. Officially they are morally bound to place the interests of their Church first in the field of education.

For those who are interested in the unabridged Catholic doctrine itself, I have included in the Notes at the end of this volume a rough translation of the *entire* text of Title XXII, "Concerning Schools," of the Catholic canon law.[12] Since the bare canon law itself can give only a small part of the total picture of educational policy, I shall ask here certain questions and give official Catholic answers which may help to make the picture complete.

(1) *Does the democratic state have the supreme right to educate its children in its own way?*

No. The primary right of education belongs to the Catholic Church "by reason of a double title in the supernatural order," and "the Church is independent of any sort of earthly power as well in the origin as in the exercise of her mission as educator." "It is the duty of the State to protect in its legislation the prior rights . . . of the family as regards Christian education of its offspring, and consequently also to respect the supernatural rights of the Church in this same realm of Christian education." "The State may . . . reserve to itself the establishment and direction of schools intended to prepare for certain civic duties and especially for military service, provided it be careful not to injure the rights of the Church or of the family in what pertains to them." "But let it be borne in mind that this institution owes its existence to the initiative of the family and the Church, long before it was undertaken by the State." All of these quotations are from Pius XI's *Christian Education of Youth*, the highest source of Catholic educational theory.[13]

(2) *Is it a mortal sin for a Catholic child to attend a neutral public school?*

Yes, without special permission from a priest, if a suitable Catholic school is available. This is the rule of Canon 1374, and the mortal sin is shared by the parent. The standard American book on canon law says that "the so-called public schools in the United States, because of their 'neutral' character, are of the kind which Catholics are forbidden to attend."[14] The latest revised Catechism of the Catholic Church in the United States says (page 198): "The Church forbids parents to send their children to non-Catholic or secular schools in which the Catholic religion is not taught, unless the bishop of the diocese grants permission because of particular circumstances."

The standard book on canon law, quoted above, after warning against the enforcement of this law too harshly, quotes favorably a decree of the Holy Office on this subject which says that parents "who, although there is a suitable Catholic school properly equipped and ready in the locality, or, although they have means of sending their children elsewhere to receive a Catholic education, nevertheless without sufficient reason and without the necessary safeguards to make the proximate danger remote send them to the public schools — such parents, if they are contumacious, obviously according to Catholic moral doctrine cannot be absolved in the Sacrament of Penance." Rebellious parents "should be absolved as soon as they are repentant." This is an intricate way of saying that Catholic mothers who send their children to public schools over the opposition of their priests may be consigned to hell. Under Canon 2319, Section 2, young

Catholic couples may be excommunicated if they make an agreement when they are married to have any of their children educated in a public school.

This is the policy of coercive pressure under which the Catholic hierarchy has established in the United States a great school system of its own which segregates about 3,500,000 Catholic children from the children of other faiths and indoctrinates them with Catholic ideology. These schools have many virtues, but democracy is not one of them. They are segregated schools controlled wholly by the priests and religious orders, and the Catholic people do not participate in their ownership. All educational policies are determined by the centralized organs of power in Rome. The Catholic parents of the United States have never been given any opportunity to vote on the wisdom of the policy of segregated education, since it was imposed upon the American Church by papal edict and by a ruling of the higher American clergy in the Third Council of Baltimore in 1884.

(3) *Do governments have the right, in attempting to give all children a democratic education, to compel Catholics to attend public schools?*

No, the law of the Church forbids this. It is a law of God that Catholic children should not attend public, neutral schools, and "If a government commands citizens to violate the law of God, they must refuse to obey." That is the rule of paragraph 247 of the latest American Catholic Catechism.[15] The Vatican persistently teaches its people that they must defy any government which attempts to enforce public education on its children. Cardinal Mindszenty directed such defiance in Hungary and was supported warmly by the Vatican; Pope Pius XI encouraged such defiance in Mexico; Cardinal Gibbons predicted such defiance in the United States in his *Retrospect of Fifty Years,* when he said:

> Similarly, for example, if the State should forbid us Catholics to continue our parochial schools, we should resist to the uttermost: for we hold that, while the State has the undoubted right to compel her future citizens to receive a certain degree of education, she has no right to deprive them of the daily religious influence which we deem necessary for their spiritual and eternal welfare, as well as for their proper training in the duties of citizenship.[16]

Pius XI stated the principle behind this policy in his 1929 letter to Cardinal Gasparri: "Logic further requires that it be recognized that the full and perfect mission to teach does not belong to the State but to the Church, and that the State may not prevent nor interfere with her in the exercise and fulfillment of that mission, not even to the extent of restricting the teaching of the Church exclusively to the teaching of religious truths."[17]

(4) *Does the Catholic Church have the right to censor public education?*

Yes, in respect to all values and teachings which may in any way conflict with Catholic doctrine and policy. This right of censorship is expressed affirmatively and negatively in various canons, agreements, and covenants. Under Canon 1374 the Catholic bishop is the sole judge of the fitness of a public school to receive Catholic pupils, and this makes him a perpetual, unofficial censor of that school. In predominantly Catholic countries like Italy, the Church makes agreements with the government, as it did in the 1929 concordat with Mussolini, for the exclusive right to teach religion and morals in the public schools, and it retains the right to discharge any teacher of religion and morals who is not satisfactory to the local bishop. In Italy there is a crucifix in every public-school classroom, and a partisan section on religion in almost every elementary-school textbook. Most Italian textbooks used in public elementary schools combine history, geography, science, and mathematics all in the same book. These books usually include religion as the first subject, and it is always specifically denominational religion with instructions for the Mass and prayers for the dead. I have just run through ten such textbooks and noted 143 pictures which would be branded as Catholic propaganda if they were introduced in American school books, and 185 pages of religious text of a Catholic character. Because of these conditions, Italian Catholics are permitted to attend Italian public schools without reproof, because these schools are essentially Catholic schools, neutral neither in subject matter nor in personnel.

In other Catholic countries such as Spain and Portugal, similar conditions exist. All Spanish public schools teach simultaneously that children must respect "His Excellency, the Caudillo, Generalissimo of the Armies on land, sea and in the air, and Chief of the Government," and the only official state religion, that of the Catholic Church. All teachers in state schools are required to take a full course in Catholic doctrine before they may teach, and all state schools must give this doctrine to their pupils. "Primary education," says the 1945 Law of Primary Education, "inspired with a Catholic sense and consistent with Spanish educational traditions, will conform to the principles of the Catholic dogma and faith and to the prescriptions of canon law."[18]

In the Spanish-speaking countries of Latin America the Church has fought to keep the same control of education as in Spain, but it has not been uniformly successful. In Mexico, when the able and progressive President Cárdenas was attempting to rescue his country from clerical domination and illiteracy, Pius XI encouraged insurrection against the government's public-school program in a thinly veiled plea for revolt in his encyclical to the Mexican bishops, *Catholic Action Plan for Mexico,* issued in March 1937. He ordered all Mexican Catholics "to keep their children as far away as possible from the impious and corruptive [public] schools," and declared that "it is quite natural that when the most elementary religious and civil liberties are attacked, Catholic citizens must not resign themselves passively to renouncing their liberties." He then continued:

You have more than once recalled to your faithful that the Church protects peace and order, even at the cost of grave sacrifices, and that it condemns every unjust insurrection of violence against constituted powers. On the other hand, among you it has also been said, whenever these powers arise against justice and truth even to destroying the very foundations of authority, it is not to be seen how those citizens are to be condemned who unite to defend themselves and the nation, by licit and appropriate means, against those who make use of the public power to bring it to ruin.[19]

The theory that the Mexican clergy represented "the nation" in defending the people against the public school was a Roman clerical fiction, since the government and the policy of President Cárdenas had been approved by the Mexican people in a democratic election.

In non-Catholic countries the Church asserts two negative educational rights, the right to keep Catholics out of public schools by priestly directives, and the right to exclude by condemnation or veto any teacher who is unfriendly to the Church, or any teaching hostile to Catholic dogma. All instruction in sexual hygiene in public schools is boycotted,[20] and also all history textbooks which expose the evil effects of clerical control on medieval culture, and books which treat of divorce or birth control in a neutral or favorable manner.

In 1950 it was Catholic pressure which forced through the New York State legislature an amendment to the state education law which said that a pupil in the public schools "may be excused from such study of health and hygiene as conflicts with the religion of his parents." This was designed chiefly to "shield" Catholic children from a little realism in sex education at the hands of trained specialists in the public schools. "The law," said the anti-Communist New York Teachers Guild of the American Federation of Labor, "is an open invitation to all religious groups to eliminate any phase of secular education not in harmony with their particular creed and ritual. This may well result in such an assault upon the practices of our secular school system as to destroy its very life."

The Vatican successfully asserts its right to extend this censorship over education even to school textbooks in American-occupied Japan. In 1948, the Catholic press issued a communiqué on this subject which, in language and tone, was strikingly similar to Kremlin statements about anti-Lysenko textbooks during the same year. Presumably the communiqué referred to Catholic schools only, but its gospel is one which Catholic authorities apply to public-school textbooks wherever they have effective power. The Catholic *Register,* in a dispatch from Tokyo, said:

Like an earlier textbook on world history, a biology text for middle schools that caused considerable anxiety to [Catholic] missioners in Japan will be withdrawn. New books are being prepared by the Catholic university in Tokyo, in conjunction with several Catholic middle schools, and will be submitted to the government. Outstanding copies of the offending biology book cannot be withdrawn because of paper shortage, but the Jesuit Father Siemes has issued a comprehensive statement regarding the materialistic errors found in the text.[21]

When Jesuits use the phrase "materialistic errors" in referring to a biology textbook, they usually mean the teaching of evolution. The Jesuits have been outstanding opponents of the theory of evolution for a long time, and they do not permit Catholic schools to teach it in the same way it is taught in public universities. "The theory of evolution," says the Catholic Catechism, "which teaches that higher forms of life develop from lower forms has offered no convincing scientific proof that the human body developed gradually from that of a lower animal. . . . The human soul, being spiritual, could not possibly have developed from a lower, material form of life."[22]

Incidentally, at the very moment when Jesuit missionaries were opening their attack on evolution in the biology textbooks of Japan, missionaries of Russian Communism across the East China Sea were launching an attack on the biology textbooks of China from another direction. The Communist-controlled Shanghai paper, *Ta Kung Pao,* according to the New York *Times,* declared in a special attack on "reactionary" textbooks in the schools of Communist China: "In dealing with Darwin's theory of evolution care should be taken to differentiate between its progressive and reactionary features. In dealing with Einstein's theory of relativity attention should be centered on those aspects in support of dialectical materialism, while the backward aspects of the theory should be refuted." The *Ta Kung Pao* announced the imposition of the Lysenko Party line on heredity in the Orient by saying: "Reactionary theories on heredity propounded by Mendel, Weismann and Morgan have already been deleted from biology textbooks for the senior and middle schools, but the progressive theory of Michurin should simultaneously be inserted to take the place of the discarded ones."[23]

Within the Catholic educational system itself, the hierarchy of the Church accomplishes the elimination of all "questionable" material from textbooks with as little fanfare as possible. The principles of control and censorship in the treatment of sociology textbooks are typical. Father William J. Kerby, founder of the department of sociology at the Catholic University of America, says: "Modern non-Catholic sociology hopes to arrive at a metaphysics through the systematic observation and interpretation of present and past social facts and processes. In the Christian-Catholic view of life, however, the social sciences are guided by a sanctioned metaphysics and philosophy. This philosophy is derived not from induction but from Revelation." And he shows how Catholic sociologists apply this principle to birth control and divorce:

> If, for instance, the sociologist proposes a standard family of a limited number of children in the name of human progress, by implication he assumes an attitude towards the natural and Divine law which is quite repugnant to Catholic theology. Again, when he interprets divorce in its relation to supposed social progress alone and finds little if any fault with it, he lays aside for the moment the law of marriage given by Christ.[24]

The formula for all Catholic sociologists and philosophers can be stated quite bluntly: You must close your mind against modern knowledge whenever it comes into conflict with Catholic belief. In sociology you must follow Pius XI and Leo XIII; in philosophy you must follow St. Thomas Aquinas.

St. Thomas was quite a revolutionist for his own day, but the Church has used his teaching as a pattern for obedience and servility. His teaching supplies a logical framework for authoritarian philosophy. Bertrand Russell's acid summary of his qualities might well be applied to both the Vatican's and the Kremlin's current attitudes toward the whole meaning of education:

> There is little of the true philosophic spirit in Aquinas. He does not, like the Platonic Socrates, set out wherever the argument may lead. He is not engaged in an inquiry, the result of which is impossible to know in advance. Before he begins to philosophize, he already knows the truth; it is declared in the Catholic faith. If he can find apparently rational arguments for some parts of the faith, so much the better; if he cannot, he need only fall back on revelation. The finding of arguments for a conclusion given in advance is not philosophy, but special pleading. I cannot, therefore, feel that he deserves to be put on a level with the best philosophers either of Greece or of modern times.[25]

Usually the Catholic acceptance of authority in place of reason is described in the Catholic educational system as a virtue. Honest scientists who disagree with the clergy are denounced as "atheists." At the very moment when the Vatican was making a world hero of Cardinal Mindszenty in his struggle for Catholic rights in Hungary, the cardinal told an American correspondent that he regarded Darwin as "a dangerous heretic who should have been burned at the stake." This same cardinal in 1945 refused to alter the Catholic description of the French Revolution in the parochial-school textbooks as "that mob movement of the late eighteenth century in France which was designed primarily to rob the church of its lands."[26]

In public universities in the United States, priest-guardians attempt to induce Catholic students to boycott any textbooks or classes which are inimical to the teachings of the hierarchy. Any professor in a public university in the United States who is scornful of St. Thomas Aquinas, or any professor who recognizes divorce as a necessary instrument of readjustment in some situations, may find his courses being deserted by Catholic students on orders from a university "counselor."

I know of several instances of this type of censorship, but I do not wish to embarrass any particular professors by making unpleasant facts public. Father Raymond P. Murray, Catholic chaplain of the municipal University of Buffalo, was indiscreet enough to put in writing his directives to all Catholic students in that university in 1946; the Church is very powerful in Buffalo because it has, apparently, a majority of the entire population.

> From time to time certain difficulties arise over certain courses given at the University. I would remind you that as Catholics we are bound in conscience by certain laws of the Church. We all know that we are forbidden to eat meat on Friday; that we must attend Sunday Mass, and make our Easter Duty. However, the Church also forbids under pain of serious sin and with censure attached, the reading of books against Faith and Morals proscribed by the Index; taking active part in Protestant church services such as singing in Protestant church choirs. Catholics are not free to take courses that deal directly with religious subjects such as courses in ethics, philosophy of religion, comparative religions, etc., if they are of a non-Catholic nature. Catholics are not permitted to use Bible textbooks not approved of by the Church. Hence in selecting your courses for the coming term, you should see that they do not conflict with your obligations as Catholics. I am available at all times at Newman Hall to consult with students concerning these matters.

Strangely enough, this type of censorship of public education is sometimes more effective in non-Catholic than in Catholic countries. In a non-Catholic country very strong pressure may be quietly exerted upon public officials and teachers without any public protest, and textbooks may be forcibly revised and courses dropped without any open scandal. When the issue of academic freedom is dramatized by a public conflict, the Church nearly always loses. Even Catholic governments hesitate to admit that their universities are cultural colonies of the Vatican.

When the Vatican was preparing the famous 1929 concordat

with Mussolini, which finally made Catholicism the official state religion, a special article — Article 33 — was inserted in a preliminary draft of the treaty, saying: "The program of textbooks of the State schools shall be revised by a mixed commission of State officials and representatives of the ecclesiastical authorities to ensure that they contain nothing contrary to religion and good morals."[27] In the final reckoning, even Mussolini had too much intellectual pride to permit the adoption of this article, and it was dropped from the last draft.

In the United States, some Church leaders engage in almost continuous sniping against the public schools as "godless," "immoral," or even "Communistic" in their emphasis. The leading diocesan weekly of the United States, *Our Sunday Visitor,* said in discussing the public schools in 1949:

> Most non-Catholics know that the Catholic schools are rendering a greater service to our nation than the public schools in which subversive textbooks have been used, in which Communist-minded teachers have taught, and from whose classrooms Christ and even God Himself are barred. According to a statement issued in a report of an Illinois Legislative Investigation Committee in August, 1949, "schools provide a most fertile field of effective activities for Communists and other subversive factors."[28]

Such loose criticism is not in itself very effective, but it becomes important and socially dangerous when coupled with the "economy" campaigns of taxpayers' groups which seek to cloak their opposition to public education behind demands for government efficiency. The National Education Association, the largest American teachers' group, was compelled in 1950 to recognize the bloc of "economy" and "anti-Communist" opponents as the foremost enemy of American public education, doubly dangerous because it masked its partisan purposes behind the most righteous slogans.[29]

Generally, in the United States, the attack on public education couples the charge that the public school breeds atheism and Communism with an oblique appeal for public money for Catholic schools. Here is a 1948 editorial headed "Stop Favoring Atheism," from the Indiana *Catholic and Record,* which represents quite accurately the standard blend of passion, prejudice and logic in the Catholic hierarchy's attitude toward public education:

Stop Favoring Atheism

We demand the separation of Atheism and State.

As matters stand today we Americans are forbidden to use money raised by public taxes to support religious education, because (according to decisions of the Supreme Court) that would be forcing atheists and religiously indifferent people to pay for what they do not believe in. But what about the Catholics and Protestants and Jews who would like to have some religion taught to their children? Have they no rights? They are being forced to pay for a godless education which they do not believe in. That's perfectly all right, it seems. It is not. It's rank injustice and discrimination.

We do not demand that the rights of atheists and unbelievers be ignored. We ask only that believers be given equal rights with unbelievers.

This can be done without uniting Church and State, for it is being done in Holland, England and Canada. In Holland, certainly not a Catholic country, almost the complete cost of denominational elementary and high schools and the larger part of the financial support for private universities is supplied from tax funds. Is there any reason why the same could not be done here?

Parents pay the taxes that support education; parents have the first obligation and right to determine the type of education their children receive; therefore, parents have the right to decide how school funds be used. This right will continue to be ignored in our country until individual communities are permitted to build the schools the parents want: secular schools for unbelievers and religious schools for believers.

The least a nation that calls itself Christian can do is stop favoring atheists. We demand separation of Atheism and State.[30]

(5) *What is the nature of academic freedom in the Catholic school system?*

It is bounded by the same type of authoritarian limitation which exists in the Communist school system. "Academic freedom gives only the right to teach the truth."[31] So declared Father Robert I. Gannon, president of Fordham University, in 1949. He might have added the inevitable Catholic corollary that supreme truth is always defined by the leaders of the Church. Teachers in Catholic institutions are free to teach anything which does not conflict with Vatican dogma or policy. There is no pretense in any Catholic institution that any teacher has a right to deviate from any major Catholic doctrine or policy and retain his position.

Virtually all teachers in Catholic institutions are of course Catholic; and, by official definition of the Catholic Catechism,

"A person who deliberately denies even one of the doctrines of the Church cannot be a Catholic."[32] No Catholic teacher is free to criticize the claim of papal infallibility, priestly celibacy, or the opposition to contraception — and remain in a teaching post at a Catholic institution. No Catholic teacher is permitted to question openly such contrived doctrines as the new dogma, proclaimed in November 1950, that the corpse of the Virgin Mary was taken up bodily into heaven by angels after her death, leaving no physical trace behind. When a Catholic teacher has forced his intellect to accept such teachings, his mind is not likely to have enough resilience left to challenge more reasonable beliefs.

Usually the limitations of freedom in Catholic education are not discussed in public in the United States because of the fear of Catholic criticism. Occasionally from the Catholic spheres of education some phrase or fact breaks through into the consciousness of the outside world which does more than a whole library to reveal the nature of the system. Such a phrase was used by Father Hunter Guthrie, president of Georgetown University in Washington, in June 1950, when he was addressing more than six thousand university graduates and their friends. Father Guthrie called academic freedom "the soft under-belly of our American way of life." He said:

> In the educational world today, we are witnessing the foolhardy attempt either to bring into being or to understand a thing which has neither form nor matter, is subject to no standard or norm, has neither limitation nor definition: the sacred fetish of academic freedom.
> This is the soft under-belly of our American way of life, and the sooner it is armor-plated by some sensible limitation the sooner will the future of this nation be secured from fatal consequences.[33]

The Washington *Post*, one of the few daily newspapers in the United States which still has the courage to speak candidly about the Catholic assaults upon the democratic spirit, replied with an editorial which ended with these words:

> We do not see how truth can be sired except by freedom — that is, by the tolerance of diversity and even of error. And we should think that an institution of learning — which is to say an institution of inquiry and challenge — can do no better than to adhere to the ideal set forth by Thomas Jefferson when he first invited scholars to join the faculty of the University of Virginia: "This institution will be based on the illimitable

freedom of the human mind. For here, we are not afraid to follow truth wherever it may lead, nor to tolerate error so long as reason is left free to combat it."

The Vatican versus the Public School in Europe

In nearly all of western Europe the struggle between the Vatican and the public school is second in importance only to the struggle between democracy and Communism. In eastern Europe the Vatican has already lost the educational battle to the Kremlin — unless an anti-Communist revolution should overthrow the satellite regimes — but the public school struggle is now in an acute stage in Belgium, France, the Netherlands, and West Germany, with the Vatican leading in Belgium and the Netherlands, holding its own in West Germany, and fighting a strong defensive battle in France. In all of these democratic countries the Church is using its power to work for the kind of special privilege which is called for by Catholic encyclicals and the canon law, but it is shrewd enough to temper its tactics to local public sentiment.

Unlike Italy, France will not permit any church to teach religion in the public schools or to display religious symbols in the public classrooms. France won the battle for separation of church and state in 1905. The public-school system, like the American system, offers free, neutral education to the children of all faiths, leaving the Catholic Church free to establish its own schools at its own expense, provided these schools meet certain minimum standards prescribed by the state. Although France is supposed to be overwhelmingly a Catholic nation, more than four out of five children of elementary-school age attend the public schools.

This defeat of Catholic power in education in one of its supposed strongholds has always been a very sore point with the leaders of French Catholicism, and they wage a ceaseless and bitter campaign against public education. In such sections as Maine-et-Loire, Vendée, Deux-Sèvres, Brittany, and Normandy, the priests virtually destroy the public schools. In many districts in these sections the public classrooms are less than half full, while the parochial classrooms are crowded. Parents who send their children to the decimated public schools are threatened with theological penalties, and graduates of Catholic schools are favored in employment. Tax strikes against the government have broken out in some districts, encouraged by Catholic bishops who are using the strikes as a weapon to force government appropriations for Catholic schools. In May 1950, according to the New York *Times,* Bishop Antoine Marie Cazaux of Luçon, while addressing a Catholic mass meeting, "urged his listeners to suspend payment of taxes until their demands had been met."[34] "Their" demands were the demands of the bishops for government money. The French hierarchy did not publicly rebuke the bishop, although it quietly called off his tax strike.

One reason for the new aggressiveness of the hierarchy is that from 1940 to 1944 Marshal Pétain, with Vatican encouragement and support, created in conquered France a virtual clerical-fascist state in which government money was paid to Catholic schools in defiance of the principles of the Third Republic. The French Catholic bishops are still living in the nostalgic afterglow of that Vichy golden age, and in their eyes Pétain has always been a great statesman and a great Catholic. They have never ceased in their efforts to get him released from prison.

Will the French hierarchy win its battle for public funds for its competing school system? One factor which is aiding the hierarchy is that it has captured certain good, democratic words in the propaganda battle and is applying them shrewdly. It calls the Catholic school *l'école libre,* and it calls the public school the state school. The Catholic schools are not free in any real sense, since they are not financially free for their students, their teachers have very limited academic freedom, and their policies are completely controlled from above by authoritarian machinery; yet the power of suggestive language is such that the undemocratic features of the system are quite effectively masked by the use of the word "free."

In terms of present political power the Vatican has only a two-to-three chance of success for its program in the French National Assembly. It can count on the solid support of the M.R.P. and a large part of De Gaulle's R.P.F. in its demands for public money, but this is not more than 40 per cent of parliamentary strength at the present time. The outcome of the battle depends chiefly on the next national election, and a shift of 11 per cent in the party proportions would bring to the Vatican one of the greatest triumphs of its political career — the restoration of the Church to a privileged position in a Catholic nation which had once defeated clerical ascendancy.

In Belgium, which is almost solidly Catholic, the Church is in a much more powerful position, with an absolute majority for the Catholic party in both houses of parliament. Catholic schools are already larger than public schools, and they receive almost equal subsidies from the state. A desperate fight is being waged between Catholic and Socialist political forces over one final concession of government funds for Catholic higher schools, with the present indications in favor of Catholic victory.

The Church's most surprising victory in the school battle in western Europe has been in the Netherlands, which is still predominantly non-Catholic — the Catholic population being about 39 per cent. There the Protestant government made the colossal blunder of subsidizing religious schools on the same basis as public schools, and having once granted such concessions to one set of religious schools, it was impossible in justice to refuse it to others. The long fight by the Catholic hierarchy for equality of government contributions to Catholic schools, which began in 1878, ended in 1920 with Catholic victory. The result has been tragic for the public schools. In 1948 the Catholic schools enrolled about 60 per cent more pupils than the public schools, and when the hierarchy's program for secondary schools is completed it is possible that the Catholic enrollment may exceed public enrollment by 75 per cent. The Protestant elementary schools are also larger than the public schools. Almost 75 per cent of all Dutch children are being taught to think of themselves first as members of a denominational segment in the community rather than as members of one cultural community. The Catholic hierarchy has achieved what it has so bitterly denounced in Catholic countries like Italy — the complete bifurcation of the national culture in the name of the superior moral worth of an outside power. The situation in West Germany is rapidly approaching the same condition, since the government supports religious-directed schools with public funds.

The British government faces a similar problem but it is not yet acute, since not more than 6 per cent of Britain's people are Catholic.[35] Great Britain has traditionally given government aid to religious schools, and it cannot consistently refuse to do for

Catholic schools what it has done for Anglican schools. For many years the British Catholic bishops managed to maintain their separate school system with the help of taxpayers' money for operating expenses, while they levied upon the Catholic people themselves the cost of the school buildings. In 1949 they decided that even this relatively small proportionate charge should be added to the British taxpayer's bill. They announced a drive "for reducing the cost of reorganizing and building Catholic schools." In plain English, they came forward with a plan to turn their financially burdensome private-school system, with its 1,038 government-aided schools and 380,000 pupils, over to the government, if the government would continue to permit Catholic religious education as usual, and would also make all teachers in Catholic schools "subject to approval, as regards religious belief, by Catholic representatives."[36] The funds of the public were to be used for the expansion and maintenance of an essentially Catholic enterprise over which the Church would continue to maintain its control. It can be imagined that no non-Catholic could gain employment in such a controlled system unless he gave tacit or overt approval to Catholic policy.

In a sense the 1949 educational plan of the British Catholic bishops went even beyond Catholic practice in Italy. It gave the hierarchy the right to ban teachers of *non-religious* subjects in a tax-supported school for failure to accept the Catholic outlook, a right which even the Church in Italy has never secured. Moreover, the Church in Italy has never been able to win official government appropriations for Catholic schools. Fortunately, all three of the leading political parties of Great Britain — Labor, Conservatives, and Liberals — promptly rejected the bishops' program. The issue, however, is still very much alive in Great Britain, and Catholic propaganda at home and in the United States is attempting to win sympathy for the hierarchy by describing the bishops' plan in the most favorable language. The plan, it is said, is a reasonable development of British tradition. Simultaneously, disparaging reports are circulated concerning the quality of British public schools. The Catholic propaganda on the subject couples praise for the moral superiority of Catholic schools with disparagement of the moral laxity of public schools.

On the whole, non-Catholic editors in Great Britain have been more courageous in speaking out against Catholic educational plans than their confreres in the United States. When England's leading Catholic prelate, Bernard Cardinal Griffin, issued a pastoral letter in February 1950, calling for the submission of all other churches to the Holy See, and at the same time made it clear that his Church was still demanding more money from British taxpayers for its schools, one of Britain's distinguished conservative journals, *The Spectator,* rebuked him for "totalitarianism pure and simple." It said:

> The pastoral letter issued by Cardinal Griffin and read in all Roman Catholic Churches last Sunday has a significant bearing on the vigorous and highly-organized demand for more public money for Roman Catholic schools. The Cardinal's declaration is as explicit as words can make it. "We Catholics," it states, "believe that our Church is the one true Church founded by Jesus Christ, whose Vicar on earth, His Holiness the Pope, speaks with an infallible voice when defining doctrines. . . . A call for reunion means an invitation to all non-Catholics to join the one true Church. It means, in other words, submission to the authority of the Holy See." This, of course, is totalitarianism pure and simple. A Church is perfectly entitled to be totalitarian. But it is clearly a very different matter when taxpayers, the vast majority of whom would firmly repudiate the doctrine voiced by Cardinal Griffin, are asked to bear the whole cost of schools where the doctrine is inculcated. That is altogether too much to ask.[37]

It is scarcely necessary to point out that where the Vatican has completely won its battle against neutral public education, the results have been disastrous. Let the former head of the Associated Press in Spain, David Foltz, describe the result in that country:

> Spain is today the one civilized country of the Western world which does not have obligatory primary education. The clergy and the Falange search for talent to improve their ranks, but most schools are reserved for the sons and servants of the oligarchy. . . . The Falange sees to political education. The Spanish clergy sees to religious education. Fortunate is the Spanish child who manages to learn how to read and write. Illiteracy is reduced only in government statistics.
>
> I have seen primary schools for more than a hundred children with only one book in the entire building. It was the teacher's text, a third-grade "encyclopedia."[38]

In general, the maintenance of a controlled private-school system under Vatican auspices has been an enormously successful device for penetration of non-Catholic countries. It fortifies the prejudices of Catholic children as a separate bloc in the population and it intensifies their denominational loyalties. It operates with a unique formula for the maintenance of power, since no other large organization in the world has ever attempted such a great experiment in foreign-controlled education.

8

Discipline and Devotion

WILLIAM JAMES ONCE WROTE a brilliant essay on "The Will to Believe," and an equally perceptive essay is needed on "The Will to Obey." To understand the driving force behind both the Kremlin and the Vatican systems of power, it is necessary to understand the devices which both systems use to develop and exploit religious devotion. In both systems the will to worship and the will to serve have been coupled with the will to obey. The most exalted altruistic motives have been skillfully woven into a code of subjection to a political-religious machine. Human weakness and human nobility have been combined in two matchless systems of personal loyalty and institutional discipline.

A great many writers have pointed out that the ecstasy of religious devotion is not confined to formal religion, and that some of the noblest defenders of faith have never acknowledged a formal creed. Psychologically the men who operate the Communist system of power today fall into this category. They are atheists, but they have frequently been called a Communist priesthood, and the description is deserved. In the beginning, as Lenin said, they were "professional revolutionists," and their successors have never ceased to be professional revolutionary missionaries in the capitalist countries whose civilizations they aim to destroy. Inside the Soviet Union they have become the established priesthood of the established church, the only church which Communism really recognizes, the Kremlin. They defend its secular altars with the same zeal that characterizes the priest's defense of the Catholic Church in countries like Spain and Portugal. As Bernard Shaw once remarked: "Communism, being the lay form of Catholicism, and indeed meaning the same thing, has never had any lack of chaplains."[1]

The young Communist who wishes to enter this Soviet priesthood must go through a process of indoctrination and training that is very much like that of a Jesuit. He must give his whole personality to the Faith without reservation. He must, as Ignatius Loyola said to his Jesuits, surrender his will to his religious superior "just as if he were a corpse."

The parallels in the operation of the two priesthoods of the Vatican and the Kremlin are so consistent that in this chapter, instead of discussing the Vatican and the Kremlin separately, I shall make the comparisons as I go along. To begin with, the Vatican and the Kremlin stand for the control of the Catholic and the Communist worlds by special classes of persons. The rulers of the Communist Party rule world Communism; the members of the Catholic priesthood rule the world of Catholicism. Both ruling classes are artificially segregated castes in the communities to which they belong. They are kept distinct in activity and status in order to increase their efficiency and prestige. Priests and nuns are segregated from normal human beings by the insuperable barrier of costume — I have seen priests in Italy playing soccer in full robes! Communist organizers do not wear special costumes, or forswear marriage, but they form a special type of power group whose way of life is quite distinctive.

Lenin, when he laid down the leadership principle for Communism before the Bolshevik revolution in his book *What Is to Be Done?*, was scornful of the idea that society could be controlled by large masses of workers, and he consistently favored the small disciplined body of propagandists "pushing on from outside." He held that without leaders "professionally trained, schooled by long experience and working in perfect harmony, no class in modern society is capable of conducting a determined struggle."[2] The Catholic Church has always recognized the validity of this reasoning as applied to the world of ecclesiastical power.

In both the Communist and Catholic systems of power the small, disciplined inner group of leaders must be chosen from above, screened from above, and directed by the hierarchy of Party or Church. To preserve vitality and prevent decadence in this ruling group, there must be a certain amount of upward mobility. New blood is necessary in any healthful organism.

But no new group must ever be permitted to displace either the Communist or the Catholic élite. The priesthood must never surrender to the masses or permit the masses to take the reins of power. The ruling caste must be essentially a self-appointed and a self-perpetuating caste. Sidney and Beatrice Webb, in describing the leadership principle in force in Russia, speak of the "vocation of leadership." Both the idea and the words are used in exactly the same way in the Catholic system of power in appealing for "vocations."

The selection of new leaders from above is the basis of both Communist and Catholic discipline, and it is the direct opposite of the process of selection in a democratic society. An American legislative representative is chosen by the voters of a certain district and is answerable to his people for all his political acts and beliefs. He does not belong to a special class in the community and he is not indoctrinated against majority control in a party or priestly school. His judgment is subjected at periodic intervals to the approval of his constituents.

This type of democratic control of the leaders by the masses is not considered a proper method by the Catholic Church or the Communist Party. The ends of Communist and Catholic activity are not determined by the masses of the people but by the élite; and only the élite are considered discerning enough to choose appropriate goals for their followers.

Usually the Communist candidate for Kremlin priesthood requires a very severe period of preliminary training before he is given any substantial recognition. The leaders must be sure of his loyalty before they can trust him. This training consists of two parts, the cultural indoctrination and the intensive practical discipline. A new Party member is often assigned to the most difficult and unpleasant tasks in order to test his loyalty and devotion, and he must accept every assignment without grumbling, and execute it as directed. Military discipline prevails in all branches of the movement even in peacetime. A new Party member in a non-Communist country may be assigned, for example, to picket in a strike which the Party favors for political reasons; or distribute handbills; or start a "spontaneous" street demonstration against a "fascist" who was a Communist hero the week before; or jab hatpins into a policeman's horse; or circulate a petition for "peace" at a moment when the Soviet Union is invading a weaker country. He is expected to obey willingly and to give passionate support to his Party's position.

To hold his allegiance to the Party line and condition him for further obedient service, the Party directs that he should attend many Party meetings until late in the night, read Party literature unceasingly, and saturate himself in Party strategy. Family responsibilities and pleasures must be subordinated to the Party's interests, and faithful members must move from city to city on Party orders, or remain stationary according to reverse orders. A French Communist Party guidebook says: "The militant called upon to choose between his family life and work for the Party has an easy choice."[3] Whether the choice is easy or not, it is universally enforced on Communist Party members throughout the world. "Practically every moment of a Party member's living day," says Ben Gitlow, former Communist Party candidate for Vice President of the United States, "is spent in purposeful activity for the Communist Party. . . . Lucky is the Party member who finds time to wipe his nose and catch more than three or four hours' sleep a day. . . . He has no time to contemplate, to think or to worry about himself. The Party winds him up and keeps him going."[4]

As a Party member progresses in discipline and responsibility, he may be assigned to types of work that are not only physically dangerous but morally treacherous. If the Party leaders desire it, he must spy on his fellow members, and even affiliate himself with internal movements of rebellion in order to destroy them. When joining the movement, he takes an oath to support the Soviet Union as the Fatherland of socialism. Accordingly, he is expected to act for the Kremlin even against his own nation whenever Moscow directs it. When the Communist forces of North Korea invaded South Korea in the summer of 1950 and the western democracies struck back, every Communist party in the world supported the Communist invasion as a "liberation" movement, and became, in effect, a fifth column in each nation.

So many former Communists have described the processes of Party discipline in their "confessions" in recent years, that it is not necessary to repeat many details here. Louis F. Budenz, former editor of New York's *Daily Worker* and now a devout

Catholic, tells how the Communist Party of the United States during the days of his membership operated an open and a secret system of training schools at the same time. The more important recruits were assigned to the secret schools. Budenz declares that the students in these secret Party schools were frequently isolated from the outside world completely for six to ten weeks. During that time, they were not permitted to leave the premises or write to friends or use their own names or receive mail. Ordinarily, married comrades were not permitted to attend the secret schools with their wives or husbands; if this rule was relaxed for some special reason, man and wife were forbidden to have sexual contact.[5]

The Two Monasticisms

Mr. Budenz, as a devout Catholic, did not draw the most obvious analogy between this type of Communist monasticism and Catholic monasticism. The great Catholic religious orders recruit and train their devotees by techniques that are strikingly similar to the methods of the secret Communist schools. In both cases there is a systematic appeal to altruism, well calculated to touch the youthful heart. The Catholic recruits are usually secured at a relatively early age, particularly the women recruits, and their sequestration is more complete and continuous than that of the Communist devotees. They are committed for life, while still young and inexperienced, to lives of sexual denial and personal isolation from normal activity.

Sometimes economic relief for their families plays a part in the vocational choice. In Catholic countries like Italy, young boys and girls are frequently recruited from poor families as early as eight or nine years of age, trained by priests and nuns in religious schools, saturated in an atmosphere of doctrinal compulsions, and then promoted to membership in religious orders almost automatically. At no point in the process are they given an opportunity to make a genuinely free occupational choice. Their whole experience has conditioned them for one calling only. They are drafted into the life of a Religious by social and cultural pressure. They are, as H. G. Wells has put it, "set aside from the common sanity of mankind from their youth up."[6]

Secular priests, it is true, are not fully and irrevocably committed to their careers until they are twenty-one, and they are not completely cut off from outside influences during their training. Also, young Catholic girls who become postulants at sixteen in a religious order are nominally free to reconsider and reverse their choices, after a period of training, before they take final vows. In practice, however, they are completely surrounded by suggestions of conformity and discipline, and during the critical "religious year" in the novitiate, they may be denied all contact with family and friends. In fact, if they show signs of wavering during this critical period, they are usually denied the right to receive visitors or to read mail or newspapers or to consult any outsider of independent judgment until "their" decision has been made. The final choice of vocation may be largely the result of continuous sequestration.

The oath of devotion in a Catholic religious order parallels that of the Communist Party. Complete submission to institutional superiors and complete surrender of the personal will are accepted as necessary Christian virtues. Ignatius Loyola, whom I have already quoted, set the tone for Catholic religious discipline when he taught his Jesuits the virtue of "absolute annihilation of our own judgment." "We must," he said, "if anything appears to our eyes white, which the Church declares to be black, also declare it to be black."[7]

In the Catholic religious orders chastity is pledged for life, often when the recruits are still too young to understand the meaning of their own renunciation. Recruiting, in fact, is largely based on the guilt feelings of youth and adolescence about sex, and the conviction of sin is systematically exploited to induce a commitment to the Religious vocation. After commitment, celibacy is skillfully associated with devotion in such a way as to sublimate sexual energy into institutional channels. Many commentators have pointed out that for male celibates the figure of the Virgin Mary, and for female celibates the figure of Christ, are used as agents for the redirection and sublimation of thwarted sexual energy. Religious orders for women carry the sexual symbolism so far that they dress their postulants in bridal costumes when they are sworn in to full membership as "brides of Christ." The psychological result of such a substitution upon a community of sex-starved young nuns has been brilliantly described by Rumer Godden in her book, *Black Narcissus*.

The requirements of community living and group segregation in the Catholic system also form a necessary part of the total discipline. The monastic economic system is essentially a communist system. Monks and nuns may not own anything except personal belongings; if they are given gifts, the favors must be turned over to their religious orders. Even teaching nuns who are placed upon the government payrolls of American states and cities must turn over their salaries to the Church, and live on the meager personal allowance of monastery life.

There is much to be said for the exalted nobility and high devotion of Catholic monasticism, but it cannot be denied that the life of the Catholic Religious is almost totally devoid of personal freedom. Freedom of reading, freedom of entertainment, freedom of movement to a new environment, freedom of marriage, and freedom of recreation are all denied as a matter of course. Secular priests have more physical freedom than members of religious orders, but scarcely any more intellectual freedom. Nuns are continuously segregated from reality by protective devices of sequestration and control. American Catholic seminary students training for the priesthood in Rome are not even permitted to go to approved motion pictures in public theaters, or to read a YMCA magazine; and, of course, they are not permitted to read ordinary newspapers freely. No cloistered nun who has taken solemn vows may ever leave a convent for a short time without a special indult of the Holy See, except in the case of imminent danger of death or other serious crisis. When she is permitted to leave, some other nun must accompany her. Religious women, appearing in churches, are forbidden by Canon 1264 to sing in a place where they can be observed.

The convents of nuns with solemn vows, according to canon law, "should be protected on every side in such a manner as to prevent, as far as possible, those within from being seen by, or seeing, persons outside." Nuns are warned "lest, from intercourse with outsiders the discipline be relaxed and the religious spirit weakened by useless conversation." Even the priestly confessor of such nuns must sit outside the enclosure and hear confession through an opening. Objects are passed through the convent gate in a wheel installed in the wall. "There is no objection," says the Congregation of the Religious, "to having a little opening in the wheel through which one may see what is being put in."[8]

When the nuns with solemn vows receive visitors in the parlor, there must be two screens, similar to the screens used in American prisons, separating the nun from the visitor. (A former priest in Italy told me how, as a small child visiting his cloistered aunt with his mother, he was permitted to squeeze between the visitors' screens and stand there for a moment so that the aging nun could feel the live, warm body of a child.)

This complete isolation and subordination of personal freedoms is taught to Catholic devotees as a useful part of Christianity. Obedience to the Mother Superior is equated with obedience to God, and rebellion against repressive discipline is described as rebellion against God. The system of discipline for nuns with simple vows is much more reasonable than for cloistered nuns, but the *principle* of the discipline remains the same. The renunciation of freedom of thought and freedom of speech is considered a virtue; the subject mind is exalted as a good thing in itself; the thwarted personality is considered holy; the withdrawal from the world's realities is described as supreme realism. Until recently, nuns who were caught in this system of discipline could not even write to a religious superior outside of their own order without the risk that their letters would be opened. Now, letters may be sent unopened to the Pope and a few other religious superiors, but all letters addressed to other persons are subject to opening and censorship.

The monastery life is a singular mixture of selflessness and egotism, of religious fanaticism and social stupidity. The service orders, particularly those of nursing nuns, are sublimely useful and worthy of the deepest admiration and respect; and usually the teaching orders are almost as praiseworthy in the completeness of their personal sacrifice. But the so-called contemplative orders are scarcely above the level of juvenile escapism. In Trappist (Cistercian) monasteries, for example, apparently stable and able-bodied men withdraw from all social responsibilities for life and dedicate themselves "silent in life-long penitential reparation for the sins of the world." They deliberately make life uncomfortable for themselves on the theory that discomfort in itself is holy penance — like that of the Hindu fakirs who sleep on beds of nails. Trappist monks rise at 2:00 A.M. instead of a healthful hour, and, if possible, never speak to their fellow members except in a special sign language. Ostensibly they scorn the world as sinful. However, they manage to circularize hundreds of thousands of people in the United States — people who live in the sinful world — with gaudy appeals for worldly money. (I have received many of these appeals because my name is on several Catholic mailing lists.) They collect enough American revenue for themselves to live on their little islands of self-absorption with reasonable security. Even the Catholic convert Thomas Merton suggests, in his book, *The Seven Storey Mountain,* the inconsistency of combining Trappist principles with such appeals for money from the outside world.

"Mortification," says the *Catholic Encyclopedia,* "is one of the methods which Christian asceticism employs in training the soul to virtuous and holy living. . . . What it slays is the disease of the soul, and by slaying this it restores and invigorates the soul's life. . . . They [the desires of the flesh] represent a twist in the nature, and must be treated as one treats a twisted wire when endeavoring to straighten it, namely by twisting it the opposite way."[9] The Church still encourages this kind of discipline by self-punishment and hardship. In a sense, the priestly schedule of endless, repetitive reading of ritual is a kind of mental self-torture, calculated to discipline the will, and at the same time to deaden the critical intellect. Few sensitive minds could survive such an erosion of energy without a fatal loss of intellectual independence.

One of the saints created by Pope Pius XII during the summer of the Holy Year of 1950 was Maria Anna de Paredes of Ecuador, whose chief claim to holiness was that she virtually achieved her own destruction at the age of twenty-seven by self-torture and starvation. She slept two or three hours a night, deprived herself of normal food, wrapped her body in strands of thistles which caused profuse bleeding, and clung for hours to a high cross on the wall of her room. Far from condemning these practices, Pius XII praised the young lady as a model of Christian womanhood when he raised her to sainthood. However, it was widely reported in Rome that he was somewhat reluctant to take the final step of canonization because of the nature of the new saint's "accomplishments." A struggle is going on inside the Church between those who recognize the facts of psychological science and those who do not. The advocates of mortification are on the defensive, for modern psychologists have analyzed the sexual significance of self-flagellation with embarrassing candor, and there are many Catholic scholars who would like to eliminate the practice entirely from Church discipline.

The Sense of Guilt

Meanwhile, in the Communist system of power, there is a similar exploitation of the sense of guilt in behalf of the authoritarian state, and a similar, but much more severe, development of the techniques of punishment. Perhaps the Russian mind has been inured to self-torture by centuries of subjection to the old Orthodox Church. In any case, the Soviet state has carried over into modern Communism a great part of the doctrinal baggage of the Orthodox theory of sin. The first law of Communist discipline is that rebellion against the authority of the Stalinist machine is not merely a mistake but a mortal sin — a mortal sin against the Soviet Fatherland and the Holy Communist Faith. The cultivation of the sense of guilt is one of the basic devices of Party discipline. Any comrade who rebels even slightly against Kremlin orders must be made to feel that he is a traitor to the working class. Psychic torture begins even before physical torture, and it is often more appallingly ruthless.

The best evidence of the success of Communist methods in producing a sense of guilt in the minds of all rebels is the Communist "confession" which has been a feature of almost every great Communist heresy trial since 1936. Fallen Communists in these famous purge trials have apparently revealed a positive pleasure in their abasement, and many observers have compared their reactions to those of religious masochists who practice self-flagellation. Whether the comparison is sound or not, it is certain that the Communists use both physical and psychic torture very effectively in producing confessions at their treason trials. They often break a rebel's body first in order to subdue his spirit, and the will to confess is frequently produced by techniques which bring the victim close to the border of insanity without leaving any mark upon his body.

Zbigniew Stypulkowski, one of the leaders of the anti-Nazi

underground in Poland, and also a leader of the old anti-Communist government of Poland, has told in detail exactly how a Soviet tribunal prepares a victim for confession before a trial. He was questioned 141 times in 70 days in the Lubianka prison in Moscow in the attempt to break his will and make him admit anti-Soviet acts which he had never committed.

> They did not actually torture us, because for this performance we must show no marks. . . . All night and day a very strong light was on in the cell. The light bulb was fixed at the door, so that it shone straight into my face when I was lying in bed. . . . During the night I had only one blanket. If I fell asleep, I automatically put my hands under the blanket. But at that moment, the warder who looked every moment through the hole in the door to see what was happening in the cell, would open the door with much noise and whisper: "That is forbidden. You must have your hands on the blanket." Of course, it interrupted my moment of rest. My fingers would become stiff and I could not sleep.
>
> To eat I got two slices of bread in the morning and at lunchtime water with some cabbage leaves in it. In the afternoon I got two spoonfuls of barley. That was all, but it was nicely served. The bread was fresh, and the soup was tasty. This stimulated my appetite and the amount was so insufficient. The light in my cell, which was on all night and all day, was very powerful; there was no escape from it. If I turned away in sleep — hiding my eyes — the warder came in whispering, "You are not allowed to sleep like this, I must see your eyes." . . .
>
> After two or three weeks, I was in a semi-conscious state. After fifty or sixty interrogations, with cold and hunger and almost no sleep, a man becomes like an automaton — his eyes are bright, his legs swollen, his hands trembling. In this state he is often even convinced that he is guilty. He believes what the judge tells him.[10]

So torture and fear break the human spirit. The slightest deviation from Party discipline in factory, army, or public office may bring swift punishment from the secret police. Any man suspected of disloyal intrigues against the Kremlin may be rounded up at any moment without any public legal proceeding and quietly put away. The secret police, now called the MVD, have the power to send any Russian to a forced "corrective" labor camp for any term up to five years without any official trial.[11] Quick vengeance may be meted out to a whole group of dissidents for the crime of one of them. Friends and families are, in Stalin's code, perpetual hostages who can be used to guarantee the loyalty of his associates. Reprisal, in fact, is the chief weapon of Stalinist terror, and it is likely that a successful revolution would have overthrown Stalin long ago if it had not been for the fear of even the most desperate rebels that their suicidal assassinations would be followed by the mass slaughter of all their friends and relatives. It is this terror which has helped to keep the same small group of men in power in the Soviet Union without any genuinely free election for almost thirty-five years.

The first great series of Bolshevik reprisals began in August 1918, when five hundred persons were liquidated for the murder of one, the head of the Cheka in Petrograd. This orgy of reprisal paled into insignificance when compared to the great Stalin purge of 1936 and 1937; this purge followed the murder in Leningrad, in December 1934, of one of Stalin's close friends, S. M. Kirov, who had been assigned the task of suppressing the Zinoviev opposition in that city. Before the purge was through, thousands of alleged "assassins of Kirov" had been shot, and hundreds of thousands sent to concentration camps. One estimate put the officers of the Red Army who were arrested or shot in that period at 20,000. Marshal Tukhachevsky, war hero, was executed in 1937 for attempting a *coup d'état*. Of the five men of the original Politburo who had operated the government through the great civil war — Lenin, Trotsky, Stalin, Kamenev, and Bukharin — only Stalin has survived; Trotsky was murdered in 1940, and Kamenev and Bukharin were shot in 1936. Thus Stalin attained his lonely eminence while the chief prosecutor at the "treason" trials, Andrei Vishinsky, shouted: "Shoot the mad dogs!"[12] To parallel such a fantastic situation in the United States, one would have to imagine Franklin Roosevelt ordering death before a firing squad for Herbert Hoover, General Marshall, and Cordell Hull.

Ostensibly the Soviet Union has a system of tribunals for all ordinary offenders, but the sins of political offenders are outside of the protection of the law. The political offender may disappear from the circle of his family and friends without a sound or a trace, and his relatives do not dare to inquire about him persistently, or challenge the Communist authorities for victimizing him. An agent of the MVD may appear at the house of any Soviet citizen in the middle of the night and take him away without explanation. Years later, the shadow of a once-normal man may appear again suddenly in the old circle. Usually his life during the period of discipline remains enveloped in silence.

No one ever speaks openly in the Soviet Union of the great system of forced-labor camps — which were established in 1922, and which have now become a basic fact in Russia's economy. Professor Warren Walsh, chairman of the Board of Russian Studies at Syracuse University, on the basis of internal Soviet data, estimates the total population of these camps at the present time at 14,000,000. The British government has secured and made public the Russian code for these labor camps. Under that code Russian workers are punished partly according to "their degree of class dangerousness." [13] If they happen to be prosperous and oppose Stalinism, they are punished as "class-hostile elements." If they are ordinary proletarians, they are punished as "unstable elements among the workers." They can be sent to a forced-labor camp as readily by an administrative government agency as by a court.

Sometimes the Kremlin victims are sent away or executed for a mere blunder in computation. The blunder, in fact, may be punished even if it is not a blunder at all but only an unfortunate revelation of truth which happens to be contrary to official theory. The directors of the 1937 census were executed, apparently because their computations did not support the optimistic preliminary estimates of Stalin and the Politburo. The well-known journalist, John Scott, has summarized in *Life* magazine [14] the classically simple stories of nine men who served as prisoners in the Soviet Union's forced-labor camps. The story of one scientist is typical:

One day [he said] I made a mistake. It was not a large mistake, but the director of the laboratory where I worked did not notice the extra zero in the final figure and incorporated it in his report. Only weeks later it was discovered, and under circumstances extremely embarrassing to the entire institute. It was therefore not surprising that when the arrests began in 1937, I was one of the first to go. I got eight years in a forced labor camp. . . .

We had to fell the trees, strip them, cut them to length and pull the logs to a designated place. My quota was six cubic meters of lumber a day. This norm was based on the productivity of a skilled woodcutter working for ten hours with sharp tools. I was inexperienced, the weather was unbelievable, the tools were scarce and dull. . . .

Almost all of us tried hard to meet the quota. Those who did were given three metal tabs by the criminal trusties who supervised us political prisoners. When you presented the tabs in the kitchen, you got a regular ration. If you failed to make six meters, you got only two tabs. If you failed to make four cubic meters, you got only one. The food you got on one tab was merely enough to keep a man alive lying in bed. Men died like grasshoppers in autumn. The young died more quickly than the old. Women survived even better than the older men.

We were not closely guarded, but whenever a man escaped his barracks everyone was called out, and every tenth man was shot. Usually the fugitive too was brought back several days later and shot before the whole camp.

Ignazio Silone, the distinguished Italian novelist who served for a time as one of the leaders of world Communism, and then deserted Moscow in disgust, has described the attitude lying behind this type of cruelty. "What struck me most about the Russian Communists," he said, "even in such really exceptional personalities as Lenin and Trotsky, was their utter incapacity to be fair in discussing opinions that conflicted with their own. The adversary, simply for daring to contradict, at once became a traitor, an opportunist, a hireling. An adversary in good faith is inconceivable to the Russian Communists. What an aberration of conscience this is, for so-called materialists and rationalists to uphold absolutely in their polemics the primacy of morals over intelligence! To find a comparable infatuation one has to go back to the Inquisition."[15]

In a sense, the Communist agitator is more like a Jesuit than a Benedictine. Jesuits are not confined to monasteries, and they circulate freely in the world as roving agents of the Faith. They are holy men of the world, even when their worldliness is dedicated to another world.[16] Communists, too, may be worldly, provided their total careers are dedicated to the cause. In Russia they often acquire luxuries and privileges which separate them from the masses of the people as effectively as if they were multimillionaires. In the Catholic system, secular priests are permitted to acquire wealth and power so long as they do not do anything "scandalous" to advertise their wealth. Conspicuous personal extravagance is frowned upon, but institutional spending for personal vanity is just as apparent in Rome as it is in Moscow, and the distance between a prince of the Church and the masses of the Italian people is just as great as between a member of the Politburo and the masses of the people of Moscow.

Both systems of discipline are remarkably successful in one

thing. They produce heroes and martyrs of sublime courage and self-sacrifice. They offer the most striking examples to the world of the dedicated personality. It would be difficult to choose between them in this respect. They serve completely different gods, but they serve these gods with the same utter devotion. The consecrated personality may wear a monk's habit in the mountains of Tibet, or the black robes of a nursing nun in a leprosarium in Africa, or the uniform of a political commissar in the Red Army.

Garrett Underhill, formerly of the War Department General Staff of the United States, has pointed out that the concept of "dedicated services" in the Red Army is essentially a religious concept and that the political commissar in that army, who may seem like a Communist spy to us, is a man committed to heroism as well as obedience:

> Along with outward displays of militarism, the idea of dedication to service is carried out in the Soviet services with an almost religious fervor. The Russians have not dared follow Napoleon's lead and become so counter-revolutionary as to re-introduce Christianity. Still the word "holy" as used in the armed forces' oath is that used by the Orthodox Russian Church. . . . This concept of dedicated services is emphasized daily. When an officer compliments a subordinate — which he must do often, for the Soviets hold praise more necessary than blame — the junior snaps smartly to attention and replies smugly: "I serve the Soviet Union." When a new group of Soviet B-29s is formed, the airmen kneel with bowed heads to receive their colors from their air division commander.[17]

How well this religious devotion paid off in the Red Army during World War II was described by Mr. Underhill in these words:

> The Germans frequently found that, if a disabled tank continued to fire until its last crew member was killed, the odds were that the tank crew included a political officer. After the Red Fiftieth Field Army was surrounded at Bryansk, the army's top military leaders and political officers drank and indulged in mutual recriminations while they awaited the Germans. But when the enemy came, they fought back to back till not a general or a senior political officer was left.

The Discipline of Exclusion

Within the Communist and Catholic systems of power there is another kind of discipline which may be described broadly as the discipline of exclusion. It is designed to keep the faithful from contamination by doctrines that are close to orthodoxy but still unorthodox. The particular sins to be avoided are democratic socialism and Trotskyism on the one hand, and Protestantism on the other. At the Kremlin there is no enemy so cordially hated as a good democratic socialist, and at the Vatican there is no opponent so roundly condemned as a militant Protestant. Good Communists and good Catholics must at all costs see that they are not tainted with these forms of heresy. To prevent the corruption of the faithful, both the Kremlin and the Vatican have developed very definite lines of doctrinal and disciplinary demarcation beyond which no faithful disciple may wander.

The Catholic discipline of exclusion against Protestantism is imposed by canon law, but it is not very often discussed openly in countries like the United States because the Church would be gravely embarrassed by the exposure of the narrowness of the official point of view. The Vatican declares that all Protestants are heretics; that Protestant clerical orders are spurious; and that all human beings who deliberately reject the Catholic form of Christianity after examining its claims are doomed to eternal perdition.[18] The fact that Protestants worship the same God and the same Christ does not in any way soften the official impeachment. In fact, Catholic literature is more caustic in attacking Protestantism than in attacking Mohammedanism or Buddhism.

In Italy, where the Church operates under the direct primacy of the Pope, many official attacks on Protestantism have been published in recent years which are wholly inconsistent with the official endorsement of tolerance spoken by Catholic bishops in the United States. I have before me as I write this chapter an official Catholic booklet, published in Pompeii under an official Imprimatur, written by a Jesuit priest, and now being widely circulated in Italy. Its subject is Protestantism, and it pictures Protestants in a large colored cartoon on the cover as hungry jackals storming the walls of St. Peter's. It describes Protestants as "disgraceful apostates of the sanctuary in whom there is not a shadow of good faith." "The heads of Protestantism," says the booklet, "were true and real criminals worthy of jail. Their principles are immoral and bring about anarchy."[19]

Under the Catholic policy of no compromise with Protestantism, no Catholic may read a Protestant Bible, or attend a Protestant religious service of any kind, or read a Protestant book of religious exposition, or sing in a Protestant choir, or be married by a Protestant clergyman, or enter his child in a Protestant school. In fact, no Catholic may marry a Protestant unless a dispensation is obtained, and this is not granted unless the Protestant bride or groom promises that all the children of the marriage shall be reared as Catholics. There is, of course, no corresponding anti-Catholic policy in the Protestant system. Protestants recognize unconditionally the marriages of their members by Catholic priests or Jewish rabbis.[20]

The discipline of exclusion and discrimination in the Catholic system is especially important because it applies not only to the ruling caste of the Church but to the 350,000,000 Catholic members throughout the world. The policy of exclusion makes of the Catholic population a biological bloc in each nation which is even more clearly separated from the rest of the community than the Communist bloc, because Communists — in countries outside of the Soviet Union — are not expressly forbidden to inter-marry with other groups. In the Catholic system interbreeding with non-Catholic families is specifically forbidden by canon law,[21] and Catholic children are taught in their schools that it is unwise to "keep company" with non-Catholics. The rule, of course, is frequently violated in countries like the United States, because the Catholic people are much more broad-minded than their priests and because they resent the narrow-minded, denominational outlook of priestly marriage rules. But the old, divisive, and narrow rule still exists on the Catholic statute books, and the priests attempt to enforce it where possible by appealing to the unconditional law of the Catholic code that a Catholic who is ostensibly married by a Protestant clergyman is not married at all. According to this rule, a Catholic who attempts marriage in this way commits so grave a sin that he incurs exclusion from the sacraments. The taboos against Catholic marriage to Jews are equally severe, and it is even more difficult to get a dispensation for marriage to a Jew than to a Protestant.

The total psychic effects of this Catholic policy of discrimination are quite incalculable. They destroy community co-operation and tolerance in countless ways. In the United States the rules of non-co-operation go so far that Catholic students attending *public* high schools are officially forbidden to attend an inter-faith baccalaureate service in a public-school auditorium.[22] The Church fears that mixing with the followers of other branches of Christendom on a level of equality will promote "indifferentism" in religion. This was the reason for the decree of the Holy Office of December 20, 1950, directing priests not to belong to Rotary Clubs, and suggesting that even Catholic laymen should regard such clubs with suspicion. The decree fell like a bombshell in American Rotary circles because few American Rotarians had realized that the Vatican's policy on such questions is so narrow. Actually, another Vatican Congregation, that of the Sacred Consistory, had ruled twenty-one years earlier that membership of priests in Rotary Clubs was "not expedient." This time, the American hierarchy, greatly embarrassed by the new revelation of reactionary thought at Rome, was notably unenthusiastic about explaining the reason for the ruling. The Rome correspondent of the National Catholic Welfare Conference said: "Rotary follows a policy of neutrality on religion and thus relegates it to a place of secondary importance or less and favors the development of religious indifferentism."[23] This was undoubtedly the official reason for the ban, but another unspoken reason was that Rotary Clubs place Protestant preachers on the same level as Catholic priests at the same luncheon table, and the Church does not like such equalitarian conduct.

This policy of separatism was underscored in 1951 in the case of the memorial all-faiths chapel erected in Philadelphia to the four American chaplains — Protestant, Jewish, and Catholic — who had died a heroic death on the troop transport *Dorchester* in 1943 by giving their life jackets to sailors when the ship was torpedoed. The building of the chapel was accompanied by an unprecedented publicity campaign for "brotherhood," and the structure was dedicated by President Truman; but no Catholic representative was present at the opening ceremonies, nor could any official Catholic altar be erected, because, as Monsignor Thomas McCarthy explained (*Time,* February 12, 1951), Catholic canon law forbids joint worship.

Naturally, since American Catholics are usually quite broad-minded and generous in their attitudes toward other faiths, they bitterly resent this narrow-minded attitude of the Vatican. But they are quite helpless in attempting to destroy such rules themselves, since they have no mechanism for modifying Catholic law. Even their bishops can do nothing more than protest mildly, keeping an eye on Rome to see how far they will be permitted to go without excommunication.

On the world level, the Catholic policy of exclusion prevents any liberal bishop of the Church from collaborating with any movement for Christian unity which is not predicated upon complete surrender to Roman supremacy. The Vatican world-wide "unity" movement, called the Unity Octave, stages a drive every year for Christian unity with the bland announcement that its object is "the return of all separated Christians to communion with the Holy See." Its American director announced early in 1951: "The reunion of Christendom can never be realized by coalescence of sects, but by return to the Church alone, never by 'comprehension' but only by conversion."[24] The Vatican will not send any delegates to discuss co-operation with other denominations at the sessions of the World Council of Churches, the Christian organization which is attempting to federate the churches of the world.

On the local level, the Catholic policy of exclusion means non-co-operation with Protestants in many community endeavors in non-Catholic countries; and in Catholic countries like Spain and Italy the policy means official government discrimination against Protestant activity. In Spain, because of Catholic pressure, Protestants are not even permitted to hold any outdoor religious celebrations or festivals.[25]

In Vatican theory the sin of Protestants is that they belong to an organization that has officially rejected Roman authority, the Voice of God on earth. Historically they are renegades, and renegades must be denounced even if their motives appear to be pure. This hatred of the renegade is even more marked in the case of a Catholic priest who has deliberately deserted his faith for heresy. Against such renegades the tactics of the church are vindictive and determined.

The general principle used in handling priests and nuns who wish to renounce their vows and return to non-clerical life is that they are not permitted to resign voluntarily if they have made some open commitment against the Catholic faith. Then they must be purged affirmatively and not permitted to resign. The most extreme types of excommunicated apostates are branded with a label of *vitandus* and expelled publicly by name with the stipulation that they are to be avoided by all the faithful. After that, no good Catholic may be seen talking with them or doing business with them in any way. If they are merchants in a Catholic community, their business is destroyed. If they are authors, their works may not be read. If they are neighbors they must not be visited. If they die and are buried by mistake in a Catholic cemetery, their bones must be dug up promptly. The only exception to the boycott rule is that when the *vitandus* is a member of a loyal Catholic family, his family may still live with him.[26]

When the Vatican is strong enough in any particular country, it writes such penalties against apostate priests into the laws of the nation. One of the prices which the Vatican extracted from Mussolini in 1929 for the signing of the Italian concordat with the Holy See was that all ex-priests should be treated by the Italian government as if they were *vitandi*. Article V of that concordat provides that "apostate or suspended priests may not be employed or continued in employment as teachers or in any office or post which brings them into direct contact with the public."[27] In spite of this provision priests are deserting the Church in Italy in considerable numbers and attempting to survive as best they can. Sometimes they are forced back into the Church under conditions of great humiliation because they cannot find work suitable for their capacities.

The experience of my Roman friend Y, a former priest, may be considered typical. Y is a cultured man of middle age who holds a doctorate in classics in addition to his theological degree from the Gregorian University in Rome. After teaching in private schools for several years, he decided, rather late in life, to become a missionary priest. He left his teaching post, studied for the priesthood, and was ordained. The war prevented his immediate assignment as a missionary, and he began teaching as a priest in a Catholic high school.

His studies had awakened various theological questions in his mind, and he began to doubt certain orthodox historical doctrines. Some of his views were discovered by his pupils and reported by their parents to the inquisitors of the Holy Office. The Holy Office discharged him as a teacher and priest and excommunicated him as a Catholic on three grounds — that he questioned the infallibility of the Pope, that he doubted the Trinity, and that he challenged the philosophy of St. Thomas Aquinas. He applied for a position in three non-Catholic schools, but in each case the school authorities did not dare to employ an ex-priest, though no question had ever been raised as to his teaching competence or his personal morality. Mimeographed letters were sent out by the Church to all parents in the district where he lived directing them not to employ him as a tutor for their children. Two strong-arm men from Catholic Action warned him not to organize the ex-priests of his region. When it was rumored that he was going to the United States to obtain help for ex-priests, the Papal Nuncio to the government of Italy, Monsignor Duca, wrote to the Ministry of Interior and the Foreign Office asking that he be denied a passport. Y is now eking out a living by tutoring a few children of Waldensians in Rome.

The Vatican directly encourages such discrimination. In defending the provision against ex-priests in the concordat, *Civiltà Cattolica*, the Jesuit magazine which probably deserves to be rated as the most intellectual organ of world Catholicism, declared, in March 1950, that "apostate and censured priests are garbage." When Church of Christ missionaries from Texas were attacked in 1950 in Frascati, near Rome, after a local priest had denounced them in a sermon, *Civiltà Cattolica* condoned the violence, deplored the fact that the government had permitted the Protestant missionaries to stay so long in Italy, and said that "nothing more has happened than a little innocuous stone-throwing."[28]

The Socialist Villains

The chief target of the parallel Communist policy is democratic socialism. Democratic socialists, according to the Kremlin, are not socialists but fascists, and no language is too strong for reviling them. They are the arch-traitors of the working class and the betrayers of Karl Marx. When the French Communist Party sent out a secret questionnaire to its members asking for autobiographical data, it grouped the following questions together: "Are there members of the Socialist Party in your family? In your wife's family? Are there Trotskyites? Are there policemen, gendarmes, or police informers in your family? In your wife's family?"[29]

No Communist caricature of an American millionaire could possibly be more vindictive than the typical Kremlin characterization of non-Communist labor leaders like Attlee and Bevin of Great Britain, or Green, Murray, and Reuther of the United States. Moscow's favorite villains of 1949 were these non-Communist leaders of American and British labor, and such European leaders as Kurt Schumacher, of the Social Democratic Party of West Germany, and Giuseppe Saragat, leader of the right-wing Socialist Workers Party of Italy.

In Kremlin theory Communist renegades, or fellow travelers who have once co-operated with the Communists and then repented, are even more vile and despicable than socialists who have never been inside the fold. When Henry Wallace turned against Soviet foreign policy after the Communist invasion of South Korea in June 1950, his character in the Soviet press was immediately transformed, and every motive which had previously been described as noble was made to seem treacherous and guileful. "Wallace is trying to mask his cowardly desertion by canting about his devotion to peace," said *New Times* of Moscow in 1950. "His subterfuges can deceive nobody. His desertion to the camp of the warmongers has shown that he was not a sincere supporter of peace, democracy, progress and the ideal for which he was campaigning only six months ago. Evidently his position is wholly and entirely determined by pecuniary and other ties with the monopoly circles which direct the present aggressive policy of the United States."[30]

After 1949 all the villains in the Communist rogues' gallery were temporarily overshadowed by the arch-villain, Marshal Tito of Yugoslavia. Within the span of a few weeks, the personality of this sturdy anti-Stalinist Communist changed in the Soviet press from that of a smiling and gracious comrade to that of a snarling and oppressive dictator. "The Tito Clique of Murderers and Spies" was the headline title of an article in the chief theoretical magazine of the American Communist Party in January 1950. It symbolized well the savage hatred of the Communist machine for any devotee who has turned renegade. Here are some samples of the Party invective directed against Tito:

> There are no national interests which Tito would not betray on the orders of Washington. . . . The imperialist servant, Judas Tito, carried out the orders of his masters to the dot. . . . The Yugoslav rulers demagogically and insolently deceive the people, alleging they are building Socialism in Yugoslavia. But it is clear to every Marxist that there can be no talk of building Socialism in Yugoslavia when the Tito Clique has broken with the Soviet Union. . . . The fascist terror dictatorship of the Tito clique against the mass of the working people is carried out for the benefit of foreign capital. . . . The anti-popular policy of this agency of imperialism should be unanimously condemned by world opinion.[31]

Of course, the Soviet discipline of exclusion is infinitely more dangerous than the Catholic discipline because it is enforced by a great military machine and it affects the free movement of several hundred million persons in the countries of the Soviet orbit. The victim of Soviet power is not only prevented from making mental excursions into the areas of liberal democracy and democratic socialism, but he is physically restrained from contacts with non-Communist civilization. No resident of the Soviet Union may leave his country without special permission, and the same prohibition is applied to the peoples of the satellite countries in the Soviet orbit. In effect, Stalin has locked the Russian door and thrown away the key. Citizens of the Soviet Union are not permitted to go abroad, and since a decree of February 15, 1947, marriage to non-Soviet citizens has been forbidden. Even the millions of Jews in Russia who would like to go to the new Jewish homeland of Israel are being prevented from leaving, perhaps because the government of the new Israel is predominantly socialist, and the Kremlin will never compromise with socialism.

The Kremlin, in its desire to maintain the purity of Communism by exclusion, has even developed recently a philosophy of inbreeding which is an exact parallel to that of the Catholic Church. It is attempting to persuade its Young Communists not to marry outside the Faith, especially if the prospective bride or groom wants marriage by a priest. In March 1950, a Young Communist from Kalingrad province asked the editors of *Kom-*

somolskaya Pravda a question: "The statutes of the Young Communist League say the members must fight against survivals of religious superstitions. I intend to marry a girl, not a YCL member, who wants a church wedding. I would like you to explain whether I can go through with this ceremony." This was the answer of the official Young Communist paper:

It seems to us, Comrade M., that you have not given the matter deep enough thought. . . .
Our youth must grow free from survivals of the old, including religious superstitions. . . . That is why the YCL obligates its members to fight religious superstitions and to explain to youth their harm. . . .
Such an act, if you perform it, directly violates the YCL statutes. It contradicts Communist ethics and is incompatible with the title of Young Communist. It would be an unprincipled act. . . .
Some young people in our country are still under the influence of religious superstitions. They go to church, participate in religious rites, avail themselves of the services of clairvoyants and believe in auguries. We must resolutely conduct patient explanatory work among these young people, answering the questions that puzzle them, and convince them of the absurdity and harmfulness of superstitions and prejudices. And now suppose that a Young Communist, instead of waging this campaign as the YCL statutes demand, gives way to these backward feelings. Judge for yourself whether one can consider such a Young Communist a progressive person in principle.
Have you thought of the social significance of such an act? One's attitude toward religion is not a private matter with a Young Communist. . . . What would the other young people think of you when they discover that you have not only failed to change your fiancee's opinions and to explain to her where she errs, but that you yourself have compromised your principles by going off to church? Do you know what young people will say about you? They will say you are not a true Young Communist.
Forgive us for our bluntness, Comrade M. . . . Try yourself to understand and to explain to your fiancee that your family will not be made strong by the church ceremony, but by deep feelings, unity of interests, and sincere friendship. That happiness is in your own hands and does not require any "heavenly" blessing.[82]

9

The Management of Truth: the Kremlin

MODERN MAN HAS LEARNED a painful lesson from the rise of dictatorships: The same machinery that has been created to spread truth throughout the world can be used with equal success for misinforming the world. In fact, the management of truth is a necessary part of the apparatus of power wherever dictatorship suppresses freedom of thought.

Hitler, Mussolini, and Stalin have given the world the greatest demonstrations in recent times of the power of systematic deception. Even the Vatican, with all its lofty moral idealism, has stooped to the use of some of the same devices. In this chapter and the next, I propose to look at some of the devices used by both the Kremlin and the Vatican to maintain themselves in power through the manipulation, the distortion, and the shading of truth.

Lying for the Faith is quite basic in Communist philosophy, and the practice goes back to pre-revolutionary days. Machiavelli acquired a certain reputation for cynicism because, as interpreter of the politics of medieval Italy, he spoke rather frankly about political motives and goals; but Machiavelli never exalted deception in human relations as systematically as Lenin. Lenin was an extremely blunt and forthright person, but he calmly brushed aside all obligations in the realm of truth-telling whenever falsehood would serve the revolution more effectively. He believed in truth, especially for school children, but according to his code the obligation to tell the truth should never be permitted to stand in the way of a Communist purpose. If truth became inconvenient it was branded as "bourgeois morality." "There are no morals in politics," Lenin said once, "there is only expediency."[1]

It should be remembered that Lenin and his associates did not acknowledge that they were evil or treacherous in making the choice for the revolution against conventional morals. In their own eyes they were serving the cause of ultimate truth, and the end justified the means. They were ready to die as conspirators for the "higher" truth, and many of them did die with all the heroism and devotion of the early Christian martyrs.

"Ilyitch never lies to us";[2] that, according to William Henry Chamberlin, is what the Communists of Russia said about Lenin and his truth-telling. Their devotion to truth, and Lenin's devotion, was an instrument of the revolution to be turned against the upper classes when it seemed appropriate. "Very frequently," said Lenin in 1920 to a Young Communist League convention, "the bourgeoisie makes the charge that we Communists deny all morality. That is one of their methods of confusing the issue. . . . We deny all morality taken from superhuman or non-class conceptions. . . . We say that our morality is wholly subordinated to the interests of the class struggle."[3]

The Kremlin's devices of deception begin with its own people. It must keep them thoroughly misinformed about their relative position in the modern world. It must teach them the inferiority of all capitalist civilizations, and it must exalt Russian accomplishments to the heavens, even if the extreme claims arouse Homeric laughter in the whole world. The Kremlin does not need to fear the effect of derision upon the Russian people because they never hear the laughter of the outside world.

A great deal of the exaggeration of past Russian accomplishments is quite new in Kremlin strategy. In the early days of the revolution nothing was too harsh to say about Russian national heroes of the past. Ivan the Terrible was really terrible, and Tsarist generals were wholly lacking in personal merit. Since then, Ivan the Terrible has become a national hero by special permission of Stalin, and a laudatory motion picture about him has been produced, which gives him a permanent place in the Russian Hall of Fame.

Stalin and his associates began to appreciate the value of using national feeling to support Communist policies in the 1930's, and during World War II, when German armies were fighting on Russian soil, there was an immense new emphasis on Soviet patriotism. A deliberate attempt was made to induce every Russian to appreciate the glory of his Fatherland. Since the war the emphasis has continued, and the revived spirit of nationalism has been systematically associated with Stalin and Communism. The campaign for glorifying national accomplishments has gone so far that it has produced a whole set of mythical facts designed to reinforce Russian national pride and, at the same time, belittle the accomplishments of all other peoples. Here are some of the typical claims about Russian national accomplishments which the Communist newspapers present as facts:

(1) *That Russia won the war.*

Yes, the Soviet Union even won the war against Japan. In general, the Russian press played down the help given to the Soviet Union throughout the war by the nations of the west. When the Red soldiers became enthusiastic about the lend-lease arms that were being sent to Russia by the United States, the Communist agitators in the army told them that it was only obsolete or discarded equipment.[4] Throughout the war, in fact, the Communist press gave the Russian people the impression that they were fighting the war almost single-handed, by emphasizing the drive for a second front and by failing to give due credit to the Allied campaigns in Africa and the Orient. When American and British troops finally made their landing in Normandy, Stalin praised the enterprise warmly, but his gratitude was very short-lived. As soon as the war seemed safely won, in 1945, Russia repudiated further help, and even during the closing months of the war *Pravda* described the Normandy landing rather patronizingly as "entering Germany by the back door." "We proved to be the only power capable, not only of halting the dark surge of fascism, but also of inflicting on it a decisive and fatal defeat,"[5] say B. P. Yesipov and N. K. Goncharov in their textbook on pedagogy, used in the training of Russian teachers. The school textbooks which had contained a favorable mention of the Normandy landing were quickly revised and virtually all mention of the American and British contribution to victory was eliminated. V-E Day, which had been made into a national holiday, was promptly abolished.

"The second front," said Marshal Sokolovsky in *Pravda* in

1949, "was opened only when it became evident that the Soviet Union was capable alone, without the help of the Allies, of defeating Fascist Germany and liberating the peoples of Europe from the Fascist-German aggressors. The Anglo-American troops landing on the European continent encountered trifling resistance from the Hitlerite Army, since the chief German forces were concentrated on the Soviet-German front."[6] This emphasis upon Russia's role in the war has been imposed upon all of the Soviet's satellites. One of the reasons given for purging Wladyslaw Gomulka, Communist deputy prime minister in the left-wing government of Poland, was that he failed to glorify sufficiently the role of the Red Army in "liberating" Poland. In Prague in 1949 the reading books for third-grade students in the schools told of the Red Army's liberation of the city without mentioning any other army — although General Patton's American forces were so close to Prague at the time of Russia's entry that he could easily have liberated the city with American troops if the Allied command had directed him to do so.

The Kremlin has even circulated a picture of the "surrender of Japan" in which Russian soldiers are thrust into the foreground as if they, in their three-week war effort, had been largely responsible for Japan's defeat. The newsreel version of the surrender entirely omitted General MacArthur and pictured a Japanese officer surrendering to a Russian general!

(2) *That the Russians discovered penicillin.*

It wasn't Sir Alexander Fleming of Great Britain who discovered penicillin, but three Russians who performed the service for mankind in 1871. That, at least, is what *Pravda* says. The names of the discoverers were Polotebnov, Manassein, and Gukovsky. For some reason or other, development was held in abeyance for about fifty years because the Russians lacked the equipment to take advantage of the discovery.[7]

(3) *That the Russians invented the airplane.*

It wasn't the Wright Brothers. A Russian scientist, it seems, designed a monoplane with three steam engines in 1882, and a Russian pilot named Golubev successfully flew it. The proof is contained in Russian newspapers printed in the year 1882, according to the newspaper published for young Communists, the *Komsomolskaya Pravda,* which has a circulation of more than one million.[8]

(4) *That the Communist system is more productive than capitalism.*

The Russian workers are told that in nations like the United States millions of workers are constantly unemployed and that the standard of living is a starvation standard. The Australian economist, Colin Clark, has revealed in careful studies that the productivity of the United States, based on real income for man-hours worked, is approximately eight and one-half times that of the Soviet Union. The New York *Times* published other figures in 1947 which showed that an American worker in that year had to work 7 minutes to earn a pound of rye bread, and a Russian worker 31 minutes; an American worker 48½ minutes for a pound of butter and a Russian worker 642 minutes; an American worker 1684 minutes for a man's woolen suit and a Russian worker 34,815 minutes.[9] Joseph Newman, New York *Herald Tribune* correspondent in Moscow for more than two years, expressed the opinion in 1949 that "the Russian is still one of the poorest supplied workers in the world."[10]

(5) *That Russia has abolished classes and class injustice.*

Many Soviet leaders have formally announced that the Soviet Union has attained the status of a "classless society," a society, according to Molotov, "which cannot exist in any other states, divided as they are into classes of oppressors and oppressed." Stalin said in 1936 that "there are no longer any antagonistic classes in [Soviet] society."[11] It is true that the Communists have abolished the classes of Tsarist society; but they have introduced a new hierarchy of ranks, titles, and uniforms into government service, and the distance between the Communist ruling group and the masses of the people seems to be almost as great as in the days of the Tsar. During the last war the ratio between the pay of the lowest second lieutenant and a private soldier in the Red Army was 57 to 1.[12]

Millions of Soviet citizens have been put into civilian uniforms which carry badges of rank in the form of collar tabs and sleeve insignia. "Thus, in effect," says Dr. Alex Inkeles of Harvard, "Bolshevik leaders have restored to the Soviet Union the system of *chiny,* or formal civil service ranks, which was a central aspect of the Tsarist system of social differentiation and had traditionally been treated by the Bolsheviks as one of the paramount symbols of class exploitation and stratification."[13] The new class system makes it possible for many Russians to earn 100,000 rubles or more a year, ten times the approximate average wage in industry, and they do not pay as high a proportion in income taxes on this excess as the average factory worker pays on his lowly wage.

(6) *That Russia has the only true democracy.*

"Unlike parliamentary democracy," said Molotov on the twenty-fifth anniversary of the Bolshevik revolution, "the democracy of the Soviets is a true democracy of the people." "Not a single capitalist state has truly universal suffrage," according to Andrei Vishinsky. "The Soviet people," said a writer in *Pravda* in 1949, "are the most advanced people of our epoch. . . . The historically doomed exploiter class" is now in its "mortal agony." And he continued:

> At one time the advanced bourgeois west laid claim to the role of the indisputable and historically-decreed "teacher" of its "pupil" — backward Russia. . . . The dialectic of history changed the roles of "teachers" and "pupils." The capitalist world is experiencing the insoluble crisis of bourgeois culture, its spiritual agony. From now on the Soviet Union is the bulwark of World Civilization and progress.[14]

In this "true democracy" of the Soviet Union, no opposition party has been permitted to offer a slate of candidates since 1917. In Communist theory this absence of an opposition is not important because numerical majorities and numerical minorities are not essential to democracy. What counts is the "democratic potential" in a nation. When the Communists did not at once capture control of East Germany and Soviet Berlin by a majority vote, Joseph Starobin, a staff editor of the New York *Daily Worker,* explained the Communist philosophy of majorities thus:

> Admittedly the Ebert [Berlin Soviet Zone] government does not represent a numerical majority; but it represents the democratic potential of Berlin, the desire for a unified city, and for a solution of the city's needs

on a unified basis, in harmony with the economy of the Soviet zone of which Berlin is a part. Only a reactionary government would represent a numerical majority. This is the Achilles heel of the whole idea of elections, it seems to me, in a nation of moral paraplegics, who need skillful democratic therapy, and not the chance to vote their gripes and their illnesses.[15]

The Cosmopolitan Villain

Since every Communist propaganda campaign must have a villain, a convenient new villain has been created in recent years, embodying the attitude toward non-Russian culture which the Kremlin wishes to suppress. It is called "cosmopolitanism." In general, a cosmopolitan is a citizen of the Soviet Union or a satellite country who does not quite appreciate the Communist claim of super-excellence for all Russian achievement. Such a person must be presented to the public as a special type of monster who lacks mental perspective and human sympathy. It must be shown that he is tainted with "bourgeois nationalism."

One of Russia's leading magazines, *Voprosy Filosofii,* defines cosmopolitanism as follows:

Cosmopolitanism is a reactionary ideology preaching renunciation of national traditions, disdain for the distinguishing features in the national development of each people, and renunciation of the feelings of a national dignity and national pride. Cosmopolitanism preaches a nihilistic attitude of the individual toward his nationality — toward its past, present and future. With lofty phrases about the community of interests of all mankind, about "world culture" and the reciprocal influence and interpenetration of cultures, cosmopolitanism conceals either an imperialistic, Great-Power chauvinism toward other nations or a nihilistic attitude toward one's own nation, a betrayal of its national interests. The ideology of cosmopolitanism is hostile to, and radically contradicts, Soviet patriotism — the basic feature which characterizes the world outlook of Soviet man.[16]

It will be seen that cosmopolitanism is any form of international sentiment which the Kremlin does not like. In practice, the crusade against cosmopolitanism imposes a kind of compulsory lying upon all the faithful. The good Communist must lie about the United Nations because it stands for "the community of interests of all mankind." He must lie about Russian accomplishments because Russia is the "socialist motherland." He must lie about capitalist achievements because capitalism is the primary devil in all Soviet propaganda.

In 1949 the drive against cosmopolitanism went so far that the Ministry of Education weeded out 139 of 350 university textbooks because "they contained elements of fawning and servility to capitalist culture . . . and did not demonstrate the priority of our natural sciences."[17] *Any* sign of loyalty to *any* non-Russian culture is suspect. One reason for the development of anti-Zionism in the Soviet Union is that Communist leaders distrust the independent Jewish spirit as too critical for "national unity." The Jews have been described as "homeless cosmopolitans," and one voluble Stalinist critic, V. B. Lutsky, has declared that the Zionist movement is "utilized at the present time as a weapon of subversive activity of Anglo-American warmongers in the countries of the world."[18] Some observers believe that this anti-Zionism has already become a new type of anti-Semitism — not, basically, religious anti-Semitism, but a distrust of Jews as persons who have a broad outlook upon international affairs and who, therefore, constitute a threat to the narrow outlook of Communist opinion.[19] There is no room in the Soviet Union today for any persons who question the Communist outlook or the Communist superiority over non-Communist cultures.

In February 1951, the Jewish Labor Committee, headed by prominent American trade unionists, voted to present the case against the Soviet's new anti-Semitism to the United Nations as a denial of human rights under its charter. The disclosures of the new Russian policy were shocking to those who had not followed the recent developments in the Soviet Union. A report of the facts disclosed that in the Soviet Union all Jewish schools had been closed, all Yiddish newspapers silenced, and all Yiddish writers liquidated. In Rumania 68,000 Jews had been expelled from the Communist Party, and all Jewish schools, newspapers and synagogues had been closed.[20]

Even the scenery of Russia and its natural splendors must not be compared invidiously with any bourgeois scenery. A fifth-grade geography textbook was eliminated from Russian schools in 1948 because it made Niagara Falls "much more interesting than Lake Baikal." Every published description of life in the west must be drawn in such a way that non-Communist civilization appears bestial and depraved.

The mere appearance of doubt about Russian superiority in

the mind of a university scholar may bring swift punishment from a cultural commission. Dr. George Lukacs, one of Hungary's most noted philosophers and president of Hungary's Academy of Sciences, was giving a lecture one night after his country had come under Communist rule when he made the statement that a Communist country was "potentially" more capable of great achievements in science and the arts than capitalist countries. That was too mild an endorsement for the members of the Central Committee of the Hungarian Communist Party. They wanted to know why Dr. Lukacs had not said that Communist countries were *actually* greater in their achievements. He must be tainted with cosmopolitanism. He was bitterly condemned, and ultimately forced to resign.[21]

The case of Eugene Varga and his compulsory prevarication is worth noting. One feature of the campaign against cosmopolitanism is that western capitalism must always be pictured as if it were in a state of approaching collapse. If it shows signs of prosperity, those signs must be described as deceptive — for collapse is just around the corner. Part of this apocalyptic theory was that western capitalism would collapse promptly at the end of the war when artificial wartime demands on production were withdrawn. Eugene Varga, member of the Soviet Academy of Sciences, challenged this notion indirectly in his own magazine and in his book, *Changes in the Economy of Capitalism as a Result of the Second World War,* and predicted that a major economic depression in capitalist countries was not probable before 1955. He suggested that America might maintain a high standard of living after the war. This was not acceptable doctrine for the Party's prophets who had been basing their political policy on the hypothesis that western capitalism would be too busy after the war with its own agonies to stop Soviet aggression. Varga was promptly denounced as a prevaricator and a tool of western influence in an economists' conference which had been called to dissect him. He stood his ground for a short time but was finally forced to recant, and his magazine was abolished.[22] He is still functioning in the Soviet Union only because he has accepted political guidance for his economic chart-making.

Meanwhile, the doctrine of internationalism in world affairs has been redefined to make Russian nationalism the only true form of internationalism. "An internationalist," says Stalin, "is he who unreservedly, without any hesitation, and unconditionally, is ready to defend the USSR because the USSR constitutes the base of the World Revolutionary movement and to defend, to advance this revolutionary movement is impossible without defending the USSR."[23] This identification of internationalism and Soviet patriotism runs through all the discussion of world policy in the Soviet press. A writer on the victory of socialism said in *Pravda* in January 1949 that the chief Communist task was the task "of arousing in the people the sacred ideas of Soviet patriotism, of burning hatred for capitalism and for all manifestations of the bourgeois ideology; of educating our people in the spirit of proletarian internationalism, and cultivating love for the party of Lenin-Stalin."[24] Democratic internationalism is never discussed in the official press except in terms of violent abuse; it is assumed that proletarian internationalism is the only genuine variety.

In accordance with this gospel the propaganda for internationalism in the satellite countries also is substantially propaganda for Russia. The Communists attempt to de-nationalize and de-westernize all their subject people, and they do this while still professing opposition to all forms of imperialism. The very word "imperialism" has been reoriented in their vocabulary until it has become exclusively a label for the non-Communist variety. The leaders still profess the gospel of Lenin that Communists "will always combat every attempt to influence national self-determination by violence or by any injustice from without,"[25] and it does not disturb their consciences because they never admit that Kremlin policy can be "injustice from without."

In Communist-controlled Hungary in December 1949, according to the New York *Times,* a Greater Budapest Library Committee was formed to "launch a book campaign to increase hatred of imperialists and their base agents and simultaneously love of the Soviet Union."[26] One of the casualties of the campaign was the Hungarian Year Book which had printed statistics of prostitution and crime which "showed the working class in an unfavorable light." Other casualties included such "western" advertising terms on signboards as "nylon" and "jeep." If Hungarians under Communist control insisted on demanding nylons and jeeps, they should at least have the good taste to find some pro-Communist names for such questionable products.

Many of us who call ourselves liberals were inclined at one time to smile rather patronizingly at Communist claims of Russian accomplishment and to consider the whole campaign against foreign superiority a passing phase of a new and immature culture. I remember that that was my own attitude when I heard exaggerated claims of Communist glories and corresponding bourgeois decadence during my brief sojourn in the Soviet Union in the 1920's. Perhaps, I reasoned, this childish egotism is merely a defense against an inner feeling of insecurity. Perhaps it will wear off as the new regime becomes more mature.

All of us who adopted this charitable attitude in the 1920's were shocked out of our complacence when Stalin, Molotov, and associates began in the 1930's to use deliberate deception and trickery on a grand scale in their international dealings. The feeling of distrust came to a climax after World War II when the Soviet regime gave so many exhibitions of crude dishonesty in international dealings that it lost any last remnant of diplomatic respectability.

In August 1939, I was living on the coast of Brittany in a seaside hotel operated by Communist-dominated labor unions of Paris. (It happened to be the cheapest hotel in the neighborhood.) To find out what was going on, I attended several Communist meetings. In the period up to August 23, before the Hitler-Stalin pact was signed, the language of every French Communist's speech was almost monotonously anti-Hitler. Fascism was the great enemy of the working class. War to the death against Hitler was the supreme duty of all good men. Suddenly, like a thunderclap, came the news of an agreement between Stalin and Hitler. It was, as later revelations made clear, a mutual spoils agreement in which Stalin pledged non-interference in Hitler's war and agreed to accept in return the Baltic States, Bessarabia, and a large part of Poland, while Hitler stole the major part of Poland.

After the deal was announced, absolute and stupefied silence reigned in French Communist circles for about forty-eight hours. The ideological floor of the world had collapsed under the French Communists' feet. Their moral values had been turned upside down, and at first they were completely bewildered; they had no words for the new language of appeasement.

Then came the slow recovery. The first day's issue of the Paris *Humanité* after the announcement of the new pact was terse and evasive. The editors did not quite dare at first to express revised opinions and abandon their old clichés. By the second day after the thunderclap, the new verbiage of deception had arrived in canned speeches from Moscow. The Party press passed along the phrases of appeasement, and all over France the Communist partisans began to express the new line. Overnight Hitler became not a unique devil but one of *several* evil men in the world. He was not necessarily the *worst* among the evil men. Communist strategy, it seems, called for a compromise on occasion even with evil. The compromise with Hitler was *temporary* and necessary, and it represented ultimate anti-fascist *grand strategy*. It *seemed* to give new strength to Hitler but that was only an *illusion,* since it gave the glorious Soviet Union breathing time to gather strength for the *ultimate* struggle for the people's democracy. British, French, and American imperialism had forced the Soviet Union into this necessary compromise. After all, imperialisms were much *alike,* and if the great Stalin could successfully compromise with one imperialism in order to defend the interests of the working class against *other* imperialisms, this was proof of sound morality and superior *wisdom.* Stalin had outwitted western capitalism, and the temporary compromise would never have been necessary *if western capitalism had stood with Stalin against Hitler at Munich.*

The Hitler-Stalin pact and the transparently deceptive defenses of the Soviet Union in 1939 proved to be the final straw for most western liberals. If they had retained any charity in their hearts for the Kremlin's ideals, the tolerance soon disappeared. To this day, one of the best tests for distinguishing an honest believer in liberal democracy from a Communist puppet is to confront him with the question: Where did you stand in regard to Stalin between August 23, 1939, when the Hitler-Stalin pact was signed, and June 22, 1941, when Hitler invaded the Soviet Union?

When Japan and Germany had been defeated in World War II, and the secret archives of the German Foreign Office were made available to the world, some of the truth about Russian foreign policy during the Hitler-Stalin period became available. Von Ribbentrop, before he was hanged at Nuremberg, revealed that Hitler and Stalin — through the good offices of Molotov and Von Ribbentrop — had made a secret deal in Moscow in 1939, not announced with the public agreement, under which Russia would get the Baltic States and Bessarabia, and Poland would be divided. The State Department later published the documents.[27] Russia, soon after Germany marched into Poland, occupied Polish territory up to the Vistula and Bug rivers, and Molotov wired "my congratulations and greetings" to Hitler on the entrance of German troops into Warsaw.

Stalin, acutely embarrassed by the need to justify in official propaganda his own and Hitler's invasions of Poland, tried to get the Führer to co-operate in a propaganda fraud "to make the intervention of the Soviet Union plausible to the masses and at the same time to avoid giving the Soviet Union the appearance of an aggressor." Hitler was asked to permit Stalin to pretend to the Russian people that the Russians were entering Poland to protect their Ukrainian and White Russian "brothers" who were "threatened" by Germany. It was conceded that this would be "jarring to German sensibilities" — but so what? Hitler did not relish being described as the imperialist villain for the Russian masses, and he never officially agreed to the fraud, but Stalin circulated the lie anyway, apologizing privately for the reflection on the pure motives of Hitler. The captured German documents show how the Kremlin, because of its complete control over the agencies of information, can manufacture and circulate successfully any propaganda fraud which will serve its purposes.

When France fell before the Nazi armies, Molotov sent Hitler "the warmest congratulations of the Soviet Government on the splendid success of the German armed forces." Russia at this time was helping Hitler with huge quantities of wheat, oil, and cotton. The records of the German Foreign Office, and the diaries of leaders like Prince Fumimaro Konoye of Japan, as well as the records of the former German Chief of Staff, General Franz Halder, show that Russia was discussing a plan to divide up a large part of the world with Germany, Japan, and Italy, and that India and Iran were to belong to the Russian sphere of power. Hitler, in a conversation with Molotov on November 12, 1940, offered the Kremlin full partnership in his Axis and suggested co-operation in opposing the United States and its "imperialistic policy" by setting up "in the whole of Europe and Africa some kind of Monroe Doctrine." He said that "the Russian people could develop without in the least prejudicing German interests," and Molotov agreed that this was quite correct and that co-operation was "entirely acceptable in principle" but that the USSR must "co-operate as a partner" in such a deal.

The deal was never consummated, not because the Kremlin had any qualms of conscience but because Stalin had angered Hitler to the point of open warfare by demanding too large a share of spoils for Russia. The Kremlin demanded as part of its sphere of influence not only India and Iran but also all the Balkans, including strategic naval bases that would have given the Soviet Union outlets to the Mediterranean and virtual command of the Bosporus and the Dardanelles. Hitler, in blind rage, committed the greatest blunder of his career by striking back with an invasion of Russia.

By the time the Korean war began in June 1950 with the invasion of South Korea by North Korean armies, the standard Soviet deceptions in diplomacy had become so notorious that the world simply jeered at them. In June 1950, said the Kremlin, the South Koreans and the United States "invaded" North Korea and started a war of aggression. The world could see the Big Lie in operation even more clearly than in 1939. In every nation which had a Communist party, the Kremlin representatives stood up and repeated the refrain in the same words. Togliatti in Italy, Thorez in France, Foster in the United States, Pollitt in England, and all the other selected Soviet agents throughout the world, each in his respective capital, repeated the refrain that the attacked were the attackers and that western imperialism was on the march against an innocent People's Republic. At a Communist rally in Rome and in the Italian Chamber of Deputies, I heard the same phrases from Communist and left-wing Socialist leaders that came from similar leaders in other capitals from Peiping to Washington. In each case the United States government, whose motives in the Korean war were irreproachable, was pictured in lurid oratory and even more lurid posters and cartoons as an ogre of aggressive imperialism whose designs included the conquest of Asia for Wall Street. When Jacob Malik of the Soviet Union imported the big lie into the Security Council of the United Nations at Lake Success, and repeated it *ad infinitum* for thirty days while he served as chairman, men were embarrassed to hear other men present such childishly specious deceptions. The Kremlin, it appeared, was wholly indifferent to the opinion of the western world so long as it could feed its own particular type of prevarication to the controlled press of its own countries.

I recite these unpleasant events not because they are news to Americans who read the newspapers but because they serve to remind us that the Kremlin has developed deceptive diplomacy to a point never before equaled in all history. Beginning with the assumption that all bourgeois values are only masks for selfish purposes, it has outstripped Talleyrand and surpassed Hitler in the prefabricated diplomatic lie. Now we can see that Stalin really meant what he said in a statement about bourgeois diplomacy in 1913: "Words must have no relation to action — otherwise what kind of diplomacy is it? Words are one thing, actions another. Good words are a mask for concealment of bad deeds. Sincere diplomacy is no more possible than dry water or wooden iron."[28] Stalin intended his statement to apply only to the capitalist diplomacy of the period, but he has always regarded all non-Communist diplomacy as hopelessly insincere, and he has never felt any obligation to adhere to promises made to bourgeois diplomats unless it suited his convenience.

Between 1939 and 1950 the Soviet Union probably broke more solemn treaties and international agreements than any other power in history in a similar span of time.

At Yalta in February 1945, the Soviet Union had participated in the pledge that the liberated peoples of eastern Europe should be free to "create democratic institutions of their own choice," and that governments should be set up "responsive to the will of the people." Russia's interpretation of that pledge was made in the words of Stalin: "Any freely elected government in these countries will be an anti-Soviet government, and we cannot allow that."[28a] The United States State Department in 1948 documented thirty-seven distinct post-war violations of agreements by the Soviet Union, and the House Foreign Affairs Committee produced fifty-two pages of a similar indictment in August 1950.[29] Worse than the specific violations was the fact that the Kremlin deliberately used its power, from the days of the Berlin air lift to the war in Korea, to make peace impossible, at the end of a war which was fought chiefly to organize the nations for permanent peace. Stalin, by treachery as well as by force of arms, added 400,000 square miles to his own territory and perhaps 30,000,000 people, not including his new, indirect dominion over great stretches of territory in Asia populated by nearly half a billion people. And, while preaching peace, he continued to maintain an army of 175 to 255 divisions, at least four times the size of the armies of the west.

The Communist Fronts

The Communist techniques of deception for political and cultural organizations inside democratic nations are worthy of P. T. Barnum at his best, combining expert showmanship with political juggling. It is part of routine Communist procedure to appropriate all the labels of conventional democratic practice and twist their meaning for Communist purposes. The conventional symbols of western thought are boldly appropriated and filled with a new and strange content. Communism is a "new" democracy and a "higher" freedom. This use of Aesopian language for the concealment of actual policy was thoroughly ventilated at the trial of eleven leaders of the American Communist Party in New York in 1949. The prosecution, in the words of Judge Medina's charge to the jury, contended that "Aesopian language, only understood by Communists thoroughly indoctrinated in the use of such verbiage, was used in their Constitution of 1945 and elsewhere, and that defendants also habitually used in their writings and teaching a species of double talk which they used to convey one meaning to themselves and their followers, but which would be otherwise understood by the uninitiate and the public at large."[30] This is a very mild description of the Communist devices of semantic deception. A glossary of Communist terms of propaganda would indicate that, in practice, the word "freedom" means freedom from capitalism, and the word "democracy" means participation in the Communist movement. Any other kinds of freedom or democracy belong to the species known as "bourgeois."

Professor Harry Schwartz, of Syracuse University, has translated some of the choicest definitions from the latest edition of the Soviet's *Dictionary of Foreign Words;* several of these appear in the New York *Times Magazine* for February 4, 1951, together with Professor Schwartz's comment that the Communist double talk about democracy reminds him of Humpty Dumpty's statement in *Through the Looking-Glass:* "When I use a word it means just what I want it to mean, neither more nor less." The Soviet definitions of *democracy* and *dogmatism* are worth quoting:

> *Democracy:* A political structure in which power belongs to the people. The Soviet Socialist democracy is a new higher type of democracy, with power actually in the hands of the people. . . . Bourgeois democracy is a form of class supremacy, the dictatorship of the bourgeoisie over the proletariat and the working masses.
>
> *Dogmatism:* Uncritical thinking based on dogma. . . . Dogmatism is characteristic of religious beliefs, metaphysical points of view, and of all theoretical systems which are dying out, reactionary, and fighting against the developing new ideas. Marxism-Leninism is foreign to any dogmatism.

If Americans were confronted by an appeal from a political party with headquarters in New York which called itself the Russian Imperialist State-Ownership Party (American Branch), they would not pay much attention to its appeals. Being confronted with a Citizens Committee for Free Milk, or a University Bureau for Free Speech, or a Clergymen's Alliance for Peace, they are sometimes betrayed by their humane and democratic sentiments into supporting Communist fronts.

Under our pure food laws a conglomerate package of meat which includes some ham may not be sold under the label of ham. It may be sold as deviled meat or luncheon meat or simply meat with ham flavor. In politics consumers are not so well protected. A Communist party controlled by a Communist central committee in Moscow may call itself a People's Party, a Progressive Party, a Labor Progressive Party, a Labor Party, a Socialist Unity Party, or a United Workers Party. In Poland in 1945 the Communists camouflaged themselves under the title of Polish Workers

Party, and then created an extra ersatz Peasant Party of their own to win votes away from the once-powerful party of the same name led by Stanislaw Mikolajczyk.[31] A "Committee to Undermine the Military Power of the United States and Great Britain Pending their Conquest by the Soviet Union" could not collect many signatures for a petition to outlaw the atomic bomb, but a "Committee of Partisans for Peace" can gather millions of signatures for such a purpose, particularly if it is headed by a number of innocent-sounding bishops.

This type of deception has become quite familiar to Americans during the great exposures of Communist activity in recent years. Occasionally those exposures have degenerated into rank hysteria and falsehood — the diatribes of Senator Joseph McCarthy of Wisconsin are not much more accurate than the Communist propaganda which he assails — but in spite of the abuses of partisan anti-Communism, the truth about Communist propaganda fronts is now quite clear. The government's list of false fronts is, as far as it goes, quite indisputable.

In most democratic countries the strategic work of Communist deception in the political and cultural fields is done by men who do not hold Communist Party cards. In fact, in countries like the United States the Communist Party is perhaps the least important instrument of Communist propaganda. Sometimes the Party itself in a certain country is operated by quite unimportant left-wing labor leaders and foreign-born Communists, while native-born and educated professionals promote the Cause in non-Communist labor unions, newspaper offices, universities, and political parties. Frequently the Communist representatives themselves demand that their ablest representatives stay outside the Party. Arthur Koestler tells how he felt quite crestfallen when he offered his soul to the Communist organization in Germany, and the Party functionary who was assigned to receive his tender of allegiance seemed not at all anxious to accept him as a full-fledged member. "If you insist," he said, "we will make you a Party member, but on condition that your membership remains secret."[32] The Party preferred to have a journalist of Koestler's rank act as an entirely "independent" foreign editor of an influential daily newspaper where his judiciously phrased opinions might sway non-Communist judgment.

Sometimes the Communist agitator in a non-Communist country acts as a conspirator with an assumed name, even when there seems to be no apparent need for concealment. Often the reason for the maneuver is that forged passports and other false documents are very useful in the Party's larger strategy. A few fictitious personalities come in handy in emergencies. Similarly the Party is extremely adept at changing the labels of false-front organizations quickly when the situation requires it. After a Communist false front has been exposed and abolished, an innocent organization almost always appears promptly in the same general area. Usually the new, innocent front makes use of the membership list of the abolished body, but no one can prove that the new and the old organizations have the same masters.

Each Communist movement in each democratic country is instructed to follow the line of deception best adapted to that country. Unfortunately for the success of these tactics, the overall policy for Communist expansion is frequently directed by men who are abysmally ignorant of the conditions of labor and culture outside of Russia. Their tendency is to interpret the whole world in terms of their narrow experience in the Soviet Union. I saw this Russian arrogance and provincialism assert itself too aggressively for success in the Chinese revolution of 1927 in Hankow. Later on, the Kremlin's agents learned to adapt their propaganda more successfully to the Asiatic mind, but anyone who has seen them perform in the earlier stages of Chinese revolutionary movements is bound to question their capacity to keep themselves subordinated enough to hold Chinese friendship permanently.

The Communist plan for a "black-belt republic" in the southern states of the United States in the 1930's was revealing proof of stupidity at central headquarters in the Kremlin. It would have been hard to suggest a solution for America's racial problem less adapted to the American situation and less appealing to the American Negro people themselves. The black-belt plan, of course, was quickly abandoned when it proved to be a propaganda dud.

Always the strategic line of deception in any country changes with the needs of the Soviet Union, but always that subordination to Soviet policy is concealed as much as possible in order to make

Communist propaganda acceptable to local opinion. Frequently the movement makes skillful use of the names of national and local heroes. The American Communist Party sagaciously declares its undying faith in the tactics of democracy at the very moment when its overlords are denying the validity of those tactics throughout the world. Jefferson and Lincoln, if Communist platforms are to be taken seriously, were simply forebears and precursors of Stalin.

Here are a few excerpts from the 1948 campaign platform of the Communist Party of the United States, published at a time when Russia was rapidly destroying the right of opposition parties to exist in nearly all of eastern Europe:

> The destruction of the rights of the Communists is the classical first step down the road to fascism. The tragedy of Germany and Italy prove this. Therefore, it is incumbent upon all Americans who hate fascism to defend the rights of the Communists, and to help explode the myth that Communists are foreign agents or advocate force and violence.
>
> We are no more foreign agents than was Jefferson who was also accused of being a foreign agent by the Tories of his day. We follow in the best tradition of the spokesmen of labor, science and culture whose contributions to human progress knew no national boundaries. "The strongest bond of human sympathy, outside of the family relation, should be one uniting all working people of all nations and tongues and kindred."
>
> It is not the Communists who advocate or practice force and violence, but the monopolists, the KKK, the lynch mobs and the fascist hoodlum gangs. . . . We condemn and reject the policy and practice of terror and assassination and repudiate the advocates of force and violence. We Communists seek only the opportunity to compete fairly in the marketplace of ideas, asking only that our program and proposals be considered on their merit. . . . We have supported every democratic movement since the Communists of Lincoln's generation fought in the Union cause during the Civil War.[33]

Probably no American historians have ever been able to identify the "Communists of Lincoln's generation" who fought in the Civil War, but such deficiencies rarely cause anxiety among Communist platform writers. They approach history with creative confidence. They can change the Party's line concerning co-operation with democracy overnight without any confession of inconsistency. A new semantic mask can be put on or taken off at will.

The current semantic mask of Soviet imperialism is "peace"

and opposition to the atomic bomb in the name of humanity. Peace congresses and people's peace fronts have blossomed throughout the world, calling upon humanity to abjure violence: the helpless and peace-loving peoples of the world are being driven to war by "Wall Street"; true believers in a people's peace should support the World Congress of Partisans for Peace, and, along with perhaps half a billion others, sign the Stockholm peace appeal to outlaw the atomic bomb.[34] But when a practical plan for controlling atomic energy for peace was offered to the Soviet Union in the United Nations, there were no Communist takers. And every peace congress under pro-Communist auspices in recent years has been quite openly a war congress for Soviet interests, cheering wildly for Communist aggression. At the "World Congress for Peace" in Paris early in 1949, when the pro-Communist delegates were calling for the victory of the Chinese Communists in war, one British delegate had the courage to challenge the demonstration by asking: "Do you want peace now?" The honest and spontaneous answer came back with a roar: "No."[35]

Usually the Communist answer to such a question is neither honest nor spontaneous — nor brief. When William Z. Foster, chairman of the American Communist Party, was asked by Senator Homer Ferguson before the Senate Judiciary Committee in 1948, "If the Soviet Union attacks the United States, would you fight against the Soviet Union?" it took him 163 words to say "No" as follows:

> This line of questioning and the campaign of hysteria surrounding the Mundt Bill is an attempt to use the big lie technique of Hitler. It is an effort to conceal the fact that the United States government, under its present leadership, has embarked on a campaign to dominate the world, the most ruthless campaign of imperialist expansion in history.
>
> But I will gladly answer that question. If there is a war, the fault will lie not with the Soviet Union but with the Wall Street monopolists. The Soviet Union could never attack the United States or any other country, because it is a Socialist state. I could not conceive of such a possibility.
>
> If despite the efforts of the Soviet government and peace-loving people everywhere to prevent it, war did come, it would be an imperialist war and we Communists would oppose it. We would work to bring it to an end as quickly as possible on the basis of a democratic peace.[36]

Professor Sidney Hook has described how the Party's shifting line in the United States can be roughly appraised according to its shifting attitudes toward Franklin Roosevelt.[37] Before 1936, Roosevelt was called a fascist because it was then the general policy of Moscow to refer to all leaders of non-Communist governments as fascist. Then Moscow swerved from this too, too solid line of condemnation and tried a popular-front policy for a few years, even permitting Earl Browder, its American leader, to write a suave book on the reform of capitalism, treating Roosevelt as a well-meaning progressive. Then came the sudden and bewildering switch to the Stalin-Hitler alliance, and from 1939 to 1941 Roosevelt became an imperialist and warmonger. Then, with Hitler's invasion of the Soviet Union and Stalin's need for American arms, Roosevelt became a savior of the world's proletariat, and even Winston Churchill was transfigured in some Soviet literature into a genial reactionary with a large and rather amiable cigar.

In fact, the shifting Soviet attitude toward Churchill paralleled that toward Roosevelt. Before 1939 he was not so bad, because he fought Chamberlain's policy of appeasement. In the May Day parade in Chicago in 1941, during the period of the Hitler-Stalin pact, he was bannered as "an imperialist pig." Two months later he was a shrewd realist because he had come to the aid of Stalin against the German invasion. After his Fulton, Missouri, speech, he reassumed the pig role.

Today, of course, with the United States engaged in a cold-hot war with the Kremlin, Roosevelt's successor in the White House is called a warmonger, while the Communist movement, now stripped of all disguises, is serving openly and audaciously throughout the world as a Russian military conspiracy. All the standard elements of military deception are used in the conspiracy. Spying, sabotage, the promotion of defeatist sentiment, and the creation of general turmoil have become accepted Kremlin weapons in western countries. If and when "peace" should be worked out temporarily, new camouflages would replace the present openly conspiratorial tactics. When the eleven top leaders of the American Communist movement were sentenced to prison in 1950, the American Communist Party blandly announced a slight alteration in some of its textbooks for agitators, eliminating from those books the phrases advocating the overthrow of government by force and violence which had led to the conviction of the Party's leaders.[38] The maneuver deceived nobody; the Party line remains unchanged. In announcing the alteration of Communist textbooks the Party said that, of course, the courts could never "stop individuals from reading and studying any and all books, including the classics of Marxism-Leninism."

The Manipulation of Dogma

Behind all of these Communist techniques of deception lies a phenomenon which is more important than the Big Lie. For lack of a better definition it may be called the manipulation of dogma.

According to Communist philosophy the incidental beliefs by which men live are subject to alteration and adjustment to suit a revolutionary purpose. If faith in the revolution remains firm, everything else may be adjusted to that purpose. A review of Kremlin activity since the October revolution in 1917 would reveal that no single moral value, no sacred socialist doctrine, has remained exempt from the process of exploitation in behalf of the power system. In Kremlin philosophy ideas and doctrines are something to be *used*, and frequently they are used mercilessly. History, philosophy, and science must serve the Faith; and if the advancement of the Faith requires the alteration of history or the redirection of science and philosophy, so much the worse for history, science, and philosophy.

In practice, any doctrine of Communism may be added to or subtracted from the approved Marxian code on orders from the Kremlin, and when such a change takes place it is so carefully manipulated that the masses of the people are frequently not aware that a doctrinal shift has taken place. They go on repeating the same creed with the same intonation, believing that all Kremlin policies are solidly based on Marxian scriptures.

In the first days of the Bolshevik revolution, Russian socialism was quite equalitarian. Then, when the near-equality of incomes proved impractical and it became necessary to compromise with tradition by creating substantial differentials in wages, Stalin suddenly announced that "socialism is inequality."[39] After that the old doctrine of equality in wages became "counter-revolution." Good socialists vied with each other in denouncing it. By 1949 the statutes of the Russian trade unions referred to "The

Socialist Principles of Pay According to the Amount and Quality of Labor."[40] This was the new verbal dress for the familiar principle of payment by results developed in the American factory system. The principle was socialist by adoption, and the paternity was concealed.

When the Bolsheviks wanted to justify the continuing dictatorship of a single political party, they did not admit that they were twisting or perverting socialism. They simply loaded down one phrase of Karl Marx, the "dictatorship of the proletariat," with the whole weight of their lop-sided policy and made that phrase bear the burden of a permanent authoritarian system of power. Incidentally, there is an exact parallel here to the technique of the Vatican in placing the entire load of Catholic imperialism upon the single scriptural statement attributed to Jesus: "Thou art Peter, and upon this rock I will build my church." Actually, Karl Marx used the phrase "dictatorship of the proletariat" only once in his whole writings and only by over-emphasis and distortion can anyone find in his works a detailed justification for continuing dictatorship. In Communist propaganda, however, a continuing dictatorship in Moscow is hailed as "applied Marxism."

The Communist philosophy of family life has undergone a similar transformation. In the early days of the revolution, when the Communists considered it advantageous to release men from "bourgeois" loyalties and traditions, they encouraged extra-marital relations and poured contempt on the institution of the bourgeois family. The new Russians were permitted to secure divorces unilaterally by postcard, and abortions were made as easily available as the removal of tonsils. When the maintenance of family life and the increase of the Russian population became important to Kremlin power, the Kremlin reversed its field and launched a campaign against promiscuity and all modern departures from sexual convention.[41]

Divorces, which jumped to 38.3 per 100 marriages in 1935, have now become difficult and expensive, sometimes costing as much as 2,000 rubles. The Kremlin has become more and more hostile to birth control. Only therapeutic abortions are permissible, and they must be surrounded with careful safeguards. Soviet writers have recently attacked the "disorderly succession of husbands and wives" and have declared that "every parent must work toward training the future citizen to be happy only in family love and to seek the joys of sex life only in marriage." [42]

Most readers will agree with this teaching, but they are bound to feel some astonishment that the regime which preaches this gospel is the same Soviet regime which stressed contrary values early in the 1920's. Those very values which the Communists extolled in the twenties are now being derided as an integral part of "bourgeois marriage," without any admission that they were once hailed as modern and revolutionary. The new Russian Puritanism has even turned its guns on the nation which once hysterically accused the Bolsheviks of nationalizing Russian women. "Why are the most unbridled sexual perversions so shamelessly relished in [the United States]?" asks Z. Guseva, in the Soviet literary magazine, *Oktyabr*. "The amorality with which the entire capitalist world is imbued is expressed with particular intensity in attitudes toward women. . . . Depravity and prostitution go hand in hand with bourgeois marriage. . . . In contrast . . . proletarian morality reflects the new relationships taking shape in the workers' environment. . . . The question is not one of the disappearance of the family under socialism, as bourgeois-anarchist 'theoreticians' prophesied, but of its further strengthening and perfection, in none other than its monogamous form." [43]

In all these deviations and reversals in policy and doctrine, the Communist parties of the world virtually always place Russian interests ahead of consistency. That is the only reasonable explanation of the present, amazing indifference of the Kremlin to birth control as a vital social remedy for overpopulation. The Kremlin has virtually instructed the Communist movements throughout the world in recent years to slight birth control as a superficial and even undesirable remedy and to concentrate on economic and political reform as "fundamental." The reasoning behind this new Russian policy is quite transparent: Russia needs manpower for war against the west, and Russia has room to expand; therefore the Soviet Union should breed as many potential soldiers as possible. In 1933 Stalin boasted of an annual increase of three million in the population of the Soviet Union, as if that were an evidence of superiority over capitalist nations which reported a smaller proportionate increase. *Pravda* in commenting on the 1939 census said that "the might and power of Socialism finds clear expression in the unprecedented rapid tempo of population increase."[44]

At the same time, the Kremlin wants social revolutions in all the western nations, and overpopulation is one of the most effective means of producing a social revolution in a country which does not have room to expand. In many of the democratic European countries the misery produced by a too-rapid increase in population is Communism's chief ally. In countries like Italy it is doing far more than squadrons of Communist organizers to force the nation toward economic collapse.

Yet the Communists in Italy, following the Kremlin line, are obviously happy about this population pressure, and are encouraging it. At a time when the educated classes of Italy are desperately anxious to combat the Vatican's propaganda against birth control, the Moscow-controlled leadership of the Communist and left-wing Socialist parties tacitly sides with the Vatican by refusing to oppose the fascist laws which make contraception a crime.

By 1949 the Soviet philosophy of family life was almost indistinguishable in some of its aspects from that of the Catholic Church. It had different objectives, of course, but its central aim was to produce more Communists, as the central aim of Catholic policy on this subject is to produce more Catholics. In the Soviet Union in 1950, Communists were awarding the title "Mother-Heroine" to any Soviet woman who would bring up ten children. Mothers of seven to nine children were receiving a somewhat lesser distinction, the Medal of Maternal Glory, and mothers of five and six children the Motherhood Medal. All of these medals were accompanied with money payments.[45] It was reported in 1947 that the Soviet government had spent 14 billion rubles in eleven years in encouraging Russian mothers to have large families.[46] Special taxes were being levied on bachelors and spinsters, and upon parents who had only two children. Even group sex education in Soviet schools was encountering serious obstacles, not entirely unlike the obstacles to scientific sex education in American public schools created by priestly propaganda.

In fact, a number of Catholic writers have hailed recent Soviet sexual philosophy as a vindication of the fundamental correctness of the Catholic position on family values. "Bitter experience," boasted the Catholic magazine *America* in 1949, "has taught the Soviet rulers what Americans have yet to learn: stable family life is essential to the continued well-being of a nation."[47] "Communism," declared Monsignor Fulton Sheen on an American radio hookup, "in its greatest defeat proclaims the victory of the family over the class, the person over the proletariat, the fireside and the child over the hammer and the sickle."[48]

Adjusted History

If a moral philosophy of life and a whole scheme of economic values can be shifted in this manner to the right or to the left, how much more easily can history be rewritten! Historical truths, like sexual values, can be redirected and redefined according to Kremlin directives. Trotsky, second only to Lenin in the Bolshevik revolution, was wiped out of Russian history books, and his role in the revolution almost completely erased from the Russian mind, by deliberate falsification. Trotsky had committed the unforgivable sin of challenging Stalin — and it was not enough to exile him and then murder him. The very historical fact of Leon Trotsky's life and work must be manipulated out of Russian memory. The mention of his name is not permissible in the Soviet Union except in terms of denunciation. I remember the horror upon the faces of some Russian friends of mine when we were viewing a demonstration in the Red Square of Moscow and I asked sardonically: "Where is Trotsky?"

The task of destroying Trotsky as a fact of Russian history has been performed, and today he has become a half-forgotten traitor in the minds of the Soviet people whose fathers honored him as the peer of Lenin. Stalin not only helped to destroy his life and his reputation, but, having once disposed of a leading rival, he calmly appropriated nearly all of his major ideas and claimed them as his own. Communist history also had to be rewritten extensively after the great purge of 1936-37 when the "old Bolsheviks" were killed off in a savage wave of reprisals. Once these men had been heroes and builders of the nation who ranked with Stalin in responsibility and far exceeded him in popularity. Stalin revised their reputation after 1936 by revising the standard *Short History of the Communist Party of the Soviet Union.*

Then he withdrew from circulation the old books that glorified the old heroes. "The new book of Communist history," says Isaac Deutscher in his biography of Stalin, "which was at once declared to be the Bible of the party, was written by Stalin's secretaries under his personal guidance."[49]

The past history of Russia and European civilization has also been rewritten in a Stalinist mold in order to group all events into a progressive Marxian sequence, culminating in "planned economy and triumphant socialist construction in the USSR." The famous Russian historian, Eugene Tarlé, had pointed out in his *Bonaparte* that the peasants of Russia "took no part" in a national war against Napoleon's invasion of the country in 1812 but left the unpleasant job to the army, and that there was "not a single national mass revolt against the French." This was an outrageous admission for a historian to make in a Communist country, so Professor Tarlé was publicly reprimanded, and promptly produced a new version of the Napoleonic invasion of Russia which was acceptable to Stalin. According to the revised history, Bonaparte encountered among the peasants an "insatiable hatred toward the usurpers, marauders and oppressors." "According to the unanimous opinion of the French," said the repentant Professor Tarlé, "absolutely nowhere except in Spain did the peasants in the villages show such desperate resistance as in Russia. . . . The *entire* war against the invading Napoleon was solidly a national war. . . . It was the people's arm that inflicted upon the greatest commander in the world's history the irreparable, fatal blow."[50]

Sometimes the Kremlin's shifts of policies and principle in a country are so abrupt and inexplicable that the sudden change exposes the movement to humiliation and ridicule. In 1946 and 1947, when Communists were co-operating with other political parties in Italy and hoping to work out a coalition which would dominate the government, the Party leaders suddenly united with their arch-enemies, the Catholic Christian Democrats, to incorporate into the new Italian constitution the Lateran agreements of 1929 between Mussolini and the Vatican. By this maneuver the Communists infuriated the Socialists and horrified the independent liberals. They executed this surrender of their principles in behalf of expediency on the theory that they might make inroads into the Catholic masses. Although Palmiro Togliatti made a forceful speech in the Constituent Assembly in Rome against the principles of the concordat, he abandoned his principles for expediency and justified his action on the ground that Communists believed in religious freedom, the separation of church and state, and the elimination of unnecessary controversy at such a moment.

It would be difficult to discover a clearer misrepresentation. The Kremlin has never stood for religious freedom as democrats understand that concept, or for the separation of church and state in reality. In the Soviet Union today, the Russian Orthodox Church is virtually an arm of the state, controlled by a joint council of Communist ministers and bishops. The very Lateran agreement, which Togliatti helped to impose upon the Italian people by his compromise with the Christian Democrats, denies the separation of church and state to Italy and perpetuates religious discrimination in favor of the Vatican. Togliatti, well trained in Moscow, felt no obligation to be either truthful or consistent when it suited his purpose to swing the whole Italian Communist movement to the right at the expense of a free culture.

Usually Communist strategy is not so transparently stupid. Frequently its adjustments and compromises have been more tactful. But the fact that such shifts in the most fundamental doctrines of the Faith can be made entirely from above, without even an admission by the Kremlin hierarchy that its creed has been altered, shows how subordinate truth has become in this particular totalitarian system of power. In the Soviet system today truth is habitually treated as a handmaiden of political strategy. All history, all science, and all learning are managed in such a way that they echo the Voice in the Kremlin. The truth has not been formally abandoned, but all truth and all moral values have become part of the Soviet apparatus of power.

10

The Management of Truth: the Vatican

SINCE PERSONAL INTEGRITY is a cornerstone of Catholic morals, the Catholic attitude toward truth is a far cry from Communist cynicism. Throughout the ages the Church has promoted honesty — or has it? The question deserves more than a casually affirmative answer. Certainly the Church has promoted and advanced *personal* honesty. Its priests and people do not intentionally deceive, and they are in good faith loyal to the highest standard of human integrity. But the social strategy of a militant and partisan institution sometimes has a moral, or immoral, character entirely apart from the consciences of its individual members. Institutional power molds men and corrupts their character. When Britain's great Catholic historian, Lord Acton, voiced his famous aphorism, "Power tends to corrupt and absolute power corrupts absolutely," he was directing his shafts at least in part against the leaders of his own Church.

As an institution in this world the Vatican has learned to manipulate and manage truth in strange ways in furthering its world-wide program. It has learned to shade history, exploit human ignorance, and disguise its undemocratic policies, all for the greater glory of truth as it is conceived by a hierarchy which accepts its chieftain as a fountain of truth.

This last strategy, the disguise of undemocratic policy, is so important in the Catholic system of power that I shall discuss it in some detail. It has been used in the United States, especially, in connection with the church-state issue. Two leading figures of American Catholicism have been particularly involved — the late governor Alfred E. Smith, and the American hierarchy's leading personage at the present time, Cardinal Spellman.

I have pointed out in Chapter 3, "The Vatican Structure of

Power," that the Vatican by its own definition is a monarchy, that it developed in a pre-democratic era, and that one of the cornerstones of its system of power has been partial union of the Church with sympathetic governments. No pope has ever repudiated this traditional policy of Church establishment, and many popes have repudiated in the most specific language the doctrine of the separation of church and state. Pius IX in his *Syllabus of Errors* in 1864 branded as one of "the principal errors of our time" the statement that "The Church ought to be separated from the State, and the State from the Church." Leo XIII in 1888 called the separation of church and state a "fatal principle."[1] No true Catholic can agree with the doctrine of church-state separation in its American constitutional form and remain loyal to Vatican policy, because the two are absolutely incompatible. The Vatican doctrine includes the claim that the state owes the Church at least partial monetary support in carrying out its mission. The American constitutional doctrine, as interpreted by the Supreme Court, excludes any such claim.

There are two ways in which this direct contradiction between Vatican and American policy on church and state can be concealed. One way is to define the Catholic doctrine in terms that have double meanings. The other is to "interpret" the Constitution so that it will say something which it does not say. The American hierarchy is using both of these devices of deception at the present time, and in addition it is attempting to minimize the fundamental clash between the theory of Vatican moral imperialism and the theory of national sovereignty.

The American hierarchy is finding it very difficult to square the world-wide record of the Vatican with American tradition. In every Catholic nation and sector in the world today, the Vatican is receiving or seeking public funds for its enterprises — Spain, Italy, Portugal, Quebec, Argentina, Belgium, Ireland, etc. Even in many non-Catholic nations and sectors, the Vatican is asking and receiving similar favors — the Netherlands, Great Britain, West Germany, Switzerland, and Ontario. It is the settled and official policy of Rome to work in every nation for a privileged imperial position, if possible guaranteed by a formal concordat. We have already seen that the privileges demanded as a matter of right by the Vatican include the exemption of priests and nuns from prosecution in government criminal courts; the receipt of public funds for schools, hospitals, and other welfare enterprises; and the complete clerical control of the marriage, separation, and divorce of all Catholics. These special privileges are characteristic and permanent features of the world policy of the Vatican as a moral empire operating in all nations by divine right.

The frank description of these facts about the Vatican's church-state policy would be very unfortunate from the hierarchy's point of view, especially in countries like the United States. The American people have accepted the doctrine of the separation of church and state as one of their most distinctive and praiseworthy contributions to social progress, and they would deal quite briskly with any church which challenged that doctrine by a frontal attack. They would not relish the thought that any American citizens should continue to be subjects of a foreign empire, even in respect to a very limited area of conduct. Hence the Catholic hierarchy in the United States has felt obligated to adopt various semantic disguises for the Vatican's church-state policy.

One of its most transparent devices is to use the word "accept" with a double meaning, and to announce that it "accepts" the American Constitution and the separation of church and state. As we shall see later, the American Catholic bishops do not, by this "acceptance," express any fundamental *agreement* with the doctrine as expounded by the Supreme Court, or pledge themselves not to fight against it. They merely accept it as a temporary condition, in the sense of admitting that they are subject to American law and have no intention of willfully violating the law, but never for a moment abandoning the Catholic ideal of a union of church and state.

Catholic clerical leaders justify their apparent equivocation on such matters by the so-called theory of *thesis* and *hypothesis*. The thesis is the truth or principle which the Church stands for eternally; the hypothesis is the truth or principle modified by circumstances. Professor George La Piana has described the distinction in these words:

> The thesis is the doctrine of the Church which, having its fountain head in the divine revelation, is eternal, unchangeable, and not affected by human events or circumstances of times and places. The hypothesis,

on the contrary, is the sum total of the circumstances of times and places which make nigh impossible, or extremely difficult or even dangerous, any effort to apply the thesis. In such cases, the Church in making agreements with the state does not insist on the application of the thesis and limits its claims according to the hypothesis.[2]

This theory makes it clear why Catholic bishops in the United States can declare, as they have done repeatedly, that they believe in the separation of church and state "without equivocation." Most people would infer from such an utterance that the hierarchy thereby commits itself without reservation to the American doctrine of the separation of church and state. Not so. The bishops accept the doctrine as a temporary hypothesis, a statement of principle which comes as near as practicable to the Catholic principle for the time being; but they do not thereby abandon the thesis.

An excellent illustration of what American Catholic bishops really mean when they "endorse" the separation of church and state appeared in the Catholic press in the United States in 1948 in a series of syndicated articles on Portugal from the National Catholic Welfare Conference News Service. They were written by a Catholic writer, Eugene Bagger. This news service is, of course, directly controlled by the Catholic bishops of the United States who *are* the National Catholic Welfare Conference. This series of articles, almost wholly favorable to the semi-fascist dictatorship of Salazar, said flatly in describing conditions in Portugal: "Separation of Church and State is maintained." In the same article the author said: "Instruction in morals, to be given in State schools to all pupils whose parents do not claim exemption, and in all orphanages, includes elements of Catholic doctrine and apologetics as well as Gospel and Church history." The children in Portuguese public schools, of course, do not receive instruction in any non-Catholic religion. And the author added, in describing the terms of the Vatican-Portuguese agreements of May 7, 1940:

> The Government subsidizes all [Catholic] missionary bodies in the Portuguese colonies; provides building sites for [Catholic] churches, schools, etc.; pays the salaries of Bishops and vicars and prefects apostolic, the expense of missionaries traveling from Portugal to the colonies and back, and missionary pensions.[3]

Such a description makes it clear what the American Catholic bishops really mean when they say that they favor the separation of church and state. They are using Catholic-Portuguese terms in speaking to an American audience which uses words in a different sense. They are willing to describe any relationship of church and state short of complete identification as "separation," and permit American non-Catholics to think that they sincerely accept separation in the American sense.

Glossary of Double Talk

The three words which are most commonly used with double meanings by defenders of Vatican policy are "freedom," "democracy," and "conscience." We have already seen that the Church teaches the limitation of intellectual freedom by denying Catholics the right to read any books or magazines which directly refute Catholic dogma or discipline. Thus the Church denies the basic ingredient of freedom of thought, which is the right to receive unrestricted information. Because this denial is in fundamental conflict with the American conception of freedom, the defenders of Catholic power consider it necessary to create a definition of freedom which will include the Vatican variety. In practice, as Dr. Paul Hutchinson of the *Christian Century* has pointed out, the Catholic leader who talks about freedom usually means the freedom of the Church, whereas the Protestant leader means the freedom of the individual.

The Catholic hierarchy recognizes the importance of individual freedom to *accept* Catholic teaching, and it has created a definition of individual freedom to conform to that notion. John Redden and Francis A. Ryan in their standard Catholic work, *Freedom Through Education,* say that: "Freedom implies the capacity to choose morally. To make this choice the individual must be able to discern between what is right and what is wrong. . . . If he chooses evil, his conduct is sinful and deserves condemnation. If he chooses good, his conduct is virtuous and merits reward. Freedom means, then, the ability to do what one ought to do: that is, to do what is right, just, lawful, and to avoid what is evil. In other words, freedom means man's power within himself to act in conformity to his rational nature." The authors go on to explain that "in order to know what one ought to do, it is necessary first of all, to know what is true. . . . There are truths in the moral order, as well as in the scientific world, which must be accepted on authority. . . . Authority, then, at times, must necessarily substitute temporarily for freedom in those matters wherein proper temporal and spiritual good makes reasonably evident the necessity for substitution."[4]

Thus, by a full circle in reasoning, the right to choose a course of action has become the duty to accept Catholic authority, and freedom has become obedience. Catholic apologetic literature is full of such sleight-of-hand transitions. Father John A. O'Brien, on page 133 of his *The Faith of Millions,* says: "There is a legitimate freedom and an illegitimate one. The first is the freedom of believing the truth. The second is the freedom of believing error, which is in reality an abuse of the mind and constitutes a form of intellectual anarchy. No one has a right to believe error anymore than one has the right to do wrong." And the definition of moral error, of course, rests with the Church.

A similar limitation is noticeable in the Catholic definition of conscience. The conscience, in Catholic terminology, is not a free organ or agent; it is an organ of ratification or agreement. "What is conscience?" asks Father John C. Heenan in his *Priest and Penitent.* "It is not a separate faculty of the soul. It is a practical judgment of the mind by which we are able to decide regarding the morality of behaviour." So far so good. But then Father Heenan goes on: "It is the application of the law of God to a particular action. It follows that when two people judge differently of the morality of a course of action, both cannot have a true conscience, unless, which would be absurd, all morality is subjective. A right conscience is one which dictates behaviour in conformity with the law of God. A false conscience allows behaviour which is contrary to the law."[5] It follows that the conscience which denies Catholic dogma has no rights because it is in error.

Thus the word "conscience," which the non-Catholic uses to describe an organ or faculty of individual judgment, becomes in Catholic semantics the collective conscience of the Catholic clergy, which is dictated by the Pope. Cardinal Gibbons, in addressing Protestants, said: "Yes, we obey the Pope, for our conscience tells us that we ought to obey the spiritual authority of the Pope in everything except what is sinful . . . while you believe in private judgment, we believe in a religion of authority which our conscience tells us is our lawful guide and teacher in its own sphere."[6] In this sense the individual Catholic conscience is simply the echo of the conscience of the priests.

The Catholic attitude toward democracy is somewhat more frank. The Vatican has always scorned democracy for itself, but it permits its priests in democratic countries a belief in limited democracy so long as it does not apply to or limit the power of the Vatican. This means in practice that a democracy or a dictatorship is good according to its attitude toward the Vatican. No American Catholic leader has ever summed up the Vatican attitude more accurately than the famous stormy petrel of New England, Orestes Brownson, who became a convert to Catholicism. In his *Quarterly* in 1845 he said: "Democracy is a mischievous dream wherever the Catholic Church does not predominate to inspire the people with reverence and to accustom them to obedience to authority."[7] Brownson is still regarded by many Catholic leaders as "the greatest all around thinker America has ever produced." These words of description are taken from the *Liguorian,* the magazine of the Redemptorist order which is now attempting to proselyte for the Faith in Brownson's home state of Vermont; and a writer in that journal adds: "Like a blacksmith, pounding out his arguments with bold and sinewy strength, this rough giant has left a treasury of perfectly wrought phrases to meet the political problems that must again and again confront the Church."[8]

"Always and everywhere," says George N. Shuster, "the essential indifferentism of the Church to forms of government or culture has abided as a principle, even though it may occasionally have been lost sight of in practice."[9] This doctrine of indifferentism means in practice that dictatorship in Spain and democracy in the Netherlands are both heartily praised by Catholic authorities because the Vatican is well treated by both, and that dictatorship in Poland and democracy in Sweden are both denounced for the contrary reason. The Vatican permits its American bishops to praise democracy heartily *for the United States,* but simultaneously praises Franco for exactly the opposite qualities.

The Brooklyn *Tablet,* leading American diocesan paper, printed in its official question-and-answer column, under the name of Father Raymond J. Neufeld, on May 28, 1949, the following revealing question and answer:

QUESTION. *Is a dictatorship morally wrong in the eyes of the Church?*
ANSWER. A dictatorship is a form of government in which one person is appointed to rule with absolute authority. Such a form of government can be morally good or evil, depending on the justice or injustice of its rule. First of all, the dictator must have a right to his position. If he came by his power unjustly, then his dictatorship is morally wrong. Secondly, the government under a dictator must acknowledge God as the supreme author of all law. No man has authority except it come from God. Thirdly, the inalienable rights of all the subjects of the government must be respected and preserved.

Dictatorship as it operates in Russia, as it operated in Germany under Hitler and in Italy under Mussolini is morally wrong. These three isms are based on the Karl Marx theory of government in which the State is supreme, going so far as to deny the existence of God. The rights of the citizenry are completely denied, since in Russia the individual is the property of the state.

The dictatorship in Spain, on the other hand, is morally good, public opinion to the contrary notwithstanding. The Franco government was established in a defense against the Russian influence in Spain. Though Franco is a dictator, he acknowledges the existence and the supremacy of God and he respects the God-given rights of the people.

Al Smith as Spokesman

In 1928 the under-cover conflict between the Catholic and the American conceptions of church and state power suddenly came into the open when one of the ablest products of machine politics and American Catholicism, Governor Alfred E. Smith, was nominated for the presidency by the Democratic Party. What happened then is history, and I do not propose to repeat it here. In 1928 I was personally very critical of the tactics used in defeating Al Smith and I deeply regretted that defeat. From the point of view of this narrative, the significant feature of the campaign was the patent dishonesty of the Catholic hierarchy in remaining silent while a Catholic candidate made public a personal interpretation of Catholic policy on church and state which did not accurately reflect the Vatican's position.

Al Smith was confronted by a series of searching questions from a distinguished New York lawyer, Charles C. Marshall, published in the *Atlantic Monthly*. He replied with a series of statements of his belief, statements that were in part directly contrary to Catholic doctrine and policy. He declared that public education was the function of the state. He said:

> I recognize no power in the institutions of my Church to interfere with the operations of the Constitution of the United States or the enforcement of the law of the land. I believe in absolute freedom of conscience for all men and in equality of all churches, all sects, and all beliefs before the law as a matter of right and not as a matter of favor. I believe in the absolute separation of Church and State and in the strict enforcement of the provisions of the Constitution that Congress shall make no law respecting an establishment of religion or prohibiting the free exercise thereof. I believe that no tribunal of any church has any power to make any decree of any force in the law of the land, other than to establish the status of its own communicants within its own church. I believe in the support of the public school as one of the cornerstones of American liberty. I believe in the right of every parent to choose whether his child shall be educated in the public school or in a religious school supported by those of his own faith.[10]

Probably Al Smith was perfectly sincere in making this statement. It is more than likely that he had never taken the time to study the policies of his own Church outside of the United States, and he undoubtedly took at face value the adroit words used by the hierarchy in presenting Vatican policies in American dress. Perhaps he had never even heard of Pius IX's *Syllabus of Errors* in which the doughty champion of blunt speaking had claimed superior rights over every temporal government by denouncing as error the statement: "In the case of conflicting laws enacted by the two powers [church and state], the civil law prevails." Such ignorance of Vatican doctrine and policy on the part of American Catholics is not uncommon, and it frequently astonishes non-Catholic observers. In Smith's case, his statement is alleged (probably correctly) to have been written by the famous chaplain, Father Duffy, whose monument now stands at the northern end of Times Square in New York. Father Duffy was such an advanced theological liberal that he was an active friend of the noted (and excommunicated) Catholic professor of the University of Rome, Ernesto Buonaiuti. Because of that liberalism he was never given due recognition by the American hierarchy after his return from World War I, and he quietly took revenge on his reactionary superiors by helping to promulgate a statement of the Catholic outlook that must have horrified the theologians of the Holy Office.

After the campaign of 1928 it soon became apparent how overgenerous Al Smith and Father Duffy had been in interpreting the doctrines of the Vatican, and also how mistaken those American Catholics had been who had accepted the Smith interpretation of papal policies as official. On February 11, 1929, the Vatican agreement with Mussolini was made public. It represented Vatican policy in the Church's home country at the most exalted level. The Church had been negotiating it at the very moment when the American hierarchy permitted Al Smith's interpretations of Catholic policy to go unchallenged. Then, within two years after the Vatican agreement with Mussolini, Pius XI underscored the Church's claims of power in the modern state by issuing two important encyclicals on *Christian Marriage* and on *Christian Education of Youth*. The three documents taken together, the two encyclicals and the consolidated Vatican-Mussolini agreements of 1929, can be put side by side with Al Smith's interpretation of Catholic doctrine with devastating effect. (The major portions of the 1929 concordat are printed in the Appendix.)

Al Smith declared that he recognized no power in the institutions of his Church to interfere with the operation and enforcement of the Constitution and laws of the United States. The Vatican in its home country has used its power to write into the Italian constitution by reference a whole set of special regulations on religion, education, and domestic relations which limit the legislative power of the Italian people. The Vatican claims that these regulations, since they are contained in a treaty with an independent foreign power (the Vatican), cannot be abrogated by a mere majority decision of the Italian people except with the Vatican's express consent.[11] Hence, the Lateran agreements, as incorporated in the present Italian constitution in 1946, give the Vatican super-national rights over education, marriage, divorce, and the public employment of ex-priests; and they give Catholicism recognition as the sole official religion of the state.

Pius XI in his 1930 encyclical on *Christian Marriage* not only disputed the right of *any* government to pass divorce laws, but asserted the supremacy of Vatican law above all other law in regard to the sterilization of the feeble-minded and, by clear implication, prohibited any Catholic judge from enforcing such a law when he said that the government's power over such a matter was a "power over a faculty which it never had and can never legitimately possess."[12]

In American Catholic schools, at the time of Al Smith's statement, the children were being taught that the Vatican had a moral right to annul the laws of the United States and other nations in several particulars. The *Manual of Christian Doctrine* of the famous Catholic teaching order, the Brothers of the Christian Schools, published in 1926 in Philadelphia with the Imprimatur of Cardinal Dougherty, contained this passage:

> Why is the Church superior to the State?
> Because the end to which the Church tends is the noblest of all ends.
> In what order or respect is the State subordinate to the Church?
> In the spiritual order and in all things referring to that order.
> What right has the Pope in virtue of this supremacy?
> The right to annul those laws or acts of government that would injure the salvation of souls or attack the natural rights of citizens.[13]

Al Smith declared that he believed in the equality of churches. This is one of the beliefs which the hierarchy denounces at every opportunity, and in Catholic countries it will never permit its people to recognize the equality of Protestantism in any way. In the Italian concordat, the Vatican not only won special treatment for itself as "the sole religion of the state"; but it won, in the Italian laws of 1930, which supplemented the concordat (now sections 402-406 of the Italian Criminal Code), a concession which read: "Whoever publicly slanders the [Catholic] religion of the State shall be punished with imprisonment for one year." The same sections of the code provide a *different* penalty for the slandering of non-Catholic religions, declaring that in such cases *"the punishment shall be diminished"* (italics added). Many prosecutions have occurred in recent years in Italy in which the defendants have been convicted of slandering the Pope, both as a religious leader and as head of a foreign power (the Vatican), but the most vicious slanders of Protestant leaders, which are circulated in official Catholic booklets, are unchallenged by the law. An even worse story of discrimination can be written about Spain, where Protestant churches are not even allowed to bear any external symbols showing that they are churches.

Al Smith declared that he believed in the absolute separation of church and state. In spite of that personal conviction, his Church was expressing at that moment opposite opinions and policies in virtually every Catholic country of the world. The 1926 *Manual of Christian Doctrine,* which I have quoted above, had this to say about non-Catholic faiths and the separation of church and state:

What then is the principal obligation of heads of States?
Their principal obligation is to practice the Catholic religion themselves, and, as they are in power, to protect and defend it.

Has the State the right and the duty to proscribe schism or heresy?
Yes, it has the right and the duty to do so both for the good of the nation, and for that of the faithful themselves; for religious unity is the principal foundation of social unity.

When may the State tolerate dissenting worships?
When these worships have acquired a sort of legal existence consecrated by time and accorded by treaties or covenants.

May the State separate itself from the Church?
No, because it may not withdraw from the supreme rule of Christ. . . .

On what conditions are civil laws binding?
. . . That the legislating power has no law contrary to the natural law, or to the positive divine law; otherwise a civil law is entirely null, and should not be observed.[14]

I have quoted these two passages from the famous *Manual of Christian Doctrine,* from the edition of 1926, to show that this was the teaching of the Catholic Church at the time Al Smith wrote his faulty analysis. *But this is also the teaching of the Catholic Church today.* These passages occur word for word in the 1949 edition of this same work, and this work is the standard manual for training American Catholic high-school students in the fundamentals of their faith *today.*

Why did the American hierarchy permit Al Smith to misrepresent some of its basic teachings by ignoring such official statements? Certainly any Catholic political leader in Europe who had made such faulty pronouncements on Catholic policy would have been promptly rebuked for departure from the Faith. The answer, I suppose, lies in the realm of larger Vatican strategy. The Vatican is operated by very practical men who have learned from necessity to adjust their policies to left-wing governments or anti-clerical parties or secular democracies without any qualms of conscience, so long as they do not lose sight of the ultimate objectives of Catholic power. The Church's leaders are able simultaneously to appear in Spain as supporters of a reactionary Catholic dictator, in Belgium as champions of monarchy, and in the United States as friends of complete democracy. In 1928, as long as the priests themselves did not officially and formally approve of Al Smith's interpretations of Catholic policy, it was considered quite feasible for the hierarchy to remain silent. The Church leaders recognized the enormous potential gains that might accrue from convincing the American people that they had nothing to fear from Vatican political designs. A charitable American press, in the case of Charles C. Marshall versus Al Smith, glossed over the fact that Marshall in his subsequent writings demolished Al Smith's picture of Catholicism.[15]

Ever since 1928 the American hierarchy has continued to picture its policy on the separation of church and state as supremely American. The apparent agreement between Vatican and American policy on this point is produced by using words in special senses. Catholic writers, for example, use the phrase "temporal power" in a narrow significance to deny that the Vatican has any temporal powers outside of its own tiny kingdom. An American Catholic leader, Father J. Elliott Ross, said in a book on *Religions of Democracy:* "The Pope has no civil or temporal authority over Catholics in the United States. It is true that the Pope is a temporal sovereign, but his temporal authority is restricted to Vatican City."[16] This sounds plausible, but it is based upon an artificially narrowed interpretation of the word "temporal." The truth is that the Pope actually has a great deal of temporal power over Catholics not only in countries which have made concordats with the Vatican, but over American Catholics as well. The whole financial administration of the American Church is controlled from Rome, and all its physical assets are, in the last analysis, owned by the Pope. Its buildings are held by bishops acting as corporate papal agents, and the Catholic people have no share in the titles.

The Pope's authority in the United States also extends into many areas which American citizens consider both temporal and political. The public school is certainly a temporal institution, and so is an American court. The Pope imposes penalties on American citizens for sending their children to public schools under certain circumstances, and he likewise imposes equally severe penalties upon American citizens for suing Catholic bishops in American courts.

American Catholics, according to Archbishop Cushing of Boston in an advertisement circulated by the Knights of Columbus, "accept the Constitution without reserve, with no desire, as Catholics, to see it changed in any feature." This also sounds exceedingly persuasive, but there is a snare in the pronouncement. Catholic leaders accept the Constitution *with the Catholic interpretation of the First Amendment*. The Catholic interpretation of the First Amendment is that the Constitution permits the federal government to pay public funds to Catholic enterprises so long as the Catholic Church is not the *sole* established church. This Catholic interpretation of the First Amendment was announced by the Catholic bishops of the United States in 1948, and all subsequent statements of the hierarchy on this problem must be read in the light of that official interpretation. The Catholic bishops still interpret the phrase "separation of church and state" to mean that the two institutions should be separated *after* their Church has succeeded in winning life-giving revenues from the government.

In their attack on the Supreme Court the bishops deplored the fact that the Court's interpretation of the First Amendment "would bar any co-operation between government and organized religion which would aid religion, even where no discrimination between religious bodies is in question." In their opinion the amendment bars only *"preferential treatment to one religion as against another,"* and they pledge themselves to "peacefully, patiently and perseveringly work" to get the Supreme Court to revise its "novel interpretation."[17] The bishops will undoubtedly encounter some difficulties in this task of persuasion, since the decision of the Supreme Court which they attack was handed down by a vote of 8 to 1. But, in the meantime, they do not morally accept even an 8-to-1 judgment, and their declarations of allegiance to the First Amendment must all be interpreted in the light of their own semantic reservation.

It should be pointed out also that while the Catholic bishops in the United States appeal to the alleged principle of the equal rights of religious groups to receive government support under our Constitution, the Church itself never recognizes the right of any other church to receive government support in any Catholic country. If the United States became a Catholic country, there is no doubt that the American bishops would soon abandon their alleged scruples on the subject and would demand government money for the Catholic Church alone.

Some Catholic writers have tried to strengthen the Catholic interpretation of the First Amendment by reinterpreting the writings of early American leaders like Jefferson and Madison to make it appear that they were perfectly willing to permit public expenditures for religious institutions in some cases. Perhaps the most extreme interpretation of this type has been made by James M. O'Neill, a Catholic teacher of oratory in Brooklyn College. In his book *Religion and Education Under the Constitution*, he takes such a bizarre position that even the Jesuit magazine *America*, which had denounced "the judicial tyranny" of the Supreme Court in the McCollum case and suggested the duty to resist such tyranny when "precious values of human life are at stake," attacked him because he "tries to prove too much."[18] That the Catholic interpretation of the First Amendment is a partisan and twisted interpretation will be evident to anyone who studies the record of the public discussions which led up to the adoption of that amendment. Our forefathers had the good sense to object to government support not only for *one* church but for *any* church. They could have provided in the Constitution — as North Carolina actually did in its constitution of 1776 — that there should be "no establishment of any one religious church or denomination in this state in preference to any other. . . ." What they said was: "Congress shall make no law respecting an establishment of religion." It is true that Jefferson's interpretation that the First Amendment aimed to "erect a wall of separation between church and state" was not written into the Constitution itself — but that interpretation was almost universally accepted by his contemporaries, and those contemporaries are more acceptable guides in such a matter than a group of present-day Catholic bishops.

In a sense the effort of some Catholic writers to shift the argument on church and state problems into constitutional channels is based on a desire to avoid direct discussion of the problem as a current reality. The main church-state issue in the United States today is not what Madison and Jefferson thought about the separation of church and state but what the American people today think about the *wisdom* of allowing any church to get support from public revenues. Even if our forefathers had all favored government financial support for churches — as some of them did — there would be a strong moral case against it today in a nation nearly half of whose people do not belong to any church. If our founding fathers had not written the First Amendment into the Constitution, we would feel compelled to write it in today. The American policy of separation has proved itself in the American experience, regardless of its constitutional sanction. It is strong enough to stand on its own legs without the help of constitutional lawyers. The rule that public money should not be paid for religious enterprises is perhaps the most distinctive and certainly one of the happiest features of our democracy, and it undoubtedly has the support of an overwhelming majority of the American people. The Catholic hierarchy is not permitted to go along with this American policy, and it embarrasses American Catholic laymen to admit that their Church is attempting to force them to make a choice between their Constitution and their Pope. Accordingly, to gloss over the unpleasant fact of this conflict and its significance, the hierarchy has evolved the theory that the Constitution does not really mean what the Supreme Court says it means. This stratagem at least postpones the unhappy day when the Catholics of the United States must make a moral choice between two sovereignties.

The Spellman-Roosevelt Controversy

The members of the American Catholic hierarchy contended with much vehemence that the defeat of Al Smith was due largely to "anti-Catholicism"; and they meant by this term personal bigotry and prejudice against Catholic citizens because they were Catholics. Unfortunately, there was some truth in their charge, and fair-minded Americans have never ceased to deplore the prejudice and passions that were aroused during the Al Smith campaign.

But there was also in the anti-Smith camp a great deal of clear-eyed and unprejudiced apprehension about the possible effect of placing in the White House a man who was even nominally a disciple of a foreign power claiming certain rights over several million American Catholics in respect to important civic responsibilities. This apprehension seemed justified when, in the 1930's and 1940's, the hierarchy began to encroach upon the constitutional principle of the separation of church and state with the active support of Catholic legislators. The erosion was at first very slight and purely local, but the process soon became national.

The hierarchy had discovered in the Al Smith campaign that the technique of camouflage and counter-attack on the church-state issue was quite feasible in dealing with an electorate unfamiliar with Catholic policies in other countries. Most Americans in 1928 did not know that the Catholic policy in Catholic countries like Spain, Portugal, and Italy flatly contradicted the picture of Catholic policy drawn by Al Smith. Although Al Smith was overwhelmingly defeated, the hierarchy did not suffer much loss of prestige. Church leaders successfully raised the cry of "anti-Catholic bigotry" against their critics, and many Americans who opposed Al Smith for perfectly honest and adequate reasons felt a little ashamed of themselves. They hesitated to be associated with denominational criticism directly or indirectly, even when the denominational critics were correct in their analysis of the potential danger to American institutions. The hierarchy took full advantage of the sensitiveness of most Americans about criticizing any church, and continued to denounce as "anti-Catholic" any leaders of public life who spoke frankly about Catholic demands on the public purse. This technique of vilification and counter-attack was well illustrated in the famous exchange of letters between Cardinal Spellman and Mrs. Roosevelt in 1949.

The immediate occasion for the Spellman-Roosevelt controversy was the fight in Congress by Catholic legislators for the inclusion of parochial schools in the program of federal aid for education. In a decision in 1948, the Supreme Court had, by implication, made direct aid to Catholic schools unconstitutional, but it had already *permitted* the use of such funds for such auxiliary services as textbooks and school buses.[19] The Catholic hierarchy, seeing the opportunity to get federal money for a vital part of the Church establishment, opened a great campaign for federal contributions for parochial school buses. Representative Graham Barden of North Carolina had introduced in Congress a bill which cut squarely across the church-state battlefield by granting federal money to public schools without mentioning Catholic schools or their bus transportation.

Mrs. Eleanor Roosevelt, in a syndicated column in June 1949, came out for the traditional American principle of the use of public funds for public schools only, and said, among other things:

Those of us who believe in the right of any human being to belong to whatever church he sees fit, and to worship God in his own way, cannot be accused of prejudice when we do not want to see public education connected with religious control of the schools, which are paid for by taxpayers' money.

The reply of Cardinal Spellman is such a classic example of the hierarchy's propaganda methods that I have included the Spellman-Roosevelt exchange in the Appendix of this book. Here, it will be worth while to list several samples of the misrepresentations used by Cardinal Spellman, and his techniques in counter-attack.

(1) *". . . you aligned yourself with the author and other proponents of the Barden bill and condemned me for defending Catholic children against those who would deny them their constitutional rights of equality with other American children."*

There is no such thing as a constitutional right of Catholic children to get public money for any part of the Catholic educational enterprise. The Supreme Court *permits* the use of public funds for such auxiliary services as textbooks and buses for Catholic schools, but the policy involved is entirely a matter of free choice and discretion. The Supreme Court has indicated that the use of public funds for textbooks and buses represents the extreme limit of special privilege for religious schools permissible under the Constitution, and it has denied the right of state legislatures to give money directly to Catholic schools for their major operations. All American children are granted equality under our laws in the American public-school system at public expense without any distinction of creed. The Barden bill preserved this tradition of equality in a traditional manner.

(2) "... *you could have acted only from misinformation, ignorance or prejudice, not from knowledge and understanding.*"

This type of attack, from a man who has never been a lawyer, legislator, parent, or educator, is worth noting.

(3) "... *the Barden bill — the now famous, infamous bill that would unjustly discriminate against minority groups of America's children.*"

The one thing which the Barden bill did not do was to discriminate against *any* minority group. It provided public assistance for public schools only, where Methodists, Catholics, and Jews could receive benefits as Americans without discrimination. To provide special benefits from public funds for denominational schools would discriminate against the approximately 46 per cent of the American people who do not belong to any church.

(4) "... *I had intended ignoring your personal attack, but, as the days passed and in two subsequent columns you continued your anti-Catholic campaign, I became convinced that it was in the interest of all Americans and the cause of justice itself that your misstatements should be challenged . . .*"

The pretense that even the most broad-minded and tolerant citizens are "anti-Catholic" if they disagree with Vatican political or educational policy is the last refuge of the hierarchy in almost every public controversy. Unfortunately, it is so effective in the United States today that no ordinary legislator dares to risk the charge by honestly challenging any Catholic leader.

(5) "*You say you are against religious control of schools which are paid for by taxpayers' money. That is exactly what I, too, oppose.*"

This is an extremely adroit misrepresentation, quite typical of the more skillful manipulations of words used in some Catholic propaganda. Throughout the whole world the Catholic Church stands for public funds for Catholic schools, and the complete religious control of those tax-supported schools by the hierarchy. It has never abandoned its demands for such support, plus Catholic control, either in the United States or in any other nation. Almost every issue of Catholic diocesan papers in the United States contains some more-or-less veiled appeal for such support. In making the statement which he did, Cardinal Spellman could salve his conscience only by putting a special, casuistic interpretation upon the ordinary meanings of words. He does not *at the present time* ask for *construction* funds from the government for Catholic schools; and when he seeks government funds for *existing* schools, he can rightly say that they are not "paid for" by taxpayers' money, since they were built originally by the contributions of Catholic members. Ergo, he believes that he cannot be accused of wanting religious control of schools "paid for" by the taxpayers. But this is a juggling of words beneath the dignity of any man claiming moral leadership. All ordinary men would take the cardinal's statement as a renunciation of the demand for public money for Catholic schools; and the cardinal's Church has never made that renunciation.

The two Catholic members of the 1947 President's Commission on Higher Education were the only members of that 26-member board who refused to approve a report in favor of the use of funds for public colleges, and they based their refusal on the fact that the report did not recommend public funds for Catholic schools also. As I write these words in Rome late in 1950, Italy's Catholic Action, the direct political instrument of the Vatican, is engaged in a campaign for precisely the objective that Cardinal Spellman "renounced." In the month of the Spellman-Roosevelt controversy, June 1949, the Belgian Catholic (Christian Social) party, with Vatican support, won a national election on the issue of public money for Catholic schools, an election which the *Catholic News* described in these words: "Prior to the general election His Eminence Joseph Ernest Cardinal Van Roey, Archbishop of Malines, had issued a call for unity among Catholics in the elections in order to overcome the leftist campaign against Catholic schools in Belgium. One of the planks of the Christian Social [Catholic] platform called for government subsidies for all free education, including Catholic schools."[20]

(6) *"America's Catholic youth helped fight a long and bitter fight to save all Americans from oppression and persecution. Their broken bodies on blood-soaked foreign fields were grim and tragic testimony of this fact. . . . Would you deny equality to these Catholic boys . . . ? Would you deny their children equal rights and benefits with other sects — rights for which their fathers paid equal taxation with other fathers and fought two bitter wars that all children might forever be free from fear, oppression and religious persecution?"*

So did Methodists, Jews, and unbelievers — but they died as Americans, and their friends who respect their memory are not using their heroism as an argument for denominational special privilege.

After this exchange, the wave of public indignation against Cardinal Spellman was so intense that he was virtually forced to apologize to Mrs. Roosevelt, hat in hand. He issued a statement which attempted to correct the unfortunate impression by saying: "We are not asking for general public support of religious schools. . . . Under the Constitution we do not ask nor can we expect public funds to pay for the construction or repair of parochial school buildings or for the support of teachers, or for other maintenance costs. . . . We are asking Congress to do no more than to continue, in its first general aid-to-education measure, the non-discriminatory policy it has followed in the School Lunch Act and other Federal laws dealing with schools and school children." Not many persons were deceived. Cardinal Spellman had no authority to alter the world policy of the Vatican which demands public money for Catholic educational enterprises. He could waive this demand as a temporary stratagem, but only the voice of the Pope could renounce the policy.

The cardinal had attempted to perform a double service by attacking Mrs. Roosevelt. He had attempted to warn all public personages in America that they might face a similar fate if they challenged the Church directly, and he had engaged in an adroit misrepresentation of Catholic financial demands. His tactics failed primarily because he faced the wrong antagonist, and because he used methods which were conspicuously crude. With a more tactful presentation, he might have succeeded against a less influential victim. The American press condemned his insolence, but scarcely any American newspapers followed through in the controversy and attempted to show how grossly he had misrepresented Catholic policy. Most editors played safe by deploring the controversy and the "misunderstanding," and left the issue itself hanging in the air. Actually, there was no misunderstanding in this famous controversy. Mrs. Roosevelt candidly and mildly stated the traditional American view of the separation of church and state. Cardinal Spellman challenged that view, and resorted to the familiar devices of smearing his opponent and understating his own claims.

The cardinal did not actually use in this particular controversy the most popular Catholic argumentative device in favor of public funds for Catholic schools. This is the argument that the Church stands for the control of education by *parents,* and against the control of education by godless politicians. Actually, as I have already made clear, Catholic parents as against their priests have no rights over the education of their children. In the final analysis, the Church stands always and everywhere for the control of education by priests, and those priests are always and everywhere under the direct rule of Roman policy.

Exploiting the Ignorant

In almost every respect the devices of deception used by Catholicism are less extreme and crude than those of Communism. The one exception is in the field of religious-commercial fraud.

I would not discuss this phase of Vatican policy if I were not convinced from observations in Italy, Mexico, and elsewhere that it is a social phenomenon of great importance in blocking man's progress toward efficient democracy. Liberals are reluctant to talk about such things because some of the practices seem to the casual observer to be an organic part of Catholic faith. My feeling is that the misrepresentation of the laws of nature and the exploitation of magic and superstition do not form a legitimate part of *any* religion. Probably the majority of educated Catholics would agree with me. Perhaps they would consider, as I do, that the exploitation of ignorant people by anti-scientific devices is an unfortunate and illegitimate *addition* to their religion.

At any rate, it would be a happy circumstance if the minds

of men could be so neatly divided into compartments that they could accept ludicrous theories of physics, medicine, and astronomy with one part of the brain, and keep the other part of the brain clearly realistic for analyzing the problems of democracy. In actual life a philosophy which drugs one part of the mind is likely to drug the other part also. If a church teaches men to accept childish superstitions about the laws of nature, that acceptance is quite likely to incapacitate the victim for serious thinking in all fields.

This, in a nutshell, is the case against the anti-scientific deceptions of the Catholic Church. They unfit men for democratic responsibilities in modern society, since ignorance is never a sound preparation for good citizenship. The net effect of Catholic policy is to keep the masses of the people in Catholic countries in a perpetually depressed cultural condition. They have an unbalanced diet of too much sentiment and too little science, and the result of their cultural malnutrition is that they are kept permanently immature because they have never learned the art of mental growth in freedom.

Many intellectuals look upon the perpetuation of mental childhood among the Catholic masses with a kind of aloof tolerance as if it were quite harmless and slightly amusing and, in any case, none of their business. It seems to me that it can be considered harmless only by those who have failed to observe its appalling effects in Catholic countries. No one can consider the phenomenon amusing who has seen a Mexican or Italian peasant give his last peso or lira to a priest to win from a pink plaster saint a special blessing for the healing of an incurable disease.

In the United States such exploitation of the poor and the ignorant is relatively inconspicuous. The American Catholic Church, surrounded by an environment of science and learning, is on its good behavior. The crudest forms of ecclesiastical fraud are avoided because of the possibility of a violently unfavorable public reaction. Perhaps that is one reason why the Vatican has never made an American-born citizen a saint. The details of the process might seem a little too outrageous for respectful treatment in a country like the United States which has a healthy skepticism concerning all matters of magic. But in all of Latin America and in much of Europe the Catholic Church is quite literally the apostle of anti-science, the accredited agency of folk superstition. On the upper cultural level the Church holds congresses of Catholic scientists, with papal blessings; but in practice the priests' acceptance of modern science scarcely extends outside of the leading cities.

The Communists have been shrewd enough to emphasize in their propaganda the most fraudulent aspects of Catholic practice. In the spring of 1950 they caught a priest in Cinost, Bohemia, faking the "miracle" of a moving cross. The priest, according to the confession reported in the United Press, admitted that he had fixed a twelve-centimeter spring to one end of a crucifix and tied the other end to a piece of rubber fastened to the canopy of the church altar, thus being able to produce the "miracle" at will from his pulpit. The Communists made a motion picture of the episode and circulated it widely. Actually the priest's promotion of the "miracle" of Bohemia was nothing unusual in the lower reaches of the European Church. Technically the Vatican repudiates such trickery, but priests are permitted and at times encouraged to play upon the lowest superstitions of their people by similar techniques.

In the summer of 1949, the New York *Times* reported a typical miraculous incident in a Polish Catholic church. Some Catholic sextons in a cathedral in Lublin reported that a picture of the Virgin Mary "shed tears of blood over the church's afflictions in Eastern Europe." When a priest wiped away a drop of blood, another appeared to take its place. The word spread throughout that section of Poland, and nearly half a million people, with their prayers and their money, came to share in the divine benefaction. "Pilgrims," said the New York *Times,* "from as far west as Poznan were standing today six abreast in a mile-long queue that stretched through the city's streets."[21]

The Italian Church's devices of deception in this field can be taken as the norm, since the Pope, as the primate of Italy, is personally responsible for the survivals of magic and sorcery in that country. The Italian Church continually exploits doubtful relics and worse than doubtful apparitions in the most commercial manner. The details would fill a library; I shall take the time here to cite only two minor examples within the range of my personal experience.

One of the leading cathedrals of Italy, in Bari, continues to sell bottles of the "sweat" of the bones of St. Nicholas, a saint associated with Christmas, who is alleged to have been "translated" about 1087. The cathedral has on exhibition one small bone of the saint in a narrow tube located under a basement altar several feet below sea level, and the hierarchy claims that this bone sweats so copiously that it yields enough divine perspiration for all the faithful who wish to purchase the perspiration at 60 lire a bottle. The "perspiration" is collected by dropping a sponge on a silver chain into the below-sea-level hole. After being assured by the monsignor of the cathedral that this "sweat" was "good for all human ailments," in the presence of two Protestant clergymen, a member of the city council, and a former superintendent of the city's schools, I purchased five bottles for my inflamed eyes, and witnessed the purchase of similar bottles by impoverished Italians suffering from serious ailments. As the "sweat" is edible, it may be used with equal success for stomach ulcers or rheumatism. Bottles of this "sweat" are now being shipped for sale to Mexico and Latin American countries with full Church approval, and the Church hopes to build up a Christmas trade in the United States.

The most famous and possibly the most lucrative miracle in Europe is the liquefaction of the blood of St. Januarius in Naples; this occurs under full official auspices two or three times a year, usually on the first Saturday in May, the 19th of September, and the 16th of December. On each of these occasions, for a period of several days, two small vials of the alleged powdered blood of the saint, beheaded about 305 A.D., become liquefied after being carried through the streets in gigantic ecclesiastical processions, headed by cardinals and other high prelates of the Church. The powdered blood in every case is sealed inside of a silver case or *teca*, looking very much like a large reading glass, and no independent critics or scientists are permitted to open the case and examine the product. The case containing the powdered blood is carried by Church prelates in the processions in such a way that only their testimony concerning the alleged liquefaction can be accepted by the vast throngs of worshipers. The priests tell the people, and the people believe, that the veneration of the blood-relics protects them from natural disasters.

This childlike attitude toward nature is cultivated among the more illiterate people by the priests, especially in many rural parts of Europe, as a means of controlling them. The priest as nature's magician uses his power to "protect" his people. His techniques are less fraudulent than they were a hundred years ago, but the difference is only a matter of degree. Eveline B. Mitford, writing in the *Monthly Review* of London in 1906 (Volume XXII), declared:

> In the present day there are 20 well-known gowns and 70 veils of the Virgin Mary, each pronounced to be the real one; 12 heads of St. John the Baptist, in tolerably perfect condition, besides numerous large fragments of his skull and seven extra jaws, each of great note, and held in much reverence in different parts of Europe. St. Julienne has 20 bodies and 26 separate heads, whilst St. George and St. Pancras each possess 30 bodies, and St. Peter has 16; St. Peter the Dominican only possesses 2 bodies, but he makes up for the deficiency in the number of his fingers, 56 of which are scattered throughout Europe.

The duplications have been reduced in recent years; the ecclesiastical mixture of magic and exploitation continues as before.

Changing Unchangeable Dogma

Many people suppose that although Catholic political policy may have no basis in Christian tradition, Catholic dogma has a clear pedigree dating back to earliest Christianity, and that all the important teachings of the Church are derived from permanent and unchangeable pronouncements of the Founder. This is just as clear an illusion as the belief that all the abuses of Communist power arise inevitably from original socialist doctrine. In both cases original dogma has been changed to meet changing circumstances. In the Vatican system, the amplified claims of dogmatic tradition and political power are interdependent, and are used to strengthen each other. As Milton said: "Popery is a double thing to deal with, and claims a two-fold power, ecclesiastical and political, both usurped, and the one supporting the other."

The student of Church history can easily discover that the power doctrines of the Vatican are contrived concepts *added to* Christianity after the fourth century as part of its working program for expansion. The Vatican system is elastic in one sense:

it permits doctrinal change by addition whenever the Vatican thinks that a change is necessary. Each consecrated doctrine, after it has become official, is described as unchangeable, but in practice the living Church always has the option of issuing a new "interpretation" which may quickly alter fundamental policy.

This is an important fact to understand because many non-Catholics think of the whole matrix of Catholic faith as one consistent creation going back to Christ. Hitler in *Mein Kampf* expressed admiration for the Church's opposition to change and said: "Here, too, one can learn from the Catholic Church. Although its structure of doctrines, in many instances, collides quite unnecessarily with exact science and research, yet it is unwilling to sacrifice even one little syllable of its dogmas."[22] Hitler failed to note how easily the Vatican can discover a "precedent" for changing an unchangeable dogma, and how smoothly the transition to a new attitude can take place in an institution in which the hierarchy controls the rhythm of change. There is not necessarily any conscious deception in this process, but only an "adjustment" to life.

The world was treated to a demonstration of this adaptability in November 1950, when Pius XII proclaimed the dogma that the Virgin Mary's body was taken up literally into heaven after her death. The strictly religious phases of this dogma are not pertinent to this discussion, but it is fair to note that a Church which can manufacture a dogma in this manner in the broad daylight of the twentieth century can easily duplicate this performance in the fields of economics and politics. Of course, all dogmas promulgated as divine truth have long traditions behind them, but the Pope is sufficiently powerful and adroit to shape the interpretations of tradition.

It is a mortal sin for a Catholic to dispute Catholic dogma when once it has been sanctified by formal papal utterance. The highest Catholic theological journals admitted in 1950 that all historical researches "add up to the fact that we do not have a genuine historical tradition on the Assumption" of the Virgin Mary into heaven, and that "in the patristic tradition of the first six centuries we find a void regarding this problem."[23] The Pope, however, blandly promulgated the dogma of the Assumption on a purely "theological" basis.

The London *New Statesman and Nation* had the temerity to draw the deadly parallel between this kind of ecclesiastical modification of history and the variety so popular in Moscow. Would any influential journal in the United States have dared to speak so candidly as this British magazine did in an editorial on "The Assumption of the Virgin"?

We have indeed returned to the Age of Faith. Moscow also builds myths in order to strengthen faith and re-writes history for her own purposes, knowing well that absolute authority demands credulity as well as obedience. Just as Rome rebuffs those liberal Christians who had naively hoped for unity in the belief that Rome was capable of compromise, so Moscow has disillusioned Socialists outside Russia who hoped that cooperation between Soviet and Western Socialists was possible after the experience of joint Resistance during the war. Moscow has proved as totalitarian as Rome. Soviet orthodoxy, however, has the advantage that the legends it invents are not incompatible with social progress and modern knowledge. They do not take away from common men the hope of a world in which life on earth may become sufficiently inspiring to make unnecessary a belief in supernatural glories.

Neither form of religion can ever unify the West, since the very essence of Western civilization from the Renaissance onwards is the right of individual judgment, the use of the critical faculty. The belief that truth has not been finally revealed, but must be discovered by a process of inquiry, experiment and reason, is basic to our civilization.[24]

The Vatican has reinterpreted Church history for its own purposes much more successfully than the Kremlin has reinterpreted the history of Russia. As we have seen, it is quite clear from the fragmentary evidence that no authentic documents corroborate the Catholic version of the Church's origin. There is no evidence that Peter ever was a pope or a bishop or that the Founder of Christianity sanctioned the system of ecclesiastical power which Rome has developed in his name. Peter may have preached and died in Rome, but beyond this relatively inconsequential and uncertain fact little is known that could associate him in any way with the Vatican claims of Roman primacy. Yet these historical deficiencies in papal pretensions are never admitted by Catholic scholars. The *Catholic Encyclopedia* in discussing the Pope says: "History bears complete testimony that from the very earliest times the Roman See has ever claimed the supreme headship, and that that headship has been freely acknowledged by the universal Church."

In 1949 the Vatican received a prodigious amount of free publicity in the press of the western world concerning approaching discoveries that would be disclosed to the world in the Holy Year as a result of excavations under St. Peter's into the alleged tomb of St. Peter.[25] The world awaited the revelations with great interest, but nothing came of them in the Holy Year except some interesting excavations which indicated that some persons were once buried under St. Peter's. No independent archeologists could be found who would certify any identifications, and even if the actual bones of St. Peter had been discovered, the discovery in itself would not have vindicated papal claims. Nevertheless Pius XII was given generous headlines when at the end of the excavations he announced as a fact that Peter's grave had been identified, and Catholic publicists proceeded to draw the traditional deductions from this alleged fact.

The truth is that the whole structure of Vatican power has virtually no support in biblical literature in spite of the papal claim that it has. The doctrines on which the power rests have grown up gradually as a result of the process of absorption and elimination, and they have survived because they have served the group in authority in the Church. (See Chapter 3.)

Many of the most important doctrines, such as purgatory, birth control, the infallibility of the Pope, the granting of indulgences for sin in return for physical acts and monetary payments, the condemnation of all divorce, the monopoly control of marriage by the priests, and the coercive power of the Papacy, have no clear sanction in original Christianity. In fact, they have nothing more to do with original Christianity than Stalin's taste in philology with original Marxism.

If this judgment seems overly emphatic, I invite the reader to take the list of doctrines and policies listed in the preceding paragraph and, one by one, check them with the Bible, trying to find any supporting evidence for their claim to be a part of Christianity. He may be astounded to find how much of Catholicism has been added to original Christianity. For the benefit of readers whose curiosity on this point is more than casual, I have listed in the Notes the doctrines, beliefs, and policies given in the preceding paragraph, together with the alleged biblical supports for those doctrines, taken chiefly from a standard modern work, *The Teaching of the Catholic Church*, edited by Canon George D. Smith.[26] The student who cares to read the Bible verses cited will find that many of them either have nothing to do with the doctrines which the Catholic hierarchy pretends to derive from them, or that they support the doctrines with inadequate or contradictory evidence.

The practice of manufacturing dogma based on fake history is especially open to challenge when the beliefs so promoted concern modern education, politics, and medicine, and when they ostensibly summon religious authority to oppose modern science and modern programs for social welfare. Under such circumstances the ecclesiastical management of truth has broad social consequences, and it is, therefore, a legitimate target for secular criticism. The most damaging doctrinal creations of this type are in the field of medicine and social hygiene, where the maintenance of medieval, anti-scientific, and, in some cases, inhuman doctrines in the twentieth century is based upon either clerical misrepresentation or the withholding of part of the truth from the Catholic people. The priestly fiction, for example, which has been used so extensively against birth control — that Jesus Christ is opposed to contraception — is just as clear a distortion of fact as the Kremlin doctrine that acquired biological characteristics are inherited. The social consequences of the Catholic fiction may be even more serious because overpopulation is a primary cause of war.

Similarly, the manufactured dogma that God will never permit therapeutic abortion, even when the failure to perform the life-saving operation will certainly result in the death of *both* mother and unborn fetus, is something more than a theological error for the thousands of Catholic mothers who are sentenced to death by this rule. It is a dogma which has no necessary connection either with Christianity or with common sense. This rule, incidentally, is almost always understated by Catholic writers in the United States, with the result that its full barbarity is disguised. Henry Morton Robinson, in his best-selling novel, *The Cardinal,* describes how his priest-hero, Stephen Fermoyle, after persuading his sister not to marry a Jew, finally consigns her to death under the Catholic rule against therapeutic abortion when she is about to give birth to an illegitimate child. She could have been saved, but in that case the child would have been born dead. The child lives and the mother dies, and the priest-hero gasps self-righteously, "I have no authority to permit murder," when he is asked to make the choice between the life of the child and the life of his sister by permitting therapeutic abortion. Actually he permits murder by negligence — the murder of his sister — because the priestly rule on childbirth prevents the saving of her life. In Mr. Robinson's illustration the act of the priest is partially redeemed by the survival of the child, but in actual practice the Catholic rule binds the doctor against a life-saving therapeutic abortion even *when the fetus is bound to die anyway*. I have discused this issue in detail elsewhere.[27]

11

The Strategy of Penetration: the Kremlin

WHY SHOULD DEMOCRACIES BE AFRAID of such totalitarian organizations as the Kremlin and the Vatican? Communists control only a minority of voters in the western nations, and in some western countries a tiny minority. The Vatican, even when it has a large and militant minority in a nation, cannot compel majorities to accept its position.

One answer to the question is that both the Kremlin and the Vatican have learned to conquer nations without majorities by using the methods of infiltration and combination. Today the most dangerous kind of imperialism is that which may develop inside a nation through the technique of penetration by a determined minority controlled by an outside power. This strategy of penetration is far more effective than the old strategy of frontal attack.

Of course there is nothing objectionable as such in the penetration of a nation by any religion or system of political ideas. Every great nation attempts to develop friendship and sympathy for its aspiration among its neighbors by cultural penetration and propaganda. The advocates of Socialism, Esperanto, existentialism, Methodism, Americanism, Catholicism, and capitalism have a right to spread their faiths without let or hindrance wherever men are willing to listen, and it would be a sorry day for world progress if they were forbidden the right to import their concepts of society into any nation merely on the ground that those concepts were foreign. The legitimate exchange of ideas, however, becomes cultural and political imperialism when the invading power is unwilling to submit its ideas and policies for free discussion and choice in the market place of ideas, or when it does not in good faith accept the laws and regulations of the democratic society into which it penetrates.

The Kremlin never accepts the laws of any democratic society in good faith because it regards rule by majorities as "bourgeois." When its leaders talk of establishing democracy in a nation, they mean the establishment of the power of a Communist minority in that nation. Self-determination, as Lenin pointed out, means "self-determination of the working class within each nationality rather than the self-determination of peoples and nationalities."[1] And if Lenin had completed his thought, he would have pointed out that the self-determination of the working class means self-determination of that inner segment of the working class which belongs to the Communist movement.

The Kremlin's techniques for conquering without majorities are positively awe-inspiring, and probably they constitute the greatest single innovation in the development of political science in our time. The Communists, of course, owe some inspiration to fascism, and fascism owes more than a little inspiration to Catholicism; but no one should belittle either the originality or the effectiveness of the Communists. I shall list here some examples of the devices of conquest by penetration with which the Communists have become the most successful imperialists in modern times.

The Controlled Political Party

The controlled political party — controlled by the Kremlin — paved the way for every Soviet conquest in eastern Europe at the end of World War II. In almost every case the controlled party marched in with the Soviet "liberating" armies or was placed in power shortly afterwards. Hungary, Poland, Yugoslavia, East Germany, Rumania, Czechoslovakia — the story of internal conquest with Kremlin help is monotonously repetitious. The Communist Party began in every case as a minority group, and conquered the majority by manipulation and pressure. The techniques of conquest were in each case essentially the same.

The controlled party which the Kremlin develops for such conquests is always a Russian party in spirit and objectives, and its leaders are usually products of special training in Moscow; but if it seems advisable, the Russian overlords are kept in the background. Sometimes the party members themselves do not know who the mysterious overlords are. Frequently the instrument of Communist penetration into a non-Communist territory is not even a party with an official Communist label. That is one reason why the mere outlawing of the official Communist Party in a country like the United States is scarcely worth the effort. Leaders of world Communism have long been trained to reorganize their movements quickly to escape prohibitive legislation. When Canada outlawed its Communist Party, the party promptly re-emerged with Communist leaders as the Labor Progressive Party of Canada. In the United States the Cominform is now in a position to use the Progressive Party in this way if the official Communist Party is outlawed.

In many countries the favorite second front for the Communists is a captured Socialist party. In principle it may be quite indistinguishable from the Communist organization, but it is frequently useful for strategic purposes, and it may provide a refuge in times of special difficulty. Italy has provided a good illustration of this technique. There the satellite Socialist Party, headed by Pietro Nenni, imitates the language, tactics, and policies of Palmiro Togliatti's Communist organization; it constitutes part of the Peoples' Bloc with the Communists, but maintains a technically independent existence.

In the satellite countries of the Russian orbit in eastern Europe, when the Soviet troops arrived in 1945, they found a Russian left-wing party ready to take over joint operation of each government. The Communists naturally claimed an important part in some of these temporary regimes, since they had played a heroic part in the resistance movement against the Nazis and they had built strong underground organizations which survived the war. In a sense, they had earned an important role in the leadership of the new Europe, and even the political parties which were most hostile to Communism respected that claim.

Sometimes the conquering Russian armies brought native Communist leaders in with them from Moscow, leaders who had received Moscow training. Dimitrov gained power in Bulgaria, Gomulka in Poland, Rakosi in Hungary, Ana Pauker in Rumania, Gottwald in Czechoslovakia, and Tito in Yugoslavia. All of them were disciplined veterans of Communism, trained in the techniques of penetration in the "university of revolution" in Moscow.

I am reluctant to put down these names because I do not know how many of them will be hanged by their former comrades before this book goes to press. Gomulka in Poland has already been demoted for "nationalism" and "deviationism"; Gottwald in Czechoslovakia has declined in favor at Moscow; and Tito lives in the shadow of a large bodyguard. Dimitrov of Bulgaria, of course, is already dead, and nobody knows whether he died a natural death.

When Allied troops moved into Europe at the end of World War II, the veteran democracies had no parallel political parties to use as instruments of American or British control. There was no Freedom Party under American auspices, with a German label, to promote democracy in West Germany. Able intelligence officers were sent from the United States to Germany, but our mild and somewhat general pleas for democracy seemed strangely ineffectual when compared with the very specific revolutionary propaganda of the Communists, and the strong survivals of Nazi prejudice. The Communists had cells in every branch of the life of every occupied nation. They presented themselves as the only hope of the working class in the fight against fascism, and the victory of Russia conferred upon them a new prestige. The international Socialist (democratic) movement failed to parallel the Communist machinery of penetration in any way.

The first task of penetration by any Communist party was to oust or discredit any non-Communist resistance movement, and in this maneuver the Communists did not consider it necessary to use any large amount of truth. Any tortured narrative of "socialist betrayal" seemed to be enough, in an atmosphere of distrust and disillusionment, to discredit the labor liberals. The Kremlin brushed aside the London-Polish Government in exile as "imperialist" and "fascist," and established its own puppet organization in Lublin, inducing Stanislaw Mikolajczyk to take a portfolio for a time, and then maneuvering him out of power in 1947.[2] This was typical of Communist invasion strategy. In all the penetrations of eastern European countries, the Communists demanded, and usually got, the key post of the Minister of the Interior, which meant control of the national police; and they also frequently captured the Ministry of Information. They were realists, and in the long run their realism paid off. With control of the police, they were always in a position to prevent a *putsch* by any opposition force, or to spring their own *putsch* if necessary at the moment when their opponents were off guard.

The first political moves of the Communists in the conquered countries of eastern Europe were almost as adroit and circumspect as their tactics in western democratic countries. They expressed eagerness to co-operate with all parties which were not tainted with fascism. In fact, they actually co-operated for a time with several new European governments in seeming good faith. It should be remembered that they had a broad base of popular support for their economic program in many parts of Europe, and that in nations like Czechoslovakia their plans for the nationalization of industry probably had majority approval long before the Russians arrived.[3] Also it should be remembered that the Russian armies came to Czechoslovakia with a special prestige because the people believed that Stalin had been willing to defend them against Hitler when Britain and France deserted them at Munich.

In each conquered country of eastern Europe, the Communists called for a prompt election as a matter of strategy, and often the first election was reasonably honest. If they won an outright majority, the rest was easy for them. If, as happened in several countries, the Communists were in a minority even when certain allies among the Socialists were included in the reckoning, they promptly set out to create a crisis which would justify a coup in the name of restoring order.

The story of Hungary may be considered typical, although Hungary had one favor which some of the other satellites were not granted: it had what one observer called the only free and unfettered elections which took place according to the Yalta Agreement.[4] When the Red Army moved into the country in 1945, it brought with it a group of Communist *émigrés* from the old Communist Hungarian regime of Bela Kun, men who had become skilled Moscow agents from years of experience. They set up a coalition government in which they treated their non-Communist associates with great politeness, but they were careful to keep control of the police for themselves. They persuaded the Social Democrats to make an agreement with them for a coalition, and with the help of this agreement they got control of the labor unions. In November 1945, they held a free election, in which they won only 17 per cent of the vote while the Smallholders Party won almost 60 per cent; but this did not daunt them. After a waiting period, the Communist newspapers announced in 1947 the discovery of a "large-scale conspiracy" connected with the Smallholders Party. Several leaders were arrested and "confessed." Disclosures of conspiracy were made while the opposition prime minister, Nagy, was away in Switzerland, and he was warned not to return to his country.

After liquidating most of the Smallholders' leadership, the Communists held another election — but they still won in coalition with the Socialists only by a very narrow margin. Then they proceeded to liquidate the other opposition parties with new "discoveries." The Hungarian Independence Party was exposed as "fascist" and deprived of forty-nine seats in parliament; the Social Democrats collapsed under pressure. The Communist government then announced that the opposition parties "have since disappeared from the political scene. The voters have come to realize that the opposition parties, Pfeiffer's Hungarian Independence Party and Barankovic's Democratic People's Party . . . had misled them . . . their real ambition was the restoration of the old regime . . . the agents of capitalists and large estate owners, the saboteurs of protection and nationalization, were seeking cover. The leaders of these parties fled from the country, deserting their followers, and the parties themselves were dissolved."

After that there was a "united list" election, and on May 15, 1949, the People's Front triumphantly captured 95.6 per cent of the vote.

In Czechoslovakia the process of conquest was more nearly legal. President Beneš gave the Communists a very substantial role in the first post-war cabinet, and they went on from there to electoral successes. The Communists and Social Democrats together won a majority in a reasonably fair election in May 1946, and the Communists became the largest single party in a new government. But Czechoslovakia revealed one difference from other conquered countries. Its Social Democrats were fairly sturdy democratic socialists who knew a dictatorship when they saw one. They realized that their democracy was being stolen from them, and they turned on the arch-traitor in their own ranks, the Socialist Zdenek Fierlinger, who had become Prime Minister, and threw him out of their party for betraying them to the Communists. They were ready to start a genuine movement for emancipation, and it might have led to Communist defeat in the elections scheduled for the spring of 1948.

When the Communists saw defeat coming, they rigged a "crisis," and with the help of some very stupid strategy on the part of Socialist ministers, they captured the government. The excuse for the capture was that when the Communists' Minister of the Interior ousted eight chiefs of police and replaced them with Communists, the national parliament ordered their reinstatement. The Communists refused, and the non-Communist Ministers, apparently believing that the Communists were still bound by gentlemanly parliamentary traditions, resigned in protest. The Communists, instead of calling for an election, walked into power in February 1948 and took over one of the most advanced and intelligent democracies in Europe. Great Britain and the United States protested, but the Communists ignored the protests. The Security Council of the United Nations would have added its protest, but the Soviet Union interposed a veto. President Beneš resigned and died soon afterwards; and Jan Masaryk, independent Foreign Minister, probably committed suicide. The new government held farcical "one-list" elections and captured almost 90 per cent of the total vote.

Czechoslovakia initially was typical of the more civilized Kremlin methods in using a controlled political party as a democratic springboard. In much of eastern Europe the Communist techniques of capture and subjection have been more abrupt and arbitrary. Once a Communist party has captured power, the Kremlin keeps control through the machinery of the state itself. Within the Russian-dominated party those members who are hostile to Kremlin power are carefully weeded out, often by the operation of party spies or government secret police. The party leader who betrays some skepticism concerning Communist tactics is usually eliminated or demoted before he has become a serious source of infection.

Through long experience as revolutionary conspirators, the Communists have learned the perfect technique to prevent a rebellion. They operate a continuous and extensive organization of informers within their own units, with special machinery for penetrating the spearheads of Communist action.[5] These inner cells of the Communist cells report only to the most secret and exalted leaders of the national Party or to the Cominform itself. Because of this inner intelligence service, the Kremlin is always able to strike first against any incipient revolt, either in the Soviet Union or in a satellite country. The potential leader of every revolt is usually spotted in advance and imprisoned or killed. Nikola Petkov, independent leader of Bulgaria's Agrarian Party, was hanged in 1947 by a Communist-dominated regime essentially for opposing the Communist regime in his country with some courage. The Communists knew that if a revolt was to come, Petkov was its logical leader. Petkov's trial showed how completely any opposition movement in any Communist-dominated country is honeycombed with Stalinist agents. Tito in Yugoslavia would undoubtedly have met the same fate in 1948 if he had not built his own partisan movement as a core of Yugoslavia's independent Communism before the Russian armies arrived in Belgrade. His spies were one jump ahead of Stalin's spies.

Communism's political strategy of penetration in non-Communist countries like Italy, France, Great Britain, and the United States differs only slightly from that in the nations of the Soviet orbit. On the upper diplomatic level, the Russian embassy in each country tends to be a dignified symbol of Communist prestige. The Russian ambassadors are naturally spokesmen for anti-capitalism and Kremlin policy, but not usually noisy or particularly provocative.

The most successful political unit of penetration in a democracy is usually the small and very well-disciplined unit of obscure devotees. It takes the form of a Communist cell, with the lines of authority for each cell running upward to a Kremlin representative and not laterally to another cell. This vertical organization of power makes it difficult for any particular cell to become a center of rebellious infection. Each cell, being completely isolated from neighboring cells, finds any organization for local independence very difficult. The few occasions when all the cell members in a certain locality get together are systematically directed and controlled by Kremlin agents. The motions, the speeches, and the resolutions at regional and national mass meetings are as thoroughly prepared in advance as the resolutions at a conference of Catholic bishops.

The former Franco-Italian Communist who writes under the pen name of A. Rossi has told, in his book *The Communist Party in Action,* the story of the techniques of penetration used by the Kremlin in France. Some of the most successful work of French Communism during World War II was accomplished by tiny cells of three to six persons, meeting secretly and often functioning as isolated bodies under a distant command. The cells acted always as "a society-within-a-society which regards itself as destined to destroy the society it is within." "Your true Communist," says Rossi, "thinks of himself as already a citizen of another polity, as subordinated to its laws even as he awaits the time when he can impose them upon others."

The program for this work of penetration by each Communist cell in France was laid down in the utmost detail by the French Communist headquarters. The work of each cell was carefully inspected and supervised. Rossi quotes the "Plan of the Organization and Activities of a Cell" drawn up by the Central Committee of the French Communist Party in 1940. The resemblance to military orders is striking, even to the use of the word "mission" for each cell's assignment. After the war the cells were enlarged to about thirty members, but their techniques did not change very much.

The cell is the Party's basic organizational unit. It is therefore imperative that each cell obey the following instructions to the letter.

A. The cell should have a maximum of six members. The resulting decentralization facilitates the holding of meetings. It also makes for improved division of labor and enables the Party to maintain a close check on each militant's performance.

B. Each cell is required to hold weekly meetings. The time and place of these meetings will be changed each week, and those who are to attend will be notified at the latest possible moment. Each meeting will adjourn at the end of 60 or at most 90 minutes.

C. The agenda for each of these meetings will be as follows: (1) questions relating to finances; (2) questions relating to the cell's operations; (3) questions relating to training and policy.

The secretary of the cell will work out a detailed agenda based on this outline, and will explain it to the comrades present at the meeting in clear and precise language.

Example: questions relating to finances (15 minutes). This will be the first item on the agenda. The treasurer must not fail to explain how important funds are to the Party, or to remind the comrades of their duty both to contribute to these funds and to collect contributions from the Party's numerous sympathizers. Everything relating to money should be taken up under this item.

Questions relating to operations (20-30 minutes). During this important phase of the meeting the cell leader, bearing in mind the Party's security regulations, should assign the members their respective tasks, and make all necessary explanations. Pamphlets; posters; slogans on walls and sidewalks. Display of map of surrounding neighborhoods; assignment of stations and streets to each member. Decision on the most favorable hour for performing each mission, *to be based on recommendations by the comrades*.

Questions relating to training and to Party policies (30 minutes). We must never forget that the cell is the Party's classroom, and that the comrades are expected to make a genuine intellectual effort to understand Party policy and Party tactics. The meeting should, to this end, discuss the Party's circulars, pamphlets, and newspapers. One of the comrades will offer a brief talk on current problems. Continuous study of the *History of the Communist Party of the Soviet Union* (*Bolsheviks*) and *Left-wing Communism: an Infantile Disorder*.

Comrades, the present situation — beyond any in the Party's history — calls for order, discipline, courage, caution. You must seek these qualities in yourselves.

Forward, comrades — to become the true élite of the people and the guarantors of the final victory.[6]

These instructions for the operation of Communist cells could be repeated verbatim for almost every non-Communist nation in the world.

The Temporary Coalition

In all of their maneuvers within democracies throughout the world, the Communists act on the assumption that a small inner core can control the larger, formless mass of any political organization by ceaseless agitation and obstruction. It is probably accurate to say that they have never won majority power in peacetime in any single nation in the world by democratic methods. But they have won so often by undemocratic methods that they may well ask: Why should we be respectful toward democracy?

The Communists, in fact, have no respect for democratic procedure in politics except to use it for Kremlin purposes. They are openly contemptuous of majorities and specialize in breaking them up by internal intrigues and continuous disorder at meetings. (I saw this happen in the American Labor Party of New York when I was a vice-chairman of that organization.) The Communists are so confident of their ability to defeat almost any majority in a democratic body that they do not hesitate to join organizations in which they are greatly outnumbered. One of their favorite devices is to form a coalition with an opposition group, and then to capture the combined group for their own purposes.

This device of the captured coalition was popular in Europe in 1945 and 1946 because both the Socialists and the Communists needed coalitions to keep reactionaries and monarchists from returning to power. Communists were frequently welcomed with open arms by non-Communist parties because they used the language of "national unity" against fascist revival. And, as I have already pointed out, the Communists had a distinguished record in several resistance movements. They were in a strategic position to exploit the confusion and instability of post-war Europe.

In each country where the Communists attempted the coalition technique, the non-Communist leftists were gently maneuvered into a position where they could be absorbed or destroyed. Some of the independent leftists, no doubt, honestly believed that they could maintain their own identity and still co-operate with the Kremlin. In the summer of 1947, Joseph Cyrankiewicz, Socialist Prime Minister of Poland in a Communist-dominated coalition, made a statement to Alexander Werth of *The Nation* which reflects the typical optimism of those who collaborated before they were swallowed up:

> We are two parties, each with its own particular "dynamics," and there are therefore inevitable difficulties; but the Communists cannot rule without the Socialists, and since there is no other practicable government formula, we are going to stick together, and relations are going to improve.

This collaboration is important not only for Poland; it is important as an example for the whole of Europe.[7]

Cyrankiewicz made it plain that the Socialists wanted a coalition with the Communists not as part of a single party but as an independent member of a partnership. The Polish Socialists had had one of the strongest social democratic parties in Europe, but a year and a half later they succumbed, and a Communist-dominated United Party of the Polish Working Classes took over the government.

The story could be repeated not only for Europe but for the United States as well. In leftist coalitions throughout the world the Socialists have never swallowed the Communists: the Communists have always swallowed the Socialists. If the Socialists refuse to be swallowed but show signs of doing their own swallowing, the Communists suddenly discover a counter-revolutionary "plot," and withdraw to avoid absorption.

The names of the coalitions and individuals in eastern Europe after World War II are tragic mileposts in the story of Communist intrigue and penetration. Mikolajczyk of Poland, Subasitch of Yugoslavia, Maniu of Rumania, Masaryk of Czechoslovakia, Petkov of Bulgaria, Tildy of Hungary, Szakasits of Hungary, Fierlinger of Czechoslovakia, Groza of Rumania, Georgiev of Bulgaria — they were all once leaders of "independent" collaborating parties, and when Communism captured their countries they were forced to choose between collaboration and extinction. In each one of their countries the Kremlin formed a collaborationist government with a co-operative front which soon became an official Communist front. In Yugoslavia, Albania, and Greece, the combination was called the National Liberation Front; in Bulgaria, the Fatherland Front; in Rumania and Finland, the National Democratic Front; in Hungary, the National Independence Front; in Poland, the Government of National Unity; in Czechoslovakia, simply the National Front.[8]

The Controlled Labor Organization

Such uniform success in political conquest could not be achieved by the organization of human beings on the political level alone. The Communists have realized that people tend to vote in elections with the particular economic or cultural bloc to which they belong, and they have shaped their program in such a way as to control certain basic economic groups for their own purposes. They have specialized in organizing mass movements of labor, culture, and sport to build up favorable public opinion and prepare the population for complete conquest. They have learned to shift their nuclei to strategic units in any situation in much the same way as a general shifts his strongest reserves to the points of danger on a battlefield.

The labor unions have been the most vulnerable groups for this Trojan-horse strategy. Since they are automatically anti-capitalist in their attitudes when they are engaged in conflict with the employers, their class objectives frequently coincide with the temporary aims of the Communist movement. Both the conservative labor union and the Communist Party attempt to improve the conditions of working people — up to a point. After that point has been reached, the Communists attempt to use labor power for complete social revolution.

Today the Communists control the largest labor organizations not only in the Soviet Union and the satellite countries of eastern Europe, but also in Italy, France, and China. The Communist-dominated C.G.I.L. in Italy is probably three times the size of its nearest non-Communist labor rival. In France the Communist-dominated C.G.T. is still the strongest labor federation — perhaps three times the size of all other labor federations combined.[9]

For a time it looked as if the Communist techniques of infiltration would succeed in the American labor movement. The internecine battle between the C.I.O. and the A.F. of L. gave the Communists a chance to assert their aggressive leadership, and they began to control considerable blocs of labor in several of our largest cities, particularly in the C.I.O. For a time they dominated a furriers' union, a transport workers' union, an electrical workers' union, a maritime union, a teachers' union, and a public employees' union. For a time also they developed tremendous power in the great new union of automobile workers.

During the high emotional period of war co-operation between the Soviet Union and the west, it also seemed for a time that Communists might capture the world labor movement. The American C.I.O., together with most of the trade unions of Europe, joined the World Federation of Trade Unions, along with the labor organizations of the Soviet Union. At W.F.T.U. conferences in Europe, addresses of solidarity and brotherhood filled the air, and for a short time "representatives" of Russian labor actually spoke words of kindness concerning their subject brothers in capitalist countries. Soon, however, the subject brothers from the west realized that, in spite of words of fellowship, the Russians regarded the W.F.T.U. as just one more agency of infiltration. In every W.F.T.U. organization throughout the world, the Communists continued to serve as Russian agents, regardless of the interests of the members. The Kremlin played its cards so crudely that by 1950 there was nobody left in the W.F.T.U. except satellite organizations. Then the unions of the west formally withdrew and at London in 1949 formed a new world-wide democratic federation of free labor — the International Confederation of Free Trade Unions.[10]

One of the determining factors in alienating western labor was the complete inconsistency of Kremlin labor policy. In every crisis in recent years the tactics of Communist labor leaders and Communist unions have been subordinated to Kremlin political strategy. Their "friendship" for democratic labor has been turned on and off by Moscow order. In 1930 they were out to destroy every labor organization in America and substitute separate Communist unions, because their provincially minded general staff in Moscow entertained the illusion that the whole American labor movement was about to collapse. When they had been cured of this aberration, they embraced American labor with equally hypocritical affection during the period of sweetness and light of the 1930's, when Earl Browder was directed to swing American Communism to the right. Their tactics in dealing with European labor have been equally treacherous and unpredictable.

During the early months of the Korean war, the Communists in Italy used the C.G.I.L. and the Communists in France used the C.G.T. primarily as instruments of political agitation and sabotage. They attempted to block the landing of American arms in Naples by a general strike, and they temporarily disrupted the public services of almost every large city in Italy in protest against "American imperialism." In 1950 one of the favorite placards carried in Italian parades of the Communist-dominated C.G.I.L. read: "President Truman is a war criminal." When a great new labor movement of Italian workers developed in opposition to such subservience to Moscow, its leaders were accused of "destroying the unity of Italian labor."

During the period of the Hitler-Stalin pact, nothing was too abusive for Communists to say about labor conditions in the western democratic nations, and no strike against such conditions could be considered unjustified. Kremlin organizers poured into American industry to foment disputes and capture union locals. In the great seaports of the United States, Soviet agents sabotaged vessels carrying arms to Great Britain and France, and created as much obstructive turmoil as they could. A Communist leader was trailed through western American cities giving detailed instructions at cell meetings for disabling railroads by the use of emery dust and steel shavings.[11]

Then, suddenly, when Russia was invaded by Hitler's forces in June 1941, and the Kremlin needed American production, the whole labor-union policy shifted. The Communist nuclei in the American unions accepted with lamb-like gratitude the very conditions that they had denounced a few months earlier. They pleaded emotionally for increased production, temporary sacrifice, and the unity of the working class.

Such reversals of policy finally revealed to American labor that, no matter how courageous and self-sacrificing certain individual Communists might be, the unions could never trust a Communist leader. The American unions proceeded to clean out Communist leadership and to expel Communist-dominated groups. The C.I.O., after a brief period of tolerance, formally ousted all Communists and Communist unions from membership in 1950. The final proof of anti-Communist housecleaning in American labor came in the summer of 1950 when even the faithful followers of the Australian Communist, Harry Bridges, finally deserted him in San Francisco at a time when he was attempting to block the United Nations' war effort in Korea.

How do Communists capture a labor union?

Usually the process is quite simple, because labor unions do not draw lines against persons on the basis of political affiliation. The man who finds work in a particular industry is usually able to walk into the front door of the recognized union in that industry. Many of the important policies of the union are determined in open membership meetings where the well-prepared newcomer can influence votes. The open membership meeting, particularly in time of strike, is fair game for any well-organized Communist minority.

The Communists in any particular union usually employ the device of the preliminary caucus. They meet in advance of regular meetings and plan a strategy for the open meeting. Then, at the meeting or convention, they use every reasonable and unreasonable device of oratory and parliamentary law to put over their program. When their opponents are in command, they specialize in continuous disorder. Frequently they win control of a labor organization by the simple device of exhausting all their enemies. They are willing to stay up late into the night in order to effect a parliamentary coup when their opponents are too tired to fight.

Most of the members of any mass organization tend to follow the lead of the most aggressive segment in that organization, and the Communists know how to trade upon that fundamental trait of human society. They bring to their task careful training and iron discipline, and usually they are effective speakers. They can think of a good non-Communist reason for the most transparently partisan edict of the Kremlin, especially after they have been carefully coached by a Party strategist in a preliminary caucus. By jumping up to speak in every labor meeting and by speaking with force on every appropriate motion, they frequently create the appearance of a strong mass movement and throw their opponents into confusion. It is commonly said that any Communist minority of 25 per cent in any union can dominate the entire membership, especially if it can capture the key offices of the organization at a single election.

Of course the Communists have more than strategy to support their position in the labor movement. They have human discontent based on social inequality. Usually they know how to play upon that discontent by picking their causes carefully and by dramatizing some actual maladjustment or injustice in society. More important still, they are genuine devotees of class power, and a labor union often needs class power to win its legitimate demands. In time of strike even the most conservative unions automatically seek militant leadership, and the Communists are there to supply that type of leadership. As professional anti-capitalist fighters they are frequently welcomed by the non-Communists in much the same way that the tough professionals of the regular army are welcomed by a company of volunteers. For the same reason, Communists are frequently chosen as shop chairmen in factories by non-Communist majorities, because they are bold fighters for labor's claims.

It is one of the ironies of the story of Communism in the labor movement that, in spite of the exalted professions of Soviet allegiance to labor welfare, the labor unions of the "Socialist Motherland" itself are oppressed and disfranchised groups which do not actually have as much freedom as unions in capitalist countries. In fact, labor unions in the Soviet Union have become primarily company unions of the totalitarian state. They do not dare to start an unauthorized strike, or attack a Kremlin political directive, or insist on the elimination of an unsound industrial practice. The living standards of their members are far below those of the west, but they dare not discuss this fact candidly in Russian labor circles.

Capturing Bourgeois Culture

The general techniques of Communist penetration into cultural units are similar to the tactics used in labor unions. The Communists attempt to duplicate in non-Communist countries the network of agencies of public opinion which have been developed in the Soviet Union for controlling all social life. Their deceptive strategy was discussed in Chapter 9. There are dancing classes and workers' universities and youth sports clubs and theatrical leagues and musical societies and art conferences, all outwardly dedicated to sports, music, etc., and all controlled by Kremlin agents and Kremlin directives. In these auxiliary societies the Communists attempt to make Communist life a whole life, appealing and well-rounded.

The emphasis of these auxiliary societies in non-Communist countries is exactly contrary to the emphasis in the Soviet Union. In Russia the appeal is for co-operation and loyalty; in the democracies of the west the aim is to stimulate social discontent with existing conditions. Reform is constantly stressed, and reform committees spring up demanding everything from the revision of school textbooks to a reduction in the price of potatoes, and frequently the accomplishments are quite substantial and genuinely beneficial to the community.

In the United States it was almost impossible for many years to organize a group in any large American city for cheaper milk or better housing or racial fair play or clean government, without encountering a well-trained inner core of Communists in the organization. In the early stages of endeavor the Communist nucleus would usually allay suspicion and create sympathy by hard work for the fundamental purposes of the group. After the Communist representatives had won the confidence of their fellow members, they might suddenly turn the organization into a puppet Communist front, passing resolutions against the atomic bomb or the "imperialist" invasion of North Korea. This type of penetration in the United States was especially successful in the 1930's before the great exposures of Communist fronts. Today western democracy is on guard, and the Communist-front organizations can claim almost no genuine supporters outside the ranks of the Kremlin faithful.

International Infiltration

Would the Kremlin have the audacity to use its familiar tactics of penetration and obstruction in the United Nations? Would it treat a world organization also as a propaganda cockpit? Those were the questions which anxious diplomats asked privately when the United Nations was formed at San Francisco. The diplomats did not have long to wait for an answer. Between 1945 and 1951, Molotov, Vishinsky, Gromyko, and Jacob Malik used the machinery of international conferences and the assembly halls of the United Nations almost continuously for the same kind of obstructive tactics that had characterized Communist strategy in the labor world.

Until 1950 many persons of intelligence had been optimistic about the possibility of assimilating the Soviet Union in a society of nations. The very fact, they argued, that Stalin had come in on the ground floor of the United Nations at San Francisco was a hopeful sign. Might not Moscow ultimately recognize in good faith the plans for a democratic parliament of man? Even the fact that Russia demanded the right to veto all basic decisions in the Security Council seemed to many charitable observers merely an evidence of temporary suspicion. After all, the United States itself was unwilling to forgo the veto as a safeguard.

As Russia blocked every move for democratic control of the atomic bomb and every attempt to reach democratic agreements for permanent peace, the western diplomats began to realize that the Russians were as contemptuous of majorities at Lake Success as they had been in eastern Europe. They looked upon the representatives of other nations in the United Nations as deluded tools of capitalism and imperialism who must be by-passed or vanquished in the onward march of Communism toward world power.

Behind the crude maneuvering of Soviet diplomats in the United Nations was the basic doctrine which made Kremlin strategy possible. The Kremlin was infallible, and it had no obligation to yield to hostile majorities anywhere. It served a higher moral purpose above bourgeois democracy, and so it had the right to enter every democratic opposition movement for the purpose of discrediting and conquering it.

The western world was reluctant to admit the truth of this simple fact, but it could not do otherwise after the sorry exhibition staged at Lake Success by the Kremlin in August 1950, when Jacob Malik of the Soviet Union for a whole month blocked the efforts of other countries to discuss the Korean issue frankly. He practiced before the Security Council of the United Nations the same crudely obstructive policies which Communist cells had been practicing in non-Communist labor unions for a generation. He mangled parliamentary law and rode roughshod over all the gentilities of human association.

The New York *Times* made an interesting comment on the reasons for Mr. Malik's conduct. It said: "This idea of the Kremlin's infallibility (and presumably Mr. Malik knows what punishment he would face if he departed from it) helps to account for the singular spectacle in the Security Council. It makes it possible to understand why a presumably intelligent man, talking to other presumably intelligent persons, can with a straight face insist for two weeks that war is peace, that self-defense is aggression, that night is day and that black is white."

Does not the claim of infallibility in *any* institution make it impossible for that institution to face problems of truth and falsehood honestly? I think that a good case can be made out of the thesis that absolute power is amoral. It knows only obedience and disobedience, not right and wrong.

In perspective that seems to be the fundamental fact behind the Kremlin strategy of penetration. It has no respect for the adverse judgments of mankind in *any* organization, democratic or undemocratic, because it is superior to and exempt from the corrective processes of democratic freedom. It considers itself the fount of all sound moral judgment. We shall see in the next chapter that that is also the fundamental belief behind the Vatican's strategy of penetration.

12

The Strategy of Penetration: the Vatican

THE MISSIONARIES OF THE KREMLIN penetrate the jungles of capitalism with the gospel of a classless society according to Lenin, and the missionaries of the Vatican penetrate all non-Catholic countries with a gospel of faith, service, and loyalty which emphasizes almost all Kremlin values in reverse. In this chapter I am interested in the machinery of power which underlies that penetration and makes it possible. The Vatican assumes the right to operate within every non-Catholic nation not only a Catholic church but also a Catholic school system, a Catholic political party, a Catholic labor federation, and a Catholic diplomatic establishment, all completely subordinate to the Roman Curia. Since I have already discussed some phases of these institutions, I shall confine myself here to political parties, labor unions, and papal diplomats, with a few incidental remarks about the Church as a biological bloc.

It is obvious that the Vatican's techniques of penetration are in sharp contrast to those of the Kremlin. The Kremlin relies on violence wherever it is deemed to be necessary; the Vatican does not — or, at least, has not done so in recent times. The Kremlin aims to destroy the governments which it cannot conquer by persuasion; the Vatican is, on the whole, law-abiding and non-revolutionary. But the Vatican has one special advantage not shared by any other church or government. Since it is a church and a state, it can enter into any nation which permits the free exercise of religion and use its machinery of power to further political as well as religious ends. Simultaneously it can use the reservoirs of religious devotion and prejudice among its people in behalf of strictly political objectives. Because of this ambidextrous facility, the Catholic leader who is attacked for the stupidity of the Church's formula on some controversial political issue can fall back on religious emotion and loyalty to disguise and defend that stupidity; and similarly when the right of a religious institution to play an aggressive role in the determination of foreign policy is questioned, the Catholic protagonist can revert to the ancient claim that his Church has always been more than a church and that it is a sovereign power with political prerogatives.

In practice anyone who questions the right of the Church to operate in a field which seems to lie close to the heart of secular democracy is accused by the Vatican of opposing the Church's "spiritual authority." That phrase, "spiritual authority," was used in this connection in October 1949, by Count Giuseppe dalla Torre, editor of the Vatican's *Osservatore Romano,* in stating the negative side of the Catholic right of penetration. "Wherever a state," he said, "putting the Catholic Church in the same category as other denominations whose clergy is autonomous and self-governing, refuses to recognize a superior spiritual authority because it is outside its jurisdiction, it not only hinders the freedom of the Catholic Church but it denies its organic structure."[1] This is at once a warning against any possible attempt by any government to force the democratization of the Catholic Church within its jurisdiction, and a backhanded statement of the right of the Vatican to enter any country with its full quota of religious, moral, cultural, and political policies.

The Priest-Diplomats

In the world of international power politics the most effective agents of the Church are its priest-diplomats. They are simultaneously politicians and missionaries, prepared to act in either role according to the demands of any particular situation, and armed with the special knowledge supplied to them by the Vatican's world-wide intelligence network. The Vatican now has thirty-six Nuncios, Internuncios, and lesser diplomats at the world's capitals who correspond in functions and rank with the ambassadors and ministers of secular nations; and twenty-three Apostolic Delegates who function as ecclesiastical representatives in countries which do not have diplomatic relations with the Holy See.[2] The regular Vatican diplomats live in elaborate establishments and maintain a considerable pomp and splendor. In most capitals they are actually the doyens of the diplomatic corps, taking precedence over the senior ambassadors of the oldest lay states. This special recognition goes back to the Congress of Vienna of 1815, and the Vatican has always insisted that this precedence should be maintained.[3]

The Vatican's diplomacy has become especially important in recent years because of the Church's active participation in the struggle against Communism. Ordinarily the Cardinal Secretary of State is the only cardinal who lives in the Vatican Palace, and he sees His Holiness every morning to discuss the world's diplomatic situation. During recent years, when Pius XII has nominally been acting as his own Secretary of State, the work of the Office has been performed by two of the Vatican's most important figures, Monsignor Giovanni Montini and Monsignor Domenico Tardini. Monsignor Montini, although still too young to succeed Pius XII, is considered by insiders as a possible future pope. He handles directly the ordinary current affairs of Vatican diplomacy, while Monsignor Tardini handles special agreements.

The Church's diplomatic establishment makes the Vatican a nerve center of political intelligence and an important factor in the manipulations of power politics. Today, for example, the Vatican through its far-flung diplomatic representatives is the leading champion of the internationalization of Jerusalem, and it is working with Moslem powers on this issue against the majority of the United Nations Assembly. It is generally acknowledged that it was Vatican diplomatic pressure which swung the votes in the United Nations Assembly on December 9, 1949, to the internationalism formula. In the close and dramatic fight between Israel and the Vatican at Lake Success, several Catholic countries were induced to switch their votes from the negative to the affirmative column by direct Vatican intervention. The final affirmative vote was assured when Cardinal Spellman wired the President of the Philippines and persuaded the Philippine regime to change its vote from abstention to Yes.[4]

The Vatican's influence on the political policies of secular states is exercised not only through its own diplomats in foreign capitals but through the diplomats of foreign powers who are assigned to the Holy See. Some thirty-six ranking ambassadors and ministers from many of the world's greatest powers now maintain their establishments near the Vatican and meet periodically with the acting Secretaries of State, or with the Pope himself if a crisis arises. Many of these nations which recognize the Vatican in this way are not primarily or even substantially Catholic nations. Great Britain, with a Catholic population of only 6 per cent, has a representative; Egypt, with 1 per cent, and Finland, with one-tenth of 1 per cent, also have ministers. The United States (at this writing), the Soviet Union and its satellites, Israel, and the Scandinavian powers do not maintain official relations.

It has been a source of great disappointment to the Vatican that no official representative from the United States has been appointed since the days when the Church controlled the Papal States of Italy. Even in those days — from 1848 to 1867 — our government did not recognize the Papal States as a church, and Seward warned our minister resident at the Holy See in 1862 that "so far as spiritual or ecclesiastical matters enter into the question they are beyond your province, for you are a political representative only." When Pius IX's regime made difficulties for a Protestant church which desired to worship outside of the American legation in Rome, Congress passed an act saying that "no money hereby or otherwise appropriated shall be paid for the support of an American legation at Rome." Since then the United States has had no official representative at the Vatican, and the Vatican has sent to Washington only religious representatives (Apostolic Delegates). Franklin Roosevelt, however, sent the Protestant business man Myron Taylor to the Vatican in 1940 as his personal representative, under the pretext that contact with the Vatican was important for purposes of cooperation in a war period; Taylor resigned in 1950.[4a]

The Vatican is so sensitive to the factors of prestige and precedence involved in full recognition that the Pope will not accept any part-time assignment of any diplomat who is also accredited to the government of Italy. He insists on full recognition as the head of an important sovereign power, and apparently he believes that the acceptance of the part-time services of an ambassador to Italy would impair the Vatican's standing in world diplomacy.

The exchange of diplomats makes it possible for the Vatican to maintain constant pressure on all secular powers in favor of any particular political policy. The Vatican's representatives mingle with government leaders at the highest level and have an unexcelled opportunity to affect their personal judgment. Pressure from the Vatican is not necessarily limited to religious matters; in middle and western Europe particularly the Vatican's finger is in almost every political pie. Its diplomats are, of course, always and everywhere vigorous propagandists against the Soviet Union. In Spain they are propagandists for Franco; in Belgium they are propagandists for the monarchy; in France they are propagandists for the separate Catholic labor movement; in Italy in 1950 they played the decisive role in "persuading" the Italian parliament to pass a new anti-divorce law outlawing the recognition of foreign divorce decrees. (They had already made Italy officially a land of no divorce.)

This pressure is not always exerted officially by the Roman diplomats themselves, but they have a large corps of bishops and priests to campaign for them in the native vernacular. Nor is the intelligence network of Vatican diplomacy limited to official diplomats. Unofficially every bishop in the world is part of the diplomatic establishment of the Vatican, and his regular reports are available in the making of foreign policy. The bishops' reports, in fact, are not confined to religious and moral problems, since they cover all matters that may affect Vatican power and prestige. Also their services as political propagandists are always available to the Vatican, even in countries where there is no Nuncio. In the United States in 1926-27, for example, virtually every Catholic bishop in the nation was a pro-war propagandist against Mexico; but there was no Nuncio at Washington to direct the diplomatic campaign, and there was no need of a Nuncio. The direction came from Rome through the "regular channels."

In matters of world political policy, all bishops, priests, and Catholic editors are, in a sense, diplomats for the Vatican who follow the papal line almost as faithfully as Communist leaders follow the Kremlin line. Before World War II, when the Vatican wanted to keep the United States from intervening in Europe, the Catholic press and the Catholic pulpit throughout the world sounded the message of non-intervention. Today the tone of the pulpit and the press is exactly the reverse, since the political interests of Vatican diplomacy call for the participation of the west in the war against Communism.

The final aim of every Vatican representative to a foreign government is the official concordat, an agreement which gives legal recognition to the special privileges of the Church in the nation. It is a full-blown political treaty between two sovereign powers, and it is executed with all the solemnity of the most important secular treaty. Usually when it is made with a Catholic country, it recognizes the Roman Catholic religion as the sole official religion of the state, and grants public money to Catholic schools, or Catholic control of the teaching of religion and morals in the public schools.

Frequently the concordat grants concessions to political rulers to exercise some power over the Church, such as the confirmation or nomination of the chief bishops in a country. In all these matters the Catholic people have no power whatever; the Vatican blandly assumes that its special representatives and bishops can bargain for the people in the same way that European diplomats once bargained for the subject peoples of their empires. The diplomacy of concordats is imperial diplomacy. Hence, the popes have always preferred to make concordats with absolute rulers because it is easier for imperial diplomats to deal directly with imperial diplomats without the intervention of annoying parliaments. The assumption that concordats may rightfully be imposed upon people from above characterized the negotiations between Pius XI and Mussolini, and as a result the future generations of Italy were bound by an agreement which, when incorporated into the constitution as it was in 1946, prevents the Italian people from passing laws in their parliament permitting divorce or otherwise contravening Catholic canon law in the field of marriage.

But the day of concordats is dying. Their popularity reached a peak in the nineteenth century when the Papacy made twenty-six leading international bargains, most of which were very favorable to its interests. Then, as democracy increased throughout the world, the people rapidly discarded the old concordats. Pius XI in his reign of seventeen years signed eighteen conventions with states, of which at least ten were major concordats; but today only one of his major concordats, that with Italy, is still functioning.[5] As democracy has increased, the people of the west, even the good Catholic people, have become more and more reluctant to bargain away any of the nation's cultural or moral rights in a treaty with a foreign government, even when that government claims exclusive jurisdiction from God. The American attitude toward such concessions is becoming general. It is part of the American tradition that the rights, privileges, and prerogatives of any church functioning on American soil should be determined directly by the people through their representatives.

The Controlled Political Party

Since political power in modern democracies is based upon political parties, the Vatican has rather reluctantly accepted the necessity of building its own political parties in order to effect its own purposes. The controlled Catholic party is a fairly recent development in Vatican strategy. Having grown up in a predemocratic era, the Papacy ignored mass political movements as long as it could gracefully do so, and bargained successfully with princes and kings. When democratic parties first began to develop in nineteenth-century Europe, the Papacy was apprehensive. The popes were quite scornful of democracy and quite frankly counter-revolutionary. As late as 1885, Leo XIII in his *Immortale Dei,* which was the nineteenth-century bible of Catholic political philosophy, spoke of democratic parties in the hostile language of a medieval prince, and declared that the doctrine of the sovereignty of the people "is doubtless a doctrine exceedingly well calculated to flatter and to influence many passions, but which lacks all reasonable proof, and all power of insuring public safety and preserving order." (It should be noted that this statement was made about one hundred years after the birth of the American Constitution; and during that entire century American Catholics had been asserting that there was no conflict between its philosophy and that of the Papacy.)

After the capture of Rome by the new Kingdom of Italy in 1870, Italian Catholics were forbidden to participate in the political life of the new nation because of the kingdom's seizure of the Papal States. Pius IX and Leo XIII tried to bring about the internal disintegration of the kingdom by directing non-co-operation for all Catholics, and all those who had taken part in the seizure of papal property were excommunicated, even the members of the new parliament. But the electoral boycott injured the Papacy more than the Italian government, and the popes finally retreated in some disorder, permitting Italian Catholics to participate in the national elections.[6]

After World War I, the Vatican under Benedict XV adopted an openly political line and entered politics in earnest, not only in Italy but also in Germany and Belgium. The Vatican had already entered politics in Catholic Austria under the leadership of Monsignor Ignatz Seipel and his bitterly anti-Socialist Catholic Party. Its greatest success there was scored in 1933 and 1934 when the nation became a clerical-fascist state under Engelbert Dollfuss and his Fatherland Front. His monolithic regime was treated by the continental Catholic press with respect and admiration as a model of Catholicism in politics, but its resemblance to Mussolini's regime greatly embarrassed British and American Catholics who were attempting to prove to their compatriots at that time that the Vatican was not pro-fascist.

Although the first Catholic ventures into European parliamentary politics ended in reactionary and anti-democratic movements, new Catholic parties with bold democratic slogans began to blossom and prosper in Europe after World War II. A little probing into the sources of strength of some of these parties would have revealed the fact that the same classes and individuals which had supported fascism had quietly moved over into the Catholic camp; but post-war Europe was so alarmed about the rising menace of Communism that it did not care to notice such things.

Today the Vatican partially controls at least seven unofficial Catholic parties in Europe, and participates indirectly through these parties in the governments of Italy, France, West Germany, Belgium, the Netherlands, Spain, and Portugal. In each one of these countries, except France, the Catholic party is far stronger than the Communist Party. In 1949 the Catholic *Register* boasted that there was a Catholic premier or vice premier in Switzerland, Lichtenstein, Monaco, Spain, Portugal, Belgium, the Netherlands, Ireland, Italy, France, and West Germany.[7]

What do these parties look like? We can take the time only for a glance at their present position.

In Belgium the Christian Social (Catholic) Party has held a majority in both houses of parliament since June 1950, when it swept into power in a national referendum on the monarchy. Since then the party has developed many conflicting internal tensions, and its continuance in power is doubtful.

In France the M.R.P. (Mouvement Républicain Populaire), which was born out of Catholic Action, has held a key place in the government for many years. Although it has only 24 per cent of the seats in the French National Assembly, it has placed such good Catholics as Georges Bidault and Robert Schuman in the premiership and the foreign office, and it continues to be the most powerful policy-making force in the government coalition. It has deliberately imitated the organization techniques of the Communist Party, with a centralized machine, training schools for its workers, and branches in all the villages and towns; and it has drawn heavily for strength on the Catholic counterparts of Communist labor and farm cells — respectively, the Jocists and the Jacists.[8] Meanwhile, the Vatican has a possible second-string Catholic party in General De Gaulle's R.P.F. (Rassemblement du Peuple Français), which follows a strong anti-Communist and pro-Catholic policy.

In Portugal, Premier Salazar's monolithic, one-party state is essentially a clerical-fascist state in which the Catholic hierarchy co-operates with the dictatorship in return for a privileged position in the national life. The dictator himself is popularly called "the little priest." His National Union Party, which has been unopposed for eighteen years, has the unofficial blessing of the hierarchy, and it reciprocates by supporting Church supervision of religious education in the public schools, the prohibition of divorce, and the full recognition of the Catholic canon law on marriage.

In Italy the strongest Catholic party in Europe, the Christian Democrat Party, holds an over-all majority in the Chamber of Deputies and completely dominates the government of Premier Alcide de Gasperi. Although the party has made Italy into a confessional state with Catholicism as the state religion, financial support for the clergy, local domination by bishops, and the recognition of Catholic marriage law, its hold on the Italian masses is distinctly precarious. It polled only 48.7 per cent of the popular vote at the 1948 national election after a campaign in which the nation was thoroughly alarmed about Communist conquest, and after both the Vatican and the United States had thrown immense resources into the struggle.

In the Netherlands, although the Catholic bloc in the population is less than 40 per cent, the Catholic Party is the largest single party in the state, polling 32 per cent of the votes at the last national election and capturing 8 of the 15 seats in the government's coalition cabinet. The party has already won its major financial objectives.

In West Germany, where the Catholic and non-Catholic population is about evenly divided, the chief political party, the Christian Democratic Union, is overwhelmingly Catholic in composition and its Catholic representatives in the Bundestag outnumber its Protestant representatives more than 2 to 1. The reshuffling of boundary lines in Germany as a result of World War II and of the post-war agreements made West Germany into a virtually Catholic, rather than Protestant, state. "The West German state," says the British journalist, Basil Davidson, "is in the most practical sense a Catholic base in Europe, in every way as self-conscious and proselytizing as, for instance, Franco's Spain."[9] The Prime Minister, Konrad Adenauer, is a Catholic, and the party — although it includes many Protestants — stands for an essentially Catholic program in education.

Franco's Spain, the most Catholic country in the world, is a clerical-fascist police state in which the Catholic hierarchy co-operates passively in the suppression of all free political activity. No political opposition has been permitted since the fascist revolution. Franco, according to the Law of Succession which was adopted by a fake "referendum" in 1947, heads the Council of the Kingdom, which also includes the Cardinal Primate of the Church. The Minister of State is a former head of Catholic Action, and the Church chooses the Minister of Education. The one recognized political party under Franco is the Falange, which prescribes a fascist uniform and which has written into its twenty-six-point program the two following points:

> Our state will be a totalitarian instrument in the service of national integrity. . . . Political parties are to be abolished.
> Our movement will incorporate the Catholic spirit in the national reconstruction.

"Of the elements supporting Generalissimo Franco," says Cyrus L. Sulzberger, chief foreign correspondent of the New York *Times,* "by all means the most important in terms of political and cultural impact is the Roman Catholic Church in Spain." [10]

This running sketch of seven Catholic political parties in Europe does not cover the many situations throughout the world where Catholic power expresses itself in blocs, coalitions, and pressure groups within other political parties, nor does it touch upon the great political activities of the Church in the iron-curtain countries or in Catholic regions like Argentina and Quebec.

A Catholic International?

The question which many observers are asking about this Catholic political development is: Will such Catholic political parties be amalgamated and fused into a Catholic international to parallel the Cominform and dominate western European politics?

The answer must be very tentative. In the past the Vatican has been extremely cautious about forming any political international because of the fear that such an organization might get out of hand. The Sicilian priest, Don Sturzo, who headed the Catholic Popular Party of Italy before Mussolini came into power, attempted to form a "white international," but his plans were rejected by Pius XI. The present Pope seems somewhat more receptive to the idea, and new moves toward a rightist international have recently been made. At least three European-wide conferences of Catholic parties have been held since 1947. The cohesive force in the new movement is anti-Communism and anti-Socialism, with Catholicism as background and atmosphere.

With the partial backing of more than 100,000,000 Catholics in western Europe, the Catholic parties are already co-operating to make the Council of Europe into an anti-Socialist force, and that is one reason why the British Labor Party is reluctant to surrender any national sovereignty to a European coalition. The Vatican must move with special caution because the democratic Catholic parties in France, Belgium, Italy, and the Netherlands refuse to have anything to do with the Catholic parties of the

Spanish and Portuguese dictators, and the Pope cannot be placed in the position of seeming to oppose his two prize Catholic countries. The Vatican may choose to co-operate with totalitarian regimes, but no Catholic politician in a European democracy can afford to co-operate if he wants labor votes. So Franco and Salazar must remain outside of the Catholic alliance for the time being.

The tentative groundwork for a Catholic international in Europe — without Spain and Portugal — has been laid in Paris, and modest offices have been opened in the headquarters of the M.R.P. under the name of Nouvelles Equipes Internationales, which means a team or clearing house. With official support from the Catholic parties in Italy, Germany, Belgium, Austria, the Netherlands, the Saar, Luxemburg, and Switzerland, and personal support from Catholic political leaders in France, Belgium, and Great Britain, as well as the backing of six exiled parties from eastern Europe, the new international is, to put it mildly, promising. Premier de Gasperi, in speaking to an international conference of the organization in Sorrento in April 1950, called upon it to formulate "plans for an over-all Christian policy" throughout Europe.[11] Thus far no detailed general program has appeared.

What are the tactics and political policies which such a Catholic international can support?

It is possible to make certain generalizations after observing the Catholic political parties in action in Europe. The first generalization is that every Catholic party must represent certain basic Vatican objectives — or it will not get Vatican support. Those objectives must always include opposition to the Kremlin, and the securing of public money for Catholic schools. A political party which stands for these two Vatican demands may have a wide latitude of choice concerning all other planks in its platfrom and still win the support of local priests with Vatican approval. It may be Socialist — the Catholic party of Bavaria is still called the Christian Socialist Party — or capitalist or monarchist or fascist (like Salazar's and Franco's parties), but the Vatican will not repudiate it if it serves as an instrument of opposition to the arch-enemy, and if it helps the Church to secure public funds. Self-interest is the Vatican's primary motive for being in politics, and in practical operation it is as consistent in pursuing that end as Tammany Hall.

In view of the present drift toward democracy as a form of government, the Vatican is now tolerating democratic governments with more charity than in the past; but its tolerance is instantly changed to hostility if a democracy opposes any special interest of the Church. Gabriel Almond of Yale University, in a significant study, "The Christian Parties of Western Europe," says that the Vatican "supports democratic governments and democratic parties when such a policy will protect or enhance the position of the Church. It will withdraw its support when democratic institutions seem to be seriously threatening Church interests, or when they prove to be too weak a reed on which to rest its fate."[12] Mr. Almond, after analyzing the activities of the Catholic parties of Europe, reaches this conclusion: "It is probable that the majority of the voters of these parties are not democrats by conviction, but this is not to say that they are convinced anti-democrats." The parties contain authoritarian elements which are ready to carry Europe back to fascism if a crisis gives them the opportunity. They are particularly strong in the rural areas of Italy, Belgium, and Germany, where, as Mr. Almond points out, "the Christian party organization is often indistinguishable from the Church apparatus. One may pass from Church to Catholic Action to Christian party and still be under the same roof and surrounded by the same faces."

Ideally, every Catholic party must support the whole Vatican political program. If it gains power, it must abolish divorce, prohibit birth control, recognize the Church as the sole state religion, suppress criticism of the Pope, prevent public Protestant ceremonies, ban all books which are on the Catholic Index, and pay the salaries of priests. But only completely Catholic nations such as Spain and Portugal ever go this far, and such extreme demands are never heard of in the Catholic political movements of nations like France, Belgium, and the Netherlands. In such countries the Catholic political parties and blocs shrewdly limit their demands to the feasible and the practical. In economic matters they are often as liberal as the Socialists, but they always attempt to prevent Socialist domination of a government.

There is something rather grimly humorous in the Church's

acceptance of alliances with Socialists in France, Belgium, and the Netherlands in order to defeat Communist power more effectively, since many popes have declared that no good Catholic can be a good Socialist. To justify this co-operation the Vatican has evolved a formula which divides socialism into two varieties, the materialist kind and the humane or Christian variety. Marx and his materialistic philosophy are still anathema, but all other brands are acceptable if not commendable, especially if they acknowledge the vague and sentimental contributions of Leo XIII and Pius XI to the literature of reform. The Catholic bishops of West Germany in 1949 actually endorsed the "Christian doctrine of socialism, as the Popes have demanded for so long." [13]

One fundamental stratagem is always apparent in the Vatican's support of a Catholic party. The support must never be official, and the connection between the party and the Church must never be too evident. "The Church stands above all political parties." That is the doctrine for public consumption, and the reason for it is quite obvious. A defeated political party might drag the Vatican down with it. If the connection between the Catholic party and the Vatican remains unofficial, the Holy See can always blame its shortcomings on human weakness. It can always maintain the fiction that it is a non-partisan organization. It attempted to maintain this fiction even in the middle of its intense campaign for Christian Democrat victory in Italy in 1948, when almost the whole energies of the Italian priesthood were diverted to political effort and when "God's own loudspeaker," Father Riccardo Lombardi, was arousing huge audiences to white-hot passion against the leftist forces.

This desire to avoid direct responsibility for political disaster explains why the Church also frowns on the political leadership of priests. When a party is led by a priest, it is difficult for the Vatican to defend its claim that the Church is above partisanship. The Catholic Popular Party which developed in Italy after World War I, and which seemed for a time to be the most logical barrier against Mussolini, was jettisoned for a good price by Pius XI partly because its leadership by the Sicilian priest, Don Sturzo, made it seem too official an instrument. The Pope forced Don Sturzo to resign partly because of this fact and partly because he decided at that moment to back Mussolini against the Italian Socialists. So he publicly reminded all Italian Catholics that it was against the moral law to make an alliance with Socialists. Since the Socialists were indispensable for any alliance that could defeat Mussolini, the Pope's action opened the door to fascist power. Pius XI, incidentally, betrayed the Catholic political movements of both Germany and Austria to dictatorships in a similar manner because he was fundamentally hostile to democracy.[14]

The wisdom of the Vatican's opposition to priests as statesmen was underscored during World War II when Monsignor Josef Tiso served from 1939 to 1945 as head of the Catholic-fascist state of Slovakia under Hitler's domination. Perhaps if the Axis powers had won the war, Tiso would have been described in the Catholic textbooks as a reasonably respectable statesman. He had never lost his standing as a priest and had never been repudiated by the Vatican publicly; in fact, he had received an Apostolic Benediction from Pius XII in December 1939.[15] It was, therefore, embarrassing for the Vatican when he was convicted of collaborating with Hitler in the deportation and murder of Jews, and was promptly hanged.

The Vatican controls its political parties by devices which are less formal than the devices used for political control by the Kremlin. There is no formal bureau for Catholic political parties in the Vatican set-up, and no official political platform. All clerical advice on all levels is given privately, except in a crisis. Each local bishop acts as a political agent for the Vatican, and supports, ignores, or opposes a Catholic party according to Vatican directives. The Vatican can destroy any Catholic political party in Europe in a few weeks by directing all bishops to order all local priests to advise their parishioners to leave the organization. This veto power on all Catholic parties makes the leaders completely obedient to the bishops whenever the bishops care to exercise their authority.

The Vatican's lay device for controlling a Catholic political party is its own world-wide lay organization, Catholic Action. This mass propaganda organization can never slip from Vatican control because it is organized hierarchically by dioceses and parishes and works under the direct supervision of the appropriate bishop or priest. In the United States it is not openly political at the present time because the Vatican is not ready for the formation of a Catholic party in America; but in countries like Italy it is the most powerful political mass movement in the nation, with the possible exception of the Communist Party. It was the primary force in winning the Italian election of 1948, and it continues today to be the strong inner core in the Christian Democrat Party, pushing it to the right and making its policies more uncompromising.

Catholic Action uses very solemn theological terms in describing itself as non-political, but its practices in many parts of Europe are almost as openly partisan as those of a political party. "It is non-political," says the Irish Catholic scholar, Professor D. A. Binchy, "only in the sense that the Catholic Church claims to be non-political; that is, it must take no part as an organization in public affairs of a purely secular nature. On the other hand in all 'mixed matters,' where Church and State claim concurrent jurisdiction, it must be prepared to support the Church's claims in the event of a dispute; still more if the State should encroach on the Church's domain or adopt any policy opposed to the traditional Christian principles of morality and government."[16] Since the Pope alone in the Catholic system of power has the right to define "traditional Christian principles of morality and government," he can use Catholic Action to support any policy which he so defines.

American Catholics know very little about the political phases of European Catholic power, and in the American Catholic press political Catholicism in Europe is represented simply as the Church's crusade to preserve the Faith against Communism. Here, for example, is a typical question and answer in the Catholic *Register* of Denver which emphasizes "atheistic Communism" as an issue:

Are pastors of Catholic churches permitted to instruct their people how and for whom to vote?

If the result of the election can have no evil effect on right faith or good morals, the pastor should not use the pulpit to discuss politics, though he may, as a private citizen, voice his views on the election outside the pulpit. If, however, the issue at stake in the election is one of vital importance to faith and morals, such as the diffusion of atheistic Communism, the pastor certainly has the right to present the facts before the people; moreover, he should do so, since he is the flock's guide in moral matters.[17]

There are very few important issues in modern politics which a priest cannot interpret as "of vital importance to faith and morals," and in European politics in recent years the leading priests in almost all countries which have Catholic parties have managed to announce their interpretations of faith and morals in striking fashion just before election time in such a way as to affect the result at the polls. Their appeals in each case have been strictly limited to the standard objectives of Catholic power, but in effect they have gone far beyond the Church's moral program and swung Catholic support to reactionary blocs. After a pastoral letter from Catholic bishops, clearly supporting the Christian Democratic Union, had defeated the Socialist Party of West Germany in the 1949 election by influencing women's votes, Kurt Schumacher, leader of the Socialists, angrily denounced the Vatican as the "fifth occupation power" in Germany, and said: "We have the impression that they [the Church leaders] would like to make a second Spain in Germany."[18]

Mr. Schumacher was angry, and he undoubtedly overstated the case against Vatican political strategy, but in perspective there was a great deal of justice in what he said. The Vatican is in its very nature an occupying power, and when it enters politics in a country, the voters of that country are quite unable to determine its program. Moreover, although a Catholic party may begin with a progressive program, the inherent conservatism of the Church nearly always pushes it to the right, and it becomes inevitably the nesting ground for all the forces of economic and political reaction. This has been the sorry fate of almost all the Catholic parties of Europe since the "model" Catholic state of Austria under Dollfuss became an essentially fascist state in 1933. The Anglican Archbishop of York expressed the apprehensions of many western democrats about this counter-revolutionary tendency of Catholic politics when he said in 1947: "The Catholic parties on the Continent are at present progressive in their programs, but they are also the only rallying grounds for the reactionaries, and in the course of time there is danger that, once again, on the Continent, Catholicism will be identified with reaction."[19]

The Controlled Labor Union

A London dispatch to American Catholic newspapers in December 1949 said: "Catholic delegates to the conference of the newly formed International Confederation of Free Trade Unions here voted to form a World Federation of Catholic Trade Unionists." Behind this dispatch lay a whole story of Vatican penetration into the labor movements of many countries.

To most non-Catholics such a dispatch would seem somewhat bizarre. They would naturally ask: Why *Catholic* labor unions? Why not Methodist or Jewish or Christian Science labor unions? The idea of religious divisions in the labor movement seems utterly repugnant to most British and American workingmen, including British and American Catholics. On the European Continent, however, the Vatican has long been active in building a labor movement of its own in exactly the way that it has built school systems of its own. For many years it failed to make substantial progress with this program, but recently it has gained new strength from the increasing fear of Communist aggression. It has asserted the theory that the Catholic labor union is the most effective competing force against Communism in any labor crisis, and by emphasizing this gospel it has succeeded in building labor organizations which claim more than three million members in European countries.

The complete story of the Vatican's attempt to penetrate the world labor movement is too long to tell here, but the high points are as follows. The nineteenth-century Church in Europe tended to be hostile to the rising power of organized labor because of the Vatican's traditional alliances with upper-class groups. When political socialism and industrial unionism began to conquer Europe simultaneously, the Vatican found itself increasingly on the defensive. Leo XIII saw the necessity of a change in policy if the Church was to hold the loyalty of the Catholic masses, and in his famous encyclical *Rerum Novarum,* in 1891, he effected a strategic about-face in the Catholic philosophy of labor by endorsing the principle of "workingmen's unions." The encyclical was a vague and sentimental appeal for justice for the workingman, which the Catholic liberals have tried vainly to inflate into a comprehensive bill of economic rights; but it had the great virtue of releasing the humane forces in the Church from bondage to reaction and prejudice. It was so vague that its arguments could be successfully used for benevolent socialism or benevolent fascism; and forty years later Pius XI in another famous encyclical on labor actually did make use of Leo XIII's pronouncements in supporting the principles of the fascist corporate state.[20]

Most of the early labor unions of Europe were predominantly Socialist. The assertion of the rights of labor in a capitalist society was closely tied up with the assertion of the ultimate ideal of Socialism, the taking over of industry by a workers' state. Although the Socialist movement was not fundamentally anti-religious in the larger meaning of that term, it was strongly anti-clerical — not only because of the Church's alliances with the upper classes but because labor leaders had come to regard the Church as an enemy of progress and science. The Vatican, fearful of the rising power of Socialist labor, decided that it must form an opposition labor movement of its own. A beginning was made in the 1890's, and in 1920 an International Federation of Christian Trade Unions was launched at The Hague. Now it is called the C.I.S.C. (Confédération Internationale des Syndicats Chrétiens), and in the autumn of 1950 its international officers at Utrecht claimed that it had 3,271,000 members, mostly in France, Belgium, Italy, the Netherlands, and Ireland. It has no strength in the United States, Great Britain, Germany, Austria, and the Scandinavian countries, and of course it has no branches in the east European countries of the Soviet orbit. In several of these countries, however, there are associations of individual Catholic trade unionists, serving as anti-Communist cells inside non-Catholic unions, and the C.I.S.C. claims more than a million of these individual Catholic unionists to reach its estimated total.

Wherever possible, the Vatican uses Catholic unions for its own purposes — for a Catholic monarchy in Belgium, for the defeat of the Communist-dominated C.G.T. in France, for the strengthening of Catholic schools in the Netherlands. But it has never been as successful in the labor movement as it has been in politics. When the non-Catholic unions of the world met in London in December 1949 to form a world democratic labor front against the Kremlin, the Vatican was cold-shouldered. The non-Catholic and many of the Catholic delegates wanted a single non-Communist federation of world labor to oppose the Communist-dominated W.F.T.U. (see Chapter 11) which they had left, but the Catholic C.I.S.C. earned the deep resentment of the delegates by holding out for the continuation of its own separate international federation of Catholic unions. Most of the labor leaders of the west, including the foremost Catholic leaders of American labor, objected strenuously to such a division along religious lines.

Now the labor organizations of the United States, Great Britain, and the continental countries of western Europe are united in a new labor international with the name International Confederation of Free Trade Unions; but the Catholic unions are outside. They were invited to join the new I.C.F.T.U. on a free and equal basis with all other unions, but it was stipulated in the invitation that their Catholic international must cease to exist within two years, and they refused to accept the stipulation.

The decision for separation was not popular even in the American Catholic press, because it revealed the narrow denominationalism of Vatican labor policy. Even in Italy there was much opposition in Catholic circles to a denominational policy, and the newly formed anti-Communist labor federation of that country, the C.S.I.L., decided to join the International Confederation of Free Trade Unions instead of the Catholic international. Nevertheless the C.I.S.C. still has enough power in several countries of Europe to divide the ranks of democratic labor effectively. In both Belgium and the Netherlands the Catholic unions are only a little below the regular, neutral unions in numerical strength, and they have majority control in several key industries. In France they are probably second in strength to the Communist-dominated C.G.T., and slightly ahead of the non-Communist Force Ouvrière. It is true that in France the Catholic unions are relatively progressive and independent, and they resent the clerical policy of labor which the Vatican is now supporting. Some of their leaders would welcome affiliation with the new non-confessional I.C.F.T.U. if they could overcome the objections of their bishops.

In the Netherlands, however, the Catholic hierarchy is fighting desperately to maintain the power of its own labor bloc, and it has brought up its heaviest theological artillery for the battle. In an edict read from all Catholic pulpits in 1946, and since repeatedly confirmed, the bishops have announced that Catholics who join the regular, non-religious federation of labor, the N.V.V., may be denied absolution in the confessional for such a sinful act.[21] The N.V.V. is not a Communist organization — in fact, it is quite definitely anti-Communist and there is a Communist rival in the field — but the Catholic hierarchy is unwilling to lose its hold over the Dutch Catholic workers by leaving them free to decide the question of labor affiliation for themselves. It even carries its narrow rule of separatism to the grave. In 1949, when the body of an N.V.V. railroad worker in Heerlen was being taken to a Catholic cemetery for burial, the flower car in his funeral cortege, containing a large wreath from the N.V.V., was stopped two hundred yards from the cemetery on orders of the Catholic authorities, and the tainted wreath was removed.[22]

It was the fear of such denominational bitterness which led the new free federation of non-Communist labor to reject for itself all religious classifications. At its organizing conference in London in 1949, Miss Maniben Kara of India gave the reply of democratic labor to denominational narrowness in a simple and moving appeal:

At the outset I must make it absolutely clear that I have nothing against Christians. I think they are good, honest and sincere citizens. I make my objection only because I think that no trade union organisation should be mixed up with any religion. On this ground I personally would not like to lay down a precedent which this Assembly later on will find it extremely difficult to adopt. I understand that the Christian Catholic trade union organisations have to take their dictation, to some extent, from their own churches. To that extent I believe that those trade union organisations are not absolutely free or democratic because it is not the will of the constituents of those organisations which really counts inasmuch as they have to depend upon an outside authority. I for one would very much like to see this International grow up into a strong organisation which will be free from any outside influences, except from those of the working classes. If we accept that as a principle I cannot understand how this Assembly can recommend the inclusion of any sect of people who owe allegiance to any outside influence other than their constituent members. . . .

If we allow the admission of trade unions based on religion, you will not be able to shut the door against Hindu trade unions, Moslem trade unions, Arab trade unions and various other trade unions which would come for affiliation before this gathering. We are living in the days of civilisation; we are going ahead; national boundaries are receding in the background. We are thinking in the terms of international politics. We are thinking in the terms of one world, and in that atmosphere we cannot possibly narrow down the scope of the Conference by having among us, or by admitting, those people who want to have a sectarian outlook.[23]

The Vatican is not moved by such an appeal because it is confident of its own special mission as adviser and guide for organized labor, and it has developed special agencies for this guidance throughout the world. Wherever possible it continues to support separate Catholic labor movements with priest-advisers for every branch; and in every situation where labor separatism is not practical, it promotes its two agencies of labor penetration into non-Catholic unions, the A.C.T.U.'s and the Jocists. The Jocists are the Young Christian Workers — under twenty-five years of age and unmarried — who use the cell technique for penetration. They claimed fifty operating cells in thirty major cities in the United States in 1948.[24] The A.C.T.U. (Association of Catholic Trade Unionists) in the United States is a typical instrument for adult penetration of non-Catholic labor organizations. It consists of Catholic devotees who are economic liberals and who work under priestly direction inside American labor unions as a kind of union within a union, attempting to swing the policies of the larger organization toward the Catholic position. In spite of much fanfare in the American and the Catholic press, the A.C.T.U. has never been of much importance in the American labor movement. It has had a maximum membership of 5,000 in a national labor union membership of nearly sixteen million. American workers deeply resent any attempt to bring denominational divisions into the labor movement. Not a single important labor leader in the United States supports A.C.T.U. vigorously, and many Catholic labor leaders openly condemn it. The reason for the condemnation is obvious — the organization in spite of its professions of helpfulness is actually creating a dual authority in the labor world, outside the unions themselves. Article VII of the constitution of A.C.T.U.'s Detroit branch accurately reflects its spirit:

> In the event of insoluble dispute over any question of policy, tactics, principle or leadership, the counsel of the Most Rev. Archbishop shall be the final determinant.[25]

Conquest by Fecundity

Perhaps the most important factor in the penetration of Catholic power into non-Catholic territory today is a phenomenon which is almost never discussed frankly in public, the stimulated Catholic birthrate. Although it is impossible to prove by scientific statistics, it seems certain that the orthodox Catholic blocs in the western democracies are outbreeding the non-Catholic blocs by a considerable margin. Catholic priests are tireless missionaries for large families, and they are much more successful in increasing the number of Catholic souls by this gospel than by the process of conversion.

They threaten married couples with perdition for the practice of contraception, and simultaneously preach the doctrine that no Catholic spouse has the moral right to refuse sexual intercourse in marriage except for grave reasons — and the reasons do not include extreme poverty. "When it is needful to speak of it," says the *Homiletic and Pastoral Review* in advising priests concerning their duty to impart sound sexual teaching in the confessional, "let him [the priest] rather show that a married person has the obligation of returning the debitum at any time that the partner demands it, unless he or she be excused for grave reasons."

This teaching, based on the theory that the production of new Catholic souls is a good thing in itself, when accompanied by the pressure of the priests against mixed marriages, tends to make the Catholic group in a non-Catholic community into a distinct biological bloc, outbreeding its competitors and gaining power proportionately at their expense. In European Catholic political campaigns the party leaders consider large families an important advertisement of their loyalty to Catholic principles. Belgian Catholic leaders have boasted of the fact that the three top leaders of the regular labor union federation have only one child among them whereas the three top leaders of the Catholic labor federation have twenty-six! When the Catholic M.R.P. was campaigning for an increased parliamentary representation in France after World War II, its statisticians, according to Gordon Wright, "proved that the M.R.P. deputies averaged 2.8 children apiece, whereas the Socialists could boast only a 1.6 average, and the Communists 1.3. No other party, observed the M.R.P., included a deputy with 13 children and four others with 10 each."[26]

Canada is rapidly becoming a Catholic nation because of this policy, and northern New England is being transformed by the Catholic overflow from Canada. French Catholic Canada is winning what the French Canadians call *la revanche des berceaux,* the revenge of the cradles. In this type of biological penetration and conquest, the Kremlin is a very poor second to the Vatican.

13

The American Answer

THE TWO PATTERNS OF POWER which I have discussed in the preceding chapters are as alike as the two poles of the earth. They occupy the opposite extremes of our moral universe but they represent the same type of intellectual climate, the climate of authoritarian rule over the human mind.

The contrasts between them are self-evident, and the battle between them is one of the irrepressible conflicts of our time. One is fighting on our side in the east-west struggle, and the other is fighting against us. One is a messenger of personal gentleness and love; the other represents ruthlessness and force. One respects the traditions and values of our economic society; the other insists on complete economic and political revolution. One teaches faith in a personal God and hope for personal immortality; the other is hostile to all the central tenets of orthodox religion.

But these contrasts represent differences in aim and purpose, or differences in temporary alignment, not differences in the permanent politics of power. As institutions in this world, the Kremlin and the Vatican are far more conspicuous in their similarities than their differences. It will pay to look back briefly over the areas I have discussed in this book and draw up a balance sheet of Vatican and Kremlin methods.

The Balance Sheet of Methods

How do the two institutions compare in the structure of power?

The Vatican is controlled by an official dictator, the Pope; the Kremlin is controlled by an unofficial but equally absolute dictator, Joseph Stalin. Neither permits any opposition party to form inside his organization. The dictator of the Vatican is infallible in all matters of faith and morals, and he has the extraordinary advantage of being able to say what faith and morals are. The dictator of the Kremlin makes no claim to personal infallibility, but his power to determine what is right and wrong in the Communist world is approximately equal to that of the Pope in the Catholic world.

The dictator of the Vatican is not chosen directly or indirectly by democratic process, since the cardinals who appoint him are themselves appointed princes, and their appointment is not ratified by the Catholic people. The dictator of the Kremlin is chosen and ratified by semi-popular agencies, but the election and the ratification are all controlled by techniques of exclusion, monopoly, and terror which make a mockery of every democratic pretense. The Pope's policies are completely undemocratic in their origin and sanction, since they are not determined or ratified by any group or agency representing the Catholic people; even the Vatican's constitutions and laws are all imposed upon the Catholic people by fiat, and they contain no bill of rights guaranteeing to Catholics as citizens freedom of thought or speech in their own organization. The Kremlin constitution and laws are nominally sanctioned by popularly elected bodies of voters, and they contain an elaborate bill of rights, but in practice the guaranties are set aside at will by the Kremlin dictatorship.

In the Kremlin system of power all adults have the right to vote, but they must not organize an opposition party for which to vote. In the Vatican system of power all the people are disfranchised, even priests in local councils if their bishops care to deny them the right to vote; no session of a General Council of the higher clergy has been called for more than eighty years. Below the top level, both dictatorships are run by committee systems in which the College of Cardinals corresponds to the Central Committee of the Communist Party of the Soviet Union, the resident (Italian) cardinals of the Roman Curia correspond to the Politburo, and the Vatican diplomats correspond to the regional agents of the Cominform.

The theory of imperialist rights under which the two dictatorships operate is essentially the same, but the territory claimed by the Vatican is much smaller than that claimed by the Kremlin.

The Kremlin does not actually recognize the sovereignty of any capitalist nation as sacred, since it operates within each nation with the purpose of controlling that nation's life completely for Communism. The Vatican claims supreme imperial power within every nation over such areas as religion, morals, education, censorship, and domestic relations, but it recognizes the limited sovereignty of civil governments over other vital areas such as military defense, public works, and the enforcement of criminal law. In carrying out its imperial policy the Kremlin's agency, the Cominform, imposes upon its national Communist parties obedience to the Kremlin in all matters of major policy, and the Vatican does likewise in ruling its own national churches.

How do the two institutions compare in their methods of deification?

The pageantry of deification in the Vatican system is more ritualistic than that of the Kremlin, but in both systems the leaders — the reigning Pope and Stalin — are primary objects of continuous and contrived adulation. Admiration for both leaders shades into veneration, and veneration into worship. Although both organizations officially disclaim deification, all printed and spoken propaganda of both exalt their respective leaders as essentially divine. Glorified biographies and pictures of the two deified chieftains are used continuously to inflate the belief in their personal virtues, conceal personal deficiencies, and build up institutional obedience. Both the Pope and Stalin are sequestered from almost all normal contacts with the world, and presented to the public only in carefully managed theatrical appearances. The Vatican adds to its pageantry of deification an elaborate constellation of ecclesiastical saints who serve as minor and supporting deities for the papal heavenly court.

How do the two institutions compare in thought control?

Both the Kremlin and the Vatican stand officially for the education of the people in "freedom," but in practice both institutions limit critical thought and speech. The Kremlin controls the dissemination of all information through press, radio, motion pictures, and books by the device of owning or controlling all business and cultural enterprises in its territory. The Vatican does not possess this power over whole nations but, through a system of internal controls, it rigidly censors the publication by Catholics of hostile attacks on any major doctrine or discipline of the Church, and it attempts to impose a similar system of censorship on non-Catholics through political and cultural pressure and legislation wherever it can marshal the requisite power. The Vatican makes the reading of any anti-Catholic work a mortal sin, and officially bans many great works of science and philosophy. The Kremlin does not officially impose such a prohibition, but it goes far beyond the Vatican in directing all Communist science, music, art, and literature into narrowly controlled Marxist channels.

Both organizations use the school as a partisan weapon and oppose the neutral public school. The Kremlin completely directs the school systems in Communist countries, eliminates all hostile teachers and textbooks, and infuses every subject with Marxist-Stalinist partisanship. In Catholic countries the Vatican makes Catholicism a part of the public-school curriculum to the exclusion of all other faiths, and in non-Catholic countries it establishes a complete segregated school system, supporting it with theological coercion.

How do the two institutions compare in discipline and devotion?

Both the Vatican and the Kremlin rule their domains through a special class of élite and dedicated personalities, the priesthood (including nuns) and the members of the Communist Party. Both enforce the most rigid discipline upon their devotees, and cultivate blind loyalty as a virtue. The Vatican goes beyond the Kremlin in prohibiting all normal sex life among its élite and in exploiting the sense of sexual guilt in the young; but the Kremlin goes beyond the Vatican in extremes of torture and punishment. Both institutions attempt to prevent a drift to democratic heresy by disciplining with unusual severity those Communists and Catholics who show sympathy with the nearest institutional competitors, Socialism and Protestantism.

How do the two institutions compare in the use of deceptive propaganda?

The Kremlin is the unchallenged champion of all time in the manufacture of the Big Lie. Its leaders hold that any deception is justified if it extends and maintains the revolution against bourgeois power. It systematically maligns all western accomplishment and exalts all Russian achievement. The Vatican's relatively mild deceptions in the field of politics consist in ecclesiastical double talk about freedom and the separation of church and state. Both organizations occasionally profess to believe in the separation of church and state but neither practices this belief; in countries of the Soviet orbit the state interferes with the Church, and in countries of the Vatican orbit the Church interferes with the state. The masking of undemocratic policies by deliberate misrepresentation and the exploitation of ignorant masses by fake medicine and fake science make the Vatican an instrument of profound moral corruption in many parts of the world.

How do the Vatican and the Kremlin compare in the strategy of penetration?

Both institutions use controlled political parties, controlled labor unions, and controlled social cells as instruments for capturing non-Catholic and non-Communist cultures. The Communist control of its parties, unions, and cells is more complete and more conspiratorial than that of the Vatican, but there is little to choose between the two networks as far as democracy is concerned. Both networks represent imperial dictatorships attempting to extend their power. The Kremlin supports its parties of penetration with armed invasion wherever feasible, while the Vatican does not. The Kremlin's conquered provinces center in eastern Europe; the Vatican's in western Europe and Latin America. Poland, Hungary, Czechoslovakia, and Rumania are prize exhibits of one class; Spain, Portugal, Quebec, and Ireland of the other. The Kremlin's two chief instruments of penetration into non-Communist countries, aside from the Communist parties themselves, are the Cominform and the World Federation of Trade Unions. The Vatican's three corresponding instruments of penetration are Catholic Action, the relatively feeble federation of Catholic political parties known as the Nouvelles Equipes Internationales, and the C.I.S.C. In the United States the Church as a biological population bloc, and the Catholic school, are more powerful instruments of penetration than any corresponding instrument of the Kremlin.

An American Policy

In confronting these parallel forms of authoritarian power, is it possible to develop a dual American policy which is reasonable and balanced, a policy which avoids the extremes of hysterical anti-Communism and of dogmatic anti-Catholicism, and yet is consistently firm?

It is hard to answer such a question briefly without appearing to be either pontifical or superficial or both, but brevity is necessary in such a summary. It seems to me that the basic elements of a consistent policy are more or less self-evident. It is bound to be a policy of constructive opposition to the political power and the authoritarian spirit of both the Vatican and the Kremlin, because they are totalitarian agencies whose aims and methods are incompatible with democratic ideals. Men who believe in government by consent of the governed, men who accept freedom of thought and freedom of information as the basic freedoms of democratic life, could scarcely be expected to view with favor two organizations which neither practice nor preach these freedoms in their own institutional life or in the nations which they completely conquer. We have a right as defenders of democracy to judge both the Kremlin and the Vatican by their products, and history shows us that the completely Catholic nation is no more democratic than the completely Communist nation. If we are asked to choose today between the Soviet Union and Catholic Spain, we will choose neither.

The negative principle in a sound policy for dealing with the Vatican and the Kremlin can well be expressed in the conventional term "containment" — containment of imperial power whether military or moral, containment of any force which is hostile to our freedoms. Democracy is inevitably bound by its own self-interest to attempt the limitation of both Vatican and Kremlin power to presently occupied territories because the two systems have been encroaching on the democratic way of life throughout the world. The encroachments, of course, have been strikingly different in kind and degree, but they challenge democratic institutions unmistakably whether they take the form of a school system which teaches the gospel of restricted and antiscientific thought, or of an invading military column. The threats in both cases are genuine threats to fundamental freedoms, and it seems clear that if we make peace with such institutions, it must be a peace of tolerance and not of approval.

But containment is a negative concept, and if democracy is to survive against aggressive forms of totalitarianism, it should choose its own timetable and plot its own intellectual offensive. "Eternal vigilance is the price of liberty" is the best expression of the goal and practice of our democratic offensive. A positive and living faith in democratic ways of thought must be reaffirmed, and subservience to authoritarian rule must be rejected if democracy is to survive in the modern world, and no cloak of religious piety or of perverted social idealism must be permitted to shield undemocratic institutions from the winds of democratic doctrine.

In the light of such a formula the American answer to Communism offers few moral difficulties if anti-Communism is not carried to the extreme where freedom of thought is destroyed. Stalin has made anti-Communism a moral and intellectual necessity for free men by his tactics since the end of World War II. The sight of Korea, Berlin, Czechoslovakia, and Hungary (to mention only a few of the controlled and devastated areas) reminds free Americans that, but for the grace of military might, there goes the United States. During the first twenty years of Soviet power, it appeared to many to be logical at times to excuse Communist tyranny on the plea that it was needed to destroy something worse, but that plea has lost all its force since the Kremlin has taken the field as the world's most rapidly expanding imperialist power. Now resistance is obligatory for all self-respecting men. We have two primary questions to ask: How can we honorably avoid war? If we cannot — how, when, and where shall the issue be joined?

The first item in a sound American policy for dealing with Communists would seem to be military preparedness, and the second, constructive work with money and technical knowledge to eliminate the inequality, race discrimination, and poverty which breed Communism as a stagnant pool breeds mosquitoes. If Communism springs from the soil of despair, the west cannot afford to abandon Marshall Plan aid, military assistance to

Europe, or the broader program of Point Four funds for backward countries which are now a prey to Communist agitation. From the point of view of sheer economy, peacetime aid is likely to be far less expensive than wartime devastation.

Common sense dictates that physical war should be delayed as long as possible and avoided even at the price of some compromise, because the weapons of war are now so destructive. When the issue is survival, men cannot afford to carry chips on their shoulders. Stalin *might* die; China *might* be incapacitated by a famine; the Politburo *might* recover a sense of proportion under pressure; there *might* be some Russian demands that could be honorably and fairly compromised. No false pride should keep us from making minor concessions when the survival of so many million lives is at stake. Moreover, we are outnumbered in the present alignment of world forces by Communism, perhaps as much as 3 to 1, certainly as much as 2 to 1, even if all of western Europe is counted on our side — and not all of western Europe *is* on our side. An even more important fact is that under present circumstances it would be physically impossible for the western democracies to control and regulate a defeated Communist world. Even if World War III ended in a victory for the democracies (and it might *not*), the result could be an inundation of a large part of the globe in a Communist-dominated chaos which would be more difficult to master than the organized terror of Kremlin power.

Such gloomy foreboding does not imply that we should shrink from the ultimate necessity of meeting the challenge of Communist power. We have put our hand to the task of organizing the world against aggression, and it is unthinkable that we should turn back after the sacrifices that have already been made.

Meanwhile, it is a truism that if we are forced to fight and win a war of bombs, the victory will be wasted unless we also win the war of ideas. It is not possible permanently to rule and regulate half of the world's population by force. Men cannot permanently be kept from joining the ranks of the Communist movement by threatening them with extinction. They must be persuaded to join the community of free men by free choice, and they must continue to like their choice. They will continue to like their choice only if democracy can produce a better solution for the problems of modern society than any other social order can produce. Thus far western democracy has produced a higher standard of life and a higher level of human happiness than Communism, but it has not displayed that passionate interest in the poverty and insecurity of the common man that will guarantee continued supremacy. So long as millions of men are poor without commensurate fault, and thousands are rich without commensurate merit, democracy will be threatened by any competing social order which offers a more logical formula for social justice. Hence the battle of democracy against Communism should be viewed not merely as a defensive battle for present values but as a continuing competition for the good society.

A Temperate Anti-Vatican Policy

Opposition without hysteria to Vatican policy in the United States involves a very different set of values from anti-Communism. America is thoroughly aroused to the dangers of Communist power, and it is politically advantageous for demagogues to rival each other in outshouting the feeble voice of Communist propaganda. American Communism is so weak that it cannot elect a single congressman, senator, governor, mayor, or city councilman in the whole nation. Even Henry Wallace in the days of his unfortunate left-wing honeymoon, with all the prestige of a former Vice President, could not poll 3 per cent of the national vote.

But Vatican power in America is pervasive and substantial, outnumbering Communist power in official membership by about 490 to 1,[1] and it is inextricably entangled with virtue and loyalty to moral values, with altruism and personal faith, and above all with the tradition of American freedom which protects both good and evil against attack if they happen to wear a religious label. Can we cut through these protective traditions and in dealing with the Vatican arrive at a policy which is not based on hypocrisy or appeasement? I am not hopeful of an honest or reasonable solution, because Catholic power makes cowards of more men in public life than we like to think.

Our first task is to break the current taboo against any frank discussion of the "Catholic question" and establish a free flow of ideas. Men should have the same right to speak without penalties on this issue that they have to speak on Communism. The pretense of the American Catholic hierarchy that every person who challenges its policies is per se "anti-Catholic" must be revealed as fraudulent nonsense. The further pretense that world Catholicism is *only* a religion and is therefore entitled to the conventional avoidance of religious argument must be dissected and destroyed with hard facts. From the point of view of western democracy, Catholicism is not merely a religion; it is also a foreign government with a diplomatic corps; an agglomeration of right-wing clerical parties and fascist governments; a cultural imperialism controlling a world-wide system of schools; a medieval medical code with comprehensive rules for personal hygiene; a network of clerical-dominated labor unions; a system of censorship of books, newspapers, films, and radio; and a hierarchy of marriage and annulment courts which compete with the courts of the people. Since all of these primarily non-devotional features of Catholic power affect the lives of non-Catholics as well as Catholics, it is right that they should be considered not merely as religion but as economics, politics, medicine, education, and diplomacy — in other words, as an organic and vital part of democratic society.

It is scarcely necessary to say that we have no excuse for suggesting that a single *right* of the Vatican in the United States be taken away. Nor must we permit the opposition to *political* Catholicism to degenerate into *religious* anti-Catholicism or personal prejudice against individual Catholics. The best aid which political Catholicism has in this country today is the Ku Klux Klan, because fanatical anti-Catholicism can be used to divert attention from the fundamentally intolerant policies of the Vatican itself. The Roman Catholic hierarchy is rightly permitted under our Constitution to establish its competing school system, its separate marriage courts, and its organs of censorship, and it is unthinkable that the rights of the Vatican to establish and extend these institutions and practices should be curtailed in any way. But tolerance need not imply approval of such tactics, and the evidence justifies a policy of temperate and constructive opposition. What form should that opposition take?

In the international sphere, the Vatican's record should lead us to be wary of any alliance with Catholic parties or governments, because those parties and governments have been too often the symbols and catch-alls of reactionary forces. We are likely to be judged in terms of the morality of our worst ally, and some of the allies of the Vatican are completely fascist. The Vatican itself, for example, has been for generations the greatest landholder in several European nations where land reform is the first requirement of social justice,[2] and in such nations we cannot afford to take sides with the landlord. Already our reputation in Europe is shockingly reactionary. We are known as an enemy of Socialism, and for the European masses Socialism is almost synonymous with social welfare. Whether we like it or not, we should be honest enough to admit what every trained observer of European politics knows — that free enterprise has already been partially dethroned in Europe and that Communism cannot be defeated on that Continent without the aid of the middle-of-the-road Socialist movement. An American policy which ties us to a reactionary clerical bloc and to anti-Socialism is destined to defeat no matter how many billions in American relief go with it. As Adolf Berle, former Assistant Secretary of State, has pointed out: "Principles aside, the pragmatic results [in the European war against Communism] suggest indeed that the chief political instrument against Stalinist Communism is precisely support of the Socialist groups." But in practice the Vatican-controlled groups are the anti-Socialist groups — as anti-Socialist as the Vatican dares to make them — and too often they are groups which betray sympathy with fascism, without rebuke from above.

When we support political Catholicism in Europe, no matter how sincerely, we identify ourselves with political reaction, and we cannot afford this kind of identification. It is not an accident that the two remaining fascist powers in Europe today are the leading Catholic powers and that their dictators continue to operate on fascist principles without excommunication.

In fact, when all of its alliances and its political philosophy are carefully considered, there is a real question whether the Vatican is a liability or an asset in democracy's war against Communism. Europe and Asia are engaged in a revolutionary process of transforming their ancient societies. On the revolutionary side in the struggle are forces of idealism and hope as well as forces of bitterness and hate. In the course of the long battle for social transformation the Vatican has become known as a counter-revolutionary force. Its reputation has not always been deserved, because many devout Catholic leaders are notably idealistic and would like to see their Church in the vanguard of every movement for intelligent social change. But, whether from choice or association or the accident of history, the Vatican has become the spiritual core of the rightist bloc in the modern world, and it stands for the old order and the old values. Reactionaries of every stripe flock to the Vatican banner automatically — and any democracy associated too closely with that banner is destined to lose the sympathy of the masses of people in both Europe and Asia.

Aside from its reputation and its unfortunate associations, the Vatican also has the fatal defect of leaving its followers unprepared to meet the forces of Communism with free intelligence. Habitual, uncritical obedience to superior authority disqualifies men as fighters against Communism because it incapacitates their minds. The Vatican has cultivated in millions of men that authoritarian mind which leans for support on received dogma. That is the type of mind on which Stalin rests his vast domain, and it is not an accident that in many parts of Europe the passage of men from Catholicism to Communism has been so effortless. When the largest Communist party outside of the Soviet Union develops in the home country of the Vatican, and captures the devotion of millions of "Catholics," the moral cannot be ignored.

The independent mind is the type of mind which spurns political Catholicism for the same reason that it spurns Communism — because it recognizes in each an enemy of freedom. As Anthony Eden has pointed out, the nonconformist is "the one kind of man who invariably rejects Communism almost without a second thought. . . . He is inherently against subjection to any hierarchy and spontaneously rejects all doctrines of infallibility. To him, democracy is a necessary form of human dignity."[3]

There is another reason why our diplomacy should be dissociated from the Vatican's position in international affairs. We are not eager for an atomic Holy War even against the Kremlin. In spite of all the Pope's eloquent appeals for peace, the world-wide point of view of Catholicism on war with the Soviet Union and Communist China is more extreme than that of any other group. In the United States it has approximated hysteria. It has become an undisguised campaign for a Holy War, with all the emotional overtones of a devotional crusade.

The Catholic senator from Wisconsin, Joseph McCarthy, received wide acclaim in the American Catholic press when he staged in 1949 and 1950 a campaign of disgraceful vilification in which he indiscriminately lumped together honest anti-Communists, moderate progressives, loyal government employees, and Kremlin spies. His campaign probably did more to discredit American democracy in Europe than any event in American politics in recent years. The Catholic Secretary of the Navy, Francis P. Matthews, former Supreme Knight of the Knights of Columbus, shocked the nation in August 1950, when he openly advocated a preventive war against Russia and was rebuked by President Truman. Boston's diocesan Catholic paper, *The Pilot*, condoned his plea and pointed out that wars of offense might be as moral as wars of self-defense under certain circumstances.[4]

No one questions the right of the Catholic press to support such leaders as McCarthy and Matthews, but men who face the realities of atomic catastrophe do not relish the thought of their nation being pushed into war on a wave of religious fury. Nor do they want American policy influenced by a non-American agency like the Vatican which may have its special selfish interests at stake. They have not forgotten that until Pearl Harbor in 1941, when Vatican interests dictated a contrary point of view, the same pressure groups which are now so favorable to intervention in Europe were strenuously opposed to intervention against fascism.

This inconsistency of attitude toward totalitarian regimes should help Americans to realize that the Vatican is motivated chiefly by self-interest. It has created an illusion of friendliness for democracy because its spokesmen have kept repeating over and over again, in one form or another, the spurious syllogism: The Church is fighting Communism; Communism is democratic America's worst enemy; therefore the Church is the true defender of democratic America. But Andrei Vishinsky has "proved" that the Communist Party is the "most democratic" party by using the same syllogism, with variations, concerning Communism and fascism: "That party is the most democratic which fights most strongly against Fascism; the Communist party is the most uncompromising opponent of Fascism; therefore it is the most democratic party."[5] Surely, the first step in a realistic American policy is to expose such fallacies thoroughly, and to judge our enemies and friends on the basis of their actual records.

The lack of a consistent American policy for dealing with the Vatican was never more clearly revealed than during the 1950-51 discussions concerning the appointment of a possible successor to Myron Taylor as the President's personal representative at the Vatican. Mr. Taylor had resigned late in 1949 after ten years of service as a presidential envoy, serving at Rome without confirmation by the United States Senate because President Roosevelt had by-passed Senate approval. Mr. Taylor's equivocal status reflected the schizophrenic attitude of American politics toward the Vatican. Since our Constitution calls for the separation of church and state and a policy of no discrimination among faiths, we have no moral right to send an ambassador to the Catholic Church as a church unless we also send an ambassador to the Archbishop of Canterbury, the Chief Rabbi of Jerusalem, and the Moscow Patriarch of the Russian Orthodox Church. But if the Roman Catholic Church is more than a church — and it *is* by its own claim and definition — then its policies in the United States should be subject to the same open criticism as the policies of any other foreign power. Any regulation or policy of the Vatican which encroaches upon the duties of American citizens to their country's laws and institutions should be opposed as consistently as any corresponding regulation or policy of the Kremlin.

Perhaps the simplest way to arrive at the essentials of an American policy for dealing with the Vatican would be to ask: What would an American ambassador to the Pope demand of the Vatican if he spoke as frankly as our ambassadors to the Soviet Union now speak to Molotov or Stalin? He would naturally protest against all those regulations and rules of Catholicism which curtail or limit the free judgment of American Catholics as citizens. He would insist that no outside power should attempt to tell American voters how to decide any American political issue, especially when the outside organization gives its members no participating rights in arriving at the decision.

To make such principles concrete, an American representative to the Vatican might begin with three immediate demands — that the Vatican cancel for the United States its rule against Catholic attendance at public schools; that the Vatican grant to all Catholic Americans the moral right to study both sides of every social question, including material critical of Catholic policy; and that the Vatican recognize American marriage and divorce as valid.

In all the three areas covered by these demands, present Vatican policy is fundamentally un-American and constitutes a direct threat to responsible citizenship. All Americans should be free to attend American public schools without penalties of any kind; no Americans should be forbidden to read and discuss freely any honest criticism of Catholic policy; and all marriages recognized by the government of the American people should be recognized by all the people. These principles are elementary in a democracy, and probably they would be recognized as just and reasonable by the overwhelming majority of the American Catholic people if those people could be given a chance to vote on the issues without ecclesiastical pressure and misrepresentation.

Then why should not American democracy make such adjustments a basic minimum for an honorable peace with Vatican power?

The mere asking of such a question reveals how far democracy is from a realistic policy in dealing with Vatican encroachments on the democratic way of life. We have permitted a confused sentimentality on so-called religious matters to blanket the discussion of some of the great moral issues of our time.

We have been thoroughly aroused to the necessity of defending our freedoms against one form of totalitarian power; we have been astonishingly apathetic concerning the perils of the other. We need to return once again to American first principles and renew the immortal sentiment of Thomas Jefferson printed at the beginning of this book: "I have sworn upon the altar of God eternal hostility against every form of tyranny over the mind of man."

Appendix

I

THE MUSSOLINI-VATICAN AGREEMENTS OF 1929

A. TEXT OF THE TREATY BETWEEN ITALY AND THE HOLY SEE (*Excerpts*)

ARTICLE I

Italy recognises and reaffirms the principle set forth in Article I of the Constitution of the Kingdom of Italy of 4 March 1848, whereby the Catholic Apostolic and Roman religion is the sole religion of the State.

ARTICLE II

Italy recognises the sovereignty of the Holy See in the international field as an inherent attribute of its nature, in conformity with its tradition and the exigencies of its mission in the world.

ARTICLE IV

The sovereignty and exclusive jurisdiction which Italy recognises to the Holy See implies that there cannot be any interference whatsoever on the part of the Italian Government, and that within Vatican City there will be no other authority than the Holy See.

ARTICLE VIII

Italy considers the person of the Supreme Pontiff as sacred and inviolable, and declares attempts against him, or incitement to commit them, punishable by the same penalties established for attempts or incitement to commit them against the person of the King. Offences or insults publicly committed in Italian territory against the person of the Supreme Pontiff with spoken or written word are punishable as such offences or insults against the person of the King.

ARTICLE XI

The Central bodies of the Catholic Church are exempt from all interference on the part of the Italian State, except for dispositions of Italian law concerning purchases by moral bodies, as well as transfer of real estate.

Article XII

Italy recognises to the Holy See the active and passive right to maintain legations according to the general regulations of international law. Envoys of foreign governments to the Holy See will continue to enjoy all of the prerogatives and immunities which accrue to diplomatic agents according to international law. Their seats can continue to remain in Italian territory, enjoying the immunity due them according to international law, even though their States shall not have diplomatic relations with Italy. It is agreed that Italy pledges for ever in every case to let pass freely correspondence of all States, including belligerents, both to the Holy See and vice versa, as well as to permit free access of bishops of the whole world to the Apostolic See.

The high contracting parties pledge themselves to establish normal diplomatic relations through the accrediting of an Italian ambassador to the Holy See and of a pontifical nuncio to Italy, who will be dean of the diplomatic corps according to the customary right recognised by the Congress of Vienna, 9 January 1815.

By reason of the recognised sovereignty, and without prejudice as set forth in Article XIX, diplomats and Holy See couriers sent in the name of the Supreme Pontiff enjoy in Italian territory, even in time of war, the same treatment due diplomats and diplomatic couriers of other foreign governments according to the regulations of international law.

Article XXIV

The Holy See, in relation to the sovereignty due to it also in the international sphere, declares that it wishes to remain and will remain extraneous to all temporal disputes between States and to international congresses held for such objects, unless the contending parties make concordant appeal to its peaceful mission; at the same time reserving the right to exercise its moral and spiritual power.

In consequence of this declaration, Vatican City will always and in every case be considered neutral and inviolable territory.

Article XXVI

The Holy See agrees that with the agreements signed today, adequate assurance is made for what is necessary for it for providing for due liberty and independence of the pastoral government of the diocese of Rome and the Catholic Church in Italy and the world, declares the Roman Question definitely and irrevocably settled and therefore eliminated, and recognises the Kingdom of Italy under the dynasty of the House of Savoy, with Rome the capital of the Italian State.

Italy in her turn recognises the State of the Vatican City under the sovereignty of the Supreme Pontiff.

The law of the 13 May 1871, No. 214, is abrogated as well as any other decree contrary to the present treaty.

B. TEXT OF THE CONCORDAT BETWEEN ITALY AND THE HOLY SEE (*Excerpts*)

Article I

Italy, according to the terms of Article I of the Treaty, assures to the Catholic Church free exercise of spiritual power, free and public exercise of worship, as well as jurisdiction in ecclesiastical matters, in conformity with the regulations of our present concordat; where it is necessary accords to ecclesiastics the defence of its authority for acts of their spiritual ministry. In consideration of the sacred character of the Eternal City, Bishopric of the Supreme Pontiff and bourne of pilgrimages, the Italian Government will engage to prevent in Rome all which may conflict with the said character.

Article III

Theological students of the last two years of preparation in theology intended for the priesthood and novices in religious institutions may, on their request, postpone from year to year until the twenty-sixth year of age fulfilment of the obligations of military service.

Clerics ordained "in sacris" and members of religious orders who take vows are exempt from military service except in case of general mobilisation. In such cases priests pass into the armed forces of the State, but maintain their religious dress, so that they can practise among the troops their sacred ministry under the ecclesiastical jurisdiction of the military ordinary Bishop. According to the terms they are preferentially attached to the health services.

At the same time, even if general mobilisation is ordered, priests exercising full Divine rights are dispensed from call to arms. . . .

Article IV

Ecclesiastics and members of religious orders are exempt from the office of jurymen.

Article V

No ecclesiastic can be employed or remain in the employment or offices of the Italian State or public bodies depending upon the same without "nulla osta" of the diocesan ordinary.

Revocation of "nulla osta" deprives the ecclesiastics of capacity to continue exercising employment or office taken up.

In any case apostate priests or those incurring censure cannot be employed in a teaching post or any office or employment in which they have immediate contact with the public.

Article VI

Stipends and other emoluments enjoyed by ecclesiastics on account of their office are exempt from charges and liens in the same way as stipends and salaries of State employees.

Article VII

Ecclesiastics cannot be required by magistrates or other authorities to give information regarding persons or matters that have come to their knowledge through the exercise of their sacred ministry.

Article VIII

In the case of the sending of an ecclesiastic or a member of a religious order before a penal magistrate for crime, the King's procurator must inform the proceedings thereof to the ordinary of the diocese in whose territory he exercises jurisdiction, and must immediately transmit to the office of the ordinary the preliminary decision thereon and, if issued, the final sentence, both of the court of first instance and the court of appeal.

In case of arrest, the ecclesiastic or member of a religious order is treated with the respect due to his state and hierarchical degree. In case of the sentence of an ecclesiastic or member of a religious order, punishment is to be undergone in places separate from those designated for laymen, unless a competent ordinary has reduced the prisoner to a lay state.

Article XI

The State recognises the holidays established by the Church, which are: All Sundays, New Year's Day, Epiphany, St. Joseph's Day (that is, 19 March), Ascension Day, Corpus Domini, the Feast of the Apostles Sts. Peter and Paul (that is, 29 June), the Assumption of the Blessed Virgin Mary (15 August), All Saints' Day, the Feast of the Immaculate Conception (8 December), and Christmas Day.

Article XIX

The choice of archbishops belongs to the Holy See. Before an archbishop, bishop, or coadjutor with the right of succession is nominated, the Holy See shall communicate the name of the chosen person to the Italian Government, in order to be sure that the Government has no objections of a political nature against such person. The formalities to this effect shall be carried out with all possible haste and with the greatest discretion, so that secrecy about the chosen candidate shall be maintained until he is formally nominated.

Article XXXIV

The Italian State, wishing to reinvest the institution of marriage, which is the basis of the family, with the dignity conformable to the Catholic traditions of its people, recognises the sacrament of matrimony performed according to canon law as fully effective in civil law. Notices of such marriages will be made both in the parish church and in the town or city hall. Immediately after the celebration of such marriage the parish priest will explain to those he has married the civil effect of matrimony, reading the articles of the civil code regarding the rights and duties of spouses and will prepare the marriage certificate, a copy of which he will send within five days to the commune in order that it may be copied into the registers by the civil authorities.

Cases concerning nullity of marriage and dispensation from marriage by reason of nonconsummation are reserved for ecclesiastical tribunals and their departments.

Article XXXVI

Italy considers the teaching of Christian Doctrine according to the forms received from Catholic tradition as the foundation and crown of public education. Therefore Italy consents that the religious teaching now imparted in the elementary schools be further developed in the middle schools according to a programme to be agreed upon between the Holy See and the State.

Such instruction will be given by masters, professors, priests, and members of religious orders approved by ecclesiastical authorities and in subsidiary form by lay masters and professors furnished with proper certificates of capacity issued by the diocesan ordinary.

Revocation of the certificate by the ordinary immediately deprives the teacher of authority to instruct. Only textbooks approved by the ecclesiastical authorities will be used in the public schools for such religious training.

Article XLII

Italy will admit recognition by royal decree of noble titles conferred by the Supreme Pontiff even after 1870 and also those to be conferred in the future. In cases to be determined such recognition will not be subject to an initial payment of tax.

II

THE ROOSEVELT-SPELLMAN CORRESPONDENCE

Mrs. Eleanor Roosevelt in her column "My Day," as published in the New York *World-Telegram* of June 23, 1949, said:

The controversy brought about by the request made by Francis Cardinal Spellman that Catholic schools should share in federal aid funds forces upon the citizens of the country the kind of decision that is going to be very difficult to make.

Those of us who believe in the right of any human being to belong to whatever church he sees fit, and to worship God in his own way, cannot be accused of prejudice when we do not want to see public education connected with religious control of the schools, which are paid for by taxpayers' money.

If we desire our children to go to schools of any particular kind, be it because we think they should have religious instruction or for any other reason, we are entirely free to set up those schools and to pay for them. Thus, our children would receive the kind of education we feel would best fit them for life.

Many years ago it was decided that the public schools of our country should be entirely separated from any kind of denominational control, and these are the only schools that are free, tax-supported schools. The greatest number of our children attend these schools.

It is quite possible that private schools, whether they are denominational schools — Catholic, Episcopalian, Presbyterian, Methodist, or whatever — or whether they are purely academic, may make a great contribution to the public school systems, both on the lower levels and on the higher levels.

They will be somewhat freer to develop new methods and to try experiments, and they will serve as yardsticks in the competitive area of creating better methods of imparting knowledge.

This, however, is the very reason why they should not receive Federal funds; in fact, no tax funds of any kind.

The separation of church and state is extremely important to any of us who hold to the original traditions of our nation. To change these traditions by changing our traditional attitude toward public education would be harmful, I think, to our whole attitude of tolerance in the religious area.

If we look at situations which have arisen in the past in Europe and other world areas, I think we will see the reasons why it is wise to hold to our early traditions.

On July 21, Cardinal Spellman sent the following letter to Mrs. Roosevelt, and released it to the press:

Dear Mrs. Roosevelt:

When, on June 23 in your column, My Day, you aligned yourself with the author and other proponents of the Barden bill and condemned me for defending Catholic children against those who would deny them their constitutional rights of equality with other American children, you could have acted only from misinformation, ignorance or prejudice, not from knowledge and understanding.

It is apparent that you did not take the time to read my address delivered at Fordham University; and, in your column of July 15 you admitted that you did not even carefully read and acquaint yourself with the facts of the Barden bill — the now famous, infamous bill that would unjustly discriminate against minority groups of America's children.

Unlike you, Mrs. Roosevelt, I did not make a public statement until I had studied every phrase of the Barden bill; nor did I take issue with a man because his faith differed from mine. We differed, Congressman Barden and I, over the unimpeachable issue of equal benefits and equal rights for all America's children.

I had intended ignoring your personal attack, but, as the days passed and in two subsequent columns you continued your anti-Catholic campaign, I became convinced that it was in the interest of all Americans and the cause of justice itself that your misstatements should be challenged in every quarter of our country where they have already spun and spread their web of prejudice. I have received hundreds of messages from persons of all faiths demanding that I answer you. I am, therefore, not free to ignore you.

You say you are against religious control of schools which are paid for by taxpayers' money. That is exactly what I, too, oppose. But I am also opposed to any bill that includes children who attend parochial schools for the purpose of receiving funds from the Federal Government while it excludes these same children from the distribution and benefits of the funds allocated.

I believe that if the Federal Government provides a bottle of milk to each child in a public school it should provide milk for all school children. I believe if, through the use of Federal funds the children who attend public schools are immunized from contagious diseases that all children should be protected from these diseases.

Taxation without representation is tyranny was the cry that roused and rallied our pioneer Americans to fight for justice. Taxation without participation should rouse today's Americans to equal ardor to protest an injustice that would deprive millions of American children of health and safety benefits to which all our children are entitled. And the Supreme Court of the United States has declared that health and transportation services and the distribution of non-religious textbooks to pupils attending parochial schools do not violate our Constitution.

"The separation of church and state is extremely important to us who hold to the original traditions of our nation," you continue. But health and safety benefits and providing standard non-religious textbooks for all American children have nothing to do with the question of separation of church and state!

I cannot presume upon the press to discuss, analyze or refute each inaccuracy in your columns — for they are manifold. Had you taken an objective, impersonal stand, I could then, in the same impersonal manner, answer you. But you did not. Apparently your attitude of mind precluded you from comprehending issues which you either rigorously defended or flagrantly condemned while ignorant of the facts concerning both the Barden bill and my own denunciation of it.

American freedom not only permits but encourages differences of opinion and I do not question your right to differ with me. But why, I wonder, do you repeatedly plead causes that are anti-Catholic?

Even if you cannot find it within your heart to defend the rights of innocent little children and heroic, helpless men like Cardinal Martyr Mindszenty, can you not have the charity not to cast upon them still another stone?

America's Catholic youth helped fight a long and bitter fight to save all Americans from oppression and persecution. Their broken bodies on blood-soaked foreign fields were grim and tragic testimony of this fact. I saw them there — on every fighting front — as equally they shared with their fellow-fighters all the sacrifice, terror and gore of war — as alike they shared the little good and glory that sometimes comes to men as together they fight and win a brutal battle.

Would you deny equality to these Catholic boys who daily stood at the sad threshold of untimely death and suffered martyrdom that you and I and the world of men might live in liberty and peace?

Would you deny their children equal rights and benefits with other sects — rights for which their fathers paid equal taxation with other fathers and fought two bitter wars that all children might forever be free from fear, oppression and religious persecution?

During the war years you visited the hospitals in many countries, as did I. You too saw America's sons — Catholic, Protestant and Jew alike — young, battered, scarred, torn and mutilated, dying in agony that we might learn to live in charity with one another. Then how was it that your own heart was not purged of all prejudices by what you saw these, your sons, suffer?

Now my case is closed. This letter will be released to the public tomorrow after it has been delivered to you by special delivery today. And even though you may again use your columns to attack me and again accuse me of starting a controversy, I shall not again publicly acknowledge you. For, whatever you may say in the future, your record of anti-Catholicism stands for all to see — a record which you yourself wrote on the pages of history which cannot be recalled — documents of discrimination unworthy of an American mother!

       Sincerely yours,
       FRANCIS CARDINAL SPELLMAN
       Archbishop of New York

Two days later, Mrs. Roosevelt sent the following reply to Cardinal Spellman:

Your Eminence:

Your letter of July 21st surprised me considerably.

I have never advocated the Barden bill nor any other specific bill on education now before the Congress. I believe, however, in Federal aid to education.

I have stated in my column some broad principles which I consider important and said I regretted your attack on the Barden bill because you aligned yourself with those who, from my point of view, advocated an unwise attitude which may lead to difficulties in this country, and have, as a result, the exact things which you and I would deplore, namely, the increase in bitterness among the Roman Catholic groups, and the Protestant and other religious groups.

I read only what was in the papers about your address and I stated in my column very carefully that I had not read the Barden bill or any other bill carefully, because I do not wish to have it said that I am in favor of any particular bill.

If I may, I would like to state again very simply for you the things I believe are important in this controversy. In the early days in this country there were rather few Roman Catholic settlements. The majority of the people coming here were Protestants and not very tolerant, but they believed that in establishing a democratic form of government it was essential that there be free education for as large a number of people as possible, so there was a movement to create free public schools for all children who wished to attend them. Nothing was said about private schools.

As we have developed in this country we have done more and more for our public schools. They are open to all children and it has been decided that there should be no particular religious beliefs taught in them.

I believe that there should be freedom for every child to be educated in his own religion. In public schools it should be taught that the spiritual side of life is most important. I would be happy if some agreement could be reached on passages from the Bible and some prayer that could be used. The real religious teaching of any child must be done by his own church and in his own home.

It is fallacious, I think, to say that because children going to public schools are granted free textbooks in some states, free transportation, or free school lunches, that these same things must be given to children going to private schools.

Different states, of course, have done different things as they came under majority pressure from citizens who had certain desires, but basically by and large, throughout the country, I think there is still a feeling that the public school is the school which is open to all children, and which is supported by all the people of the country and that anything that is done for the public schools should be done for them alone.

I would feel that certain medical care should be available to all children, but that is a different thing and should be treated differently. If we set up free medical care for all children, then it should not be tied in with any school.

At present there are physical examinations for children in public schools which are provided without cost to the parents, but there is nothing to prevent people who send their children to private schools from making arrangements to pay for similar examinations for their children.

I should like to point out to you that I talked about parochial schools and that to my mind means any schools organized by any sectarian group and not exclusively a Roman Catholic school. Children attending parochial schools are, of course, taught according to the tenets of their respective churches.

As I grow older it seems to me important that there be no great stress laid on our divisions, but that we stress as much as possible our agreements.

You state: "And the Supreme Court of the United States has declared that health and transportation services and the distribution of non-religious textbooks to pupils attending parochial schools do not violate our Constitution." None of us will presume to decide questions which will come up before the Supreme Court of the United States, but all of us must think seriously about anything which is done, not only in relation to the specific thing, but in relation to what may follow after it and what we think will be good for the country.

Anyone who knows history, particularly the history of Europe, will, I think, recognize that the domination of education or of government by any one particular religious faith is never a happy arrangement for the people.

Spiritual leadership should remain spiritual leadership and the temporal power should not become too important in any church.

I have no bias against the Roman Catholic Church and I have supported Governor Smith as Governor and worked for him as a candidate for the office of President of the United States. I have supported for public office many other Roman Catholic candidates.

You speak of the Mindszenty case. I spoke out very clearly against any unfair type of trial and anything anywhere in any country which might seem like attack on an individual because of his religious beliefs. I cannot, however, say that in European countries the control by the Roman Catholic Church of great areas of land has always led to happiness for the people of those countries.

I have never visited hospitals and asked or thought about the religion of any boy in any bed. I have never in a military cemetery had any different feeling about the graves of the boys who lay there. All of our boys of every race, creed and color fought for the country and they deserve our help and gratitude.

It is not my wish to deny children anywhere equal rights or benefits. It is, however, the decision of parents when they select a private or denominational school, whether it be Episcopal, Wesleyan, Jewish or Roman Catholic.

I can assure you that I have no prejudice. I understand the beliefs of the Roman Catholic Church very well. I happen to be a Protestant and I prefer my own church, but that does not make me feel that anyone has any less right to believe as his own convictions guide him.

I have no intention of attacking you personally, nor of attacking the Roman Catholic Church, but I shall, of course, continue to stand for the things in our Government which I think are right. They may lead me to be in opposition to you and to other groups within our country, but I shall always act, as far as I am able, from real conviction and from honest belief.

If you carefully studied my record, I think you would not find it one of anti-Catholic or anti-any-religious group.

I assure you that I have no sense of being "an unworthy American mother." The final judgment, my dear Cardinal Spellman, of the worthiness of all human beings is in the hands of God.

With deepest respect, I am

Very sincerely yours,

ELEANOR ROOSEVELT
(MRS. FRANKLIN D. ROOSEVELT)

Bibliography

Annuario Pontifico. Tipografia Poliglotta Vaticana, 1950.
Armstrong, Hamilton Fish. *Tito and Goliath.* The Macmillan Company, 1951.
Ashby, Eric. *Scientist in Russia.* Penguin Books (Harmondsworth, Middlesex), 1947.
Barghoorn, Frederick C. *The Soviet Image of the United States.* Harcourt, Brace and Company, 1950.
Barmine, Alexander. *One Who Survived.* G. P. Putnam's Sons, 1945.
Bartoli, Giorgio. *The Primitive Church and the Primacy of Rome.* Hodder and Stoughton (London), 1910.
Berman, Harold J. *Justice in Russia.* Harvard University Press, 1950.
Bernhart, Joseph. *The Vatican as a World Power.* Longmans, Green and Company, 1939.
Betten, Francis. *The Roman Index of Forbidden Books.* B. Herder Book Company, 1912.
Binchy, D. A. *Church and State in Fascist Italy.* Oxford University Press, 1941.
Blanshard, Paul. *American Freedom and Catholic Power.* Beacon Press, 1949.
Blau, Joseph L. *Cornerstones of Religious Freedom in America.* Beacon Press, 1949.
Blueprint for World Conquest as Outlined by The Communist International. Introduction by W. H. Chamberlin. Human Events, 1946.
Bouscaren, T. Lincoln. *Canon Law Digest.* Two volumes. Bruce Publishing Company, 1934, 1943.
Bouscaren, T. Lincoln, and Ellis, Adam C. *Canon Law: Text and Commentary.* Bruce Publishing Company, 1946.
Budenz, Louis F. *Men Without Faces.* Harper and Brothers, 1950.
———. *This Is My Story.* Whittlesey House, 1947.
Butts, R. Freeman. *The American Tradition in Religion and Education.* Beacon Press, 1950.
Carlyle, R. W. and A. J. *A History of Medieval Political Theory in the West.* Six volumes. W. Blackwood and Sons (London), 1936.
Catechism of Christian Doctrine. (Baltimore Catechism.) St. Anthony Guild Press (Paterson, New Jersey), 1949.
Catholic Almanac, 1950. St. Anthony Guild Press (Paterson, New Jersey), 1950.
Chamberlin, William Henry. *The Russian Revolution.* Two volumes. The Macmillan Company, 1935.
———. *Soviet Russia.* Little, Brown and Company, 1930.
Cianfarra, Camille M. *The Vatican and the Kremlin.* E. P. Dutton and Company, 1950.
———. *The Vatican and the War.* E. P. Dutton and Company, 1945.
Codex Iuris Canonici. Typis Polyglottis Vaticanis, 1947.
Coulton, G. G. *Inquisition and Liberty.* W. Heinemann, Ltd. (London), 1938.
Counts, George S., and Lodge, Nucia. *The Country of the Blind.* Houghton Mifflin Company, 1949.

———. *I Want to Be Like Stalin.* John Day Company, 1947.
Curtiss, John S. *Church and State in Russia, 1900-1917.* Columbia University Press, 1940.
Dallin, David J. *The Real Soviet Russia.* Yale University Press, 1944, 1947.
Deane, John R. *The Strange Alliance.* Viking Press, 1946.
Deutscher, Isaac. *Stalin: A Political Biography.* Oxford University Press, 1949.
Duchesne, Louis. *Early History of the Christian Church.* Three volumes. Longmans, Green and Company, 1924.
Durant, Will. *The Age of Faith.* Simon and Schuster, 1950.
Emerton, Ephraim, editor. *The Correspondence of Pope Gregory VII.* Columbia University Press, 1932.
Fischer, John. *Why They Behave Like Russians.* Harper and Brothers, 1947.
Fischer, Louis. *The Soviets in World Affairs.* Two volumes. Jonathan Crowe (London), 1930.
Five Great Encyclicals. Paulist Press, 1947.
Florinsky, Michael T. *World Revolution and the U.S.S.R.* The Macmillan Company, 1933.
Foltz, Charles, Jr. *The Masquerade in Spain.* Houghton Mifflin Company, 1948.
Gibbons, James Cardinal. *A Retrospect of Fifty Years.* Two volumes. John Murphy Company (Baltimore), 1916.
Gitlow, Benjamin. *The Whole of Their Lives.* Charles Scribner's Sons, 1948.
God That Failed, The. Symposium edited by R. H. S. Crossman. Harper and Brothers, 1950.
Gunther, John. *Behind the Curtain.* Harper and Brothers, 1949.
Harper, Samuel N., and Thompson, Ronald. *The Government of the Soviet Union.* D. Van Nostrand and Company, 1949.
History of the Communist Party of the Soviet Union. Edited by the Central Committee. International Publishers, 1939.
Hook, Sidney. *From Hegel to Marx.* Humanities Press, 1950.
Howell Smith, A. D. *Thou Art Peter.* C. A. Watts and Company (London), 1950.
Hughes, Emmet. *Report From Spain.* Henry Holt and Company, 1947.
Hughes, Philip. *A Popular History of the Catholic Church.* The Macmillan Company, 1949.
Husslein, Joseph. *Social Wellsprings.* (Encyclicals.) Two volumes. Bruce Publishing Company, 1942.
Index Librorum Prohibitorum. Typis Polyglottis Vaticanis, 1948.
Inkeles, Alex. *Public Opinion in Soviet Russia.* Harvard University Press, 1950.
Kravchenko, Victor. *I Chose Freedom.* Charles Scribner's Sons, 1946.
La Piana, George. "A Totalitarian Church in a Democratic State." *Shane Quarterly,* April 1949.
Lea, H. C. *A History of the Inquisition of the Middle Ages.* Three volumes. Harper and Brothers, 1888.
Lenin, V. I. *Religion.* (Pamphlet.) International Publishers, 1933.
———. *Selected Works.* Twelve volumes. International Publishers, 1935.
Manhattan, Avro. *The Vatican and World Politics.* Gaer Associates, 1949.
Manual of Christian Doctrine. 62nd edition. Christian Brothers (122 West 77th Street, New York), 1949.
Marshall, Charles C. *The Roman Catholic Church in the Modern State.* Dodd, Mead and Company, 1931.

Mazour, Anatole G. *An Outline of Modern Russian Historiography*. University of California Press, 1939.
Mikolajczyk, Stanislaw. *The Rape of Poland*. Whittlesey House, 1948.
Moehlman, Conrad. *The Wall of Separation Between Church and State*. Beacon Press, 1951.
Moore, Barrington, Jr. *Soviet Politics — the Dilemma of Power*. Harvard University Press, 1950.
Moore, Thomas E. *Peter's City*. The Macmillan Company, 1930.
Mosely, Philip E., editor. *Soviet Union Since World War II*. (Volume 263 of Annals of the American Academy of Political and Social Science.) 1949.
Nazi-Soviet Relations, edited by R. J. Sontag and J. S. Eddie. United States State Department, 1948.
Rossi, A. *The Communist Party in Action*. Yale University Press, 1949.
Salvemini, Gaetano, and La Piana, George. *What to Do With Italy*. Duell, Sloan and Pearce, 1943.
Schlesinger, Arthur, Jr. *The Vital Center*. Houghton Mifflin Company, 1949.
Schwarzschild, Leopold. *The Red Prussian*. Charles Scribner's Sons, 1947.
Shotwell, James T., and Loomis, Louise. *The See of Peter*. Columbia University Press, 1927.
Smit, J. O., and Vanderveldt, J. H. *Angelic Shepherd: The Life of Pope Pius XII*. Dodd, Mead and Company, 1950.
Smith, George D., editor. *The Teaching of the Catholic Church*. Two volumes. The Macmillan Company, 1949.
Smith, Walter Bedell. *My Three Years in Moscow*. J. B. Lippincott Company, 1950.
Snow, Edgar. *The Pattern of Soviet Power*. Random House, 1945.
Sorokin, Pitirim. *Russia and the United States*. E. P. Dutton and Company, 1944.
Sprigge, Cecil J. S. *The Development of Modern Italy*. Yale University Press, 1944.
Stalin, Joseph. *Leninism*. Two volumes. G. Allen and Unwin (London), 1933.
Stalin's Kampf, edited by M. R. Werner. Howell, Soskin and Company, 1940.
Stokes, Anson P. *Church and State in the United States*. Three volumes. Harper and Brothers, 1950.
Thompson, R. W. *The Papacy and the Civil Power*. Harper and Brothers, 1876.
Timasheff, Nicholas S. *The Great Retreat*. E. P. Dutton and Company, 1946.
Towster, Julian. *Political Power in the U.S.S.R., 1917-1947*. Oxford University Press, 1948.
Trotsky, Leon. *The History of the Russian Revolution*. Three volumes. Simon and Schuster, 1932.
Vyshinsky, Andrei. *The Law of the Soviet State*. The Macmillan Company, 1948.
Walsh, Warren B., and Price, Roy A. *Russia: A Handbook*. Syracuse University Press, 1948.
Williams, Melvin J. *Catholic Social Thought*. Ronald Press, 1950.
Wolfe, Bertram. *Three Who Made a Revolution*. Dial Press, 1948.
Wright, Gordon. *The Reshaping of French Democracy*. Reynal and Hitchcock, 1947.
Zirkle, Conway, editor. *Death of a Science in Russia*. University of Pennsylvania Press, 1949.

Notes

(Books listed in the Bibliography are referred to by the author's surname and, where necessary, his initial or a short title.)

Chapter 1
PATTERN AND PANORAMA

1. The committee included Arthur Schlesinger, Jr., James Burnham, and James T. Farrell. Its statement was printed in full in the *Information Service Bulletin* of the Federal Council of Churches, November 18, 1950.
2. New York *Times*, November 17, 1950.
3. *Blueprint*, p. 207.
4. Lenin, *Selected Works*, XI, 658. For first quoted sentences and opinions, see pp. 660, 664.
5. Stalin, p. 70.
5a. Bishop Ivan Bucko, described in the *Catholic News* of January 20, 1951, as "the only Ukrainian Bishop to have escaped the Soviet regime," estimated that before World War II there had been 6,000,000 Ukrainian Catholics in Russia and Central Europe, including East Germany, Hungary, and Czechoslovakia. He said: "My people cannot resist Soviet persecution much longer. I fear the Ukrainian Catholics will sooner or later go over to the Orthodox faith."
6. See Dallin, chap. 4; Karpovich, in *Russian Review*, Spring 1944; Chamberlin, *Soviet Russia*, chap. 13; and Timasheff, chap. 8.
7. New York *Times*, August 29, 1950.
8. Curtiss, p. 187.
9. Florinsky, p. 19.
10. "Political Parties in the Russian Duma," by Warren B. Walsh, in *Journal of Modern History*, June 1950.
11. Sorokin, p. 94.
12. Louis Fischer, I, 522.
13. Pius XI, *Atheistic Communism* (pamphlet), Paulist Press, p. 5. Original text in *Apostolicae Sedis*, March 31, 1937; translation in Husslein, II, 341; and in *Five Great Encyclicals*, p. 177.
14. The story, chiefly from the Vatican's point of view, is told in a recent book by Camille M. Cianfarra, Vatican correspondent of the New York *Times*: *The Vatican and the Kremlin*.
15. New York *Times*, April 26, 1950; and *Times* Index for August 1950. For a contemporary summary of the battle, see Arnaldo Cortesi, New York *Times*, February 13, 1949.
16. The Catholic population of the world has been variously estimated by Catholic authorities from 330,000,000 (*What Is Catholic Action?*, 1940, p. 50) to 375,000,000 (estimate of the 1950 *Catholic Almanac*).

With the recent losses in eastern Europe, it is likely that 350,000,000 is a generous estimate, and it should be remembered that about 27 per cent of these estimated numbers are children below thirteen, since all baptized infants are counted in the Catholic totals. The membership estimate of 25,000,000 for Communist parties is from an article in the New York *Times* of April 23, 1950, by Harry Schwartz, an authority in this field.

17. Gunther, p. 190.
18. See the very interesting interview with Archbishop Stepinac by Cyrus Sulzberger in the New York *Times* of November 13, 1950. The official Tito case against Archbishop Stepinac was published in booklet form by the Yugoslav Embassy in Washington in 1947 as *The Case of Archbishop Stepinac*.
19. The full official decree in Latin is in the *Acta Apostolicae Sedis*, July 24, 1949; the English text in the New York *Times* of July 14, 1949; and the principal text with Catholic comment in *America* of July 30, 1949.
20. *America*, August 20, 1949; and New York *Times*, August 6, 1949.
21. Quoted in the New York *Times*, July 31, 1949.
22. *Ibid.*, August 17, 1949.

Chapter 2

THE KREMLIN STRUCTURE OF POWER

1. Wolfe, p. 20.
2. See *American Sociological Review*, August 1950, article by Alex Inkeles.
3. Towster, p. 205. For the most part, in this description of the framework of the Soviet government, I have followed Towster. Harper and Thompson's standard work reprints the present Constitution of the Soviet Union.
4. Quoted by Towster, p. 186, from 1923 statement.
5. Moore, p. 233.
6. Stalin, *Constitution*, p. 29, quoted in Towster, p. 194.
7. New York *Times*, June 12, 1950 (editorial); for 1950 election figures, see issue of March 16, 1950.
8. Quoted in New York *Times*, November 8, 1949.
9. April 25, 1949, quoted by *Current Digest*, Vol. I, No. 17, p. 43.
10. Stalin, II, 44.
11. See *The Election to the Russian Constituent Assembly of 1917*, by Oliver H. Radkey, Harvard University Press, 1950.
12. *History*, p. 305.
13. Walsh and Price, p. 43.
14. Inkeles, p. 68.
15. *Trud*, May 11, 1949.
16. W. B. Smith, p. 26.
17. Lenin, *Selected Works*, II, 17.
18. S. Abalin, *Pravda*, January 12, 1949. For current history of the international, see New York *Times*, October 6, 1947, and October 9, 1949.
19. Gitlow has discussed this incident; Budenz has described it in some detail in *This Is My Story*.
20. *The Communist International*, March 5, 1934.
21. New York *Times*, October 6, 1947.
22. See Armstrong.

Chapter 3

THE VATICAN STRUCTURE OF POWER

1. G. D. Smith, II, 731.
2. In article on "Papacy."
3. For a discussion of this passage and the place of Peter in the early church see E. F. Scott, D.D., *The Nature of the Early Church,* Charles Scribner's Sons, 1941. Dr. Scott says about the famous passage in Matthew 16: "As it stands, however, it is more than suspicious. Mark, on whom Matthew is dependent throughout the chapter, knows nothing of this addition, and it is quite out of keeping with the incident to which it is attached. Peter had earned no special privilege by his confession, for he had only acted as spokesman for the whole band of disciples. Nor can Jesus have been in the mood to congratulate him for he was accepting the Messiahship as a terrible burden from which there was no escape." See also Howell Smith, chapter on "The Evolution of the Papacy"; and *The See of Peter* by James T. Shotwell and Louise R. Loomis.
4. Carlyle, Vols. I, II. The claims of Gregory VII are discussed in Vol. II.
5. *Encyclopedia Britannica,* "Empire." See also Emerton.
6. In his *Unam Sanctam.*
7. *Encyclopedia Britannica,* "Italy."
8. *Manual of Christian Doctrine,* p. 128.
9. Shotwell and Loomis, in their detailed and authoritative summary of the available evidence for the Petrine tradition in the Bible and elsewhere, say (p. 6): "For any connection of Peter with the city of Rome the witness of the New Testament is vague and inconclusive . . . taken by itself it is insufficient to *prove* anything." The authors list in translation all the documents on which the Church relies for its claim that Peter actually headed a hierarchy in Rome. The earliest documents are so indefinite that they can be used as effectively in opposition to Vatican claims as in support of them. A letter of about 95 A.D., ascribed to Clement of Rome, mentions Peter by inference as a good apostle and great pillar of the Church who "by reason of unrighteous envy endured not one nor two but many trials, and so, having borne his testimony, he passed to his appointed place of glory." A letter of Ignatius, second bishop of Antioch, written about 116 A.D. to his churches, says: "I do not command you as Peter and Paul did. They were apostles." Ignatius in greeting the Roman Christians in a flowery passage speaks of the Roman church as "preeminent in the land of the Romans, worthy of God, worthy of honor, worthy of blessing, worthy of praise, worthy of prosperity, worthy in her purity and foremost in love." Shotwell and Loomis say of this passage (p. 241): "This is the first of several obscure and vague passages in the early Fathers that testify to a prominence or leadership of the Roman church but leave one uncertain as to the exact nature or extent of the distinction." The authors point out (p. 61) that it was not until 354 A.D. that "we find Peter definitely and positively styled the first bishop of Rome."
10. See Smit and Vanderveldt for the official biography of Pius XII.
11. Bernhart, p. 428.
12. *Catholic Almanac,* 1950, p. 109.
13. Page 99.

14. Vol. X, p. 418.
15. Vol. IV, p. 321.
16. G. D. Smith, II, 725.
17. Page 487. Published by McVey, Philadelphia, 1901.
18. Chap. 2, quoted in *The Exposition of Christian Doctrine.*
19. *Five Great Encyclicals,* p. 136.
20. La Piana, p. 81.

Chapter 4
THE DEVICES OF DEIFICATION

1. Barmine, the former Brigadier General in the Red Army, who had many contacts with Stalin, says on page 259 of his *One Who Survived:* "We knew him as a slow and plodding thinker, cautious and suspicious . . . he is swift and ruthless once he begins to act."
2. *Stalin's Kampf,* p. 244. See also Deutscher.
3. Lenin, *Religion,* pp. 41 ff.
4. Counts and Lodge, *Country,* p. 75, quoted from *History of the U.S.S.R.* (edited by A. Pankratova), III, 310-11.
5. Snow, p. 145.
6. New York *Herald Tribune,* January 7, 1951.
7. *The God That Failed,* p. 194.
8. New York *Times,* December 25, 1949. Albanian reference, December 1, 1950.
9. *Political Affairs,* January 1950, p. 2.
10. New York *Times,* December 19, 1949.
11. *Soviet Literature,* No. 4, 1950.
12. New York *Times,* December 12, 1949.
13. *Pravda,* December 20, 1949, article on "Our Stalin," by Arkady Perventsev. Quoted in *Current Digest,* Vol. I, No. 52.
14. *VOKS Bulletin,* 1949, II, 56. This is published by the USSR Society for Cultural Relations with Other Countries. The editor is Vladimir Kemerov.
15. *Pravda,* August 28, 1936. Quoted by Eugene Lyons in the *American Mercury.*
16. *Pravda,* December 21, 1949.
17. Schlesinger, p. 75.
18. G. D. Smith, II, 685, describes the distinctions as roughly corresponding to the Latin theological terms, *dulia* for the saints, and *latria* for God.
19. An example was described in *Osservatore Romano,* July 28, 1950.
20. Most of these generalizations about the Pope and his power flow inevitably from the Catholic thesis that he is God's Vicar on earth and that he has infallible judgment in determining what is right and wrong. The Very Reverend H. A. Ayrinhac in his *Constitution of the Church in the New Code of Canon Law* (p. 32) says: "In religious and ecclesiastical matters the Pope has no superior but God; all the members of the Church, moral bodies as well as physical persons, are subject to him. He can dispense from, change, abrogate, all ecclesiastical laws, whether enacted by particular Bishops, Popes or General Councils." Canons 218-221 give the Pope jurisdiction over the universal Church by divine law. (See Bouscaren and Ellis, pp. 154 ff.) Leo XIII laid down the rule in his *Chief Duties of Christian Citizens* that all Catholics owe obedience to the Pope "as to God Himself." His right to excommunicate, coupled with his infallibility,

give the Pope the power to commit any soul to hell. Crimes and penalties, as well as the rules for absolution and forgiveness, are described in Canons 2195 to 2414, and the Pope is the complete dictator over this penal machinery — if he cares to exercise his dictatorship. See Bouscaren and Ellis (pp. 895 ff.) for a chart of *Latae Sententiae* excommunications and suspensions. The Pope's power to dispense, commute, or annul a promise is expressed in Canon 1320; his power over dispensation from impediments is described in Canon 1040; the rule concerning his resignation is in Canon 221; the nine-day funeral rule is described in Bouscaren and Ellis, p. 155; the rule of burial in an elevated place, in the same work, p. 699; the Pope's right to depose emperors and free their subjects from allegiance has been asserted many times, notably by Gregory VII in his letter to the people of Constance, recorded in Emerton, p. 54. Moehlman quotes the famous eleventh-century paragraph from the *Dictatus Papae*, on which my list is partially based: "The Pope alone may use the imperial insignia; all persons shall kiss the foot of the Pope alone; the Pope has the power to depose emperors; his decree can be annulled by no one; he can be judged by no one; the Roman church has never erred, according to the testimony of the holy scriptures; by the Pope's command or permission subjects may accuse their rulers; he has the power to absolve subjects from their oath of fidelity to wicked rulers."

21. Quoted by permission from *Ceremonies of Beatification and Canonization,* Society of St. John, Desclees and Company, Tournai, Belgium, 1950.

Chapter 5

THE KREMLIN AND THOUGHT CONTROL

1. B. Moore, p. 125, from *Directives of the Communist Party of the Soviet Union on Economic Questions,* Moscow, 1931.
2. Last proposition of the *Syllabus of Errors,* printed in Marshall. For sources of Stalin's attack, see B. Moore, p. 157.
3. Quoted by J. A. Brown, Jr., in *Russian Review,* January 1950, article on "Public Opinion in the Soviet Union."
4. *Ibid.,* p. 38.
5. Vyshinsky, p. 617.
6. Inkeles, pp. 207 ff., discusses letters in the Soviet press.
7. The *New Republic* of March 21, 1949, pointed out that the New York *Daily Worker* was caught flat-footed on the expulsion of Miss Strong from Russia three days after a reviewer in the *Worker* had said: "Anna Louise Strong would long ago have received the Pulitzer Prize for foreign news reporting, if the Pulitzer Prize Committee were not guided by political considerations."
8. Towster, p. 304. Berman discusses the whole Soviet legal system.
9. No. 2, 1948.
10. See Timasheff, p. 210.
11. Quoted by A. M. Egolin, Corresponding Member of the Academy of Sciences of the U.S.S.R., in *The Ideological Content of Soviet Literature,* Public Affairs Press, p. 16.
12. *Ibid.,* pp. 9, 13.
13. Inkeles, p. 144.
14. Margaret K. Webb, in *Virginia Quarterly Review,* Autumn 1950.

15. Translated in *Current Digest*, Vol. I, No. 18.
16. *Ibid.*
17. *Annals of the American Academy*, November 1938.
18. *The Listener* (B.B.C.), March 30, 1950.
19. *Saturday Review of Literature*, December 4 and 11, 1948. See also Bertram Wolfe, "Science Joins the Party," in *Antioch Review*, Spring 1950.
20. *VOKS Bulletin*, No. 56, 1949.
21. *Pravda*, August 15, 1948, quoted by Counts and Lodge, *Country*, p. 213.
22. *Pravda*, August 27, 1948, quoted by Counts and Lodge, *Country*, p. 223.
23. Zirkle, p. 314.
24. *Saturday Review of Literature*, December 11, 1948.
25. *New Republic*, December 5, 1949.
26. *Bolshevik*, 1944, Nos. 19-20, p. 61, quoted by Inkeles, p. 257.
27. The words are from a statement attacking an ill-fated opera; the statement, by the Central Committee of the All-Union Communist Party, was published in *Sovietskaia Muzyka*, No. 1, 1948, pp. 3-8, as quoted by Counts and Lodge, *Country*, pp. 160 ff.
28. *Ibid.*, quoted by Counts and Lodge, *Country*, p. 174.
29. New York *Times*, March 27, 1949.
30. *The Nation*, September 21, 1948.
31. *Soviet Literature*, No. 4, 1950, Moscow.
32. See article, "Literary Tightrope Walking in the U.S.S.R.," by Vera Sandomirsky, in *Antioch Review*, Winter 1950-51.
33. References to first four authors, New York *Times*, December 26, 1948; last three, *The Nation*, February 11, 1948.
34. *Time*, February 19, 1951.
35. New York *Times*, July 31, 1949.
36. *Ibid.*, October 9, 1949.
37. See Inkeles, chaps. 16-18.
38. Counts and Lodge, *Country*, p. 144.
39. *Pravda*, January 31, 1950, quoted by *Current Digest*.
40. Eisenstein died two years later.
41. *Pravda*, July 6, 1950, quoted in *New Leader*, October 30, 1950.
42. *Literaturnaya Gazeta*, New Year's Issue, 1949, quoted in *Foreign Affairs*, July 1950.
43. New York *Herald Tribune*, December 15, 1949.

Chapter 6

THE VATICAN AND THOUGHT CONTROL

1. Lea, I, 555.
2. Coulton, *The Inquisition* (New York, 1929), p. 74. See also Durant, chap. 28, for a review of the early Inquisition. With slight exceptions I have followed Catholic sources in my description. See *Catholic Encyclopedia*, "Inquisition."
3. Lea describes methods of torture in detail (Vol. I, pp. 421 ff., 553), giving a table of costs for the burning of four heretics in 1323.
4. *Catholic Encyclopedia*. See also Lea, I, 215.
5. *History of England*, chap. 1, p. 47.
6. Bouscaren and Ellis, p. 711.
7. Marshall reprints the *Syllabus of Errors*.

8. The original statement in *Civiltà Cattolica* (XCIX, 29 ff.) was reprinted in part in *Time*, June 28, 1948. Father Murray's criticism of it, and the two quotations from *Razón y Fe*, CXXXIV (1946), 148-171, and *Razón y Fe* (1948), 518-539, are contained in a valuable article by Father Murray in *Theological Studies*, September 1949. Father Murray's somewhat liberal views do not seem to represent the Vatican, and his most reactionary critic, Father Francis J. Connell, has recently been made dean of the School of Sacred Theology of the Catholic University in Washington.
9. *Freedom of Worship* (Paulist Press), p. 10. This revealing pamphlet is reprinted in Stokes, Vol. III, Appendix V.
10. Quoted by Robert Duffus, in New York *Times*, July 20, 1947.
11. Catholic *Register*, June 19, 1949.
12. Page 143. Published by Sheed and Ward, New York, 1927.
13. London *Times*, October 28, 1949.
14. Bouscaren and Ellis, p. 711.
15. 1950, p. 504. This *Almanac* has a good summary of Church law on censorship. See also the *Catholic Encyclopedia*, "Censorship."
16. *Index*, p. 139.
17. Budenz, *Story*, p. 187.
18. Howell Smith, p. 799.
19. See *Catholic Encyclopedia*, "Censorship," and also "Modernism"; also Bouscaren and Ellis, pp. 734, 735, for requirements concerning the anti-modernist oath. An interesting contemporary account of the modernist battle against Pius X is *Modernism*, by A. Leslie Lilly, Charles Scribner's Sons, 1908. Professor La Piana has eloquently told the story of Ernesto Buonaiuti in the *Harvard Divinity School Bulletin* for June 3, 1947.
20. *Atlantic Monthly*, January 1948.
21. *Christian Crisis* (The Macmillan Company, 1940), p. 163.
22. Bouscaren and Ellis, p. 713.
23. See the 1950 articles by Sam Pope Brewer in the New York *Times*.
24. New York *Times*, October 16, 1949, and February 8, 1951.
25. There is a startling inconsistency between the standards imposed on motion pictures in the United States and in European countries by Catholic censorship agencies. Since there is no central Index for undesirable films, many pictures which are praised by Catholic critics in one country are banned by Catholic censors in another.
26. Lea, III, 613.
27. *Editor and Publisher*, August 12, 1950.

Chapter 7

THE KREMLIN AND THE VATICAN VERSUS
THE PUBLIC SCHOOL

1. Chamberlin, *Soviet Russia*, pp. 286-87.
2. Sorokin, pp. 144 ff.
3. See an important article in the *American Sociological Review* of August 1950 by Alex Inkeles, "Social Stratification and Mobility in the Soviet Union: 1940-1950." The fee for attendance in the eighth, ninth, and tenth grades in Moscow is 200 rubles a year; for higher grades, 400 rubles. The official exchange rate is about four rubles to the dollar.

4. Inkeles, p. 262.
5. *Modern Nationalism and Religion,* p. 96.
6. As translated in Gury's *Doctrines of the Jesuits,* p. 607.
7. National statistics on illiteracy are not always reliable or comparable. The *Encyclopedia Britannica Year Book, 1950,* using the latest available figures from national governments, puts the illiteracy rate in Portugal at 54%; Spain 46%; and Southern Italy "the great majority." UNESCO's latest figures, summarized in the *National Education Association Journal* for December 1950, show an illiteracy proportion in Brazil of 57%; Chile 28%; Colombia 44%; Peru 57%; Venezuela 57%; pre-revolutionary Poland 23%. A few predominantly Catholic countries in the world are able to boast a low illiteracy rate, e.g. Belgium 8%; Ireland 12%; and Hungary 15%. According to the *Encyclopedia Britannica,* the predominantly Protestant countries of Europe — Denmark, Germany, the Netherlands, Norway, Sweden, Switzerland, and Great Britain — have less than one-half of 1 per cent illiteracy. Illiteracy estimates for the United States have not been brought up to date recently — 4% is probably a maximum estimate.
8. See Timasheff, p. 210.
9. Fischer, *Why They Behave Like Russians,* p. 64.
10. Quoted by Counts and Lodge, *Country,* p. 263.
11. Address by A. G. Kalashnikov, "Thirty Years of Soviet Education," Moscow, 1947, quoted by Counts and Lodge, *Country,* pp. 262 ff.
12. The Catholic canon law on education, in rough translation of the Latin text in *Codex Iuris Canonici,* reads as follows:

Canon 1372

All the faithful should be instructed in such a way, from early youth, that nothing should be taught them which is contrary to the Catholic religion; and honest customs and religious and moral instruction should have a particular place. Not only the parents but those who according to paragraph 1113 act in their place have the right and the serious duty to care for Christian education.

Canon 1373

In every elementary school, religious instruction should be imparted to children according to their age. Children attending middle and higher schools should receive a more perfect instruction in religious doctrine, and those responsible for religious leadership in that place should see that it is carried out by priests notable for their zeal and instruction.

Canon 1374

Catholic children must not attend non-Catholic, neutral, or mixed schools, that is, such as are also open to non-Catholics. It is for the bishop of the place alone to decide, according to the instructions of the Apostolic See, in what circumstances and with what precautions attendance at such schools may be tolerated, without danger of perversion to the pupils.

Canon 1375

The Church has the right to create schools of all types, not only elementary ones but middle and higher schools as well.

Canon 1376

Only the Holy See has the right to create a Catholic university or faculty. A Catholic university or faculty, even if founded by a religious order, must have its statutes approved by the Holy See.

Canon 1377
Nobody has the right to confer academic degrees valid for the Church if he has not obtained the right from the Holy See.

Canon 1378
Doctors of ecclesiastical science have the right to wear, except during the holy functions, a ring with a stone and a doctor's hat. Besides, those prescriptions have to be followed which state that for certain offices and functions those who have obtained a degree or a license are to be preferred, under equal conditions and according to the judgment of the bishop.

Canon 1379
In places where there are no Catholic schools, neither elementary nor middle schools, it must be seen to, especially by the bishop, that they are founded. In the same way, where there are no Catholic universities, it is to be wished that in that nation or region Catholic universities should be founded. The faithful should not fail to give their help for the foundation and maintenance of Catholic schools.

Canon 1380
It is to be wished that the bishop should send clerics who excel in piety and mental ability to universities or faculties founded or approved by the Church, to study philosophy, theology, and ecclesiastic law and to obtain the degrees.

Canon 1381
The religious instruction of children is, in all schools, subject to the inspection and authority of the Church. It is the right and the duty of the bishop to watch that in the schools of his territory nothing should be taught or nothing happen which is against faith and good morals. The same authorities have the right to approve books and religious instructors; and they may for religious and moral reasons remove teachers or books.

Canon 1382
The bishops or their delegates may visit all schools, oratories, places of recreation, and service as well as religious and moral institutions. Non-religious schools are exempt from these visitations except internal schools of religious orders.

13. *Five Great Encyclicals;* also in Husslein, II, 87 ff.
14. Bouscaren and Ellis, p. 74.
15. Page 201.
16. Gibbons, I, 252.
17. *Current History,* August 1929, p. 849.
18. Emmet Hughes, p. 66.
19. Husslein, II, 383 ff.
20. The Catholic bishops of the United States in their official statement on education, November 18, 1950 (New York *Times,* November 19), said: "We protest in the strongest possible terms against the introduction of sex instruction into the schools." They also said: "Fathers and mothers have a natural competence to instruct their children with regard to sex."
21. May 3, 1948.
22. Page 40.
23. New York *Times,* December 19, 1949.
24. *Catholic Encyclopedia,* "Sociology," as quoted by Williams, pp. 90, 95.

25. *History of Western Philosophy*, p. 475.
26. Ruth Karpf in *The Nation*, January 1, 1949.
27. Binchy, p. 456.
28. September 4, 1949.
29. New York *Times*, July 4, 1950.
30. As quoted in the Brooklyn *Tablet*, November 2, 1948.
31. New York *Times*, January 26, 1949.
32. Page 118.
33. The address was quoted in the *New Republic* of June 26, 1950.
34. New York *Times*, May 30, 1950, dispatch by Michael Clark.
35. The British *Catholic Directory* for 1951 claimed 2,808,596 Catholics in Great Britain at the end of 1949, but this does not include continental Catholic refugees, who may bring the total to 3,000,000.
36. Brooklyn *Tablet*, November 12, 1949. The Catholic case may be found in *America*, April 23, 1949, and December 3, 1949; and in an *America* pamphlet, *The Right to Educate;* also in the Brooklyn *Tablet*, December 10, 1949.
37. February 24, 1950.
38. Foltz, p. 110.

Chapter 8

DISCIPLINE AND DEVOTION

1. *The Intelligent Woman's Guide to Capitalism and Socialism*, p. 185.
2. Pages 114-15.
3. Rossi, p. 171.
4. Gitlow, p. 237.
5. Budenz, p. 99.
6. *Crux Ansata*, p. 137.
7. Constitution of the Jesuits, par. vi, cap. 1, sec. 1.
8. Bouscaren, *Digest*, I, 315. An English translation of "Canonical Legislation Concerning Religious" is obtainable in pamphlet form from Libreria Editrice Vaticana, Vatican City.
9. Volume X, "Mortification."
10. *The Listener* (B.B.C.), June 8, 1950.
11. Dallin, p. 239 (and other sources). The Cheka, organized in December 1917, became the O.G.P.U. and the O.G.P.U. became the N.K.V.D. in 1934. The N.K.V.D. became the M.V.D. in March 1946.
12. Deutscher, p. 380. Souvarine estimates that Stalin, after the murder of Kirov, "sent some 100,000 innocent inhabitants of Leningrad" to Asia.
13. Dallin (chap. 11) gives several estimates of the forced-labor totals in the Soviet Union, ranging as high as 15 to 20 million. Most estimates are considerably below that figure, but there is no doubt that the number of prisoners in the forced-labor camps is prodigious. Harry Schwartz, in the New York *Times* of December 17, 1950, described a Soviet document recently made public by the State Department, "State Plan for the Development of the National Economy of the U.S.S.R. in 1941," which showed that the N.K.V.D. (now the M.V.D.) was one of the chief employers and producers in the nation. The report indicated that at that time the slave labor in this miniature police state within the police state of the Soviet Union produced one-sixth of the total new construction in the nation, and about 2 per cent of all industrial production.

14. *Life,* September 26, 1949. The quotation from John Scott's article is reprinted by permission of the author and *Life.*
15. *The God That Failed,* p. 106.
16. Professor E. K. Francis of Notre Dame, in a valuable analysis of Catholic religious orders in the *American Journal of Sociology* for March 1950, says: "The Jesuits are not so much brethren as comrades-at-arms, sometimes described as a corps of officers destined to lead the people's army of the militant church."
17. New York *Times,* October 16, 1949.
18. The official doctrine, on page 130 of the Catechism, declares that the phrase "Outside the Church there is no salvation" applies with full severity only to "those who through their own grave fault do not know that the Catholic Church is the true Church or, knowing it, refuse to join it." The Catechism adds: "Those who are outside the Church through no fault of their own are not culpable in the sight of God because of their invincible ignorance." The American Church is embarrassed by this rule, which penalizes honest intellectuals who have studied the Catholic point of view and rejected it. The Massachusetts hierarchy expelled Father Leonard Feeney of Cambridge in the famous Boston heresy case of 1949 for insisting upon its literal interpretation. Actually, there is no doubt that Father Feeney was technically correct in his interpretation of Catholic law, but the Vatican has created enough loopholes in its rules to allow some charity for all but willful opponents. For the Catholic side of this controversy, see *America,* April 30, 1949; for Father Feeney's point of view, see *The Loyolas and the Cabots,* by Catherine Goddard Clarke (Ravensgate Press, Boston, 1950).
19. *Alla Chiesa Credo, ai Protestanti No!,* by P. Vittorio Genovesi, S.J. The subtitle is "Catechismo Cattolico Antiprotestantico." It was published in 1949 in Pompeii and distributed by P. Armando Jue, S.J., Via S. Sebastiano 48, Naples, Imprimatur Robertus Ronca. According to Canon 2314 (Bouscaren and Ellis, p. 861), any Catholic who joins a non-Catholic sect is "ipso facto infamous."
20. The Catholic rules of exclusion summarized in this paragraph are contained in the following canons and commentary, as published in Bouscaren and Ellis: (1) Protestant Bible, Canon 1399, p. 726; (2) Protestant religious service, Canon 1258, p. 646 ("It is illicit for Catholics in any way to assist actively or take part in sacred worship of non-Catholics"); (3) Protestant book of exposition, Canon 1399, p. 728; (4) same as 2; (5) Protestant marriage, Canon 1063, p. 462; (6) Protestant school, Canon 1374, p. 704.
21. Canon 1060 reads: "The Church everywhere most severely forbids the contracting of marriage between two baptized persons of whom one is a Catholic whereas the other is a member of a heretical or schismatic sect."
22. This rule is based on Canon 1258. *America* of July 1, 1950, gives several illustrations of the fine distinctions imposed upon baccalaureate services because of the rule.
23. The full text of the Vatican ruling against American Rotary Clubs was published in *Osservatore Romano,* January 12, 1951, and in the Denver Catholic *Register* in English translation, January 21, 1951. The key sentence reads: "Members of the clergy may not belong to the Rotary Club association or take part in its meetings; laymen are to be urged to observe

the provisions of Canon 684 of canon law." Canon 684 reads: "The faithful deserve praise when they join associations which have been erected, or at least recommended by the Church. They should beware of associations which are secret, condemned, seditious, or suspected, and of those which strive to withdraw themselves from the legitimate supervision of the Church." The earlier (and milder) ruling against Rotary Clubs was dated February 4, 1929, and is printed in Bouscaren, I, 617.
24. *Catholic News,* January 13, 1951.
25. Perhaps the best recent description of the working of this rule is in a series of articles by Winfred Ernest Garrison in the *Christian Century,* fall of 1950, partially summarized in *Time,* November 13, 1950.
26. *Catholic Encyclopedia,* "Excommunication," divides victims into two classes — the *tolerati,* or excommunicated persons whom the faithful are not obliged to avoid; and the *vitandi,* who must be shunned "either in regard to sacred things or (to a certain extent) profane matters." The rule concerning the digging up of bones is in Canons 1172 and 1175 (Bouscaren and Ellis, pp. 595-96).
27. See Appendix for excerpts from the concordat.
28. July 5, 1950, p. 169.
29. Rossi, p. 167.
30. No. 47, 1950, p. 31.
31. *Political Affairs.*
32. Issue of March 21, 1950, from *Current Digest,* Vol. II, No. 12, p. 41.

Chapter 9

THE MANAGEMENT OF TRUTH: THE KREMLIN

1. Quoted by David Spitz, *Antioch Review,* Winter 1949-50.
2. Chamberlin, *Soviet Russia,* p. 89.
3. Lenin, *Religion,* p. 47.
4. See Barghoorn, chap. 3, "The American War Effort."
5. Counts and Lodge, *I Want,* p. 62.
6. Quoted from *Pravda* of May 9, 1949, in *Foreign Affairs,* July 1950, p. 631.
7. See *The Nation,* August 21, 1948; and N. S. Timasheff, in *Russian Review,* July 1949.
8. *Komsomolskaya Pravda,* January 9, 1949, cited by N. S. Timasheff, in *Russian Review,* July 1949.
9. The Clark estimate was in the New York *Times,* August 21, 1949; the 1947 *Times* figures were by Will Lissner, and were summarized in *Time,* December 29, 1947.
10. New York *Herald Tribune,* November 4, 1949.
11. Stalin, *Problems of Leninism,* p. 571.
12. Walter Kerr, *The Russian Army,* p. 7.
13. *American Sociological Review,* August 1950.
14. *Pravda,* January 16, 1949, in *Current Digest,* Vol. I, No. 3, p. 49.
15. *Daily Worker,* December 12, 1949.
16. No. 2, 1948, quoted by W. W. Kulski, in *Foreign Affairs,* July 1950.
17. *The Listener* (B.B.C.), March 30, 1950.
18. New York *Times,* September 25, 1949.
19. Peter Viereck in the appendix of his *Conservatism Revisited* has documented this new anti-Semitic trend.

20. New York *Times,* February 17, 1951.
21. New York *Herald Tribune,* Joseph Newman, November 7, 1949.
22. See Barghoorn, p. 201; and N. S. Timasheff, in *Russian Review,* July 1949.
23. *Selected Works* (Russian edition), X, 51, quoted in *Political Affairs,* January 1950.
24. *Pravda,* January 16, 1949, in *Current Digest,* Vol. I, No. 3, p. 49.
25. Lenin, *Selected Works,* II, 322.
26. New York *Times,* December 19, 1949.
27. *Nazi-Soviet Relations.* For the following quotations see pp. 78, 91-95, 154. For Hitler conversation, pp. 226 ff. See also a recent work by A. Rossi, *The Russo-German Alliance,* Beacon Press, 1951.
28. Dallin, p. 90.
28a. Quoted by Philip Mosely, *Current History,* XV, 131. See also article by Robert G. Neumann, in *Review of Politics,* April 1949.
29. *Background Information on the Soviet Union in International Relations,* Committee on Foreign Affairs, House of Representatives, 1950.
30. New York *Times,* October 14, 1949.
31. See Mikolajczyk, *The Rape of Poland.*
32. *The God That Failed,* p. 37.
33. New York *Times,* August 7, 1948.
34. Moscow's *New Times,* No. 47 (1950), announced signatures up to November 1950 of 223,500,000 in China; 16,884,787 in Italy; 6,000,000 in Japan; and "one in every three voters" in Vienna.
35. New York *Times,* April 24, 1949.
36. *Daily Worker,* May 31, 1948.
37. New York *Times,* February 27, 1949.
38. *Ibid.,* August 18, 1950.
39. See Dallin, chap. 6, and Moore, chap. 10.
40. *Trud,* May 11, 1949.
41. Timasheff, chap. 8, has an extended discussion of the new family values, and Berman has a chapter on "Law and the Family."
42. *Current Digest* article by A. S. Makarenko, quoted by Jerry Tallmer, in *The Nation,* November 26, 1949.
43. *Current Digest,* September 13, 1949, quoted in *The Nation.*
44. Dallin, p. 104.
45. W. W. Kulski in *Foreign Affairs,* July 1950; and Berman, p. 242.
46. New York *Herald Tribune* report summarized in *Catholic News,* July 12, 1950.
47. *America,* August 20, 1949.
48. March 9, 1947, for the National Council of Catholic Men.
49. Page 382.
50. Mazour, pp. 97-98.

Chapter 10

THE MANAGEMENT OF TRUTH: THE VATICAN

1. In his encyclical on *Human Liberty,* Paulist Press, p. 25.
2. La Piana, p. 82.
3. The syndicated series began in the *Catholic News* of November 13, 1948; the quoted article was No. 8 in the series.
4. Pages 5-9.

5. Page 113.
6. Gibbons, I, 231.
7. This is quoted on page 17 of a valuable study, "Religion and Civil Liberty in the Roman Catholic Tradition," by Winfred Ernest Garrison, in *Church History*, October 1946.
8. October 1950.
9. *The Catholic Spirit in America,* p. 155.
10. Marshall's open letter was in the *Atlantic Monthly* of April 1927; Smith's reply in the issue of May 1927; and Marshall's rejoinder of April 17, 1927, was printed in a small book by Charles C. Marshall, published by Dodd, Mead and Company in 1928, *Governor Smith's American Catholicism.* The best statement of Marshall's case, however, is in his 1931 work, *The Roman Catholic Church in the Modern State.*
11. This claim was made many times in 1950, when Italian liberals were attempting to persuade the Chamber of Deputies to face the scandalous divorce situation in Italy, under which literally millions of Italians are living in extra-marital unions because they cannot legally terminate marriages which have already been discarded in fact.
12. *Five Great Encyclicals,* p. 96.
13. 1949 edition, p. 132.
14. 1949 edition, pp. 133, 174.
15. Henry Morton Robinson, in his novel *The Cardinal,* presents a caricature of Marshall under the name of Hubbell K. Whiteman, and pretends that Marshall distorted the Catholic position on church and state by representing the Pope "as a foreign suzerain with the final word over American affairs." Actually Marshall was scrupulously careful to point out that the doctrine of the two powers of the Church "makes the Roman Catholic Church *at times* sovereign and paramount over the State."
16. Page 101. Father Ross also says on page 93: "Furthermore the Pope's infallible authority does not extend to temporal subjects. Since it is restricted to what has been revealed in Scripture or in Tradition it has no power of new revelation." This appears to be a purely verbal and imaginary limitation upon the Pope's powers in view of the recent promulgation of the doctrine that the body of the Virgin Mary has been taken up literally into heaven. The "tradition" in this case was merely rumor.
17. Text in *Catholic Almanac,* 1949, pp. 86 ff.; also in New York *Times,* November 21, 1948.
18. *America's* attack on the McCollum decision was in the issue of May 21, 1949; the editor's criticism of Professor O'Neill was in the issue of April 23, 1949. Butts has valuable material on this subject, and Moehlman's new study of this field offers a complete refutation of O'Neill. Leo Pfeffer, writing in the *Columbia Law Review* for January 1950, scores "the lack of legal training" of O'Neill and criticizes his analysis of the First Amendment as "permeated with blind spots, unsubstantiated assertions, contradictions and quotations dismembered from context." O'Neill's book in manuscript was used by the appellees in the McCollum case, and the Supreme Court rejected its arguments in favor of Jefferson's wall of separation between church and state.
19. See *American Freedom and Catholic Power,* chap. 5.
20. *Catholic News,* July 2, 1949.
21. New York *Times,* July 11, 1949.
22. Page 682.

23. *American Ecclesiastical Review,* August 1950, study by Father Alfred C. Ruch.
24. September 26, 1950.
25. Perhaps the most striking free publicity was in *Life,* which headed its 15-page spread with the streamer: "The Search for the Bones of St. Peter; Vatican Diggings Have Already Led to Startling Finds." The New York *Times* of April 9, 1950, was relatively almost as generous.
26. The following biblical verses have been cited by Catholic authorities as supporting evidence for the doctrines listed. Nearly all of them are taken from Volume II of *The Teaching of the Catholic Church,* edited by Canon George D. Smith, and published under official Imprimatur in 1949 by Macmillan.

    Purgatory. Matthew 12:32. 1 Peter 3:19. 1 Corinthians 15:29. John 5:25, 28.
    Infallibility of the Pope. Matthew 16:18-19; 18:18-20. John 21:15.
    Divorce. Mark 10:2-12. Luke 16:18. Matthew 5:31-32; 19:3-12. 1 Corinthians 7:10-15. Genesis 2:24.
    Priestly control of marriage. Ephesians 5:25-32. Genesis 1:28. 1 Corinthians 7:3, 10-15.
    Indulgences. Matthew 16:19; 18:18. John 20:21-23. Ephesians 1:7.
    Birth Control. Genesis 38:7-30; 1:28.
    Coercive Power of the Papacy. Matthew 16:18-19; 18:15-20. 1 Corinthians 5:1-15. Acts 15:28-29. 1 Corinthians 7:10-15. Romans 13:1. Matthew 22:21.
27. See *American Freedom and Catholic Power,* chaps. 6, 7.

Chapter 11

THE STRATEGY OF PENETRATION: THE KREMLIN

1. Lenin, *Selected Works,* II, 322.
2. See Mikolajczyk; and also Armstrong.
3. See Gunther; also "Marxism in Action," by Paul E. Zinner, in *Foreign Affairs,* July 1950; also two articles by Stephen D. Kertesz, in *World Politics,* April and July, 1950.
4. See article, "The Methods of Communist Conquest: Hungary," by Stephen D. Kertesz, *World Politics,* October 1950.
5. Rossi, Gitlow, and Budenz all discuss these phases of Communist strategy.
6. Rossi, p. 200. Reprinted by permission of Yale University Press.
7. September 6, 1947.
8. See Mosely, special issue of the *Annals,* an indispensable summary of post-war developments in eastern Europe. I am indebted to the article by C. E. Block for the names cited. See also the *Review of Politics,* April 1949, for an article, "United States Foreign Policy and the Satellites," by Robert G. Neumann.
9. In West Germany and Austria, Communist, Socialist, and Catholic union members are all in the same federations together. Adolf Sturmthal has summarized many of the facts about European labor unions in an article, "Democratic Socialism in Europe," in *World Politics,* October 1950.
10. Official I.C.F.T.U. Report, November-December 1949, London. Permanent headquarters, 24 Rue du Lombard, Brussels.
11. An interesting summary of such tactics then and now was made in a series

of articles by Fendall Yerxa and Ogden R. Reid in the New York *Herald Tribune,* beginning November 29, 1950.

Chapter 12

THE STRATEGY OF PENETRATION: THE VATICAN

1. *United Nations World,* October 1949.
2. *Annuario Pontifico,* 1950, pp. 825-47. I have subtracted diplomatic vacancies.
3. Even today, when the Vatican has the world's smallest official state, the Holy See does not offer to step down from a position of seniority which it gained during the days of the Papal States in Italy. If the United States granted full recognition and received a Papal Nuncio in return, this Nuncio would be the head of the diplomatic corps in Washington.
4. Sweden recognized that the Vatican is the chief power blocking a Jerusalem settlement by officially appealing to the Holy See on December 6, 1950, to change its policy. See New York *Times,* December 8, 1950.
4a. See Stokes, II, 88-90; III, 910.
5. Professor La Piana in *The Nation,* May 4, 1946, also lists the concordats of the Vatican with Latvia in 1922 and Lithuania in 1927, and declares that the 1928 concordat with Poland was "the most favorable ever obtained by the Church in any country." For a general discussion of concordats, see *Catholic Encyclopedia,* "Concordat." For a list of concordats of Pius XI, see *His Holiness Pope Pius XI* by Monsignor Fontenelle, p. 192.
6. See Manhattan, chap. 9. Sprigge's description of the rise of modern Italy is notable. Salvemini and La Piana have written what is probably the best summary of the Vatican and the post-war Italian political situation. See also *The Nation,* December 11, 1948; and a series of articles by Percy Winner in the *New Republic,* beginning November 7, 1949.
7. November 11, 1949.
8. Wright, pp. 76 ff., has an excellent description of M.R.P. methods of operation in recent years.
9. *The Nation,* February 17, 1951.
10. The quotations in this paragraph are taken respectively from the Brooklyn *Tablet* of March 17, 1951, and from the New York *Times* of February 8, 1951. A good description of Franco's tactics in "consolidating" Spain politically with the help of the clergy can be found in Foltz.
11. New York *Times,* April 5, 1950.
12. In *World Politics,* October 1948.
13. New York *Times,* August 1, 1949. For anyone familiar with papal pronouncements on Socialism, this is a little hard to swallow. Pius XI in his encyclical *Reconstructing the Social Order,* after praising the moderate tendencies of some Socialists, still concluded: "We pronounce as follows: whether Socialism be considered as a doctrine, or as a historical fact, or as a movement, if it really remain Socialism, it cannot be brought into harmony with the dogmas of the Catholic Church, even after it has yielded to truth and justice in the points We have mentioned; the reason being that it conceives human society in a way utterly alien to Christian truth." *Five Great Encyclicals,* p. 157.
14. See Salvemini and La Piana, chap. 5. The Catholic writer William Teeling, in his *Pope Pius XI and World Affairs,* p. 121, says: "The Church

denied, not once but a hundred times, that the Popular Party was actually the Catholic Party, but for all practical purposes this was the case." Teeling believes that Pius XI, because he "considered Socialism only the vanguard of Communism," jettisoned Don Sturzo's movement to avoid a possible Socialist-Catholic alliance in Italy.
15. Catholic *Register,* April 4, 1948.
16. Binchy, p. 497.
17. Catholic *Register,* August 7, 1949.
18. See New York *Times,* August 1, 1949; and Helen Booth, in *The Nation,* October 8, 1949.
19. New York *Times,* October 2, 1947.
20. In his *Reconstructing the Social Order* (printed in *Five Great Encyclicals,* p. 150), Pius XI neatly avoided clear commitments, but the meaning of his recommendation was that the fascist corporative organizations were worthy of support if they were partially directed by Catholic Action. He definitely praised "repression of Socialist organizations and efforts."
21. This was admitted by leaders of the organization when I visited their international headquarters in Utrecht in October 1950. It was also brought into the open by the Dutch labor leader, A. Vermeulen, in Geneva in January 1949, at a conference of the International Labor Organization. Vermeulen charged that the policy of the Dutch Catholic bishops was in violation of the principle of free association of the I.L.O.'s charter. The practice was described by Faith Williams in a general review of Catholic unions in Europe in the *Monthly Labor Review* of the Department of Labor, December 1949.
22. *De Vakbeweging,* April 5, 1949.
23. Official Report, p. 65.
24. *Catholic Almanac,* 1949, p. 441.
25. New York *Daily Compass,* November 27, 1949.
26. Wright, p. 105.

Chapter 13

THE AMERICAN ANSWER

1. J. Edgar Hoover of the Federal Bureau of Investigation estimated the number of Communist Party members in the United States at 55,000 on May 2, 1950 (New York *Times,* May 3, 1950). The number of Catholics in the United States is, in round figures, 27,000,000. Even if we concede that half of the baptized Catholics pay no attention to their Church, and that there are ten times as many sympathizers with Communism as Party members, Catholic power still outweighs Communist power in the United States by about 25 to 1.
2. This is true of Italy today; and it was true of Hungary before the Communist conquest, and of Mexico before the revolution.
3. *Foreign Affairs,* April 1951.
4. Boston *Herald,* August 2, 1950.
5. Quoted by Philip Mosely, in *Current History,* XV, 131.

Index

Abortions, therapeutic, 206, 241
Academic freedom: in Catholic schools, 151; in Soviet Union, 137
Acton, Lord, 212
Adenauer, Konrad, 272
Agitators, Communist, 35, 137
Agitator's Guidebook, 31, 35
Albania, 72
Albigenses, 106
Almond, Gabriel, 275
American Ecclesiastical Review, 79
American Federation of Labor, 255
American Labor Party, 255
American Textile Company, 130
Americanism, 4
Anti-Catholicism, 228, 296
Anti-modernist oath, 122, 322
Anti-religion, 8
Anti-science, 233
Apostolic Delegates, 264, 266
Aquinas, Saint Thomas, 110, 137, 148, 179
Argentina, 128, 213
Ashby, Eric, 83
Asia, 297
Association of Catholic Trade Unionists, 284
Assumption of Virgin Mary, 119, 238-239
Atheism, 151
Atheistic Communism, 12
Atlantic Monthly, 123, 220
Atomic bomb, 261
Augustine, Saint, 106
Austria, 270, 279
Avignon, 52

Baccalaureate services, 176
Bagger, Eugene, 215
Baltic States, 13
Baltimore, Council of, 63, 143

Barden, Graham, 229
Barden bill, 230
Barghoorn, Frederick C., ix
Bari, Italy, 236
Bedoyere, Michael de la, 123
Belgian Catholic Party, 231
Belgium, 153, 155, 213, 224, 231, 267, 270-271, 273
Belgrade, Yugoslavia, 250
Bellarmine, Robert Cardinal, 110
Benedict XV, Pope, 12, 60, 270
Beneš, Eduard, 248
Beria, L. P., 74
Berle, Adolf, 297
Berlin, 5, 188
Bernhart, Joseph, 54
Bible, 45, 175, 240
Bidault, Georges, 271
Binchy, D. A., 278
Birth control, 119, 208, 285
Bishops, Catholic: appointment of, 63; public statements of, 215-216, 324
Blötzen, Rev. Joseph, 110
Bohemia, 235
Bolsheviks, 11, 12
Bolshevism, 7 ff.
Boniface VIII, Pope, 46
Bouscaren, T. Lincoln, 61
Brewer, Sam Pope, 127
Bridges, Harry, 257
British Labor Party, 273
Brooklyn *Tablet,* 219
Brothers of Christian Schools, 58, 222
Browder, Earl, 39, 204, 256
Brownson, Orestes, 218
Budapest, 192
Budenz, Louis F., 118, 162, 163
Buffalo, University of, 149
Bulgaria, 13, 250
Buonaiuti, Ernesto, 121, 220
Burbank, Luther, 92

333

Caius, 52
Calvin, John, 106
Canada, 245
Canon law, 60; on education, 323-324
Canonization of saints, 80 ff., 167
Cárdenas, Lazaro, 145
Cardinal, The, 241, 329
Cardinals, 49, 54-55, 77
Catechism, 58-59, 142, 147
Catholic Action, 14, 179, 231, 271-272, 275, 278, 291
Catholic Almanac, 56
Catholic Church: and national churches, 15; bishops of, 63, 215-216; courts of, 62; democracy in, 58; General Councils of, 51, 57; government of, 49 ff.; in eastern Europe, 13, 17; in Tsarist Russia, 8; laymen of, 61, 122; membership of, 6, 316-317
Catholic Encyclopedia, 57, 109-110, 167, 239
Catholic Index, 116 ff., 275
Catholic international, 274
Catholic parties, 296
Catholic people, 4, 51, 110
Catholic Popular Party (Italy), 273, 276
Catholic press, 79
Catholic *Register,* 270, 278
Catholic schools: in Catholic law, 61; in Europe, 153 ff., 274; in Hungary, 18; in United States, 58
Censorship: external, 125; in Italy, 117; internal, 115; of books, 107, 116, 126, 146; of education, 144; of films, 125, 322
Chamberlin, W. H., 184
Chaplains, 176
Charlemagne, 46-47
Chiaurelli, M., 73
Chicherin, G. V., 12
China, 16, 100; Communists in, 87, 100, 201; labor in, 255
Christian Century, 216
Christian Democrat Party (Italy), 20, 117, 271
Christian Democratic Union (West Germany), 272, 279
Churchill, Winston, 204
Civiltà Cattolica, 111, 112, 179
Clark, Colin, 187

Classes, social: in Soviet Union, 86, 187; in Tsarist Russia, 24
Clement of Rome, 52
Columbia University, 6
Cominform, 26, 40 ff., 54, 245, 291
Comintern, 38 ff.
Communism: and Catholicism, 6; and Pius XI, 12; international organization of, as religion, 65; strength of, in Italy, 20
Communist cells, 250; in labor unions, 257
Communist control of labor, 255, 258-259
Communist fronts, 198 ff., 260
Communist international, 38
Communist parties: and dictatorship, 85; and intelligentsia, 28; Central Committee of, 36, 96; discipline of, 161 ff.; in Soviet Union, 26 ff., 31, 33; in United States, 39, 72, 198, 204; membership of, 16, 34
Communist penetration, 250-251; into social units, 259-260
Concordats: between Vatican and Mussolini, 13, 55, 150, 178, 211, 222, 304-306; official, 268 ff.; with Rumania, 15
Confédération Internationale des Syndicats Chrétiens, 281, 291
Congress for Cultural Freedom, 5
Congress of Industrial Organizations, 255, 257
Congress of Vienna, 265
Connell, Rev. Francis J., 113, 114, 322
Conscience, 217
Constance, Council of, 47, 58
Constantine, Emperor, 45
Constitutions: of Soviet Union, 27 ff.; of United States, 213, 220, 225, 227
Containment, American policy of, 292
Cosmopolitanism, 189
Counter-reformation, 47
Counts, George S., 94, 137
Croatia, 18
Croce, Benedetto, 118
Cushing, Richard C., Archbishop, 80, 225
Cyrankiewicz, Joseph, 253-254
Czechoslovakia, 13, 15, 20, 139, 244, 247-249

INDEX

Dailey, Kenneth, ix
Daily Worker, 118, 188
Dale, Sir Henry, 95
Darling, Edward, ix
Darwin, Charles, 69
Davidson, Basil, 272
DeGaulle, Charles, General, 271
Deification, techniques of, 65 ff.
Democratic centralism, 38
Democracy, 2, 3, 5; and Pius XII, 128; Catholic attitude toward, 218; in Catholic Church, 58; in Soviet Union, 27 ff., 188
Deutscher, Isaac, 210
Dewey, John, 118
Dictatorship: Catholic explanation of, 219; in Soviet Union, 32; of proletariat, 84, 206; of Vatican and Kremlin, 43
Dimitrov, Georgi, 245-246
Divorce: and censorship, 119; condemnation of, 240; in Catholic law, 61, 62, 214; laws of, 221, 267
Dogma, 237-238, 241; manipulation of, 205
Dollfuss, Engelbert, 270, 279
Don Basin, 101
"Donation of Constantine," 47
Dougherty, Denis Cardinal, 222
Duffy, Father, 220
Duma, Russian, 11, 23, 24
Djugashvili, Josef. *See* Stalin

Education, 131 ff.; canon law on, 141, 323-324
Egolin, A. M., 89
Egypt, 266
Eisenstein, Sergei, 102
Elections: as Communist strategy, 247; in Italy (1948), 22, 63, 271; in Soviet Union, 30
Ellis, Adam C., 61
Encyclopedia Britannica, 44, 48
Ethiopia, 13
Evolution, 122, 146, 147
Excommunication, 19, 327
Ex-priests, 178

Fadeyev, Alexander, 99
Faith and morals, 279
Falange, 157
Fascism, 65, 246-247, 253

Fatherland Front, 270
Feeney, Rev. Leonard, 326
Fierlinger, Zdenek, 249, 254
Finland, 266
First Amendment (to U. S. Constitution), 225-227
Fischer, John, 136
Fischer, Louis, 12
Florinsky, Michael, 11
Foltz, David, 157
Forced labor (in Soviet Union), 87, 171, 172, 325
Foster, William Z., 203
France, 16, 20, 117, 134, 148, 153, 154, 267, 270-271, 273; Communist control of labor in, 255; Communist penetration in, 250-251
Franco, Francisco, Generalissimo, 2, 3, 10, 113-114, 218, 267, 272, 274
Freedom of speech: in Catholic philosophy, 113; in Soviet Union, 85
Freedom of thought, 216
French Communist Party, 251
French Revolution, 148

Galileo, 94-95, 119
Gasparri, Pietro Cardinal, 144
Gasperi, Alcide de, 271, 274
Gelasius I, Pope, 46
Genetics, 92 ff.
Genoa Conference, 12
Georgetown University, 152
Georgiev, 254
Germany: East, 13, 139, 188, 244; West, 16, 213, 270, 272, 276, 279
Gibbons, James Cardinal, 143, 217
Gide, André, 72
Gitlow, Benjamin, 162
Godden, Rumer, 164
Gomulka, Wladyslaw, 186, 245-246
Gorky, Maxim, 70
Gottwald, Clement, 245-246
Graham, Rev. Aelred, 43, 58
Great Britain, 22, 117, 155, 213, 266; Communist penetration in, 250
Greek Orthodox churches, 11
Green, William, 180
Gregory VII, Pope, 46
Gregory IX, Pope, 107
Griffin, Bernard Cardinal, 157
Gromyko, Andrei, 260
Groza, 254

Gunther, John, 18
Guthrie, Rev. Hunter, 152

Hapsburg monarchy, 18
Heenan, Rev. John C., 217
Henry IV, Emperor, 46
Heresy, 106; in Boston, 326
History: in Soviet Union schools, 41; distorted, 209-210
Hitler, Adolf, 72, 194, 238, 277
Hitler-Stalin pact, 17, 40, 193 ff., 204, 257
Holy Office, 19, 21, 110, 116-117, 142, 179, 221
Holy Roman Empire, 48
Holy Year, 66, 77-78, 80
Hook, Sidney, 203
Hoover, J. Edgar, 332
Hugo, Victor, 118, 134
Hungary, 13-15, 17, 100, 148, 244, 247, 248
Hutchinson, Paul, 216
Huxley, Julian, 95-96

Ignatius of Antioch, 52
Illiteracy, 323; in Catholic countries, 134; in Soviet Union, 134; in Tsarist Russia, 133
Imprimatur, 124
Independence Party (Hungary), 248
Independent Labor Party (Great Britain), 39
Index, Catholic, 116 ff., 275
Indifferentism, 218
Indulgences, 240
Infallibility, papal, 46, 52, 58, 59, 68, 75, 76, 121, 179
Inkeles, Alex, 188
Innocent III, Pope, 44, 108
Inquisition, 6, 106 ff.
International Confederation of Free Trade Unions, 256, 280
International Federation of Christian Trade Unions, 281
Ireland, 16, 100, 125, 213, 270
Irenaeus, 52
Israel, 265
Italy, 3, 16, 20, 55, 63, 117, 119, 126, 134, 144, 213, 222, 267, 270-271, 273; Church of, 235; Communist control of labor in, 255; Communist penetration in, 250; Kingdom of, 12, 48, 128, 269; Papal States of, 48, 266, 269
Ivan the Terrible, 184
Izvestia, 85, 89

Jacists, 271
James, William, 159
Januarius, Saint, 236
Japan, 22, 146, 186, 194
Jefferson, Thomas, 226-227, 301
Jerusalem, internationalization of, 265
Jesuits, 34, 110-112, 146, 160, 164, 172
Jesus Christ, 44, 75, 83, 164
Jews: and anti-Zionism, 190; and marriage, 175; in Soviet Union, 181; in Tsarist Russia, 24
Joan of Arc, 130
Jocists, 271, 284
Joint Committee on Slavic Studies, x

Kamenev, L., 68, 170
Kara, Maniben, 283
Kerby, William J., 147
Kirov, S. M., 170
Knox, Rev. Ronald A., 114
Koestler, Arthur, 99, 250
Komsomols, 35
Korea, 162, 180, 196, 256-257, 261
Kremlin, 260, 263; and deception, 183 ff.; and thought control, 84 ff.; infallibility of, 261; political party of, 243-244; strategy of penetration of, 262
Ku Klux Klan, 202, 296
Kun, Bela, 247

Labor unions: Catholic, in France, 20; in Soviet union, 36, 137; Communist technique in, 258-259; under Communist control, 254-255; Vatican penetration into, 280
La Piana, George, ix, 214
Laski, Harold, 69
Latin America, 145, 234, 236
Lea, H. C., 108
Legion of Decency, 125
Lenin, Nikolai, 7-9, 12, 23, 25, 32, 38, 44, 66, 70, 72, 160, 184, 244
Leo III, Pope, 46

INDEX

Leo XIII, Pope, 76, 148, 213, 269, 276, 280-281
Lichtenstein, 270
Lodge, Nucia, 94, 137
Loisy, Alfred, 121
Lombardi, Rev. Riccardo, 276
London, 283
London *Times*, 115
Lovestone, Jay, 39
Loyola, Ignatius, 160, 164
Lublin, Poland, 235
Lukacs, George, 191
Lysenko, Trofim D., 91 ff., 147

MacArthur, Douglas, General, 186
McAvoy, Rev. T. T., 121
McCarthy, Joseph, 200, 298
Macaulay, Thomas B., 109
Madison, James, 227
Malenkov, G. M., 74
Malik, Jacob, 260-261
Maniu, Iuliu, 254
Mao Tse-tung, 100
Maritain, Jacques, 124
Marriage: in Catholic law, 61-62, 214; in Soviet Union, 206 ff.; intercourse in, 285; mixed, 175, 285; monopoly control of, 240; of Young Communists, 182; to Protestants, 175
Marshall, Charles C., 219, 224
Marshall Plan, 293
Marx, Karl, 7, 25, 33, 66, 68-69, 84, 206, 276
Masaryk, Jan, 254
Matthew, Gospel of, 44-45, 52
Matthews, Francis P., 299
Medina, Judge Harold, 198
Mein Kampf, 238
Merton, Thomas, 167
Mexico, 143, 145, 236, 267
Michurin, I. V., 91-92, 94, 147
Middle Ages, 47-48
Mikolajczyk, Stanislaw, 246, 254
Mill, John Stuart, 118
Milton, John, 107, 237
Mindszenty, Joseph Cardinal, 14, 18, 143, 148
Modernism, 121
Molotov, V., 195, 260, 300
Monaco, 270
Monasticism, 163, 165 ff.
Montini, Monsignor Giovanni, 265

Moore, Barrington, Jr., 30
Morgan-Mendel theories, 95
Morrison, Charles Clayton, 226
Moseley, Philip, 91
Moscow, 260
Motherhood, in Soviet Union, 208
Muller, H. J., 94, 96
Munich, 247
Murray, Rev. John C., 112-113, 322
Murray, Philip, 180
Murray, Raymond P., 149
Music, in Soviet Union, 96
Mussolini, Benito, 55, 221, 268, 273, 276-277

Naples, 236
Nation, The, x, 99, 253
National Catholic Welfare Conference, 176, 215
National Education Association, 150
Negroes, 201
Nenni, Pietro, 245
Netherlands, 16, 153, 155, 213, 218, 270, 272-273, 282
Neufeld, Rev. Raymond J., 219
New Statesman and Nation, 239
New York *Times*, 21, 31, 72-73, 79, 100, 126, 128, 130, 192, 199, 235, 261, 273
Nicholas, Saint, 236
Nicholas II, Tsar, 23-25
Nobility, in Russia, 24
Nouvelles Equipes Internationales, 274, 291
Nuncios, papal, 264, 267
Nuns, 63, 160

O'Brien, Rev. John A., 217
Octobrists, 35
O'Neill, Eugene, 99
O'Neill, James M., 226, 329
Ontario, 213
"Operation Mental Hygiene," 5-6
Opium, 7
Origen, 52
Orwell, George, 65
Osservatore Romano, 19, 79, 89, 264
Our Sunday Visitor, 150

Pacelli, Eugenio. *See* Pius XII
Paine, Tom, 117
Papacy, 44 ff., 48, 75, 268-270

Papal States of Italy, 48, 266, 269
Pauker, Ana, 245
Paul IV, Pope, 116, 126
Paul, Saint, 44
Pavelitch, Ante, 18
Penetration, 243; Kremlin strategy of, 262; by Vatican, 263
Pétain, Henri, 154
Peter, Saint, 44, 51-52, 206, 239; bones of, 240; claims about, 318
Petkov, Nikola, 250, 254
Philology, in Soviet Union, 102-103
Pioli, Giovanni, x
Pius VII, Pope, 46
Pius IX, Pope, 47, 52, 59, 85, 111, 213, 220, 269
Pius X, Pope, 122
Pius XI, Pope, 12-13, 60, 142-145, 148, 221, 268, 273, 276-277, 281
Pius XII, Pope, 53 ff., 66, 77, 81, 127-128, 167, 238, 265, 277
Point Four program, 294
Poland, 8, 13, 15, 20, 100, 169, 195, 218, 244; Catholic Church in, 235; political parties in, 254
Politburo, 36 ff.
Popes, 224, 235, 239; and democracy, 128; and peace, 17; in Rome, 45; power of, 51 ff., 77, 224, 319-320
Portugal, 16, 128, 134, 144, 213, 215, 270-271, 275
Prague, 186
Pravda, 21, 37-38, 71, 74, 79, 86, 89, 90-91, 94, 98, 103, 185, 188, 192
Price, Roy A., 34
Priests, 160 ff.; and censorship, 118, 120; in Catholic Church, 50; in Soviet Union, 8
Progressive Party, 245
Prokofiev, Sergei, 97-98
Protestantism, 140; attitude of Catholics toward, 174
Public schools, 131 ff.; in Catholic law, 61, 142-143; in France, 153; in Great Britain, 156; in Hungary, 18; in Italy, 144; in Netherlands, 155; in Russian satellite countries, 100; in Soviet Union, 90; in Spain, 145, 157
Purges: by Kremlin, 68, 168; by Vatican, 17, 19, 21

Quebec, 213
Quotidiano, 89, 126

Rakosi, 245
Red Army, 170, 173, 186-187, 247
Redden, John, 216
Reformation, 47, 140
Reform committees, 259
Relics, 236-237
Religion: and Lenin, 70; in Tsarist Russia, 8
Religious fraud, 233
Religious freedom, in Soviet Union, 9, 10
Resistance movements, 246, 253
Reuther, Walter, 180
Ribbentrop, Joachim von, 195
Robinson, Henry Morton, 241, 329
Roman Catholic Church. *See* Catholic Church
Roman Curia, 54
Roman Empire, 43, 45
Roman Rota, 62
Roosevelt, Eleanor, 227-229, 232-233, 306-312
Roosevelt, Franklin D., 204, 266
Ross, Rev. J. Elliott, 224
Rossi, A., 251
Rotary Clubs, 176, 326-327
Rumania, 13, 72, 80, 139, 190, 244; Orthodox Church of, 15, 168
Russell, Bertrand, 6, 118, 148
Russian language, 103
Russian Orthodox Church, 8, 10-11, 211
Russian Revolution, 23, 25, 84
Ryan, Francis A., 216

Sabotage, 257
Saint Peter's (Rome), 44, 76-77, 240
Saints, canonization of, 80 ff., 167, 234
Salazar, Antonio, 271, 274
San Francisco, 260
Schlesinger, Arthur, Jr., 75
School Lunch Act, 232
Schumacher, Kurt, 180, 279
Schuman, Robert, 271
Schwartz, Harry, 199
Scott, John, 171
Secret police, 170 ff., 249

INDEX

Security Council of United Nations, 261
Seipel, Monsignor Ignatz, 270
Separation of church and state, 213 ff.; in France, 153
Servetus, Michael, 106
Seward, William Henry, 266
Sheen, Monsignor Fulton J., 209
Shell Oil Company, 100
Shostakovich, Dimitri, 97-98
Shuster, George N., 218
Silone, Ignazio, 40, 172
Simonov, Konstantin, 99
Sixtus V, Pope, 44
Slovakia, 277
Smallholders Party (Hungary), 248
Smith, Alfred E., 212, 219, 222-224, 227-228
Smith, Canon George D., 241
Smith, Walter Bedell, 37, 75
Snow, Edgar, 71
Social democrats, 84
Socialism: and Catholic Church, 60, 331; and early Christianity, 75; and Communists, 179 ff.; and United States, 297
Socialists, 247, 249, 253-254, 276, 281
Sociology, 148
Sokolovsky, Vasili, Marshal, 185
Sorokin, Pitirim, 11
Soviet Union: and Catholic Spain, 292; and Jews, 190; constitutions of, 27 ff., 86; elections in, 30, 31; expansion of, 16; films in, 101; government of, 26 ff.; law of, 88; literature of, 89, 99; music in, 96; newspapers in, 87, 89-90; philology in, 102-103; religious freedom in, 9-10; science in, 93
Spain, 2, 16, 66, 109, 113, 125, 128, 134, 144, 157, 213, 222, 224, 267, 270, 272, 275, 279, 292
Spellman, Francis Cardinal, 80, 212, 227-233, 265, 306-312
Stalin, Joseph, 2, 8, 26, 30, 39, 66, 67 ff., 91, 94, 103, 197, 260, 300
Starobin, Joseph, 188
Stepinac, Archbishop, 14, 18
Sterilization, 221
Strong, Anna Louise, 87
Sturzo, Don Luigi, 273, 276

Subasitch, 254
Sulzberger, Cyrus L., 72, 127, 273
Sweden, 218
Switzerland, 213, 270
Syllabus of Errors, 111, 213, 220
Sylvester, Harry, 123
Szakasits, 254

Tammany Hall, 35, 275
Tardini, Monsignor Domenico, 265
Tarlé, Eugene, 210
Taylor, Myron, 266, 300
Teacher's Guild (New York), 146
Tertullian, 52
Theodosius the Great, 45
Tiflis, 67
Tildy, 254
Tiso, Monsignor Josef, 277
Tito, Marshal, 18, 39, 42, 180, 245-246, 250
Togliatti, Palmiro, 196, 245
Torquemada, 109
Torre, Count Giuseppe dalla, 264
Torture, 108-109, 169
Towster, Julian, 29
Toynbee, Arnold, 5
Toynbee, Philip, 129
Trade unions. *See* Labor unions
Trilling, Lionel, 129
Trotsky, Leon 7, 9, 23, 68, 170, 209
Truman, Harry S., 2, 256
Tsaro, 9-10, 70
Tukhachevsky, Marshal, 170
Tyrrell, George, 121

Ukraine, 8
Unam Sanctam, 46
Underhill, Garrett, 173
Union of Militant Godless, 9
United Nations, 197, 260-261; Security Council of, 249, 261
United States: and Catholic censorship, 117; and Vatican, 22; Communist penetration in, 250; Constitution of, 141, 213, 220, 225, 227; increasing power of, 22

Van Roey, Cardinal, 231
Varga, Eugene, 191
Vatican: and thought control, 105 ff.; as counter-revolutionary force, 298;

congregations of, 49 ff.; diplomatic representation of U. S. at, 266; diplomats of, 264; double talk of, 216; imperialism of, 55, 57; penetration by, 263, 280-281; political party of, 269; Secretary of State of, 265; strength of, in Europe, 16
Vatican City State, 48
Vatican Council of 1870, 58
Vavilov, Nicolai, 92
V-E Day, 185
Virgin Mary, 164, 235; assumption of, 119, 238-239
Vishinsky, Andrei Y., 86, 113, 170, 260, 299

Waldensians, 107
Wallace, Henry, 180
Walsh, Warren B., ix, 34, 171
Washington *Post,* 2, 18, 152
Washington-Rome Axis, 21

Wells, H. G., 163
Webb, Sidney and Beatrice, 161
Werth, Alexander, 99, 253
Wolfe, Bertram, 24
World Congress for Peace, 203
World Federation of Trade Unions, 255-256, 282, 291
World War I, 2, 11, 22
World War II, 2, 13, 71, 184

Yalta conference, 197
York, Archbishop of, 279
Young Christian Workers, 284
Young Communists, 35, 74, 181
Yugoslavia, 13-14, 39, 42, 104, 180, 244

Zaslavsky, David, 103
Zhebrak, Anton, 94
Zinoviev, G., 68, 170
Zirkle, Conway, 94